Reading German

A COURSE BOOK AND REFERENCE GRAMMAR

Waltraud Coles

Bill Dodd

OXFORD UNIVERSITY PRESS

1997

Oxford University Press, Great Clarendon Street, Oxford OX2 6DP

Oxford New York
Athens Auckland Bangkok Bogota Bombay
Buenos Aires Calcutta Cape Town Dar es Salaam
Delhi Florence Hong Kong Istanbul Karachi
Kuala Lumpur Madras Madrid Melbourne
Mexico City Nairobi Paris Singapore
Taipei Tokyo Toronto Warsaw
and associated companies in
Berlin Ibadan

Oxford is a trade mark of Oxford University Press

Published in the United States
by Oxford University Press Inc., New York

British Library Cataloguing in Publication Data
Data available

Library of Congress Cataloging in Publication Data
Reading German: a course book and reference grammar
Waltraud Coles, Bill Dodd.
  Includes bibliographical references and index.
  1. German language–Readers. 2. German language–Grammar.
3. German language–Textbooks for foreign speakers–English.
I. Dodd, Bill (W. J.), 1950– . II. Title.
PF3117.C66   1997   438.6'421–dc21   97-28216

ISBN 0–19–870004–0 (Hbk)
ISBN 0–19–870020–2 (Pbk)

10 9 8 7 6 5 4 3 2 1

Typeset by J&L Composition Ltd, Filey, North Yorkshire
Printed in Great Britain on acid-free paper by
Bookcraft (Bath) Ltd., Midsomer Norton

STANDARD

READING GERMAN

For **OLIVER COLES** *and* **MARIA DODD**

Authors' Preface

We hope this book will prove both useful and enjoyable. Our aim in writing it has been to provide a practical and structured guide to reading authentic German texts. The twin aims of the book are to develop the user's reading skills to the point where, with the aid of a good dictionary, he or she can tackle previously unseen authentic texts with confidence; and to act as a reference work for independent reading. We have written *Reading German* for students and teachers in universities and institutions of higher learning and for independent learners who need to develop or maintain a good standard of reading competence in German. We have designed the book to be of use to a wide variety of users, including those with little or no formal understanding of German grammar or indeed of grammatical concepts in general.

As practising teachers of reading courses in UK universities it quickly became apparent to us that there was a need for a new reading course and indeed a new approach to German grammar which catered specifically for the needs of English-speaking readers of German as a foreign language. This book brings together a new kind of 'reading grammar' of German and a structured reading course which will enable students to develop and enhance their reading skills.

We would like to express our thanks to all those who helped to shape this book. The late Eva Paneth provided an important early stimulus and focus for our ideas. It was as a result of discussing our early drafts with Eva that we began to elaborate the principles of a user-oriented reading grammar which underpin this book. Our students at Birmingham and, particularly, at Durham, provided invaluable feedback on early drafts, sometimes pointing out problems and even solutions that were obvious to the users, if not to the authors. Travel grants from the University of Birmingham helped the Birmingham author to meet his Durham colleague. Several colleagues in the UK and the United States provided helpful criticism of the manuscript at various stages, whether as readers for OUP or simply out of collegial interest. We would particularly like to mention John Klapper and Christine Eckhard-Black. A special debt of thanks is due to Frances Morphy, commissioning editor at OUP, for her guidance and unstinting support. We are indebted to all of the above for making the book possible in its present form. A final word of thanks must go to our families, who gave up many hours of family life so that we could write and re-write this book.

WALTRAUD COLES, *Durham*

BILL DODD, *Birmingham*

Contents

About this Book

The book has four main sections:

The Reading Course

A structured course in 16 chapters takes the user from beginner's level towards independent reading (with the aid of a good dictionary) of complex authentic German texts. The first nine chapters develop close reading skills by systematically working through short texts and focusing on the recognition of key grammatical structures. Chapter 10 (on reading strategies) forms something of a bridge between this first stage and the later chapters, in which the focus changes to practising a wide variety of reading strategies when tackling longer texts.

Each chapter of the reading course contains a set of exercises, and a key is provided at the end of this section. A system of cross-references enables the user to study a particular grammatical feature more fully in the Reference Section.

The Reference Section

The numbered sections (R1–R191) give a detailed description of the grammatical structures of written German presented from a 'recognition' point of view (that is to say, as they are encountered by real readers reading real texts), as well as other relevant information, e.g. on cognate words, 'false friends' and other problem words, and on how to get the most out of your dictionary. Many of the illustrations in the Reference Section are taken from the authentic texts contained in the Text Corpus. This means that these grammatical examples can be located and studied in their full context. Sometimes the examples contained in the Reference Section show a variation on the pattern which actually occurs in the text corpus. In this case, the user will learn to study the full context and see whether/how a change of meaning is produced. It should be noted that the style of the cross-reference (e.g. [T12:3]) is the same for 'verbatim' and 'approximate' examples.

Further Exercises

This section contains a set of exercises (E1–E59) on important aspects of the grammar which may need reinforcing. These exercises can be done independently of the reading course, and are cross-referenced to the relevant parts of the Reference Section so that the user can focus on recognizing particular structural features. A key is provided at the end of this section.

The Text Corpus

This consists of 23 authentic German texts (T1–T23) taken from a wide range of sources and on a wide range of subjects. Each sentence in each text is numbered, and each text has a parallel English translation on the facing page.

In writing the book, we recognize that there are different reasons for wanting or having to read German, different institutional settings in which this may be done, and different types of student with different learning styles, varying experience of foreign languages and varying prior knowledge of German. Accordingly, the book has been designed so that different groups of learners can use it in different ways. Depending on the user's prior knowledge of German and reading ability in German, there are several ways of working through the book. For example, here are four possibilities:

■ Route 1

For beginning learners:

The user works through the chapters of the Reading Course, doing the exercises in each chapter and looking up the Reference Section where indicated. Particular attention should be given to the first nine chapters, and to the outline of reading strategies in Chapter 10.

Each of the first nine chapters focuses on a short text (Text A), which illustrates a number of grammatical features which are then described in the chapter; and concludes with a test text (Text B) containing these grammatical features for the reader to tackle independently. Text A is printed with a parallel translation; Text B is in German only. (It is translated in the key to the exercises for that chapter.)

■ Route 2

For readers who already have a basic competence in German:

The user finds an appropriate chapter of the Course at which to begin (i.e. a chapter in which unfamiliar grammar points are discussed) and works through the rest of the Course. In this case the user should read Text A and Text B in the earlier chapters and make sure that they contain no unfamiliar structures.

■ Route 3

For readers who have progressed through the structured course and who wish to practise their close reading skills in German further:

The user works through the Further Exercises section (E), looking up the equivalent part of the Reference Section (R) where necessary.

This is also a possible point of entry for learners who have a reasonable command of German and who wish to identify areas of the grammar which they need to focus on in order to improve their close reading skills. These students will be guided to the relevant entries in the Reference Section for further information.

■ Route 4

For readers who have worked through the course and the exercises section and who feel they are in a position to tackle previously unseen authentic texts:

The user works through the Text Corpus (T), with or without the aid of the parallel translations.

This is also a possible point of entry for students with a good working knowledge of German who wish to refresh their reading skills. These students are also recommended to work through Chapters 10–16, which are designed for practising 'higher' levels of reading competence.

The texts in the Text Corpus are entirely separate from the texts used in the course chapters, and are intended to expose the user to a variety of topics and text types. Students who have reached this level should feel confident about reading other authentic texts, using the Reference Section for support.

Part I

Reading Course

List of Chapter Topics

1

1 Mehr als   100 Millionen Menschen **sprechen** Deutsch als
*More than 100 million   people   **speak**   German as*

2 Muttersprache.   Aber nicht alle deutschsprechenden
(their) mother tongue. But   not   all   German-speaking

3 Leute   **wohnen** in Deutschland. In Österreich, in einem
*people **live**   in Germany.   In Austria,   in one*

4 Teil der Schweiz   und in Liechtenstein   **spricht** man
*part of Switzerland   and in Liechtenstein   one **speaks***

5 auch Deutsch.   Außerdem   **findet** man   deutschsprachige
*also German.   In addition one **finds**   German-speaking*

6 Bevölkerungsgruppen   in vielen   anderen   Ländern.
sections of the population   in many   other   countries.

1.0 Reading the above text you will note a number of differences between the English and the German. The most obvious difference concerns spelling.

■ All German NOUNS are spelt with an initial capital letter.
For example: Millionen, Menschen, Leute, Teil, Länder

■ German has letters which do not exist in English. For example in the above text: Österreich, außerdem, Bevölkerungsgruppen, Ländern. There are four letters the English alphabet does not have:

　ä Ä　ö Ö　ü Ü　ß

ß (called ess-tsett) is similar to **ss**. It only exists in lower case.
Straße (street) can be written Strasse.

The two dots above the vowels a, o, u are called an UMLAUT. An umlaut changes the sound of the vowel. For reading purposes a vowel with an umlaut is a different letter from the vowel without an umlaut, e.g.:

　　Kuchen *cake*   zahlen *to pay*   fallen *to fall*
　　Küchen *kitchens* zählen *to count* fällen *to fell*

If a particular word cannot be found in the dictionary or if the meaning found does not fit the context, it may be because the umlaut has been overlooked.

📖 Also allow for the effects of the spelling reform introduced in 1996. For further information on the spelling reform see **R191**.

The letter **ß** is treated as **ss** in dictionaries.
ä, ö, ü are listed with/after **a, o, u**, e.g. **zählen** immediately follows **zahlen**

✎ **1a.** Practise using your dictionary by looking up the following words containing these special German letters:

Ärger, höflich, Bühne, verträglich, Fuß, Maßnahme, rußig

It is also important not to mix up the letter sequence **ie** and **ei**.

✎ **1b.** Look up the following words in your dictionary.

Leid—Lied, Reise—Riese, verschließen—verschleißen, lieb—Leib, Wiese—Weise

1.1 The Finite Verb in the Present Tense

sprechen, wohnen, spricht, findet are the FINITE VERBS in Text A. There are FINITE and NON-FINITE forms of the verb. Here are examples from English:

	FINITE	NON-FINITE	
He	speaks		German.
They	speak		German.
He	spoke		German.
		INFINITIVE	
He	wants	to speak	German.
He	can	speak	German.
		PAST PARTICIPLE	
He	has	spoken	German.

The form of a finite verb can tell us whether it is singular or plural, and it shows the tense (e.g. present, past).

The finite verb plays the central role when working out the meaning of a sentence and you have to be able to spot finite verbs and to interpret the information they contain.

📖 You now need to read **R21–8**.

So, **sprechen** and **wohnen** are PLURAL forms in the PRESENT TENSE, **findet** and **spricht** are SINGULAR forms in the PRESENT TENSE.

Bearing in mind what you have read about verb ENDINGS and PRONOUNS, now attempt Exercise 1c.

✎ **1c.** Identify the finite verbs in the following sentences.

1. Ich spreche Deutsch, Spanisch und Englisch.
2. In Deutschland verstehen viele Leute Englisch.
3. Wir leben seit 1993 in Österreich.
4. In vielen anderen Ländern hört man diese Sprache.
5. Er liest ein Magazin in seiner Muttersprache.
6. Im Sommer fährt er nach London.
7. Sie begrüßt unsere amerikanischen Freunde.
8. Den Text übersetze ich ins Englische.

📖 You now may want to know what these finite verbs mean in English. Read **R169** for information on how to look up finite verbs in the dictionary.

✎ **1d.** Now look up the verbs you underlined in exercise 1c, i.e. first work out the infinitive form, then look up the meaning.

1.2 Sentence Patterns

When you read *speak* (sprechen) in the first sentence you will naturally want to know WHO (SUBJECT) *speaks* WHAT (OBJECT). *More than 100 million people* (mehr als 100 Millionen Menschen) is the subject. *German* (Deutsch) is the object.

In addition to the subject and the object there is, of course, further important information given in this sentence: *as their mother tongue* (als Muttersprache).

In the second sentence (Aber nicht alle deutschsprechenden Leute wohnen in Deutschland.) the finite verb is 'wohnen' (*live*). This verb follows a pattern different to the one for 'sprechen' in the first sentence. wohnen (*live*) requires a WHO (*Not all German-speaking people*) and a WHERE (*in Germany*) to form a complete sentence.

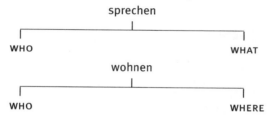

There is a limited number of patterns of this kind and they are determined by the meaning of the finite verb.

The finite verb in the third sentence (In Österreich . . . spricht man auch Deutsch.) is again *speak*, now in the singular form: 'spricht'. The object is the same as in the first sentence: Deutsch (*German*).

The subject this time is 'man' (*one*). The core of the sentence thus reads: *One speaks German (German is spoken)*. Note that wherever **man** appears it is always the **subject**.

There is also some additional information given on WHERE one speaks German, i.e. *in Austria, in one part of Switzerland, and in Liechtenstein*. Phrases of this kind, giving information on the WHERE, WHEN, HOW, etc. are called ADVERBIAL PHRASES.

📖 Later on in the course you may wish to read more on sentence patterns. This information is given in **R81** and **R82**.

1.3 Word Order (1)

Note the difference in WORD ORDER between German and English when the sentence does *not* start with the subject:

I	II		
In Österreich	**spricht**	**man**	Deutsch.
	VERB	SUBJECT	
In Austria	**one**	**speaks**	*German.*
	subject	verb	

In German, the finite verb is always the 'second idea', i.e. it appears in Position II, in a simple sentence like this one. This means that the subject comes after the finite verb if the sentence starts with an adverbial phrase (as in the sentence above) or with an object.

For more detailed information on the word order in this kind of sentence you can read **R3** and **R4**.

1e. Look again at exercise 1*c* and work out for each sentence whether the subject, an object or an adverbial phrase appears in Position I. Use your dictionary if necessary.

1.4 Negation (1)

nicht (Text 1A, line 2) means *not* wherever it appears in a text.

Later on in the course you may wish to read **R124** and **R125** for further examples and other types of NEGATION.

1.5 Compound Nouns (1)

Bevölkerungsgruppen   (Text 1A, line 6)
Bevölkerung – s – gruppen
population   groups/sections
i.e. *groups/sections of the population*

COMPOUND WORDS are a particular feature of German and long ones can appear quite unmanageable. However, there is a simple principle: the last part of the compound determines the basic meaning and the preceding parts modify this basic meaning.

R181 will give you more detailed information on compound words.

1f. You can guess the meaning of the following compounds.

1. Autoindustrie
2. Interpretationsproblem
3. Informationsmaterial
4. Computerexperte
5. Computerexpertenkonferenz

Now try to work out this one!
Flughafenrestaurantmanagerausbildungsprogramm

1.6 Connectors (1)

und (*and*) in Text 1A, line 4, is a so-called CONNECTOR which can link either individual words (Schweiz **und** Liechtenstein) or it can link whole sections of sentences.

For a list of CONNECTORS see **R160**.

Note: CONNECTORS are traditionally called 'co-ordinating conjunctions'.

1.7 What you should now be able to do: Check-list

Having worked through Chapter 1 you should now

- be able to recognize the following words and know their English meaning.

NOUNS	Millionen, Menschen, Deutsch, Muttersprache, Leute, Deutschland, Österreich, Teil, Schweiz, Liechtenstein, Bevölkerungsgruppen, Länder
PRONOUNS	ich, er, sie, wir, man
VERBS	sprechen/spricht, wohnen, finden/findet
ADJECTIVES	deutschsprechend(en), deutschsprachig(e), viel(en), ander(en)
OTHER WORDS	nicht, und, mehr, aber, alle, auch, in, außerdem

- be aware of words with an UMLAUT or ß and know where to look up such words in the dictionary

- know that in statements the FINITE VERB is always in Position II

- be able to spot FINITE VERBS in the PRESENT TENSE and work out their INFINITIVES

- know the difference between a SUBJECT, OBJECT, and ADVERBIAL PHRASE

- be able to work out COMPOUND words

- recognize 'nicht' as a NEGATION word

- recognize 'und' as a CONNECTOR and know where to find a list of other connectors

1.8 Now test your knowledge and skills on a new text. Start by finding the finite verbs. Use your dictionary where necessary.

TEXT 1B

In der Bundesrepublik Deutschland spricht man nicht nur Deutsch. Viele Ausländer wohnen in Deutschland und sie sprechen natürlich ihre eigene Muttersprache. Man hört z.B. (zum Beispiel) Türkisch, Griechisch, Spanisch, Italienisch und Polnisch. In Deutschland verstehen und sprechen viele Leute Englisch. Im Osten des Landes war (*was*) Russisch früher die Hauptfremdsprache.

2

Here is TEXT 1A again. Can you read it now, without having to use the dictionary?

Mehr als 100 Millionen Menschen sprechen Deutsch als Muttersprache. Aber nicht alle deutschsprechenden Leute wohnen in Deutschland. In Österreich, in einem Teil der Schweiz und in Liechtenstein spricht man auch Deutsch. Außerdem findet man deutschsprachige Bevölkerungsgruppen in vielen anderen Ländern.

TEXT 2A

1 Natürlich **spricht** man   die Laute der deutschen Sprache nicht
*Of course one does not **pronounce** the sounds of (the) German (language)*

2 überall   gleich   **aus**.   Selbst innerhalb Deutschlands
everywhere (in) the same (way).   Even   within   Germany

3 **hat** man schon immer   viele verschiedene Dialekte **gesprochen**.
*one **has**   always   **spoken**   many different   dialects.*

4 Deshalb **können** sogar Ausländer mit guten Deutschkenntnissen
Therefore   even foreigners with a good knowledge of German

5   nicht immer alles sofort **verstehen**,
***can** not   always   **understand** everything straight away,*

6 und manchmal **gibt** es   echte Kommunikationsschwierigkeiten.
*and sometimes there **are** real   communication problems.*

2.1 Word Order (2)

Note the word order in these sentences from the above text:

I	II	III	IV
Natürlich	**spricht**	man die Laute . . . nicht überall gleich	**aus**.
. . . innerhalb Deutschlands	**hat**	man . . . viele verschiedene Dialekte	**gesprochen**.
Deshalb	**können**	. . . Ausländer . . . nicht alles . . .	**verstehen**.

The words which appear at the end of these sentences must be read together with the finite verb in position II.

📖 If you have not already read **R3** and **R4**, do so now before moving on to a detailed look at the above examples in the next section.

2.1.1 Separable Verbs

               II   IV
Natürlich   **spricht**   man die Laute . . . nicht überall gleich   **aus**.
*Of course one does not **pronounce** the sounds . . . in the same way everywhere.*

spricht, as we have seen in Ch. 1, means *speaks*. However, in the sentence above **spricht** is used together with **aus** and although **aus** appears at the end of the sentence it is an integral part of the verb **sprechen**. With the prefix 'sprechen' acquires a new meaning: **aussprechen** means *to pronounce*.

Such verbs where one part can be split off are called SEPARABLE VERBS. There are many of these in German. They are listed in the dictionary with the prefix attached to the infinitive form, e.g. **aussprechen**.

📖 If you would like more information on separable verbs you can read **R39**. A list of PREFIXES is given in **R174**.

✍ **2a.** Read the following sentences with the help of a dictionary.

1. Sie laden den Computer ins Auto.
   Sie laden die Amerikaner zur Party ein.
   Sie laden die Batterie auf.
2. Die Firma kündigt 500 Arbeitern.
   Die Firma kündigt 500 Arbeitern eine Gehaltserhöhung an.
3. Sie schreibt ein Wort.
   Sie schreibt ein Wort ab.
4. Wir fahren nach Berlin.
   Wir fahren um 14.30 Uhr ab.
5. Er kommt im Sommer nach Hamburg.
   Er kommt am 24. Juli an.

2.1.2 The Compound Past I

II   IV

In Deutschland **hat** man immer viele Dialekte **gesprochen**.
*In Germany one **has** always **spoken** many dialects.*

hat gesprochen *has spoken* is a so-called COMPOUND TENSE, i.e. a tense form which uses an AUXILIARY verb (here: **hat** *has*).

📖 If you wish to get an overview of the German tenses read **R23**.

In the above example we are dealing with the COMPOUND PAST I, also called the PERFECT TENSE, which uses an auxiliary verb together with a PAST PARTICIPLE (here **gesprochen** *spoken*).

For this tense English uses only one auxiliary verb (*have*). German, however, uses either **haben** or **sein**. Both, however, function like *have* when used in the compound past.

📖 For a list of German auxiliary verbs see **R31**.

📖 If you would like further information on the compound past tenses ('perfect', 'pluperfect'), read **R33**.

📖 You now need to familiarize yourself with the patterns of participle forms. See **R34**. **R170** tells you how to look up past participle forms in the dictionary.

✒ **2b.** Now work out the meaning of the following sentences.

1. In Deutschland hat er Deutsch gesprochen.
2. Von 1985 bis 1994 habe ich in Berlin gewohnt.
3. Er hat die Information nicht gefunden.
4. Wir haben den Dialekt nicht verstanden.
5. Ich habe den Brief gestern beantwortet.
6. Die Amerikaner haben den Prototyp produziert.
7. Er hat das Wort nicht richtig ausgesprochen. (see **R171–2**)
8. Diese Bevölkerungsgruppe ist im 19. Jahrhundert nach Amerika gekommen.
9. Die Studenten sind nach Portugal gefahren.
10. Er ist gestern angekommen. (see **R171–2**)
11. Die Engländer sind gestern nach Spanien gereist.
12. Sie ist nicht zur Bibliothek gegangen.

2.1.3 Modal Verbs (1)

       II   IV
Deshalb **können** Ausländer nicht alles **verstehen**.
       can   *understand*
*Therefore foreigners **cannot understand** everything.*

können *can* and verbs like *want, must, may, should* are called MODAL VERBS. They have to be read together with the INFINITIVE (i.e. the basic form as given in the dictionary) of another verb which appears at the end of the sentence. In the singular the above sentence reads:

Deshalb **kann** ein Ausländer nicht alles **verstehen**.
*Therefore a foreigner **cannot understand** everything.*

📖 Now read **R63**.

📖 **Note**: Singular present tense forms of modal verbs are **irregular**. They don't look like the present tense forms given so far. For an overview of all modal verb forms see **R66**.

📖 **R69** gives the meanings of the modal verbs.

✒ **2c.** Read the following sentences. Use a dictionary if necessary.
1. Der Student will nächstes Jahr Portugiesisch lernen.
2. Ich kann nicht Spanisch sprechen.
3. In England soll man Englisch sprechen.
4. Ausländer können diesen Dialekt nicht verstehen.
5. Wir können dieses Wort nicht korrekt aussprechen.
6. Man muß den Prototyp jetzt testen.
7. In diesem Restaurant darf man Alkohol trinken.
8. Aber man muß nicht Alkohol trinken. (see **R69**)

2.2 Nouns

German NOUNS belong to one of three groups: masculine, feminine and neuter. Looking at the noun itself one cannot usually tell to which group it belongs. Instead this is signalled by the form of preceding words like *the*, *a*, *no*, *this*, *some*, *his* etc. Such words are called DETERMINERS, e.g.

the dialect	**der** Dialekt	
a dialect	**ein** Dialekt	**masculine**
no dialect	**kein** Dialekt	
the language	**die** Sprache	
a language	**eine** Sprache	**feminine**
no language	**keine** Sprache	
the country	**das** Land	
a country	**ein** Land	**neuter**
no country	**kein** Land	

In the **plural**, however, these distinctions disappear and one determiner form is used only:

the dialects/languages/countries	**die** Dialekte/Sprachen/Länder
no dialects/languages/countries	**keine** Dialekte/Sprachen/Länder

Read **R178**, which explains how the dictionary indicates whether a noun is masculine, feminine, or neuter.

Note: The order masculine, feminine, neuter ('der, die, das') is the one traditionally used in grammars of German. However, some of the tables in the Reference Section of this book use the order 'der, das, die' where this shows up an important pattern. ➜**R97, 99, 108, 110.**

2d. Check in the dictionary whether the following nouns are masculine, feminine or neuter.

1. Problem   5. Computer
2. Kenntnis   6. Wort
3. Laut   7. Gruppe
4. Frage   8. Antwort

Sometimes the same noun form can belong to more than one group. We then have different nouns with different meanings, e.g.

der Kiefer   *the jaw (bone)*
die Kiefer   *the pine tree*

Check these nouns in your dictionary:

9. Leiter   11. Steuer
10. Teil   12. See

Only some nouns tell us by their form itself, to which group they belong. The most important group are nouns ending in:

-heit, -keit, -in, -ion, -schaft, -tät, -ung

They are are always **feminine**.

The form of a determiner can change according to how the noun it precedes is used in the sentence, e.g.

Dies**er** Dialekt [SUBJECT] ist kompliziert.

This dialect is complicated.

Dies**er** Mann [SUBJECT] spricht dies**en** Dialekt [OBJECT].

This man speaks this dialect.

To the German reader **dieser** signals that **Dialekt** and **Mann** (both masculine nouns) respectively are the subject, whilst **diesen** marks the following noun as an object.

(In English we find special forms for subjects and objects for pronouns only: **He** [SUBJECT] introduces **him** [OBJECT] to his professor.)

However, if the noun which follows **dieser** is feminine it has to be read differently: dies**er** **Frau** signals that 'Frau' is **not** the subject, e.g.

Der Dialekt **dieser Frau** ist kompliziert.

*The dialect **of this woman** (this woman's dialect) is complicated.*

📖 The system of marking the difference between the subject and non-subject forms is called the CASE system. Read **R90** and the first half of **R92** for more information on this.

Then look at **R97** which gives all determiner forms for the subject (NOMINATIVE) and non-subject (ACCUSATIVE, DATIVE, GENITIVE) cases. Familiarize yourself with this table. Ignore the column headed MAIN FUNCTIONS in the first instance.

You will note that some determiner forms are specifically **non**-subject forms: dies**em**, dies**en**, dies**es** + [NOUN]**es**.

Others, however, are the same for subject and non-subjects, e.g.

Dies**e** Frau [SUBJECT] spricht dies**e** Sprache [OBJECT].

This woman speaks this language.

Note that since German allows the word order OBJECT/VERB/SUBJECT the above sentence could also look like this:

Dies**e** Sprache [OBJECT] spricht dies**e** Frau [SUBJECT].

This woman speaks this language,

i.e. *This language is spoken by this woman.*

In such cases common sense and context help you to interpret the sentence correctly.

📖 If, later on, you wish to get further information on how to interpret determiner forms read **R102** and **R103**.

✎ **2e.** Check in the dictionary whether the following nouns are masculine/feminine/neuter and then with the help of the table in **R97** decide whether the noun is a subject or non-subject or whether it could be either.

	masc.	fem.	neut.	SUBJECT	NON-SUBJECT
1. dies**em** Dialekt	✔				✔
2. d**er** Mutter					
3. jen**es** Land					
4. ein**er** Bedeutung					
5. jed**er** Student					
6. dies**es** Problems					
7. manch**en** Freund					
8. jen**em** Buch					
9. ein**e** Komposition					
10. dies**er** Mensch					

Unlike in English there are several ways in which the PLURAL of a noun is formed, e.g.

Dialekt	>	Dialekt**e**	(*dialects*)
Sprache	>	Sprach**en**	(*languages*)
Land	>	L**ä**nd**er**	(*countries*)

📖 **R179** lists all plural form indicators.

If the plural form of a noun is given in a text, you have to be able to recognize the plural indicators so that you can discount them before looking up the singular form in the dictionary.

✎ **2f.** Practise this with the following nouns:

PLURAL	SINGULAR	PLURAL	SINGULAR
1. Gruppen		6. Bevölkerungen	
2. Wörter		7. Computer	
3. Mütter		8. Bücher	
4. Probleme		9. Konstruktionen	
5. Millionen		10. Kenntnisse	

Note that there are some masculine nouns which have -(e)n added in all non-subject forms in the singular as well as in the plural, e.g.

| der Mensch | (subject, singular) |
| den Mensch**en** | (object, singular) |

Be careful not to mistake these forms for plural forms (die Menschen).

📖 If, later on, you wish to find out more about this read **R101.2**.

2.3 Verb Idioms with es (1)

Es gibt   manchmal echte Kommunikationsschwierigkeiten.
There are sometimes real   communication problems.

There are some phrases involving **es** and a verb which have a meaning other than the literal translations. The most frequent one is **es gibt**.

> **es** *it*   **gibt** *gives*

However, **es gibt** usually means ***there is/there are***.

For future reference note: 'es gibt' also appears in the PAST TENSE forms:

> **es hat . . . gegeben**   *there has/have been*
> **es gab**   *there was/were*

📖 **R42** gives other such verb idioms with **es**.

2.4 What you should now be able to do: Check-list

Having worked through Chapter 2 you now should

■ be able to recognize the following words and know their English meaning.

NOUNS	Laute, Sprache, Dialekte, Ausländer, Deutschkenntnisse, Kommunikationsschwierigkeiten
PRONOUNS	sie (plural)
VERBS	aussprechen/spricht . . . aus/hat gesprochen, können, verstehen
ADJECTIVES	deutsch(en), verschieden(e), gut(en), echt(e), gleich
OTHER WORDS	natürlich, überall, mit, immer, alles, sofort, manchmal, deshalb, innerhalb
PHRASES	es gibt

■ know that in German there may be some words at the end of a sentence (the VERB COMPLETION) which have to be read together with the FINITE VERB

■ be able to spot SEPARABLE VERBS and know how to look them up in the dictionary

■ be able to deal with the COMPOUND PAST TENSE, i.e. to spot and correctly interpret AUXILIARY VERBS and PAST PARTICIPLES

■ know about MODAL VERBS, what they look like and how to read them in conjunction with the INFINITIVE at the end of the sentence

■ know that German NOUNS belong to one of three groups: masculine (der), feminine (die), neuter (das)

■ be able to recognize *-heit*, *-keit*, *-in*, *-ion*, *-schaft*, *-tät*, *-ung* as feminine noun endings

■ know how to find out from the dictionary whether a noun is masculine, feminine or neuter

■ recognize DETERMINERS (see **R97**)

■ know that the different functions of a NOUN (e.g. whether it is the SUBJECT or an OBJECT) can be signalled by the form of the DETERMINER

■ know which determiner forms are specifically NON-SUBJECT forms

■ know that there are several ways in which the PLURAL of nouns is formed in German and be familiar with the most common forms

■ be able to spot the fixed phrase 'es gibt' and its other tense forms 'es hat gegeben', 'es gab'

2.5 Now work out the meaning of a new text with the help of a dictionary. Again start by finding the finite verb, then check if there are any verb completions at the end of the sentence which have to be read together with the finite verb. If you are not quite sure yet about the procedure read again **R4**.

TEXT 2B

Letzten Sommer sind wir nach Osteuropa gefahren. In diesem Teil der Welt finden große Veränderungen statt, und man kann dort viel Interessantes erleben und entdecken. Mit der Sprache gibt es natürlich manchmal Schwierigkeiten. Aber trotz der Verständigungsprobleme haben wir dort viele nette Leute kennengelernt. Mit einer Familie haben wir besonders Freundschaft geschlossen [Freundschaft schließen *to make friends*]. Die Kinder dieser Familie wollen uns an Ostern in England besuchen. Sie kommen am 24. April in London an.

3

Read TEXTS 1A and 2A again:

Mehr als 100 Millionen Menschen sprechen Deutsch als Muttersprache. Aber nicht alle deutschsprechenden Leute wohnen in Deutschland. In Österreich, in einem Teil der Schweiz und in Liechtenstein spricht man auch Deutsch. Außerdem findet man deutschsprachige Bevölkerungsgruppen in vielen anderen Ländern.

Natürlich spricht man die Laute der deutschen Sprache nicht überall gleich aus. Selbst innerhalb Deutschlands hat man schon immer viele verschiedene Dialekte gesprochen. Deshalb können sogar Ausländer mit guten Deutschkenntnissen nicht immer alles sofort verstehen und manchmal gibt es echte Kommunikationsschwierigkeiten.

TEXT 3A

1 Die internationale Stellung der deutschen Sprache **hat** sich
*The international position of the German language **has***

2 im Verlauf unseres Jahrhunderts sehr **verändert:**
***changed** a lot in the course of our century.*

3 Bis in die dreißiger Jahre **galt** sie als
*Until the Thirties it **was regarded** as*

4 wichtigste Sprache der Wissenschaft — dann
the most important language of science — then

5 **überflügelte** Englisch das Deutsche bei weitem. In Osteuropa
*English **overtook** German by a long way. In Eastern Europe*

6 **war** Deutsch bis zum Zweiten Weltkrieg die traditionelle
*German **was,** up to the Second World War, the traditional*

7 Verbindungssprache. Danach **strich** man es
*lingua franca. After that one **deleted** it*

8 zugunsten von Russisch aus den Lehrplänen. Heute
in favour of Russian from the syllabuses. Today

9 **ist** die deutsche Sprache dank der veränderten Situation
*the German language **is** — thanks to the changed situation*

10 in Osteuropa als wirtschaftliche
in Eastern Europe — important again as a business

11 Kontaktsprache zwischen Ost und West wieder wichtig.
contact language between (the) East and West (of Europe).

Adapted from: Ulrich Ammon, 'Die deutsche Sprache: Lingua Franca im Schatten von Englisch?,' Deutschland, Zeitschrift für Politik, Kultur, Wirtschaft und Wissenschaft, (Feb. 94).

3.1 The Tenses

In the above text three different TENSE forms are used: the PRESENT TENSE, the COMPOUND PAST TENSE I (also called PERFECT TENSE), and the SIMPLE PAST TENSE (also called IMPERFECT TENSE). In the first two chapters we looked at the present tense and the compound past I. If you are still unsure about the various tenses read again **R23**.

3.2 The Simple Past Tense

galt (line 3), **überflügelte** (line 5), **war** (line 6), and **strich** (line 7) are SIMPLE PAST TENSE forms.

Now read **R29** and **R30**. Pay special attention to the way STRONG VERBS form their simple past tense. If you are not yet quite sure how to look up these forms in the dictionary read again **R169**.

3a. Now look up the infinitives of **galt, überflügelte, war, strich**, either in **R46** or in the list of Strong and Irregular Verbs in your dictionary.

3b. The following sentences are similar to the ones given in exercise **1c** in Chapter **1**. But this time the finite verbs are in the simple past tense. Again work out the infinitives.

1. Er sprach Deutsch, Spanisch und Englisch.
2. Viele Leute verstanden auch Englisch.
3. Wir lebten vier Jahre in Österreich.
4. Man hörte diesen Dialekt oft.
5. Er las ein Buch in seiner Muttersprache.
6. Letzten Sommer fuhr er nach London.
7. Sie begrüßte unsere amerikanischen Freunde.
8. Den Text übersetzte ich ins Englische.

You have now looked up all forms of the verb **sprechen** (*to speak*), i.e. **spricht, sprach, gesprochen** (*speaks, spoke, spoken*).

If you wish to get an overview of the patterns verbs may follow in both English and German, read **R35**.

3.3 The Use of Tenses (1)

It is important to note that there are also differences between English and German in the USE of tenses. Compare:

*Since 1980 he **has been living** in Berlin.* (Compound Past I)
Seit 1980 **wohnt** er in Berlin. (Present Tense)
(Lit: *Since 1980 he **lives** in Berlin*)

R37 and **R38** explain the main differences.

3.4 Verbs with a Reflexive Pronoun

... hat **sich** verändert (*has changed*) (lines 1 and 2)

The word **sich** is a so-called REFLEXIVE PRONOUN and here it is an integral part of the verb phrase. Verbs with **sich** are called REFLEXIVE VERBS. There are many of these in German.

📖 Read **R40** and **R41** to find out more about these verbs.

📖 Read **R169** if you are not quite sure yet how to look up these verbs in the dictionary.

✎ **3c.** Some of the following sentences contain verbs with a REFLEXIVE PRONOUN. With the help of the dictionary work out the meaning of these constructions.

1. Er behauptete das Gegenteil.
   He . . . . the opposite.
   Sie behauptete sich in der Diskussion.
   She . . . . in the discussion.

2. Dann ergaben sich neue Probleme.
   Then new problems . . . .
   Nach drei Monaten ergab sich die Armee bedingungslos.
   After three months the army unconditionally . . . .

3. Er interessiert sich für moderne Kunst.
   He . . . . in modern art.

4. Sie meldeten sich für einen Deutschkurs an.
   They . . . . for a German course.

5. Sie beschwert sich immer über seinen Dialekt.
   She always . . . . about his dialect.

3.5 Verbs with an Inseparable Prefix

überflügelte (*overtook*) (line 5)

über is here an **in**separable prefix, i.e. it appears in all tense forms attached to the verb.

📖 **R174** lists separable and inseparable prefixes. It will save you time in the long term if you begin to memorize them.

✎ **3d.** Find the infinitives of the following verbs. Don't forget to detach the prefix before looking up the basic form in **R46** or in the list in your dictionary.

1. versprach
2. überfuhr
3. verhielten
4. bedachte
5. verhörte

✎ **3e.** Now look up the meanings of the verbs in **3d**. Don't forget to reattach the prefix to the infinitive of the basic form before looking up the word in the dictionary.

3.6 Pronouns (1)

Bis in die dreißiger Jahre galt **sie** als wichtigste Sprache der Wissenschaft. (lines 3 and 4):
*Until the Thirties **it** was regarded as the most important language of science.*

Chapter 2 explained that German nouns belong to one of three groups: masculine, feminine, and neuter. If a PRONOUN (in the above example *it*) replaces the noun, it is also either masculine, feminine, or neuter.

	NOUN		PRONOUN	
masculine	der ein kein	Dialekt Dialekt Dialekt	er	*it*
feminine	die eine keine	Sprache Sprache Sprache	sie	*it*
neuter	das ein kein	Land Land Land	es	*it*

Note: here **er**, **sie** and **es** all mean *it* in English.

However, sometimes **er**, **sie**, and **es** also refer to people and then these pronouns mean *he*, *she*, *it*, or, in the plural, *they*:

der Mann	*the man*	**er**	*he*
die Frau	*the woman*	**sie**	*she*
das Kind	*the child*	**es**	*it*
PLURAL: **die** Studenten	*the students*	**sie**	*they*

Note: **sie** can be either singular or plural. Check whether the finite verb is in the singular or plural, e.g.

Sie spricht Englisch.	***She speaks** English.*
Sie sprechen Englisch.	***They speak** English.*

📖 See **R98** for a list of pronouns.

✎ **3f.** What do the PRONOUNS mean here: it/he/she/they? Tick the right one.

	it	he	she	they
1. **Er** (dieser Dialekt) ist sehr kompliziert.				
2. In Österreich sprechen **sie** (die Menschen) Deutsch.				
3. **Er** (der Ausländer) spricht kein Englisch.				
4. **Sie** (die Laute) sind nicht überall gleich.				
5. **Sie** (die Mutter) kann Deutsch sprechen.				
6. **Es** (das Land) hat sich sehr verändert.				

3.7 Fixed Phrases involving Verbs

sie **galt als**   wichtigste   Sprache der Wissenschaft. (lines 3 and 4):
it ***was regarded as***   *the most important language of science.*

gelten als *to be regarded as*

It can be difficult to identify fixed phrases in which a verb is closely tied to some other word (here **als** *as*) in terms of its meaning (in English for example 'believe **in**', 'think **of**' etc). The German word order allows these other words to appear in another part of the sentence, split off from the verb. The above sentence could also read:

Als wichtigste Sprache der Wissenschaft **galt** sie bis . . .

Check in your dictionary how **gelten als** is listed.

Read **R175** for further examples.

3.8 'als'

The word **als** has many meanings and functions. **R163** lists in alphabetical order such words with multiple functions. Look up **als** in this list. Then do the following exercise:

3g.   Which is the correct translation of **als**? Tick the right box.

A. than
B. when
C. as (in the capacity of)
D. is regarded as
E. as (if)

1. Er arbeitet als Lektor an der Universität.
2. Sie gilt als kompetent.
3. Er spricht so, als ob er Experte wäre (*were*).
4. Als er in Österreich wohnte, . . .
5. Diese Sprache ist komplizierter als Deutsch.

A	B	C	D	E

3.9 'man'

Man strich   Deutsch aus den   Lehrplänen. (lines 7–8)
One deleted   *German from the*   *syllabuses.*

Phrases with **man** are usually best rendered with a PASSIVE construction in English: *German **was deleted** from the syllabuses.* See **R78.1**.

Auch in Österreich **spricht man** Deutsch.
*In Austria too German **is spoken**.*

3.10 Adjectives (1)

■ die **deutsche** Sprache (line 9)
the German language

die Stellung der **deutschen** Sprache (line 1)
the position of the German language

The ADJECTIVE in both these phrases is **deutsch** (*German*). This is the form of the word as you will find it in the dictionary. However, adjectives carry slightly different endings depending on the role of the noun following the adjective, e.g. whether it is a subject or object. These endings do not change the meaning of the adjective.

■ die Sprache ist **wichtig**. (line 11)
the language is important

When an adjective comes after the noun it refers to, it has no ending added. If **wichtig** appeared before Sprache the phrase would read: die **wichtige** Sprache

■ Deutsch als **wichtigste** Sprache (lines 3 and 4)
German as the most important language

The **-st** signals that the ADJECTIVE is here used in the SUPERLATIVE form.

■ Note the superlative form for ADVERBS and post-noun ADJECTIVES.

Er spricht **am** deutlich**sten**.
He speaks most clearly (of all).

Diese Sprache ist **am** wichtig**sten**.
This language is (the) most important (of all).

■ The COMPARATIVE is formed by adding **-er**.

Diese Sprache ist **wichtiger**.
This language is more important.

Das ist eine **kompliziertere** Sprache.
This is a more complicated language.

Er spricht **deutlicher** als sein Freund.
He speaks more clearly than his friend.

■ As in English there are also irregular patterns. Consult your dictionary.

gern — lieber — am liebsten

Er spricht **gern** deutsch.
He likes to speak German.

Er spricht **lieber** deutsch.
He prefers to speak German.

Er spricht **am liebsten** deutsch.
Most of all he likes to speak German.

📖 **R106–9** give further information on adjectives.

3.11 Prepositions and Determiners

In 2.2 we saw that the form of a determiner can tell us whether the following noun functions as a subject or an object.

If the determiner is preceded by a PREPOSITION (i.e. words like *in, on, at, to, with*, etc.) this also affects the form of the determiner, e.g.

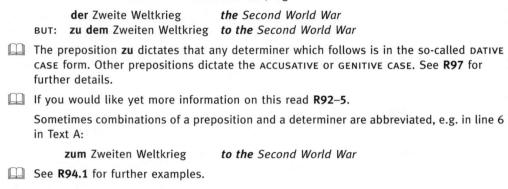

| | **der** Zweite Weltkrieg | *the Second World War* |
| BUT: | **zu dem** Zweiten Weltkrieg | *to the Second World War* |

The preposition **zu** dictates that any determiner which follows is in the so-called DATIVE CASE form. Other prepositions dictate the ACCUSATIVE or GENITIVE CASE. See **R97** for further details.

If you would like yet more information on this read **R92–5**.

Sometimes combinations of a preposition and a determiner are abbreviated, e.g. in line 6 in Text A:

zum Zweiten Weltkrieg   *to the Second World War*

See **R94.1** for further examples.

3.12 What you should now be able to do: Check-list

Having worked through Chapter 3 you now should

- be able to recognize the following words and know their English meaning:

NOUNS	die Stellung(-en), der Verlauf(⸚e), das Jahrhundert(-e), das Jahr(-e), die Wissenschaft(-en), Englisch, Osteuropa, der Zweite Weltkrieg, die Verbindungssprache(-n), Russisch, der Lehrplan(⸚e), die Situation(-en), die Kontaktsprache(-n), →**R179** for plural indicators
PRONOUNS	er, sie, es, sie (plural),
VERBS	sich verändern, überflügeln, war, streichen, ist,
ADJECTIVES	international, wichtig, traditionell, verändert, wirtschaftlich
OTHER WORDS	unser, sehr, in, bis, heute, zwischen, wieder
PHRASES	gelten als

- know how the SIMPLE PAST TENSE is formed
- be able to spot finite verbs in the SIMPLE PAST TENSE and work out their infinitives
- be aware of the differences between English and German in the use of tenses
- be able to recognize verbs with a REFLEXIVE PRONOUN and work out their meanings
- recognize INSEPARABLE PREFIXES of verbs
- be able to interpret whether a particular PRONOUN refers to an object or a person
- know that phrases with 'man' are often best read as a PASSIVE in English
- be able to look up fixed phrases involving verbs, such as 'gelten als'
- be able to work out the basic form of ADJECTIVES, i.e. without any endings
- be able to spot COMPARATIVE and SUPERLATIVE forms of adjectives and adverbs
- know that PREPOSITIONS dictate a particular CASE form and be able to recognize common PREPOSITIONS (See **R94, 95**).

3.13 Now work out the meaning of the following text with the help of a dictionary.

TEXT 3B

Friedrich der Große von Preußen (1740–86) sprach und schrieb lieber französisch als deutsch. Diese Haltung war im 18. Jahrhundert am Hof und in Teilen der Bildungsschichten vorherrschend, nicht nur in Deutschland, sondern fast überall in Europa. Französisch dominierte als internationale Sprache. Dies änderte sich im Verlauf des 19. Jahrhunderts. Dann büßte Frankreich seine dominante politische Stellung auf dem europäischen Kontinent ein, und die Bedeutung von Deutsch als internationale Sprache nahm langsam zu.

Adapted from: Ulrich Ammon, 'Die deutsche Sprache: Lingua Franca im Schatten von Englisch?', *Deutschland, Zeitschrift für Politik, Kultur, Wirtschaft und Wissenschaft*, 1 (Feb. 94).

....

This is TEXT 3A again. Can you remember what it meant? Bearing in mind the structural points discussed in the last chapter, try to read it again. Use the dictionary if necessary.

Die internationale Stellung der deutschen Sprache hat sich im Verlauf unseres Jahrhunderts sehr verändert: Bis in die dreißiger Jahre galt Deutsch als wichtigste Sprache der Wissenschaft. Dann überflügelte Englisch das Deutsche bei weitem. In Osteuropa war Deutsch bis zum Zweiten Weltkrieg die traditionelle Verbindungssprache. Danach strich man es zugunsten von Russisch aus den Lehrplänen. Heute ist die deutsche Sprache dank der veränderten Situation in Osteuropa als wirtschaftliche Kontaktsprache zwischen Ost und West wieder wichtig.

TEXT 4A

1 **Steht** Deutsch heute im Schatten von Englisch?
*Does German **stand** today in the shadow of English?*

2 Wenn man die heutigen Verhältnisse
*If one **compares** the present conditions/state of affairs*

3 mit den früheren **vergleicht, muß** man unumwunden
*with (the) former (ones), one **must** quite frankly*

4 die Frage **bejahen.**
answer** the question **in the affirmative.

5 Deutschsprachige Wissenschaftler, vor allem
German-speaking scientists, above all

6 Naturwissenschaftler, **veröffentlichen** heute oft genauso-
*natural scientists, **publish** nowadays often just as*

7 viel auf englisch wie auf deutsch. Aber Deutsch **bleibt**
*much in English as in German. But German **remains***

8 als Wissenschaftssprache **interessant,**
***interesting** as (a) language of science*

9 weil in dieser Sprache zahlreiche klassische, bahnbrechende
because in this language numerous classical, pioneering

10 Theorien **formuliert wurden,** z. B. Albert Einsteins
*theories **were (have been) formulated,** e.g. Albert Einstein's*

11 Relativitätstheorie, Max Webers oder Karl Marx'
theory of relativity, Max Weber's or Karl Marx's

12 sozialwissenschaftliche Theorien oder die Philosophien, die
social science theories or the philosophies which

13 Wittgenstein und Heidegger **entwickelten.** Obwohl die meisten
*Wittgenstein and Heidegger **developed.** Although most*

14   dieser Texte   in englischer Übersetzung **vorliegen,**
*of these texts **are available** in (an) English translation*

15   **lohnt sich** doch für viele Akademiker   **die Mühe,**
it is   *for many academics, nevertheless, **worth the effort***

16   diese Texte im Original   **zu lesen.**
***to read** these texts in the original.*

Adapted from: Ulrich, Ammon, 'Die deutsche Sprache: Lingua Franca im Schatten von Englisch?, *Deutschland, Zeitschrift für Politik, Kultur, Wirtschaft und Wissenschaft*, 1 (Feb. 94).

4.1 Word Order in Yes/No Questions

Steht Deutsch   heute im Schatten von Englisch? (line 1)
***Does** German **stand** today in the shadow of English?*

In so-called YES/NO QUESTIONS (i.e. questions which can be answered by either yes or no) the finite verb is found in Position I, usually followed by the subject. No auxiliary verb (English: *does*) is used in German.

 4a.   Compare the word order in the following sentences. Which are STATEMENTS and which are YES/NO QUESTIONS? Add a question mark or a full stop as appropriate.

1. In Österreich spricht man Deutsch
   Spricht man in Österreich Deutsch

2. 90 Millionen Menschen sprechen Deutsch als Muttersprache
   Sprechen 90 Millionen Menschen Deutsch als Muttersprache

3. Ist Deutsch heute als Wirtschaftssprache wichtig
   Heute ist Deutsch als Wirtschaftssprache wichtig

4. Galt Deutsch bis in die dreißiger Jahre als wichtigste Wissenschaftssprache
   Deutsch galt bis in die dreißiger Jahre als wichtigste Wissenschaftssprache

5. Die internationale Stellung der deutschen Sprache hat sich sehr verändert
   Hat sich die internationale Stellung der deutschen Sprache sehr verändert

4.2 Word Order in Questions with a Question Word

In questions with a so-called QUESTION WORD (e.g. **wann** (*when*), **warum** (*why*), **was** (*what*), **wie** (*how*), **wieviel** (*how many*), **wo** (*where*), etc.), the finite verb follows the question word, e.g.

I   II
Wo   **spricht**   man Deutsch als Muttersprache?
Where does one speak German as the mother tongue?

Wann   **war** Deutsch als Wissenschaftsprache wichtig?
When was German important as the language of science?

4b. Here are examples of both types of questions. Work out their meanings. Use a dictionary if necessary.

1. Warum muß man diese Frage bejahen?
2. Hat Albert Einstein diese Theorie formuliert?
3. Wann veröffentlichte er diese These?
4. Wo findet man deutschsprachige Bevölkerungsgruppen?
5. Liegt dieser Text in englischer Übersetzung vor?
6. Spricht man in der Schweiz auch Deutsch?
7. Was hat er letzten Sommer gemacht?
8. Wie spricht man dieses Wort aus?
9. Gab es viele Kommunikationsschwierigkeiten?
10. Kannst du dieses Wort verstehen?

4.3 Sentences and Clauses

The complex sentence in lines 13, 14, 15, and 16 is split into three sections (called CLAUSES) separated by commas:

Obwohl die meisten dieser Texte in englischer Übersetzung vorliegen,
Although most of these texts are available in English translations,

lohnt sich doch für viele Akademiker die Mühe,
it is, nevertheless, worth the effort for many academics,

diese Texte im Original zu lesen.
to read these texts in the original.

Only the second clause could be read on its own as a sentence with a complete meaning. Such 'independent' clauses are called MAIN CLAUSES. The other two clauses could not stand as sentences on their own; they are dependent on the main clause. Therefore they are called DEPENDENT CLAUSES. However, they add important information to the information contained in the main clause.

4.4 Word Order in Dependent Clauses (1)

Obwohl die meisten dieser Texte in englischer Übersetzung **vorliegen**,
***Although** most of these texts **are available** in English translations,*

The first dependent clause starts with a so-called CONJUNCTION (**obwohl** *although*). For a list of conjunctions see **R143**.

In this type of clause the finite verb (here: **vorliegen** *are available*) appears in final position at the very end of the clause.

In TEXT 4A there are two other dependent clauses starting with a conjunction:

Wenn man die heutigen Verhältnisse mit den früheren **vergleicht,**
*If one **compares** the present conditions with the former (ones),*

. . ., **weil** in dieser Sprache zahlreiche Theorien veröffentlicht **wurden.**
*. . ., **because** in this language numerous theories **were (have been)** published.*

Note: If the dependent clause precedes the main clause the finite verb of the main clause comes straight after the comma, i.e. straight after the finite verb of the dependent clause:

Wenn man die heutigen Verhältnisse . . . **vergleicht, muß** man . . .
Obwohl die meisten dieser Texte . . . **vorliegen, lohnt** sich . . .

For detailed information on dependent clauses read **R141–4.**

4c. First decide which of the following clauses are dependent clauses by spotting the conjunction and the finite verb in final position. Then work out the meaning of the entire sentence. Use a dictionary if necessary.

1. Obwohl er sein Buch schon 1982 veröffentlichte, kannte ich seine Theorie nicht.
2. Er hat Deutsch gelernt, weil er dieses Buch im Original lesen will.
3. Ich weiß (→note in **R28**), daß man in Österreich Deutsch spricht.
4. Als er in Berlin wohnte, lernte er schnell Deutsch.
5. Wenn er diesen Dialekt spricht, verstehe ich ihn nicht.

4.5 Word Order in Dependent Clauses (2): zu + Infinitive Clauses (1)

. . ., diese Texte im Original **zu lesen.**
*. . . **to read** these texts in the original.*

The second dependent clause in the complex sentence in 4.3 is a so-called ZU + INFINITIVE CLAUSE where the ZU + INFINITIVE (**zu lesen** *to read*) takes up the position at the end of the clause.

Such clauses are traditionally split off from the main clause by a comma. However, the spelling reform of 1996 (see **R191**) did away with this tradition. Therefore, if you read post-1996 texts, you have to be prepared for ZU + INFINITIVE clauses not being split off by a comma.

If you wish to read more about ZU + INFINITIVE clauses see **R149** and **R150.**

4d. Work out the meaning of the following sentences. Use a dictionary if necessary.

1. Die Mühe lohnt sich(,) dieses Buch zu übersetzen.
2. Ist es wichtig(,) Deutsch zu lernen?
3. Diese Sprache schnell zu lernen(,) ist sehr schwierig.
4. In dieser Situation ist es leicht(,) neue Leute zu treffen.
5. Er hat die Absicht(,) dieses Buch im Original zu lesen.

4.6 Relative Clauses (1)

. . . die Philosophien, **die** Wittgenstein und Heidegger **entwickelten**.
. . . *the philosophies **which** Wittgenstein and Heidegger **developed**.*

RELATIVE CLAUSES give further information on preceding nouns (or, sometimes, preceding clauses). The word order is the same as for dependent clauses introduced by a conjunction, i.e. the finite verb appears in the final position at the end of the clause.

The RELATIVE PRONOUN (above: **die** *which*) appears straight after the comma and, depending on the context, invariably means ***which/that/who***. However, the relative pronoun may act as the subject or as the object of the verb in the relative clause. Here are some examples:

der Student, **der** Deutsch lernt, . . .   *the student **who** is learning German*
der Student, **den** ich besuche, . . .   *the student **whom** I am visiting*
der Student, **dem** ich schreibe, . . .   *the student **to whom** I am writing*
der Student, **dessen** Adresse ich habe, . . .   *the student **whose** address I have*

Note that most relative pronouns look like determiners. But there are also some specific forms (e.g. **dessen**).

📖 Read **R147–8** and **R110–14** for more detailed information on relative clauses.

✎ **4e.** Work out the meaning of the following relative clauses.

1. . . . der Dialekt, den man im Süden von Deutschland spricht.
2. . . . die Sprache, die er nicht verstanden hat.
3. . . . Wissenschaftler, die Artikel veröffentlichen.
4. . . . die Situation, die sich geändert hat.
5. . . . Deutsch, das man aus den Lehrplänen gestrichen hat.

4.7 Review of Types of Clauses

We have now looked at most types of clauses. Can you remember their structures?

Here is an exercise to help you to test your recognition. If you are not yet quite sure about how to distinguish between them, look again at the appropriate sections in the Reference Section. [Conjunctions: **R143**, Relative Pronouns: **R110**, Connectors: **R160**, zu + Infinitives: **R149**, Question Words: **R10.8**, and for an overview of VERB-FINAL clauses: **R11–14**]

✎ **4f.** A. Remember, the finite verb is the key to the sentence. So start by underlining all finite verbs, then mark any conjunctions, relative pronouns, connectors, zu + infinitives, question words.

B. Then decide what type of clause you are dealing with.

A.

1. Hast du seinen Dialekt verstanden?

2. Wo spricht man diese Sprache?

3. Wenn man diesen Dialekt nicht kennt, kann man das nicht verstehen.

4. Er will jetzt in dieses Land reisen und diese Sprache lernen.

5. Weil er dieses Buch, das er auf Englisch gelesen hat, jetzt im Original lesen will, lernt er diese Sprache.

6. Obwohl diese Sprache schwer ist, hat er die Absicht, sie schnell zu lernen.

B. Write down the type of clause you are dealing with, e.g. Dependent Clause, Relative Clause, Question with a Question Word, etc.

1. . . . .

2. . . . .

3. . . . . . , ...

4. . . . .

5. . . . . , ... , ...
. . . , ...

6. . . . . , ... , .
. . . .

4.8 Passive Constructions (1)

weil in dieser Sprache zahlreiche Theorien **formuliert wurden**. (lines 9–10)
*because many theories **were formulated** in this language.*

This is a PASSIVE construction. [ACTIVE: *Someone formulated theories.*] The auxiliary verb **werden** (For forms see **R31**.) is used together with a past participle.

In the sentence above the simple past tense form is used (*were formulated*).

Here are some other tense forms of the same sentence in the singular and in the plural:

PRESENT

Die Theorie **wird formuliert**.   Theorien **werden formuliert**.
*The theory **is being formulated**.*   *Theories **are (being) formulated**.*

COMPOUND PAST I

Die Theorie **ist formuliert worden**.   Theorien **sind formuliert worden**.
*The theory **has been formulated**.*   *Theories **have been formulated**.*

FUTURE I

Die Theorie **wird formuliert werden**.   Theorien **werden formuliert werden**.
*The theory **will be formulated**.*   *Theories **will be formulated**.*

also with a MODAL VERB

Die Theorie **muß formuliert werden**.   Theorien **müssen formuliert werden**.
*The theory **must be formulated**.*   *Theories **must be formulated**.*

For all other tense forms and further information on the passive with **werden** see **R74** and **R75**.

✍ **4g.** What do these sentences mean? Use a dictionary if necessary.

1. In Österreich spricht man Deutsch.
   In Österreich wird Deutsch gesprochen.
2. Er hat den Text ins Deutsche übersetzt.
   Der Text ist ins Deutsche übersetzt worden.
3. Wann wurde diese Theorie von Einstein formuliert?
   Wann formulierte Einstein diese Theorie?
4. Von welchem Verlag war dieses Buch veröffentlicht worden?
   Welcher Verlag hatte dieses Buch veröffentlicht?
5. Diese Frage kann jetzt beantwortet werden.
   Man kann diese Frage jetzt beantworten.

4.9 What you should now be able to do: Check-list

Having worked through Chapter 4 you now should

■ be able to recognize the following words and know their English meaning:

NOUNS   der Schatten (-), das Verhältnis (-se), die Frage (-n), der Wissenschaftler (-), der Naturwissenschaftler (-), die Wissenschaftssprache (-n), die Theorie (-n), die Philosophie (-n), der Text (-e), die Übersetzung (-en), der Akademiker (-), die Mühe (-n), das Original (-e)

VERBS   stehen, vergleichen, bejahen, veröffentlichen, bleiben, formulieren, entwickeln, vorliegen, sich lohnen, lesen

ADJECTIVES   heutig, früher, interessant, zahlreich, sozialwissenschaftlich

CONJUNCTIONS   wenn, weil, obwohl

OTHER WORDS   oft, oder, für

PHRASES   vor allem, genausoviel wie

■ know about the WORD ORDER in Yes/No Questions

■ know about the WORD ORDER in questions with a Question Word

■ know that there are MAIN CLAUSES and DEPENDENT CLAUSES

■ be able to recognize CONJUNCTIONS (see **R143**)

■ know about the WORD ORDER in DEPENDENT CLAUSES

■ know about ZU + INFINITIVES

■ know what RELATIVE PRONOUNS look like and recognize RELATIVE CLAUSES

■ recognize PASSIVE constructions with 'werden' and know how to read them

4.10 Now work out the meaning of the following text. Use a dictionary when necessary.

TEXT 4B

Zahlreiche Fremdwörter wurden in den letzten Jahrzehnten aus dem Englischen in deutschsprachige wissenschaftliche Texte übernommen. Warum soll das aber ein Problem sein? Die Antwort ist einfach: Diese Wörter werden oft orthographisch, phonetisch und grammatisch gar nicht an die deutsche Sprache angepaßt, sondern ganz in englischer Form übernommen. Solche Texte, die viele solche Fremdwörter enthalten, werden oft kritisiert, weil die Kommunikation zwischen Wissenschaftlern und Laien in Deutschland durch die englischen Termini erschwert wird.

Adapted from: Ulrich Ammon, 'Die deutsche Sprache: Lingua Franca im Schatten von Englisch?', *Deutschland, Zeitschrift für Politik, Kultur, Wirtschaft und Wissenschaft*, 1 (Feb. 94).

5

· · · · · · · · · · · · · · · · · · ·

Read TEXT 4A again:

Steht Deutsch heute im Schatten von Englisch? Wenn man die heutigen Verhältnisse mit den früheren vergleicht, muß man unumwunden die Frage bejahen. Deutschsprachige Wissenschaftler, vor allem Naturwissenschaftler, veröffentlichen heute oft genausoviel auf englisch wie auf deutsch. Aber Deutsch bleibt als Wissenschaftssprache interessant, weil in dieser Sprache zahlreiche klassische, bahnbrechende Theorien formuliert wurden, z. B. Albert Einsteins Relativitätstheorie, Max Webers oder Karl Marx' sozialwissenschaftliche Theorien oder Ludwig Wittgensteins und Martin Heideggers Philosophien. Obwohl die meisten dieser Texte in englischer Übersetzung vorliegen, lohnt sich doch für viele Akademiker die Mühe, diese Texte im Original zu lesen.

TEXT 5A

1 Es **gibt** zwei Hauptgründe dafür, daß Deutsch
*There **are** two main reasons for the fact that German **was** not **able to***

2 seine Spitzenstellung als internationale Wissenschaftssprache
***hold** its top position as (an) international language of science.*

3 nicht **halten konnte**. Erstens **sind** Deutschland und das
First Germany and

4 wissenschaftlich ebenfalls bedeutsame
German-speaking Austria, which as far as science is concerned is just as

5 deutschsprachige Österreich durch
important, were ruined by

6 den Ersten Weltkrieg **ruiniert worden**. Deutschland **hatte** nach dem
*the First World War. Germany **had** after the*

7 Krieg nicht die Ressourcen, um die wissenschaftliche
*war not the resources (in order) **to advance** (the) scientific*

8 Entwicklung weiterhin **voranzutreiben**. Der zweite, noch
developments further. The second, even

9 einschneidendere Grund **war** der Nationalsozialismus, durch den
*more decisive reason **was** (the) National Socialism, because of which*

10 zahlreiche Wissenschaftler aus Deutschland und Österreich
numerous scientists from Germany and Austria were

11 **verjagt** oder **umgebracht wurden** und durch dessen Folgen
***forced to leave** or (were) **murdered** and as a result of which*

12 weitere nach dem Krieg **gezwungen waren**,
*more **were forced** after the war*

13 **zu emigrieren**, weil sie in ihrem zerstörten Land
***to emigrate,** because they **had** no longer in their destroyed country*

14 keine Arbeitsmöglichkeit   mehr **hatten**.
the opportunity to work.

Adapted from: Ulrich Ammon, 'Die deutsche Sprache: Lingua Franca im Schatten von Englisch?' *Deutschland, Zeitschrift für Politik, Kultur, Wirtschaft und Wissenschaft*, 1 (Feb. 94).

5.1 Phrases involving Prepositions (1)

Es gibt zwei Hauptgründe da**für**, daß . . . (line 1)

PREPOSITIONS (words like *in*, *on*, *at*, etc.) can be linked to nouns (e.g. *interest **in**, reason **for**) or to verbs (e.g. *to agree **on**, to search **for***). If the phrase is not completed in the same clause but in the next one, i.e. if the answer to the question *interest **in*** or *search **for*** WHAT is not given before the comma, in German **da** (or **dar** if the preposition starts with a vowel) is added to the preposition as a kind of stand-in word.

So the literal meaning of the above is:

*There are two main reasons for [**this** /it/the fact], that . . .*

However, phrases of this kind involving da + PREPOSITIONS are often rendered better by not trying to find an equivalent word for **da** in English, but to search for the appropriate English phrase, e.g.

*There are two main reasons **why** German was not able to . . .*

📖 **R155** will give you further information on this kind of construction. For lists of prepositions see **R94** and **R95**.

✎ **5a.**   Work out the meaning of the following sentences.

1A. Er hat Angst vor dem Examen.

1B. Er hat Angst davor, daß er das Examen nicht besteht.

2A. Sie denkt nicht an diese Tatsache.

2B. Sie denkt nicht daran, daß es in Österreich viele Dialekte gibt.

3A. Ich begann den Vortrag mit der Erklärung der Hauptpunkte.

3B. Ich begann den Vortrag damit, daß ich die Hauptpunkte erklärte.

4A. Wir glauben nicht an seinen Entschluß, Deutsch zu lernen.

4B. Wir glauben nicht daran, daß er Deutsch lernen will.

5A. Er träumte von einer Europareise.

5B. Er träumte davon, eine Europareise zu machen.

6A. Er besteht auf einer sofortigen Lösung des Problems.

6B. Er besteht darauf, daß das Problem sofort gelöst wird.

5.2 Extended Adjective Phrases (1)

Deutschland und das **wissenschaftlich ebenfalls bedeutsame** deutschsprachige Österreich
*Germany and (the) **in scientific terms just as important** German-speaking Austria*

The adjective phrase printed in bold gives further information about the noun which follows, i.e. *German-speaking Austria*. This kind of construction is sometimes found in English too, e.g.

a *frequently visited*	German-speaking country
this *often* discussed	problem
his *sometimes rather unhelpful* comments	

In written German this kind of EXTENDED ADJECTIVE PHRASE (EAP) occurs very frequently, especially in academic German, formal documents, and the quality press.

In English such phrases are usually rendered by a relative clause:

Germany and (the) German-speaking Austria, **which in scientific terms (** lit.: *scientifically)* **is just as important**.

📖 Read **R115** for further information.

✎ **5b.** Work out the meaning of the following phrases. If necessary use a dictionary.

1. ein **besonders für Dialektsprecher kompliziertes** Problem
2. die **im Westen unveränderte soziale** Situation
3. viele **für Wissenschaftler interessante** neue Theorien
4. manche **für diesen Dialekt klassischen** Aussprachprobleme
5. eine **für Sprachwissenschaftler** wichtige Frage

5.3 zu + Infinitive Clauses (2)

In Chapter 4.5 ZU + INFINITIVE clauses were introduced. In lines 7–8 in TEXT 5A we find another zu + infinitive clause, but this time the clause is introduced by the word **um** *in order to.*

. . . **um** die wissenschaftliche Entwicklung **voranzutreiben**.

. . . *in order to advance* the scientific development.

Note: Because **vorantreiben** is a separable verb **zu** appears between the prefix and the stem. See **R39**.

📖 Read **R151** for further information on such 'introduced' zu + infinitive clauses.

✎ **5c.** Now work out the meaning of the following sentences with zu + infinitive clauses.

1. Er lernt Deutsch, um diesen Text im Original zu lesen.
2. Um diesen Dialekt verstehen zu können, muß man viele Jahre im Land gelebt haben. (See **R7** for Word Order)
3. Um diesen Satz ins Englische zu übersetzen, brauche ich ein Wörterbuch.
4. Er braucht Zeit, um diese neue Theorie zu formulieren.
5. Um dieses Ziel zu erreichen, muß er viel arbeiten.

5.4 The Use of Tenses (2)

The core information in the sentence in lines 3–6 of Text 5A reads:

Deutschland u. Österreich sind durch den Ersten Weltkrieg **ruiniert worden**.

(Lit.:) *Germany and Austria **have been ruined** by the First World War.*

The tense used in German is the Compound Past I. In English, however, the past tense reads better:

*Germany and Austria **were ruined** by the First World War.*

📖 **R37** and **R38** give further information on the differences in the use of the tenses. If you have not yet read them, do so now.

5.5 Adjectives (2): The Comparative

Der zweite, noch einschneidend**ere** Grund (lines 8–9)
*The second, **even more decisive** reason*

As shown in 3.9, the -**er** signals the COMPARATIVE form. However, sometimes -**er** is simply an adjective ending.

Compare the following sentence with the one above:

ein zweit**er**, einschneidend**er** Grund
*a second **decisive** reason*

📖 Read **R107.1** for further information.

✎ **5d.** Underline the comparative -**er** indicators only:

   1. die früheren Verhältnisse
   2. bedeutsamere Theorien
   3. ein interessanter Grund
   4. kompliziertere Sprachen
   5. ein schwieriger Anfang

5.6 Relative Clauses (2)

der Nationalsozialismus,
durch den zahlreiche Wissenschaftler . . . verjagt oder umgebracht wurden und
durch dessen Folgen weitere . . . gezwungen waren zu emigrieren (lines 9–12)
National Socialism,
because of which *(lit.: through which) numerous scientists were forced to leave or were murdered and*
as a consequence of which *(lit.: through whose consequences) more were forced to emigrate*

Here the relative pronouns (**den, dessen** *which, whose*) are preceded by a preposition (**durch**). The above relative clauses are quite difficult to translate into English. So here are a few more straight-forward examples of this kind of construction:

> das Auto, **mit dem** er nach Deutschland fuhr,
> *the car **with which** he drove to Germany*
>
> die Übersetzung, **von der** er sprach,
> *the translation **of which** he spoke*
>
> der Freund, **von dessen** Problemen er nichts wußte,
> *the friend **of whose** problems he did not know anything*

📖 If you would like more information on this kind of construction read **R114** and **R147**.

✎ **5e.** Work out the meaning of the following relative clauses.

1. . . . die Theorie, von der er gesprochen hat.
2. . . . eine Möglichkeit, an die er nicht gedacht hat.
3. . . . dieser Wissenschaftler, für den er den Text übersetzt hat.
4. . . . seine Freunde, mit denen er nach Osteuropa fuhr.
5. . . . das Land, aus dem sie verjagt wurden.

5.7 Negation (2)

kein-, as shown in 2.2, means *no*. So **keine Möglichkeit** means *no opportunity*. But now look at lines 13–14 in Text 5A:

> . . ., weil sie . . . **keine** Arbeitsmöglichkeit **mehr** hatten.
> *. . ., because they **no longer** had the opportunity to work.*

Both **nicht** and **kein** can be used in combination with other words in fixed phrases. In such combinations the meaning may differ from the meaning of the individual words.

mehr means *more*.
BUT: **nicht/kein . . . mehr** means *no longer*
keine Möglichkeit mehr means *no longer any opportunity*

📖 See **R126** for further examples of such phrases.

✎ **5f.** Work out the meaning of the following sentences:

1. Er wohnt nicht mehr in Berlin.
2. Hat Deutsch keine Bedeutung mehr als Wissenschaftssprache?
3. Es gibt jetzt keine Kommunikationsschwierigkeiten mehr.
4. Gibt es Deutsch nicht mehr im Lehrplan?
5. Arbeitet er nicht mehr an der Universität?

5.8 Logical Connectors (1)

Text 5A, line 1: Es gibt **zwei** Hauptgründe . . . *(There are **two** main reasons . . .)*
line 3: **Erstens** . . .   *(**First** . . .)*
line 8: Der **zweite** [. . .] Grund . . .   *(The **second** reason . . .)*

The recognition of LOGICAL CONNECTORS [here: erstens *first(ly)*] helps you to see more clearly how a text is structured. This enables you to follow more easily the arguments put forward in the text, thus speeding up the reading process.

📖 See **R139** for a list of common logical connectors.

5.9 What you should now be able to do: Check-list

Having worked through Chapter 5 you now should

■ be able to recognize the following words and know their English meaning:

NOUNS	der (Haupt)grund (⸚e), die (Spitzen)stellung (-en), die Wissenschaftssprache (-n), der (Welt)krieg (-e), die Entwicklung (-en), der Nationalsozialismus, die Folge (-n), die (Arbeit)[s]möglichkeit (-en)
VERBS	halten, ruinieren, vorantreiben, verjagen, umbringen, zwingen, emigrieren
ADJECTIVES	bedeutsam, wissenschaftlich, zahlreich, zerstört
CONJUNCTIONS	daß
OTHER WORDS	erstens, zweite
PHRASES	ebenfalls

■ know how to deal with a da + PREPOSITION before a *daß*-Clause or a *zu* + INFINITIVE CLAUSE

■ be able to work out the meaning of simple EXTENDED ADJECTIVE PHRASES

■ recognize zu + INFINITIVE clauses introduced by '*um*' and know how to translate them into English

■ be aware that here are differences in the USE of TENSES in English and German

■ be able to recognize the COMPARATIVE *-er*

■ be able to recognize RELATIVE CLAUSES introduced by a PREPOSITION

■ know that '*nicht mehr*' or '*kein* + NOUN *mehr*' mean '*no longer*'

■ realize that the recognition of LOGICAL CONNECTORS helps one to see the structure of a text more clearly

5.10 Now work out the meaning of the following text with the help of a dictionary. Watch out, lines 2–3 contain an Extended Adjective Phrase.

TEXT 5B

Spanisch und Arabisch wurden Amtssprachen der Vereinten Nationen, weil sie staatliche Amtssprachen zahlreicher Länder sind. Durch diese bevorzugte Stellung in einer in vieler Hinsicht so wichtigen Organisation wie den Vereinten Nationen wird wiederum die internationale Stellung der Sprachen gestärkt. Sie spielen dann z. B. eine größere Rolle in der sprachlichen Ausbildung von Diplomaten. Um die Rangstufe von Deutsch in der Amtssprachenskala zu bestimmen, muß man die Anzahl der Länder wissen, in denen Deutsch die staatliche Amtssprache ist.

Adapted from: Ulrich Ammon, 'Die deutsche Sprache: Lingua Franca im Schatten von Englisch?', *Deutschland, Zeitschrift für Politik, Kultur, Wirtschaft und Wissenschaft*, 1, Feb. (94)

Read TEXT 5A again:

Es gibt zwei Hauptgründe dafür, daß Deutsch seine Spitzenstellung als internationale Wissenschaftssprache nicht halten konnte. Erstens sind Deutschland und das wissenschaftlich ubenfalls bedeutsame deutschsprachige Österreich durch den Ersten Weltkrieg ruiniert worden. Deutschland hatte nach dem Krieg nicht die Ressourcen, um die wissenschaftliche Entwicklung weiterhin voranzutreiben. Der zweite, noch einschneidendere Grund war der Nationalsozialismus, durch den zahlreiche Wissenschaftler aus Deutschland und Österreich verjagt oder umgebracht wurden und durch dessen Folgen weitere nach dem Krieg gezwungen waren, zu emigrieren, weil sie in ihrem zerstörten Land keine Arbeitsmöglichkeit mehr hatten.

TEXT 6A

1 Professor Ammon **behauptet**, der Rangverlust von Deutsch als
*Professor Ammon **argues** that the decline in the standing of German as*

2 Wissenschaftssprache **habe** seine tiefere Ursache im Rangverlust
*a scientific language **has** its deeper roots in the decline in the status*

3 der Wissenschaft in den deutschsprachigen Ländern.
of the natural sciences in the German-speaking countries.

4 An ihrer Stelle **hätten** die USA, d. h. ein englischsprachiges Land,
Instead (lit. *in their place*) *the USA, i.e. an English-speaking country, **had***

5 die wissenschaftliche Führung in der Welt **übernommen**.
***taken over** the scientific leadership of the world.*

6 Ein grober, aber doch brauchbarer Indikator für diese
A crude but none the less effective indicator of this

7 Verschiebung **sei** der Anteil der deutschsprachigen
*shift **is** (to be found in) the proportion of German-speaking*

8 und der englischsprachigen Wissenschaftler an den Nobelpreisen. Hier
and English-speaking scientists (who have won) Nobel prizes. Here

9 **gebe** es eine deutliche Parallele: **Während** 1920 noch 44% der
*there **is** a clear parallel: While in 1920 44% of the*

10 Nobelpreisträger für Naturwissenschaften
*Nobel Prize-winners in the natural sciences **were** still*

11 deutschsprachiger Herkunft **waren**, und nur 33,3% englischsprachiger
of German-speaking origin, and only 33.3% of English-speaking

12 Herkunft, **betrug** z. B. 1980 der Anteil deutschsprachiger
origin, in 1980, for example, the proportion of German-speaking

13 Naturwissenschaftler nur noch 11,9%, aber der Anteil der
*natural scientists **was** only just 11.9%, but the proportion of*

14 englischsprachigen Nobelpreisträger **war** auf 64,1% **gestiegen**.
*English-speaking Nobel Prize-winners **had risen** to 64.1%.*

Adapted from: Ulrich Ammon, 'Die deutsche Sprache: Lingua Franca im Schatten von Englisch?', *Deutschland, Zeitschrift für Politik, Kultur, Wirtschaft und Wissenschaft*, 1 (Feb. 94).

6.1 Non-Factual Verb Forms (1)

All verb forms which have appeared in the texts so far are the ones used for FACTUAL statements. However, if writers want to make a hypothetical statement or want to show that they are passing on someone else's words, a different verb form may be used.

Line 1 in the above text starts with:

Professor Ammon **behauptet** *Professor Ammon **says/claims/argues***
What follows therefore is really very like a verbatim quote and to indicate this we find in line 2:

the NON-FACTUAL verb form: . . . das **habe** seine tiefere Ursache im. . .
instead of the factual form: . . . das **hat** seine tiefere Ursache im. . .

Note that even without the introductory phrase (*Prof. A. says*), das **habe** . . . would be enough to signal that someone else's words are being reported.

In lines 4–5 we read: . . . die USA **hätten** . . . übernommen.
The factual form would be: . . . die USA **haben** . . . übernommen.

In line 7: Ein Indikator **sei** der Anteil an Nobelpreisen.
Instead of: Ein Indikator **ist** der Anteil an Nobelpreisen.

In lines 8–9: Hier **gebe** es eine Parallele.
Instead of: Hier **gibt** es eine Parallele.

After this last sentence the verb forms used are again factual verb forms: **waren** (line 11), **betrug** (line 12), **war** (line 14). This signals to the reader that the writer now reports facts rather than what someone else has written or said.

In English, reports are often marked by shifting the tense of the verb back, e.g.:

'*This **is** important nowadays.*'
*(He argued) this **was** important nowadays.*

but there are no equivalent separate (special) forms for non-factual statements. You would have to repeatedly bring in phrases such as 'X argues/claims', ' X's idea that', etc. if you wanted to achieve the same kind of effect the use of non-factual verb forms has in German, that is, to mark a sentence or passage clearly as an indirect report.

📖 Now read **R62**, points 1, 2, and 3. **R48** lists the most important non-factual verb forms. **R54** gives you more information on indirect reports.

6a. Bearing in mind all you have read about non-factual verb forms, decide

A. which of the following finite verbs are non-factual,
i.e. which of these sentences could be preceded by
Man hat mir gesagt, . . . (*I was told [that]* . . .) and

B. how these sentences would read in English.

1. Der Student spreche gut Englisch.
2. Diesen Dialekt finde ich kompliziert.
3. Die deutsche Sprache habe sich verändert.
4. Er veröffentlicht viel auf Englisch.
5. Sie hätten diese Sprache nicht verstanden.
6. Er muß diese Theorie exakter formulieren.
7. Dieser Wissenschaftler arbeite auch an diesem Projekt.
8. Wir haben mit vielen Menschen gesprochen.
9. Das Buch sei noch nicht ins Englische übersetzt worden.
10. Diesen Dialekt könne sie nicht verstehen.

6.2 Word Order in Indirect Reports

Compare:

Professor Ammon behauptet,   der Rangverlust von Deutsch   **habe** . . .
Professor Ammon argues   ***that** the decline in the standing of German has* . . .

In this example, there is no equivalent for the word *that* in the German version. The word order in the clause which follows **Professor Ammon behauptet,** is the normal verb-second main clause order:

II

der Rangverlust von Deutsch **habe** . . .

Read **R10.5** for further information on word order in indirect reports.

However, the sentence could also read:

Professor Ammon **behauptet, daß** der Rangverlust von Deutsch seine tiefere Ursache im Rangverlust der Wissenschaft in den deutschsprachigen Ländern **habe**.

Note that the addition of the word 'daß' has turned this clause into a dependent one and therefore the finite verb now appears at the end of the clause. Both German versions, i.e. the one with and the one without daß, read the same in English.

 6b. The following Text is text A from Chapter 5 rewritten as if it were an indirect report. Underline all finite verb forms, then compare them with the ones used in the original Text A in Chapter 5 given below.

Es gebe zwei Hauptgründe dafür, daß Deutsch seine Spitzenstellung als internationale Wissenschaftssprache nicht habe* halten können. Erstens seien Deutschland und das wissenschaftlich ebenfalls bedeutsame deutschsprachige Österreich durch den Ersten Weltkrieg ruiniert worden. Deutschland habe nach dem Krieg nicht die Ressourcen gehabt, um die wissenschaftliche Entwicklung weiterhin voranzutreiben. Der zweite, noch einschneidendere Grund sei der Nationalsozialismus gewesen, durch den zahlreiche Wissenschaftler aus Deutschland und Österreich verjagt oder umgebracht worden seien und durch dessen Folgen weitere nach dem Krieg gezwungen gewesen seien, zu emigrieren, weil sie in ihrem zerstörten Land keine Arbeitsmöglichkeit mehr gehabt hätten.

* This is an unusual position of the finite verb. Normally, in a dependent clause (here introduced by **daß**), the finite verb comes last. See **R67** (Dependent Clause).

Es gibt zwei Hauptgründe dafür, daß Deutsch seine Spitzenstellung als internationale Wissenschaftssprache nicht halten konnte. Erstens sind Deutschland und das wissenschaftlich ebenfalls bedeutsame deutschsprachige Österreich durch den Ersten Weltkrieg ruiniert worden. Deutschland hatte nach dem Krieg nicht die Ressourcen, um die wissenschaftliche Entwicklung weiterhin voranzutreiben. Der zweite, noch einschneidendere Grund war der Nationalsozialismus, durch den zahlreiche Wissenschaftler aus Deutschland und Österreich verjagt oder umgebracht wurden und durch dessen Folgen weitere nach dem Krieg gezwungen waren, zu emigrieren, weil sie in ihrem zerstörten Land keine Arbeitsmöglichkeit mehr hatten.

6.3 Common Abbreviations

■ d.h. (line 4) stands for **das heißt** (*i.e.* or *that means/that is to say*)

■ z.B. (line 12) stands for **zum Beispiel** (*e.g.* or *for example*)

6.4 Conventions Concerning Numbers etc.

Compare:

■ German: 33,3%   English: 33.3%

Note: In German a comma is used instead of a decimal point. So, if someone writes you a cheque for 1,000 DM, you are not going to be much richer. For it to mean **one thousand** it would have to look like this: 1 000 DM or 1000 DM or 1 000, –.

■ Während 1920 . . . (line 9)
*While **in** 1920 . . .*

. . . betrug 1980 der Anteil . . . (line 12)
. . . *the proportion **in** 1980 was . . .*

Note: In German no word for *in* is used.

6.5 Differences in the Use of Words like 'the'

Compare:

> der Anteil **der** deutschsprachigen Wissenschaftler
> *the proportion of (the) German-speaking scientists*

German sometimes uses a determiner, in the above example **der**, where English does not. This is especially true when nouns denote abstract concepts, for example: die Zeit *time*, der Krieg *war*. In such cases you have to judge from the context whether der Krieg, for example, means *war* (in general) or *the war* (a particular one). You have already come across examples of this in earlier texts. For example in Text 5A, line 9: der Nationalsozialismus *Nazism*.

6.6 Aspects of Word Formation (1)

Compare the following words, most of which appear in Text 6A. They are all derived from the word:

	wissen	*to know*
das	**Wissen**	*knowledge*
die	**Wissen**schaft	*science*
der	**Wissen**schaftler	*scientist*
	wissenschaftlich	*scientific*
die	**Wissen**schaftssprache	*scientific language*
die	Natur**wissen**schaft	*natural science*

By understanding what various suffixes and prefixes signal you can often work out the meaning of a particular word without having to consult a dictionary. Indeed, since dictionaries cannot list all possible derivatives, you may anyhow have to work out some derivatives from scratch. For example, the suffix **-schaft** indicates that you are dealing with an abstract noun and the suffix **-lich** signals that the word is an adjective.

Read **R184** for further information on aspects of Word Formation.

6c. Work out the meaning of the words followed by a question mark. Consult **R185** and **R186** where necessary.

1. Freundschaft (Ch. 2, Text B) means *friendship*
   freundlich? unfreundlich?
2. veröffentlichen (Ch. 4, Text A, line 6) means *to publish*
   Veröffentlichung? unveröffentlicht?
3. Schwierigkeiten (Ch. 2, Text A, line 7) means *difficulties*
   schwierig?
4. bedeutsam (Ch. 5, Text A, line 4) means *important, significant*
   Bedeutung?
5. Entwicklung (Ch. 5, Text A, line 8) means *development*
   entwickeln? unterentwickelt?

6.7 -in: denotes a female

Compare:

		PLURAL
der Wissenschaftler	*male scientist*	die Wissenschaftler
die Wissenschaftler**in**	*female scientist*	die Wissenschaftler**innen**
der Amerikaner	*American man*	die Amerikaner
die Amerikaner**in**	*American woman*	die Amerikaner**innen**
der Ausländer	*foreigner (male)*	die Ausländer
die Ausländer**in**	*foreigner (female)*	die Ausländer**innen**

✎ **6d.** Masculine or Feminine, Singular or Plural? Tick the right box.

	MASCULINE	FEMININE	SINGULAR	PLURAL
1. Sprachwissenschaftlerin				
2. Nobelpreisträgerinnen				
3. Österreicher				
4. Akademikerinnen				
5. Verleger				

6.8 What you should now be able to do: Check-list

Having worked through Chapter 6 you now should

- be able to recognize the following words and know their English meaning:

NOUNS	der (Rang)verlust (-e), die Ursache (-n), die Stelle (-n), die Führung (-en), die Welt (-en), der Indikator (-en), die Verschiebung (-en), der Anteil (-e), der (Nobel)preis (-e), die Parallele (-n), die Herkunft (¨e),
VERBS	behaupten, übernehmen, betragen (as in: der Anteil betrug), steigen
ADJECTIVES	tief, grob, brauchbar
CONJUNCTIONS	während
OTHER WORDS	nur

- know that there are NON-FACTUAL as well as FACTUAL verb forms and know how to interpret these forms

- be able to recognize again the NON-FACTUAL forms which appear in Text 6A

- be aware of the word order in indirect reports

- recognize **d. h.** and **z. B.**

- know about conventions concerning numbers

- be familiar with the basic principles of word formation and able to work out simple derivatives

- recognize **-in/-innen** as feminine noun endings

6.9 Now work out the meaning of the following text with the help of a dictionary.

TEXT 6B

Professor Ammon schreibt, daß die Rolle von Deutsch als internationale Sprache sich im Verlauf unseres Jahrhunderts verändert habe. Aus einer Weltwissenschaftssprache sei eine Wirtschaftssprache von regionaler Bedeutung geworden. Als wirtschaftliche Kontaktsprache fungiere Deutsch hauptsächlich zwischen dem deutschen Sprachgebiet und den Nachbarregionen.

Die deutschsprachigen Länder seien natürlich interessiert daran, die internationale Stellung der deutschen Sprache zu sichern. Eine starke internationale Stellung der eigenen Sprache habe unverkennbare Vorteile für ein Land: Sie erleichtere die Kommunikation mit anderen Ländern und erfordere weniger Fremdsprachenlernen im eigenen Land.

Adapted from: Ulrich Ammon, 'Die deutsche Sprache: Lingua Franca im Schatten von Englisch?', *Deutschland, Zeitschrift für Politik, Kultur, Wirtschaft und Wissenschaft*, 1 (Feb. 94).

7

Read TEXT 6A again:

Professor Ammon behauptet, der Rangverlust von Deutsch als Wissenschaftssprache habe seine tiefere Ursache im Rangverlust der Wissenschaft in den deutschsprachigen Ländern. An ihrer Stelle hätten die USA, d. h. ein englischsprachiges Land, die wissenschaftliche Führung in der Welt übernommen.

Ein grober, aber doch brauchbarer Indikator für diese Verschiebung sei der Anteil der deutschsprachigen und der englischsprachigen Wissenschaftler an den Nobelpreisen. Hier gebe es eine deutliche Parallele: Während 1920 noch 44% der Nobelpreisträger für Naturwissenschaften deutschsprachiger Herkunft waren, und nur 33,3% englischsprachiger Herkunft, betrug z. B. 1980 der Anteil deutschsprachiger Naturwissenschaftler nur noch 11,9%, aber der Anteil der englischsprachigen Nobelpreisträger war auf 64,1% gestiegen.

TEXT 7A

1 Eine Sprache **ist** im wörtlichen Sinne international, wenn sie
A language   is in the literal sense international, if   it

2   zwischen Bürgern verschiedener Nationen **verwendet wird.**
is used between citizens of different   nations.

3 Aber der Begriff **setzt** außerdem **voraus,** daß es sich um
But the term   presupposes also,   that they are

4 Muttersprachler verschiedener Sprachen **handelt.**
native speakers of different   languages.

5 Wenn Deutsch nur   zwischen Deutschen und
*If   German only **were (to be) used** between Germans   and*

6 Österreichern oder deutschsprachigen Schweizern verwendet **würde,**
Austrians   or   German-speaking   Swiss people,

7 **könnte** man kaum   von einer internationalen Sprache **sprechen;**
*one **could**   hardly **speak** of an   international language;*

8 erst wenn eine Sprache   mit oder unter   Anderssprachigen
*only if a language   **is being used** with or amongst speakers of other*

9   **verwendet wird, ist** sie   eine wirklich internationale
*languages   **can it be called** a   truly   international*

10 Sprache **zu nennen. Sind** die   verschiedensprachigen Partner
*language.   If the (lit.:) different-speaking partners   **are***

11 nicht Bürger verschiedener Staaten, so **wird** die Sprache zwar
*not citizens of different states,   the language **is,**   it's true,*

12   interlingual,   aber noch nicht international **verwendet.**
being used 'interlingually', but not yet internationally.

Adapted from: Ulrich Ammon, 'Die deutsche Sprache: Lingua Franca im Schatten von Englisch?', *Deutschland, Zeitschrift für Politik, Kultur, Wirtschaft und Wissenschaft*, 1 (Feb. 94).

NAPIER UNIVERSITY L.I.S.

7.1 'of'

a.

Bürger	der	Nationen
citizens	*of the*	*nations*

Sprecher	dieser	Sprachen
speakers	*of these*	*languages*

Bürger	jener	Staaten
citizens	*of those*	*states*

Where English uses **of** to link two nouns, German uses the GENITIVE case forms to indicate this link (see **R97**).

b. If there is no determiner present on which to mark the genitive case, it is instead marked on the adjective, e.g.

zwischen Bürgern	verschieden**er**	Nationen	(line 2)
between citizens	*of different*	*nations*	

Muttersprachler	verschieden**er**	Sprachen	(line 4)
native speakers	*of different*	*languages*	
i.e. speakers	*of different*	*native languages*	

Bürger	verschieden**er**	Staaten	(lines 10–11)
citizens	*of different*	*states*	

Note that this applies to *all* cases, e.g.

mit dies**em** komplizierten Dialekt (Dative)
mit kompliziert**em** Dialekt
durch dies**e** komplizierten Dialekte (Accusative)
durch komplizier**te** Dialekte

See **R108** for a table of adjective endings.

c. If there is no adjective either to mark the case on, the preposition **'von'** (an alternative form to the genitive) is used.

zwischen Bürgern	**von**	Nationen
between citizens	*of*	*nations*

Muttersprachler	von	Sprachen
native speakers	*of*	*languages*

Bürger	von	Staaten
citizens	*of*	*states*

7.2 Verb Idioms with 'es' (2)

es handelt sich um (Text 7A, lines 3–4) is a frequently used phrase for which there are many different readings in English.

Look up this phrase in your dictionary. It is usually listed under the entry for the verb **handeln**.

✎ **7a.** Work out the meaning of the following sentences.

1. Es handelt sich hier um ein altes Problem.
2. Handelt es sich um eine neue Theorie?
3. Es handelt sich nicht um eine Kommunikationsschwierigkeit.
4. Weißt du, um was es sich handelt?
5. Es kann sich hier nur um eine Sache handeln.

7.3 Non-Factual Verb Forms (2)

6.1 dealt with non-factual verb forms in indirect reports. Special non-factual verb forms are also used if a statement is a hypothetical one, e.g. in Text 7A:

wenn sie zwischen Bürgern verschiedener Nationen verwendet **wird.** (lines 1–2)

Wenn Deutsch nur zwischen Deutschen und Österreichern . . . verwendet **würde, könnte** man kaum von einer internationalen Sprache sprechen; (lines 5–7)

wenn can mean *when, whenever,* and *if.* The second sentence is a supposition, a hypothetical conditional clause. This is signalled by the non-factual form of the verbs. Compare:

FACTUAL   **wenn** Deutsch verwendet **wird**   *if/when German is used*

NON-FACTUAL   **wenn** Deutsch verwendet **würde** *if German were used*

FACTUAL   man **kann**   sprechen *one can speak*

NON-FACTUAL   man **könnte** sprechen *one could speak*

Note that **würde/n** can usually be read as *would/were*.

📖 **R48** and **R53** will give you further information.

✎ **7b.** The following sentences all have non-factual verb forms. Work out the meaning of these sentences.

1. Wenn er mehr Zeit hätte, würde er das Buch lesen.
2. Wenn du ihm eine Fahrkarte schicken würdest, käme er nächste Woche.
3. Sie würde die Prüfung bestehen, wenn sie mehr lernte (or: lernen würde).
4. Wenn er dieses Experiment alleine durchführen könnte, müßte ich nicht nach Berlin fahren.
5. Er hätte gute Karrierechancen, wenn er English spräche.
6. Es wäre besser, wenn sie im Seminar nicht immer so dominieren würde.
7. Wenn er keine Arbeitsmöglichkeit mehr hätte, wäre er gezwungen zu emigrieren.
8. Wenn diese Wörter an die deutsche Sprache angepaßt wären, könnte man sie nicht mehr als Anglizismen erkennen.
9. Die Kommunikation zwischen Wissenschaftlern und Laien würde durch diese Termini erschwert werden.
10. Wenn man die Stellung der deutschen Sprache sichern wollte, müßte man jetzt Maßnahmen ergreifen.

7.4 'If'- Clauses without wenn

Sind die verschiedensprachigen Partner nicht Bürger verschiedener Staaten, so **wird** die Sprache zwar interlingual, aber noch nicht international verwendet. (lines 10–12)

If a sentence starts with a finite verb, it could mean, as we have seen in 4.1, that one is dealing with a yes/no question. However, in that case there ought to be a question mark. The above sentence in fact is an 'if-clause without if'. In English we have the same kind of construction:

Were they not citizens of different states, they would not be able to . . .

instead of

If they were not citizens of different states they would not be able . . .

The German sentence above could thus be rewritten:

Wenn die verschiedensprachigen Partner nicht Bürger verschiedener Staaten **sind**, so **wird** die Sprache zwar interlingual, aber noch nicht international **verwendet**.

Note:

■ The form of the finite verbs in this kind of sentence can be either factual or non-factual.

■ Often **so** or **dann** are inserted after the comma, between the two finite verbs. These two words in this position usually have no equivalent in the English reading.

📖 Read **R16** and **R144.2** for further information.

✍ **7c.** Work out the meaning of these sentences.

1. Hätte er mehr Geld, dann gäbe es keine Probleme.
2. Kommt er nicht heute, so kommt er vielleicht morgen.
3. Bestimmt man die Rangordnung, so muß man auch diesen Aspekt beachten.
4. Liest man diesen Text im Original, so ist man überrascht von seiner Komplexität.
5. Wäre er hier, so würde er das Problem erklären.
6. Würden keine Ausländer im Land wohnen, wäre unsere Kultur ärmer.
7. Enthielte dieser Artikel nicht so viele Fremdwörter, so würde man ihn besser verstehen.
8. Wüßte sie seine Adresse nicht, dann könnten wir keinen Kontakt aufnehmen.
9. Beobachtet man diese Entwicklung über einen längeren Zeitraum, kommt man zu einem anderen Schluß.
10. Handelte es sich hier um eine internationale Sprache, gäbe es dieses Problem nicht.

7.5 zwar (line 11)

📖 This has two distinct meanings. Look up **zwar** in **R163**.

7.6 Aspects of Word Formation (2)

mit oder unter **Anderssprachigen** (line 8)
*with or amongst **speakers of other languages***

You will not find the noun **Anderssprachigen** in the dictionary: **anders**, the dictionary will tell you, means *different*; **sprachig**, you already know that **deutschsprachig** (Ch 1, Text A, line 5) means *German-speaking*, so literally it means *'different-speaking'*. The fact that it is spelt with a capital means that this word is now used as a noun, i.e. it means *different-speaking 'ones'*, i.e. *people*. Note that the word nevertheless retains its adjective ending (-**en**), just as if it actually were followed by a noun:

mit oder unter Anderssprachig**en**

mit oder unter anderssprachig**en** Menschen

Adjectives used as nouns are very common in German texts.

Here are two more examples:

der Dialog mit **Andersdenkenden**

denken means *to think*

denkend means *thinking* (see **R43**)

*the dialogue with **differently-thinking people**, i.e. those who think differently*

Sprachbegabte verstehen diesen Dialekt.

Sprach from **Sprache** means *language*

begabt means *talented, gifted*

***People who have a talent for languages** understand this dialect.*

See also **R180**.

7d. Now work out the meaning of the following sentences. Most dictionaries will list at least part of the word.

1. Der Artikel wendet sich besonders an **Umweltbewußte.**
2. Wissenschaftlich **Gebildete** reagieren anders.
3. **Unbefugte** dürfen hier nicht parken.
4. **Teilzeitbeschäftigte** bekommen diesen Bonus nicht.
5. Das ist ein großes Problem für **Verhaltensgestörte.**

7.7 Passive Constructions (2)

ist . . . zu + Infinitive

This is a construction with a PASSIVE meaning.

erst dann **ist** sie eine wirklich internationale Sprache **zu nennen.** (lines 9–10)
*only then **can it be called/is it to be called** a truly international language.*

In 3.9 we saw that 'man' is usually best rendered with a passive construction in English. In the above example we have a different construction with a PASSIVE meaning:

ist/sind/war/waren . . . **zu** + INFINITIVE usually means *is/are/was/were to be* OR *can be/ must be etc* + PAST PARTICIPLE

Read **R78.2.**

7e. Translate the following sentences.

1. Dieser Text ist schwer zu verstehen.
2. Dieser Text war einfach zu übersetzen.
3. Seine Kollegen sind nicht von der Bedeutung dieses Projekts zu überzeugen.
4. Die Folgen dieser Entscheidung waren damals noch nicht abzusehen.

7.8 What you should now be able to do: Check-list

Having worked through Chapter 7 you now should

- be able to recognize the following words and know their English meaning:

NOUNS	der Sinn (-e), der Bürger (-), der Begriff (-e), der Muttersprachler (-), der Anderssprachige (-n), der Staat (-en)
VERBS	verwenden, voraussetzen, nennen
ADJECTIVES	wörtlich, verschiedensprachig
CONJUNCTIONS	wenn
OTHER WORDS	kaum, erst, zwar, noch nicht, aber
PHRASES	es handelt sich um

- recognize the different ways German uses to render 'of' (Genitive forms)
- recognize the phrase 'es handelt sich um' and know how to render it in English
- know that non-factual verb forms are used for the Conditional and be able to recognize these forms
- know about 'if-clauses without if'
- have looked up **zwar** in **R163** and know about the two different meanings
- know that nouns can be derived from adjectives and be able to work out the meaning of such derivatives
- know about the various constructions with a passive meaning and be able to recognize them

7.9 Now work out the meaning of the following text with the help of a dictionary.

TEXT 7B

Mein Freund möchte Deutsch lernen, und er glaubt, es wäre möglich, das in einem Sommer zu schaffen. Wenn sich Sprachen wirklich so schnell lernen ließen, bräuchte man sich nicht jahrelang in der Schule abzumühen. Zwar schaffen es Sprachbegabte und gut Motivierte bestimmt, sich ein Grundwissen innerhalb kurzer Zeit anzueignen. Will man aber eine Sprache wirklich beherrschen, dauert es oft Jahre. Wenn er einige Monate in einem deutschsprachigen Land verbringen könnte und dort eine Sprachenschule besuchen würde, hätte er vielleicht bessere Chancen. Aber das würde natürlich viel Geld kosten, und das könnte er sich gar nicht leisten.

Er hat mich gebeten, ich solle ihm beim Deutschlernen helfen. Ich könnte ihm vielleicht meine alten Lehrbücher leihen. Aber es wäre bestimmt besser, wenn er an einem Sprachkurs teilnehmen würde.

Here is TEXT 7A again:

Eine Sprache ist im wörtlichen Sinne international, wenn sie zwischen Bürgern verschiedener Nationen verwendet wird. Aber der Begriff setzt außerdem voraus, daß es sich dabei um Muttersprachler verschiedener Sprachen handelt. Wenn Deutsch nur zwischen Deutschen und Österreichern oder deutschsprachigen Schweizern verwendet würde, könnte man kaum von einer internationalen Sprache sprechen; erst wenn sie mit oder unter Anderssprachigen verwendet wird, ist sie eine wirklich internationale Sprache zu nennen. Sind die verschiedensprachigen Partner nicht Bürger verschiedener Staaten, so wird die Sprache zwar interlingual, aber noch nicht international verwendet.

TEXT 8A

1 Deutsch **kommt** heute von unerwarteter Seite
*German **is coming** nowadays **under pressure** from an unexpected*

2 **unter Druck.** Die offiziellen Kontakte der Europäischen Union
quarter. The official contacts of the European Union

3 zu Osteuropa **finden** überwiegend auf englisch oder
*with Eastern Europe **take place** predominantly in English or*

4 auch auf französisch **statt.** Beide Sprachen **spielen** nämlich als
*also in French. Both languages **play** (you see) as*

5 Arbeitssprachen in der Europäischen Union eine größere Rolle als
working languages in the European Union a greater role than

6 Deutsch. So **kommt** es häufig **vor,** daß die
*German. Thus it **happens** frequently, that the partners from Eastern*

7 besser deutsch als englisch oder französisch
Europe who speak better German than English or French

8 sprechenden Partner aus Osteuropa in ihren Kontakten zur
*are **compelled** in their contacts with the*

9 Europäischen Union zur Verwendung von Englisch oder Französisch
European Union to use English or French.

10 **gezwungen sind.** Dieser Umstand **ist** schon öfter
*This (circumstance) **has** already frequently **been***

11 von deutscher Seite **kritisiert worden,** ohne daß sich bisher
***criticized** by Germany (lit.: the German side), without there*

12 etwas **geändert hätte.** Die deutsche Regierung **befindet** sich
***having been any change** so far. The German government **finds** itself*

13 in einem gewissen Dilemma: Sie **möchte** einerseits
*in a certain dilemma: It **does** not **wish,** on the one hand,*

14 die weitere Entwicklung der Europäischen Union nicht durch
to impede the further development of the European Union through

15 sprachenpolitische Querelen **belasten**, aber andererseits doch
quarrels over language policy, but on the other hand (nevertheless)

16 die internationale Stellung der deutschen Sprache **stützen**.
would like to support the international position of the German language.

Adapted from: Ulrich Ammon, 'Die deutsche Sprache: Lingua Franca im Schatten von Englisch?', *Deutschland, Zeitschrift für Politik, Kultur, Wirtschaft und Wissenschaft*, 1 (Feb. 94).

8.1 Word Order (3): Positions II + IV

II IV
Deutsch **kommt** heute von unerwarteter Seite **unter** Druck. (lines 1–2)

In 2.1 some examples were given for the kind of words which can appear in Position IV (the VERB COMPLETION) and which have to be read in conjunction with the finite verb in Position II. In the above sentence Position IV is taken up by yet another type, i.e. the noun part of a fixed phrase.

Phrases like **unter Druck kommen** (*to come under pressure*) have to be read as one unit, even if the noun part of the phrase (**unter Druck**) comes at the end of the sentence.

📖 Read **R176**.

📖 **R6** lists all the different types of verb completion.

✎ **8a.** Work out the meaning of the following sentences containing such phrases where the noun part can appear in Position IV.

1. Beide Sprachen spielen auch in diesem Kontext eine große Rolle.
2. Die deutsche Regierung befindet sich auch hier in einem gewissen Dilemma.
3. Dieser Meinungsunterschied kommt auch vor allem hier zum Ausdruck.
4. Diese Ankündigung versetzte viele Nationen in Erstaunen.
5. Vielleicht kommt sein Plan nächstes Jahr zur Durchführung.

8.2 Word Order (4): Variations

Compare:

II IV
Beide Sprachen spielen in der E. U. eine große Rolle.

with

Beide Sprachen spielen in der E. U. eine **größere** Rolle **als** Deutsch. (lines 5–6)

If there is a COMPARATIVE with **als** (above: eine größ**ere** Rolle **als** *a greater role than*) the verb completion, normally the last word at the end of the clause, is followed by **als** . . .

📖 See also **R10.6**.

✎ **8b.** Sentences 2–4 from exercise 8a have been slightly altered to include a comparative. Work out the new meanings.

2. Die deutsche Regierung befindet sich auch hier in einem schlimmeren Dilemma als die anderen Länder.

3. Dieser Meinungsunterschied kommt hier mehr zum Ausdruck als in anderen Ländern.

4. Diese Ankündigung versetzte viele Nationen in größeres Erstaunen als erwartet.

5. Vielleicht kommt sein Plan nächstes Jahr früher zur Durchführung als dieses Jahr.

8.3 Extended Adjective Phrases (2)

die **besser deutsch als englisch oder französisch sprechenden** Partner (lines 6–7)

The phrase in bold gives further information about the noun (Partner) which follows. As explained in 5.2, such phrases are best rendered by a relative clause in English:

*the partners, **who speak better German than English or French***

The extended adjective phrase given above differs from the ones given in 5.2 by having a PRESENT PARTICIPLE [see **R43**], (sprech**end**) + adjective ending (-en) at the end of the phrase. There are also extended adjective phrases involving PAST PARTICIPLES.

📖 Read **R116–17**.

✎ **8c.** First find the present participle or the past participle, then work out the extent of the extended adjective phrase, and then give the English meaning of the following sentences.

1. In diesem Teil der USA wohnen auch deutschsprechende Bevölkerungsgruppen.

2. Er liest einen in englischer Übersetzung vorliegenden Text.

3. Der Artikel handelt von den in diesem Teil der Welt zur Zeit stattfindenden Veränderungen.

4. Auch dieses auf französisch geschriebene und 1922 veröffentlichte Buch befaßt sich mit diesem Problem.

5. Er stützt sich auf diese von ihm falsch verstandene Theorie.

6. Dieser von deutscher Seite oft kritisierte Umstand erschwert die Kommunikation.

7. Er spricht von einer sich in einem gewissen Dilemma befindenden Regierung.

8. Sie möchten eine die weitere Entwicklung der Europäischen Union belastende Situation vermeiden.

9. Der Autor wünscht sich eine die internationale Stellung der deutschen Sprache stützende Lösung dieses Problems.

10. Ich kenne nur eine vor vielen Jahren schlecht übersetzte Version dieses Buches.

8.4 Differences in Usage: Nouns in German/Verbs in English

See Text A, lines 9–10:

Sie sind **zur Verwendung von** Englisch gezwungen.
*They are forced **to use** (lit.: **to the use of**) English.*

Formal German favours phrases with nouns whereas in English the same meaning may often better be rendered by a verb. The noun may be a derivative of the verb:

Verwendung *the use*
verwenden *to use*

📖 Read **R176** and **R184**.

✍ **8d.** Now work out the meaning of the following sentences. Would you use a verb or a noun in the English rendering?

1. Er hat gestern diese Anordnung getroffen.
   (**anordnen** means *to arrange*)
2. Sie hoffen auf eine baldige Veränderung der Situation.
   (**verändern** means *to change*)
3. Sie haben Beobachtungen über diese Entwicklung angestellt.
   (**beobachten** means *to observe*)
4. Er hat auf diesem Gebiet schon seit Jahren Forschungen durchgeführt.
   (**forschen** means *to research*)
5. Das Erlernen der deutschen Sprache erfordert viel Zeit und Geduld.
   (**erlernen** means *to learn*)

8.5 Non-Factual Verb Forms (3)

ohne daß sich bisher etwas **geändert hätte.** (lines 11–12)

The use of the non-factual form **hätte** implies that not only has no change happened so far but that it is uncertain when or even if such a change will occur at all. In English there is no equivalent form for this and the sentence may be rendered:

but as yet there has been no change

but without there having been any change so far

📖 The uses of non-factual verb forms are listed in **R52–61**.

8.6 Connectors and Logical Connectors (2)

II
Sie **möchte** einerseits die weitere Entwicklung der Europäischen Union **nicht** durch
IV
sprachenpolitische Querelen **belasten, aber** andererseits doch die internationale
IV
Stellung der deutschen Sprache **stützen.**
*It does not want, on the one hand, to impede . . . , but on the other hand [**it would like**] to support . . . .*

In the German sentence there is no equivalent for *[it would like]*. This is because **sie möchte** applies both to **belasten** and to **stützen**. The two infinitives are linked by the connector **aber** *(but)*. Note that only the first infinitive (belasten) is negated.

The paired logical connectors **einerseits** . . . **andererseits** also help to balance the structure of this sentence to give it the sense: 'does not want A but does want B'.

📖 Read **R137.3**.

✎ **8e.** Note the connectors. Underline the finite verb and the verb completion. Then work out the meaning of the sentences.

1. Er will seine Forschungsarbeit bald abschließen und dann schnell veröffentlichen.
2. Ich habe seine Theorie gestern zum ersten Mal gehört, aber gleich verstanden.
3. In diesem Kapitel möchte ich vier Fälle genau beschreiben und dann Schlußfolgerungen ziehen.
4. Dieses Wort wird nur in dieser Gegend verwendet und nur von wenigen Leuten richtig ausgesprochen.
5. In dieser Zeit wurden viele Wissenschaftler aus dem nationalsozialistischen Deutschland verjagt oder sogar umgebracht.

Note that, as well as the connector **aber**, the sentence in 8.6 has a pair of LOGICAL CONNECTORS:

Sie möchte **einerseits** die weitere Entwicklung der Europäischen Union nicht durch sprachenpolitische Querelen belasten, **aber andererseits** doch die internationale Stellung der deutschen Sprache stützen.
on the one hand, . . . but on the other hand

Recognizing such logical connectors greatly helps the reader to clearly see how a sentence or text is structured.

📖 **R139** lists pairs and sequences of logical connectors.

8.7 doch

. . . , aber andererseits **doch** die internationale Stellung der deutschen Sprache stützen. (line 15)
*. . . , but on the other hand (**nevertheless**), [would like] to support the international position of the German language.*

doch belongs to a group of words which for comprehension and translation purposes can often be disregarded.

📖 Read **R140**.

8.8 Differences in Usage: Adjective in German/Noun in English

sprachenpolitische Querelen (line 15)
lit: *language political (= language-policy) quarrels* i.e. ***quarrels over language policy***

It happens quite often that (compound) adjectives like the one above have to be read as nouns in the equivalent English phrase.

 8f. Try to work out the meaning of the following phrases.

1. nationalpolitische Fragen
2. mehrjährige Erfahrung
3. dieser gesellschaftskritische Artikel
4. eine wirtschaftspolitische Debatte
5. schulpolitische Probleme

8.9 What you should now be able to do: Check-list

Having worked through Chapter 8 you now should

- be able to recognize the following words and know their English meaning:

NOUNS	die Seite (-n), der Kontakt (-e), die Arbeit (-en), der Partner (-), die Verwendung (-en), der Umstand (˙e), die Entwicklung (-en), die Europäische Union, Osteuropa
VERBS	stattfinden, vorkommen, zwingen, kritisieren, ändern, sich befinden, belasten, stützen
ADJECTIVES	offiziell, groß, häufig, überwiegend, besser, weiter, politisch
OTHER WORDS	beide, nämlich, öfter, ohne, bisher
PHRASES	einerseits/andererseits, unter Druck kommen, eine Rolle spielen

- know that the noun part of a fixed phrase can appear as the verb completion in Position IV at the end of the clause
- recognize comparatives with 'als' and know that 'als . . .' appears after the verb completion
- recognize extended adjective phrases involving participles and know how to render them in English
- know that in some phrases where German uses a noun English often prefers a verb
- know that one finite verb may have more than one verb completion, and that the completions are usually linked by a connector
- know that there are logical connectors
- know that there are certain words which can be disregarded for comprehension purposes

8.10 Now work out the meaning of the following text with the help of a dictionary.

TEXT 8B

Deutschland hat jetzt den Ruf, das in den Wissenschaften am weitesten fortgeschrittene Land zu sein, und das mit Recht. Denn aus allen Ländern gehen lernbegierige Studenten dorthin, um auf deutschem Boden weitere Untersuchungen in allen Zweigen der Wissenschaft zu machen. Auch von unseren Studenten werden die tüchtigsten, nachdem sie ihren Kursus in der Universität durchgemacht haben, gewöhnlich nach Deutschland geschickt. . . . Nicht nur in den Wissenschaften, sondern auch in Handel und Gewerbe, im Fabrikwesen und in der Industrie . . . sind die Deutschen so fortgeschritten, daß die englische Regierung . . . untersuchen ließ, was eigentlich die Ursache sei. . . . Die Berichte aller zur Untersuchung nach Deutschland gesandten Berichterstatter bestätigen übereinstimmend, daß der Grund . . . den Fortschritten der Wissenschaften zuzuschreiben ist. Aus all dem geht klar hervor, . . . daß es . . . von größtem Vorteil ist, die deutsche Sprache zu lernen.

Ein Zitat aus dem Jahre 1898: *Zeitschrift für Deutsche Sprache*, Japan

Adapted from: Ulrich Ammon, 'Die deutsche Sprache: Lingua Franca im Schatten von Englisch?', *Deutschland, Zeitschrift für Politik, Kultur, Wirtschaft und Wissenschaft*, 1 (Feb. 94).

9

As texts get structurally more complicated it becomes difficult to give the translation in parallel lines. Therefore, for the following text, you will find the English version after the German original.

Start your reading of the text by marking all structurally important words and constructions you recognize, such as finite verbs, verb completions, relative pronouns, connectors, conjunctions, extended adjective phrases, etc. Also note all the words you already know the meaning of. They will give you clues to what the text might roughly say before looking at it in detail. Then compare the German text with the translation given below.

TEXT 9A

In seinem Artikel berichtet Professor Ammon, daß sich Goethe zum Thema der Bedeutung der deutschen Sprache geäußert haben soll, und zwar in einem Gespräch mit einem englischen ,,Ingenieuroffizier".

Dieser war nach Weimar gekommen, um Deutsch zu lernen, und er
5 berichtete dem Dichter, ,,daß jetzt fast kein junger Engländer von guter Familie ist, der nicht Deutsch lernte". Goethe hat sich darüber anscheinend nicht gewundert, denn er äußert, ,,daß [,] wenn einer jetzt das Deutsche gut versteht, er viele andere Sprachen entbehren kann", da ,,wir die vorzüglichsten Werke in guten deutschen Übersetzungen
10 lesen können".

Wenn auch die von Eckermann 1825 aufgezeichnete Äußerung Goethes sich nicht dahingehend überbewerten läßt, als hätte Deutsch damals eine dem Französischen ebenbürtige internationale Rolle gespielt, so stimmt sie doch mit anderen Beobachtungen darin
15 überein, daß die Bedeutung von Deutsch als internationale Sprache im 19. Jahrhundert allmählich zunahm.

Adapted from: Ulrich Ammon, 'Die deutsche Sprache: Lingua Franca im Schatten von Englisch?', *Deutschland, Zeitschrift für Politik, Kultur, Wirtschaft und Wissenschaft*, 1 (Feb. 94).

In his article Professor Ammon reports that Goethe is said to have made a remark on the topic of the importance of the German language, in fact in a conversation with an English 'engineering officer'.

The latter had come to Weimar to learn German and told the poet: 'that (there) is practically no young English gentleman [*lit.*: from a good family] who is not learning German'. Apparently this did not surprise Goethe, since he comments: 'If someone now understands German well, he can make do without many other languages', because 'the most excellent works are available [*lit.*: we can read] in good German translations'.

Although [*lit.*: Even if] Goethe's remark, recorded by Eckermann in 1825, should not be taken to mean [*lit.*: must not be given too much importance to the effect] that German at the time equalled French as an international language [*lit.*: played an international role equal to French], it provides further evidence [*lit.*: it agrees/tallies with other observations to the effect] that the importance of German as an international language was gradually increasing in the nineteenth century.

9.1 Modal Verbs (2): sollen/wollen/müssen + nicht

As you have seen so far, most modal verbs are quite straightforward to deal with. There are some, however, which occasionally cause problems:

> . . ., daß sich Goethe zum Thema . . . geäußert haben **soll,** (lines 1–2)

This does NOT mean

> *that Goethe should have expressed an opinion on this topic*

BUT

> *that Goethe **is said to** have expressed an opinion on this topic*

sollen, wollen, müssen + nicht are often wrongly interpreted. **sollen** and **wollen** can cause problems because both have two entirely different meanings. Be particularly careful if they appear with a past participle and either 'haben' or 'sein', as in the above example. **müssen + nicht** is often misread as 'must not'.

📖 Study the table in **R69**, paying special attention to **sollen, wollen, müssen**.

✎ **9a.** What do the modal verbs mean in the context of the following sentences? Some are quite straightforward, others may be interpreted in two different ways. Also be careful when translating sentences 4 and 6.

1. Er soll nächste Woche hierher kommen.
2. Der Angeklagte will zur fraglichen Zeit zu Hause gewesen sein.
3. Wir wollen nächstes Jahr eine Reise nach Österreich machen.
4. Er muß nicht Deutsch lernen.
5. Sie soll sich schon erkundigt haben.
6. Der Aufsatz muß nicht heute abgegeben werden.
7. Er will Millionär sein.

9.2 Pronouns (2): dieser, einer, etc.

> **Dieser** war nach Weimar gekommen, (line 4)

Determiners are frequently used as PRONOUNS, i.e. without a following noun. The forms of these pronouns are mostly identical with the determiner forms (**R97**), e.g.

> **Dieser (Mann)** war nach Weimar gekommen,
> *This (man/one), he [and in* Text 9A: *the latter] had come to Weimar*

There are a few exceptions. For example Text 9A, line 7:

> wenn **einer** jetzt das Deutsche gut versteht,
> *if **someone** now understands German well*

Compare with:

> wenn **ein** (Mann) jetzt das Deutsche gut versteht,

📖 See **R99** for other exceptions.

9b. What do the underlined pronouns mean? Translate the following sentences.

1. <u>Manche</u> finden es schwierig, Sprachen zu lernen.
2. Wenn man mit <u>denjenigen</u> spricht, die das Land kennen, . . .
3. Wir können nicht <u>jeden</u> fragen.
4. Ich habe mit <u>ihm</u> bezüglich <u>dessen</u> gesprochen.
5. <u>Jeder</u> hat diesen Text verstanden.
6. Ist das sein Buch oder ist es <u>mein(e)s</u>?
7. Sie sagt genau <u>dasselbe</u>.
8. Er hat <u>keinem</u> von seinem Vorhaben erzählt.

9.3 da + Preposition (2)/Preposition and Pronoun

Goethe hat sich **darüber** . . . nicht gewundert. (lines 6–7)
*Goethe was not surprised **about this**.*

sich wundern über means *to be surprised about/at.*

Note the difference between *to be surprised about **something***:

Er wundert sich **darüber**.
He is surprised about this.

*and at **somebody***:

Er wundert sich **über ihn**.
He is surprised at him.

da + PREPOSITION is used whenever the reference is not to a person.

da + PREPOSITION words have other functions too. For more information see **R163** and **R136**.

9c. If you replaced the underlined words with a pronoun construction which would it be? Tick either A or B.

	A	B
1.　　A: **darauf**　B: **auf ihn**		
Sie konzentriert sich jetzt ganz auf <u>ihre Arbeit</u>.		
Sie konzentriert sich jetzt ganz auf <u>ihren kranken Vater</u>.		
2.　　A: **darauf**　B: **auf ihn**		
Sie verlassen sich auf <u>seine Hilfe</u>.		
Sie verlassen sich auf <u>ihren Sohn</u>.		
3.　　A: **darüber**　B: **über ihn**		
Er beschwerte sich über <u>seinen Nachbarn</u>.		
Er beschwerte sich über <u>den Lärm</u>.		
4.　　A: **davor**　B: **vor ihm**		
Das Kind fürchtet sich vor <u>der Prüfung</u>.		
Das Kind fürchtet sich vor <u>dem strengen Lehrer</u>.		
5. A: **dafür**　B: **für ihn**		
Diese Studentin interessiert sich für <u>Thomas Mann</u>.		
Diese Studentin interesiert sich für <u>diesen Roman</u>.		

9.4 Quotation Marks

See TEXT 9A:

> „daß jetzt fast kein junger Engländer von guter Familie ist, der nicht Deutsch lernte"
> „daß [,] wenn einer jetzt das Deutsche gut versteht, er viele andere Sprachen entbehren kann"
> da „wir die vorzüglichsten Werke in guten deutschen Übersetzungen lesen können"

Note the different way German indicates the beginning and end of a quotation.

Other conventions found in German print are:

>>	<<
>	<
<<	>>
<	>

9.5 Verbs Dictate Case

Text 9A, lines 4 and 5: er berichtete **dem** Dichter *he told the poet*

Why **dem** Dichter? Just as prepositions dictate the form of the following determiner and noun/pronoun, so do VERBS.

📖 Read **R93**.

 9d. Translate the following sentences. Note the case form of the underlined objects.

1. Sie folgte ihrem Mann nach Deutschland.
2. Ich vertraue ihm ganz.
3. Er ist nie einer politischen Partei beigetreten.
4. Der Vorsitzende hat allen Kollegen herzlich gedankt.
5. An diesem Tag gedenken wir der Opfer der Katastrophe.
6. Sie bedarf jetzt seines Mitgefühls.
7. Er erklärte dem Professor seine Theorie.
8. Dieses Verhalten schadet ihrem Ruf.
9. Politiker sollen dem Volk dienen.
10. Er ist des Mordes angeklagt.

9.6 Passive Constructions (3) sich + lassen + Infinitive is a Construction with a Passive Meaning

In 7.7 we looked at one construction with a passive meaning: ist . . . ZU + INFINITIVE. In Text 9A, lines 11–12, there is another construction with a passive meaning. Slightly simplified it reads:

> diese Äußerung Goethes **läßt sich** nicht **überbewerten**
> *this remark by Goethe can/must not be overrated*

📖 Read **R78.3**.

✎ **9e.** What do the following sentences mean?

1. Diese komplizierte Frage läßt sich nicht mit einem Wort beantworten.
2. Die Ursachen haben sich erst nach einer genaueren Untersuchung feststellen lassen.
3. Trotz größter Anstrengungen ließ sich dieses Unglück nicht verhindern.
4. Läßt sich überhaupt eine Erklärung dafür finden?
5. Welche Aufgabe läßt sich schneller durchführen?

📖 **R78** lists all such constructions with a passive meaning.

✎ **9f.** Can you give one single English reading for all four sentences?

1. Diese Sprache läßt sich leicht lernen.
2. Diese Sprache ist leicht zu lernen.
3. Diese Sprache ist leicht (er)lernbar.
4. Man kann diese Sprache leicht lernen.

9.7 als ob/als + Non-Factual Verb

als hätte Deutsch damals eine . . . internationale Rolle gespielt,

or it could also read:

als habe Deutsch damals eine . . . internationale Rolle gespielt,

or:

als ob Deutsch damals eine . . . internationale Rolle gespielt **habe/hätte**,
Lit.: *as if German had at the time played an international role*

Note: **als** followed by a verb in the non-factual form always has the same meaning as **als ob** (*as if*).

📖 Read **R59** for further information on this kind of construction.

✎ **9g.** What do these sentences mean?

1. Er tat so, als hätte er die genaueren Umstände gekannt.
2. Es sah nicht so aus, als ob sie ihn schon früher gekannt habe.
3. Sie spricht die Sprache so perfekt, als wäre es ihre Muttersprache.
4. Sie tat so, als käme sie nur zufällig vorbei.
5. Man darf das nicht so interpretieren, als ob er nicht wüßte, was er machte.

9.8 Complex Sentences

In 4.3 to 4.7. we looked at different types of dependent clauses. In Text 9A, lines 11–16, we have a combination of clauses forming a COMPLEX SENTENCE:

Wenn auch die Äußerung Goethes nicht dahingehend überbewertet werden darf, als hätte Deutsch damals eine dem Französischen ebenbürtige internationale Rolle gespielt, so stimmt sie doch mit anderen Beobachtungen darin überein, daß die Bedeutung von Deutsch als internationale Sprache im 19. Jahrhundert allmählich zunahm.

Such complex sentences are best dealt with by first of all working out the structure of the entire sentence first. Now you must read **R162** where the conventions used in this book are explained.

The complex sentence above starts with a dependent clause introduced by the conjunction **wenn**:

<**Wenn**> . . . **nicht überbewertet werden** ⃞darf⃞,

This is then followed by another clause dependent on the first clause:

<**als**> **hätte . . . gespielt,**

Also note the extended adjective phrase within the clause:

eine **dem Französischen ebenbürtige** internationale Rolle

Then the main clause follows which is linked to the preceding dependent clause by 'so' (see **R144.2**):

so ⃞**stimmt**⃞ **. . .** ⃞**überein**⃞,
(**übereinstimmen** means *to agree, to concur*)

This in turn is followed by the last dependent clause:

<**daß**> **. . .** ⃞**zunahm**⃞.

Now read **R159** to see how a complex sentence can be broken down to see its various 'layers'.

Look at the above sentence again:

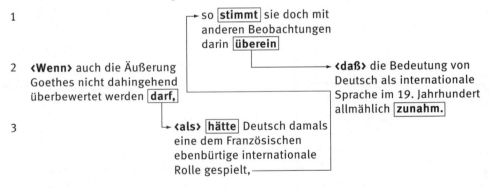

The structural core of this complex sentence, the main clause, reads:

it (i.e. Goethe's remark) agrees with other observations

the following dependent 'daß'-clause then explains what these observations were:

that the importance of German as an international language gradually increased in the nineteenth century

whilst the first two dependent clauses qualify the remark made by Goethe:

Although Goethe's remark should not be taken to mean that German at the time equalled French as an international language

9h. Here are three complex sentences. Can you work out their structures? What do they mean?

1. Erst wenn man eine Fremdsprache lernt, wird man sich der Eigentümlichkeiten der eigenen Sprache bewußt, weil man erst dann in der Lage ist, wirklich Vergleiche anzustellen.

2. Seit es ein seit 1980 geltendes Gesetz gibt, das die Gleichbehandlung von Männern und Frauen am Arbeitsplatz sicherstellt, haben sich die Ausbildungschancen für Mädchen und Frauen deutlich verbessert, weil den Frauen seither alle Ausbildungsstätten offenstehen.

3. Obwohl das Abschlußzeugnis der Gymnasien, das sogenannte Reifezeugnis oder Abitur, grundsätzlich alle zum Studium an einer Universität berechtigt, ist ein Studium genau nach Wunsch nicht immer möglich, weil die Zahl der Abiturienten so stark gestiegen ist, daß Aufnahmebeschränkungen eingeführt werden mußten, um den starken Andrang auf bestimmte populäre Studienfächer zu regulieren.

If you want to practise further how to analyse complex sentences, go to the Further Exercises Section (**E47** to **E51**).

9.9 What you should now be able to do: Check-list

Having worked through Chapter 9 you now should

- be able to recognize the following words and know their English meaning:

  NOUNS   der Artikel (-), das Thema (Themen), die Bedeutung (-en), das Gespräch (-e), die Familie (-n), das Werk (-e), die Äußerung (-en), die Rolle (-n), die Beobachtung (-en), das Jahrhundert (-e)

  VERBS   berichten, äußern, kommen, lernen, sich wundern über, entbehren, aufzeichnen, überbewerten, übereinstimmen, zunehmen

  ADJECTIVES   jung, vorzüglich, viel, ebenbürtig

  OTHER WORDS   anscheinend, damals, allmählich, und zwar, mit, fast

- know that you need to bear in mind their special meanings when you come across the modal verbs **sollen/wollen/müssen + nicht**

- know that determiners can be used as pronouns and that in most cases the forms are the same

- know that some pronouns differ: **einer, ein(e)s, dessen, deren, denen**

- know that **da + Preposition**-words can be pronouns referring to things or states rather than persons

- know that in German quotation marks at the beginning of a quote can be found at the bottom of the line

- know that verbs dictate case

- recognize **sich + lassen + Infinitive** as a passive construction with the meaning *can/must be*

- recognize als **ob/als + non-factual verb** as an 'as if' construction

- be able to analyse the structure of complex sentences and know how to read them

9.10 Now work out the meaning of the following text with the help of a dictionary.

Text 9B

Vor hundert Jahren schien es noch so, als wüßte man genau, wann die deutsche Geschichte begonnen hat, und zwar im Jahre 9 n.Chr., als drei römische Legionen von Arminius, einem Fürsten vom germanischen Stamm der Cherusker, im Teutoburger Wald besiegt wurden. Jener wurde dann später als erster deutscher Held gefeiert, und man baute ihm sogar ein riesiges Denkmal. Bis heute weiß man aber nichts Genaueres über ihn und kann darüber nur Vermutungen anstellen.

Was aber den Anfang der deutschen Geschichte betrifft, so weiß man heute, daß sich die Dinge nicht so einfach darstellen lassen, denn die Entstehung des deutschen Volkes war ein Prozeß, der sich über Jahrhunderte hinzog. Das Wort „deutsch" ist wahrscheinlich erst im 8. Jahrhundert erschienen und soll zunächst nur die Sprache bezeichnet haben, die von bestimmten Völkerschaften gesprochen wurde. Erst sehr viel später wurde dann die Bezeichnung „deutsch" auf diejenigen, die diese Sprache benutzten, und schließlich auch auf ihr Wohngebiet („Deutschland") übertragen.

Adapted from: *Tatsachen über Deutschland*, ed. A. Hoffman, Societäts-Verlag, Frankfurt/Main (1992).

10

Effective Reading Strategies

10.1 Reading as a Skill

The aim of this chapter is to encourage learners to examine their own reading techniques and to work on improving them. The main point to note is that reading is a skill which can be practised and improved.

Research into effective reading in a foreign language suggests that learners with good reading skills in their first language are able to transfer these skills to reading the foreign language and that this helps them to make good progress towards fast and effective reading in the foreign language. On the other hand, learners who make slow progress in learning to read a foreign language often have poorly developed strategies for reading in their first language. Thus, being aware of your reading techniques in English can help you to become a more effective reader of German.

10.2 'Reading for Structure' and 'Reading for Meaning'

Effective reading is a combination of two processes, which are sometimes called 'bottom–up' and 'top–down'.

'Bottom–up' processing is essentially 'reading for structure'. The reader focuses on the forms and structures in the text at a very local level, such as letters and words, and builds up the message of the text from these units. Important skills at this level are letter- and word-recognition (see **E1–3**), and the recognition of larger structures such as phrases and clauses. In German, more attention needs to be paid to the ends of words, clauses, and sentences than is the case in English. Obviously, the early stages of reading in a foreign language will involve focusing on this kind of detail to a much greater extent than one is used to in reading one's first language. This is why the first nine chapters of this course have concentrated on this kind of 'reading for structure'.

The 'top–down' approach, on the other hand, is firmly focused on 'reading for meaning'. In reading the text, the reader focuses on the meaning, remembering clearly the meanings which have been expressed so far and making predictions about what meanings might be expressed next. Readers who are competent at approaching a text in this way tend to use 'bottom–up' processing to check whether the assumptions they are making about what the text is saying are actually correct. Clearly, this is the type of reading strategy used by more advanced readers, and the next five chapters will focus on developing these kinds of reading skills.

An over-reliance on 'bottom–up' processing is natural and almost inevitable in the early stages of learning to read in a foreign language, but this can lead to comprehension problems. 'Losing the thread' or 'getting stuck' on a particular word is often a sign that the reader is not focusing on the general picture of what the text 'is about' and where the meaning is going. Consequently, most learners will benefit from consciously working on their 'top–down' reading skills. These are discussed in the following sections (especially 10.3–10.7).

10.3 Pre-Reading Skills

Even before you start reading the text, you will probably have a rough idea of what it is about – an economic report, a narrative with certain principal characters, a description of some event or process. Instead of launching straight in 'cold' on reading it, it is generally advisable to take a few moments to gather your thoughts and make a few elementary predictions about the content and the key words. This simple pre-reading exercise will help to activate your prior knowledge about a particular subject, to organize your thinking about it, and to predict some of the vocabulary, arguments, and other features which you might find. This kind of pre-reading exercise may require only a minute or two but can save a lot of time later, since your reading of the text will be more efficient because it is more focused on the content. The remaining chapters in this course contain exercises in pre-reading skills.

10.4 Skimming

Skimming through a text is a way of investigating it without reading it closely, in order to get an overall impression of what kind of text it is and what it is about. You do not even need to look at its parts in sequence. At a very basic level, you can let your eye travel over the text without making any special effort to read particular words or sentences. At the very least this will give you an idea of how long the text is, how it is structured (does it have subheadings?), and whether there are any non-linguistic sources of information such as numbers, dates, pictures, graphs, and tables which will give you a first orientation. All of this puts you in a better position to read the text intensively, to decide whether you need to read it at all, and if so to decide whether some parts of the text are more important than others. In the process you will almost certainly notice the occasional word which you recognize or can guess. Equally valuable, you may notice that a certain unfamiliar word occurs repeatedly and decide to look it up before you start reading the text closely. The information gained in this way can be used to make better predictions about the text.

When skimming a text it is useful to train yourself to pick out certain features which are easily accessible:

a. *Internationalisms and cognates* (see **R165**). These are words which look like English words and often have a meaning which is the same as or is related to the English word, e.g.

> *finden* to find; *organisieren* to organize; *Organisation* organization; *organisch* organic; *Argument* argument; *Universität* university; *unter* under; *Nacht* night; *jung* young.

Being aware of these correspondences between English and German will help you to recognize and remember a great many words, but a little caution is needed, especially with 'false friends' (see **R164**) – i.e. words which look like English words but have a different meaning altogether. The best guide to the meaning of any such German word is always its context. You cannot assume, for example, that the German word 'Argument' has all the senses of the English word 'argument'.

b. *Nouns*. Since all nouns in German begin with a capital letter, it is relatively easy to skim through a text and pick them out. This will usually provide a very strong first orientation.

c. *Words which you already know and are sure of*. See below, 10.8.

In addition, it is worth while learning to spot the following on a skim-reading:

d. *Negatives*. 'nicht', 'kein', 'kaum', etc., which are important because they can affect the meaning fundamentally (see **R124–34**).

e. *Logical connectors*. 'jedoch', 'darüber hinaus', 'außerdem', etc., which are important because they give important information about the logical connections between different parts of the text (see **R138–9**).

10.5 Scanning

Sometimes we need to read a text because it may contain some particular piece of information which we are interested in. The remainder of the text is less important to us, and may even be of no interest. Scanning the text involves skimming quickly through it to determine whether it contains what we are looking for, and if so, where exactly it is to be found. This may involve looking quickly through the text for key words or for other information such as dates, figures, or proper names. It would be inefficient to start reading the text intensively from the beginning. Having located the passage or passages we need, we can then start reading them more closely. Particular types of text – such as a list of contents or some journal articles – lend themselves very well to scanning. The remaining chapters of this course contain exercises in scanning for information.

10.6 Predicting the Meaning

Good readers not only focus on meanings, they build up a mental picture of what the text is likely to say next. Effective reading involves making good predictions about where the text is going next and also about the likely meaning of any unfamiliar word or group of words.

Making good predictions is a skill that comes from learning to stand back from a text and think about the content in more general terms. Pre-reading techniques (see 10.3) are important here. Another technique is regularly to make a mental note of the content of larger stretches of text – paragraphs, for instance. Focusing on units larger than the sentence makes it easier to follow the overall message of longer texts and the way the meanings are developed section by section. This in turn makes it easier to solve 'local' problems at the level of word, phrase, or sentence.

10.7 Tackling Difficult and Unknown Words (Guessing)

You will almost certainly be reliant on a bilingual dictionary, especially in the early stages of learning to read in German, and it is important to acquire good dictionary skills (see **R166–83**).

Developing your 'top–down' reading techniques can also help in finding the most appropriate dictionary translation for the particular context, and in any case you will need to develop strategies for tackling words which cannot be found in your dictionary. There are two approaches:

a. Look at the word closely to see whether you recognize parts of the word which you know or which you can find in the dictionary. A knowledge of word-formation patterns in German is valuable here (see **R184–6**).

b. Look at the context for clues and make basic guesses about the *kind* of meaning the word could have.

The second of these is the more important. You should resist any initial temptation to stop reading when you come across an unfamiliar word, since valuable clues as to its meaning are often found in the rest of the sentence, or in the next sentence. The single most important piece of advice in these circumstances is to *keep on reading*, to focus on meaning rather than structure, and to look for clues in the following words and the following sentence.

Good readers learn how to make good guesses, and guessing well is often quite a simple matter. It is often not necessary to get the *exact* meaning of a word in order to comprehend the text. Indeed, a useful strategy for tackling a 'difficult' word is to miss it out and mentally read a 'blank'. This prevents you becoming fixated ('getting stuck') on the word and helps you to focus on the immediate and general context. It is often possible then to guess the *kind* of meaning the offending word probably has. We use this kind of guessing technique occasionally when reading in our native language (for instance, a difficult text about some technical area we are not familar with). We need to employ it much more, of course, when reading in a foreign language. See the exercise on guessing at the end of this chapter.

10.8 Building a Vocabulary

Building a vocabulary of key words will improve reading efficiency enormously and save time checking in dictionaries. There are two principal areas:

a. Items of general vocabulary which are likely to feature in a wide variety of texts: all auxiliary verbs (**R31**) and modal verbs (**R65, R69**), connectors (**R160**) and conjunctions (**R143**), 'logical connectors' (**R138–9**), pronouns (**R25, R98–100**), determiners (**R97**), prepositions (especially those in **R95** and **R94.2–3**, negation words (**R124–9**), as well as common verbs and nouns. If you find yourself looking up the same word more than once in the dictionary, this is a sign that you should probably make an effort to remember it.

b. Items of specialized vocabulary in the field in which you are engaged, e.g. art history, politics, engineering, etc.

It is a good idea to keep a vocabulary book in which you record words you want to remember. There are also several basic vocabulary books on the market. If you would like to test your vocabulary retention on the first nine chapters of this course, see the exercise on vocabulary at the end of this chapter.

10.9 'How Well am I Following This?'

It is always useful to consciously monitor your comprehension of a text. To do this, make a point of asking yourself whether the text is saying the kind of thing you would expect it to say. Does the meaning you have got from the passage you are reading fit in with what you know so far? Does it make sense or nonsense? There may be a tendency when reading in a foreign language to settle for something that does not quite make sense. Monitoring the quality of your comprehension will alert you to points at which your reading is faulty. But remember that for most purposes you do not need to understand 100 per cent of a text.

10.10 Intensive (Sentence-by-Sentence) Reading

Of course, intensive reading cannot be dispensed with, but it is worth remembering that *although the text is linear, your reading of it does not have to be.* You can move backwards and forwards through the text as you build up an understanding of its content. Ask yourself how much of your reading in your first language is strictly sequential. Your aim in reading German should be to transfer the full range of successful techniques you already have for reading in your first language. If this survey of reading strategies indicates that you could perhaps improve your reading techniques in English, this is probably the single most effective way of improving your reading performance in the foreign language at this stage.

The previous chapters of this course have concentrated on developing the relevant intensive reading skills for German, with the main focus on clause structure and sentence structure. You will already know that reading German sentences efficiently often entails mentally rearranging the word order. Similarly, it may seem logical to read one sentence at a time and not to start reading the next sentence until you have read all the words of the current sentence. But if this is your only reading strategy or the one you employ nearly all the time, your progress towards becoming an effective reader in German may be slower than it needs to be.

10.11 How Much of the Text do You Need?

There are some kinds of text, such as poems and other literary texts, which you need to read closely to appreciate them fully. They often contain fine nuances. However, reading for information does not usually require such a high level of attention. It is usually possible to follow the sense of a text reasonably well without processing all words with the same intensity. Effective first-language readers can process the meaning without paying close attention to every word.

Reading in a foreign language, one tends to be nervous about passing over words which might radically affect the message of the text, and to begin with this usually means that readers are processing more of the text than they really need to. It is also likely that 'bottom–up', sequential reading will be important at the beginning of a text, but that comprehension will improve as you get further into a text. So you may start off reading quite intensively and then become more confident about making predictions as to the meaning.

While it is difficult to give clear guidelines as to which words can be given less attention in a German text (but see **R140**), you should already be able to guess a good number of words which belong to structures you have learned, as well as many function words like prepositions. To test this idea, here is a familiar text (from Chapter 4) with about one-third of its words missing. Without rereading the full text, see how much of the meaning you can get:

> Steht Deutsch heute -- Schatten --- Englisch? Wenn man --- heutigen Verhältnisse mit --- früheren vergleicht, muß man ---------- --- Frage bejahen. Deutsch --------- Wissenschaftler, vor allem Natur --------------, veröffentlichen ----- --- ----------- --- englisch --- --- deutsch. Aber Deutsch ------ --- Wissenschaftssprache interessant, weil -- ------ ------ ---------- klassische, ------------ Theorien formuliert ------, z. B. ------ Einsteins Relativitätstheorie, --- Webers ---- ---- Marx' ---------------------- Theorien oder die Philosophien, die Wittgenstein und Heidegger ------------. Obwohl --- meisten ------ Texte in englischer Übersetzung --------, lohnt sich doch --- viele Akademiker --- ----, diese Texte -- Original zu lesen.

Of course, the missing words have not been chosen at random, and part of the skill in reading a foreign language lies in learning which words in a text deserve more attention than others. This is also a text which you have read before. But you can learn to tackle new texts in this way once you have acquired a basic competence in 'reading for structure'. At this stage of the course, you may already have this basic competence. You can practise this technique on any text. Perhaps you would like to rehearse it on another familiar text before moving on to an unseen text. A good exercise is to take a text and see how many words or parts of words you can delete without destroying the gist. Even if you learn to pass over 10 per cent of the text in this way, you will improve your reading speed without losing comprehension. In addition, you should try this exercise on an English text and compare the results with those from a German text.

Exercises

Guessing difficult words (10.7)

Imagine you are a foreign reader of English. There are several words which could fill the gaps in the following English texts, and the foreign learner would not necessarily have to know the 'difficult' word in order to follow the sense:

While German was ----(1)---- an international language particularly in the ---(2)--- of science, its present international standing seems to be based ---(3)--- on the economic strength of the German-speaking countries. (Ulrich Ammon, 'To What Extent is German an International Language?', in P. Stevenson (ed.), *The German Language and the Real World*, Clarendon Press, Oxford, 1995, 51)

. . . language is not a 'natural' vehicle for nationalism: nationalists have ----(4)--- language only when it suited their purposes. During the most excessive period of German nationalism the German language was -----(5)---- to a subordinate role in the ideological system, because the Nazis stressed primordial ties rooted in the -----(6)----- concept of an eternal and unalterable (superior) race, which is -----(7)----- rather than acquired. (Florian Coulmas, 'Germanness: Language and Nation', in P. Stevenson (ed.), *The German Language and the Real World*, Clarendon Press, Oxford, 1995, 66)

The point of this exercise is that turning the difficult word into a 'gap' can make intelligent guessing easier.

Vocabulary test (10.8)

In working through the first nine chapters of the course you have should have been learning vocabulary items. It is essential that you make a conscious effort to learn vocabulary. Here is a short test. Without referring to the earlier chapters of this course, give the meaning of the following German words:

a. Nouns: Sprache; Krieg; Wissenschaft; Jahrhundert; Schatten; Bevölkerung; Osten; Ausländer; Kommunikationsschwierigkeit; Bedeutung.

b. Verbs: verstehen; veröffentlichen; lesen; wohnen; entdecken; ankommen; zunehmen; bejahen; vorantreiben; emigrieren.

c. Adjectives and adverbs: wichtig; interessant; europäisch; überall; sofort; langsam; heute; verschieden; wirtschaftlich; wieder.

The remaining chapters of this course build on the important close-reading skills you have been practising so far. A basic strategy for tackling texts for the first time is set out in the next chapter, which contains a selection of short texts for you to work on. Chapters 12–16 contain longer and more complex texts and detailed suggestions on how to work through them.

The aim of these final chapters is to develop your competence to the point where you can tackle quite sophisticated German texts independently. At some point during the next five chapters you should begin to look at the texts in the Text Corpus at the back of this book and try your reading skills on them, with or without the aid of the parallel English translation.

The texts in Chapters 15 and 16, in particular, are quite challenging even for many German readers who do not have higher education. Written German does not come any harder than this. So you should not be discouraged if you find them difficult. If you are able to work through them with some success, however, you will have reached a very high level of competence indeed.

11

····················

Five Short Texts

This chapter contains five short texts on which to practise your independent reading skills, before progressing to longer and more complex texts in Chapters 12 to 16. It also sets out a suggested method for approaching new texts, and especially the kind of longer text contained in the following chapters.

As you begin to tackle longer and more sophisticated German texts for the first time you should try to develop a clear set of reading strategies. The rationale for these strategies has already been introduced in Chapter 10. As you work through the texts in the later chapters of this course you may decide to adapt some of the reading strategies set out there, depending on which of them you find most helpful. The important point is that you should begin to develop a set of conscious strategies of your own for tackling German texts.

Working with a Text in Three Stages

The remaining chapters of this course will work with a method of tackling a text in three main phases: pre-reading, intensive reading, and post-reading. Before reading these texts intensively, practise the 'pre-reading' exercises described below. After reading them, do the 'post-reading' exercises. This will involve going back over part or all of the text to check that you have understood details properly.

Pre-reading

There are many strategies which can help to improve your understanding of the text before you actually begin to read it intensively. Before you read the texts in this chapter you should practise the following simple pre-reading routine:

1. Spend a minute or two calling to mind (in English) everything you know about the topic being discussed in the text. Focus particularly on the important vocabulary that comes to mind when you do this.

2. Skim the text (do not try to close-read it) and note any special features that strike you. These can include subheadings, graphs, highlighted words (e.g. italics), brackets, numbers.

3. Skim the text again, this time looking for any words which 'jump out' because they are already familiar, or look guessable.

These simple exercises should be done without reading the text closely, i.e. 'word by word, sentence by sentence'. Simply let your eye travel over the text, from beginning to end and then back again. Further suggestions for you to try at the pre-reading stage are set out in later chapters.

Intensive reading

You should then attempt a 'close-reading' of each text. At this stage you will need to recall the reading skills you have practised in the first nine chapters of the course. You may also want to consult the Reference Section to look up particular grammar points, and cross-references to the Reference Section are provided with the texts in this chapter. In the following chapters, cross-references to the Reference Section are found in the post-reading exercises.

Selected vocabulary items are given next to the text and in the order of occurrence in paragraph grouping to save you looking everything up in a dictionary, but you may still need to use a dictionary, and the form of the word given in the vocabulary list is not always the same as that used in the text, so that occasionally you will need to make connections between German words for yourself. Vocabulary items which you have already seen in the first nine chapters of the course will generally not be included in these lists, since vocabulary learning is part of your task in each chapter of the course.

Note that the genders of nouns are given in the glossaries as '-r' (for masculine), '-e' (feminine), and '-s' (neuter); and that separable verbs are shown with a mark between the verb stem and the separable prefix, like this: aus'scheiden.

Post-reading

Finally, you should go back over sections of the text to make sure you have understood it correctly. You may be able to recall particular pieces of information, and you should be able to find the place in the text where a particular piece of information is contained, and check that you have understood it correctly. Each text has a number of post-reading (comprehension) exercises to be attempted at this stage. Going back over a text in this way helps to consolidate what you have learned and this is important in steadily improving the level of your reading competence in German.

Each text in this chapter is an entry from a lexicon, and gives basic information about a topic. These are:

    Ancient Rome
    bacteria
    inflation
    research and development
    the sonata

You should select at least **two** of these texts – one from an area where you think your general knowledge is good, and one from an area in which your general knowledge is less good. (You can of course read all of them if you want to!)

Now select the first text you are going to read and start the 'pre-reading' exercises. Work through the three stages before you move on to your second text.

Ancient Rome

1 **Rom.**—Die Stadt Rom soll 753 v. Chr. von **Romulus und Remus** gegründet worden sein, doch beginnt die sicher bezeugte römische Geschichte erst im vierten
5 Jahrhundert v. Chr. Damals war Rom eine Republik und breitete seine Herrschaft immer weiter aus. Als **Gaius Julius Caesar** (100 bis 44 v. Chr.) die Alleinherrschaft übernahm und damit die republi-
10 kanische Staatsform zerstörte, gehörten die Länder rund um das Mittelmeer fast alle zum **Römischen Reich**. Es reichte zeitweilig von England, dem Rhein und der Donau im Norden bis zur Sahara im
15 Süden, von Portugal im Westen bis zum Euphrat im Osten. Caesars Neffe **Augustus** begründete das Kaiserreich, das den Mittelmeerländern lange Zeit den Frieden bescherte. Seit 395 n. Chr. war das
20 Römische Reich endgültig in eine westliche und eine östliche Hälfte geteilt.

Als das Ende des Altertums nimmt man das fünfte Jahrhundert n. Chr. an, als der westliche Teil des Römischen Reichs wäh-
25 rend der unruhigen Zeit der Völkerwanderung sich auflöste. Im Jahr 476 n. Chr. setzte der germanische Heerführer **Odoaker** den letzten weströmischen Kaiser ab.

gründen *to found*
bezeugen *to document*
damals *at that time*
aus'breiten *to extend, expand*
-e Herrschaft *supremacy*
übernehmen *to take over*
zerstören *to destroy*
gehören + zu *to belong to*
-s Mittelmeer *the Mediterranean*
-s Reich *empire*
reichen *to reach, extend*
zeitweilig *for a time*
-r Neffe *nephew*
-r Kaiser *emperor*
-r Friede *peace*
bescheren *to bring, present with*
endgültig *finally*
-e Hälfte *half*
teilen *to divide*

-s Altertum *antiquity, ancient history*
an'nehmen *to assume, suppose*
-r Teil *part*
-e Ruhe *peace, tranquillity*
-s Volk *people, ethnic group*
wandern *to migrate*
sich auf'lösen *to dissolve, break up*
ab'setzen *to depose*
-s Heer *army*

line 1	soll ➔ **R69**
line 2	worden ➔ **R74–5**
line 3	die sicher bezeugte ➔ **R109**
line 4	erst ➔ **R163**
line 7	immer weiter ➔ **R107**
lines 17–18	den Mittelmeerländern ➔ **R96**
lines 18–19	den Frieden ➔ **R101.3**
lines 22 f.	als ➔ **R163**

Schüler-Brockhaus. Sachwissen von A bis Z (Compact Verlag, Munich, 1980).

Note: Words printed in bold indicate that there is a relevant entry to be found in the **Schüler-Brockhaus**.

Post-reading exercises

1. What is the significance of the date 753BC?

2. What is said about the fourth century BC?

3. What was the extent of the Roman Empire at its height?

4. What do you think 'Alleinherrschaft' means (line 8**f)**?

5. What date is usually regarded as the end of antiquity?

6. What happened in AD 395?

7. Who was Odoaker and what did he do?

Bacteria

Bakterien.—Bakterien—das ist die Mehrzahl von »Bakterium«—sind sehr kleine Lebewesen, die nur aus einer Zelle bestehen und die man mit bloßem Auge
5 nicht sehen kann. Erst unter dem Mikroskop kann man sie nach ihrer Form unterscheiden. Stäbchenförmige Bakterien nennt man **Bazillen**, kugelförmige werden **Kokken** genannt und korkzieher-
10 artige heißen **Spirochäten**.

Bakterien gibt es fast überall: in der Erde, im Wasser und in der Luft. Sie sind für das Leben der Menschen, der höheren Tiere und Pflanzen sehr wichtig. Bak-
15 terien machen den Erdboden fruchtbar, sie sorgen dafür, daß tierische und pflanzliche Abfälle zerfallen. Manche leben im Darm und helfen bei der Verdauung, indem sie solche Stoffe für den Körper
20 verwertbar machen, die sonst unverarbeitet wieder ausgeschieden würden. Einige sind gefährliche Krankheitserreger und verursachen ansteckende Krankheiten, z. B. die Tuberkulose.
25 →Acker, ansteckende Krankheiten, Tuberkulose, Verdauung, Zelle

-e Mehrzahl *plural*
-s Lebewesen *organism*
bestehen + aus *to consist of*
unterscheiden *to distinguish*

-r Stab *stick*
-e Kugel *ball, sphere*
-r Korkzieher *corkscrew*

fruchtbar *fertile*
sorgen + für *to be responsible for*
-r Abfall *waste*
zerfallen *to decay*
-r Darm *intestine*
verdauen *to digest*
-r Körper *body*
verwerten *to use, exploit*
verarbeiten *to process*
aus'scheiden *to eject*
gefährlich *dangerous*
-e Krankheit *illness*
erregen *to arouse*
an'stecken *to infect*

line 5   erst → **R163**
line 16 sorgen dafür, daß → Chapter 5.1
line 17 manche → **R135.4**
line 19 indem → **R143**
line 21 ausgeschieden würden → **R74, R47**

Schüler-Brockhaus. Sachwissen von A bis Z (Compact Verlag, Munich, 1980).

Note: Words printed in bold indicate that there is a relevant entry to be found in the **Schüler-Brockhaus**.

Post-reading exercises

1. What do bacilli look like?

2. What do cocci look like?

3. What do spirochaete look like?

4. Where are bacteria found?

5. What effect do they have on soil?

6. How do bacteria help digestion?

7. What kind of illnesses do some bacteria cause?

Inflation

Inflation.—Das Wort kommt aus dem Lateinischen und bedeutet »Aufblähung«; gemeint ist die Aufblähung der umlaufenden Geldmenge, die bewirkt, daß das Geld immer weniger wert wird, daß man also für denselben Betrag immer weniger kaufen kann. Folgen der Inflation sind zunächst Teuerung, zugleich auch die Entwertung der Ersparnisse und die sogenannte »Flucht in die Sachwerte«; das heißt, daß viele Leute Dinge erwerben wollen, deren Wert auf jeden Fall erhalten bleibt, z. B. Grundstücke oder Kunstwerke. Daraus ergibt sich wieder, daß die Preise solcher Dinge noch schneller steigen als die aller übrigen Waren.—Wenn man von »der« Inflation spricht, meint man im allgemeinen die Geldentwertung nach dem Ersten Weltkrieg in Deutschland, die 1923 ihren Höhepunkt erreichte und mit der Schaffung zuerst der **Rentenmark** und dann der **Reichsmark** (RM) abschloß. Eine Billion—1 000 000 000 000—alte Vorkriegsmark wurden damals zu einer RM. Die Geldentwertung nach dem Zweiten Weltkrieg endete 1948 mit der **Währungsreform** und der Einführung der **Deutschen Mark** (DM).—Eine langsame Geldentwertung mit Teuerungsraten von jährlich etwa 5% nennt man »schleichende Inflation«. Darüber ist man seit 1973 in vielen westlichen Ländern weit hinaus gekommen.

→Deutschland, Geld, Markt, Preis, Weltkrieg

um'laufen *to circulate*
-e Menge *quantity*
bewirken *to bring about*
-r Betrag *sum of money*
teuer *expensive*
zugleich *at the same time*
entwerten *to reduce in value*
sparen *to save*
-e Flucht *flight, refuge*
-r Sachwert *material good, asset*
erwerben *to acquire*
erhalten *to retain*
-s Grundstück *plot of land, real estate*
-e Kunst *art*
sich ergeben + aus *to result from*

schaffen *to create*
ab'schließen *to conclude, close*
-e Währung *currency*

schleichen *to creep*
über + hinaus *beyond*

line 3   gemeint ist → **R19** (no. 16)
line 6   also → **R164**
lines 6–7 immer weniger → **R107**
line 12   deren → **R110**
line 14   daraus → **R136**
line 16   als → **R10.6**
line 32   darüber → **R136**

Schüler-Brockhaus. Sachwissen von A bis Z (Compact Verlag, Munich, 1980).

Note: Words printed in bold indicate that there is a relevant entry to be found in the **Schüler-Brockhaus.**

Post-reading exercises

1. What is the origin of the word 'inflation'?
2. What are the initial consequences of inflation?
3. What kind of goods retain their value?
4. What happens to the price of these things?
5. What do Germans usually mean by 'the' inflation?
6. What is 'schleichende Inflation'?
7. Translate the final sentence of this text.

Research and Development

1 Ziel von Forschung und Entwicklung
(FuE) ist es, das richtige Produkt zum
richtigen Zeitpunkt anzubieten bzw.
geeignete Produktionsmethoden zu
5 entwickeln oder zu optimieren. Zum
Bereich FuE zählt man auch noch die
Aktivitäten nach dem Verkauf eines Pro-
duktes, die darauf gerichtet sind, den
Kunden Voraussetzungen für Service,
10 Wartung und Entsorgung anzubieten.

In bezug auf FuE sollten die Unternehmen unter anderem folgende Punkte
beachten:
(1) Märkte wandeln sich: ständige Kon-
15 takte mit dem Betrieb und den Pilotkunden sind daher für das FuE-Team
unerläßlich.
(2) Nicht alles muß im eigenen Haus
entwickelt werden. Universitäten und
20 Fachhochschulen sowie die sonstigen
Forschungsinstitute sollten als mög-
liche Kooperationspartner immer
geprüft werden.
(3) In jede FuE-Strategie sind Service,
25 Beratung und Entsorgung mit einzubeziehen.
(4) Die interne und externe Kommunikation ist nicht Aufgabe des FuE-Teams,
sondern des Managements.

forschen *to research*
-s Ziel *goal, objective*
an'bieten *to offer*
geeignet *appropriate*
-r Bereich *area*
zählen *to count*
verkaufen *to sell*
richten + auf *to aim at*
-r Kunde *customer*
-e Voraussetzung *(necessary) precondition*
in bezug auf *concerning*
-s Unternehmen *firm*
beachten *to pay attention to*
sich wandeln *to change*
ständig *constant*
-r Betrieb *factory, company*
unerläßlich *indispensable*

-e Fachhochschule *vocational university*
prüfen *to examine*
beraten *to advise*
entsorgen *to remove worries*
ein'beziehen *to include*
-e Aufgabe *task, job*

line 3   anzubieten → **R39, R149**
lines 4–5   zu entwickeln → **R149**
lines 8–10   darauf gerichtet . . .,. . . zu → **R149,**
             R155
line 11   sollten → **R69**
line 14   wandeln sich → **R41.2**
lines 15–16 mit . . . den Pilotkunden → **R105**
line 16   daher → **R138.3**
line 21   als → **R163**
lines 24–25 sind einzubeziehen → **R78.2**

Jakob Wolf, *Lexikon Betriebswirtschaft*, (Wilhelm
Heyne Verlag, Munich, 1995).

Post-reading exercises

1. What is the German word for 'development'?

2. What is the German verb 'to develop'?

3. What is the objective of R&D?

4. What is said about universities?

5. What is said about internal and external communication?

6. What is said about service?

7. What is the meaning of the word 'Pilotkunde' (line 15f.)?

Sonata

Sonate.—Die Sonate ist ein Musikwerk für Instrumente, häufig für Klavier allein komponiert, oder für ein anderes Instrument mit Klavier (z. B. Violine und Klavier). Im 18. Jahrhundert erhielt sie eine ganz bestimmte Form. Die Sonate der Zeit, in der **Joseph Haydn** (1732 bis 1809), **Wolfgang Amadeus Mozart** (1756–1791) und **Ludwig van Beethoven** (1770–1827) lebten, besteht aus drei oder vier verschiedenartigen Stücken, die man Sätze nennt. Die Bezeichnungen für die Sätze stammen aus der italienischen Sprache. Der erste Satz ist gewöhnlich mit **Allegro** (schnell) überschrieben. Der zweite ist meist ein langsamer Satz, Andante (gehend) oder **Adagio** (langsam und ausdrucksvoll) genannt. Ihm folgt in vielen Sonaten der tänzerische dritte Satz, häufig ein **Menuett** (französischer Tanz) oder das schnelle **Scherzo** (sprich skerzo). Der letzte Satz, das **Finale** (Schluß), wird sehr schnell gespielt. Die Sätze der Sonate sind nach bestimmten Gesetzen aufgebaut. Der erste Satz, oft auch der letzte, hat eine besondere Form und wird als der eigentliche **Sonatensatz** bezeichnet. Er besteht aus drei Teilen. Im ersten Teil erscheinen zwei gegensätzliche musikalische Gedanken, die »Themen« der Sonate. Der Komponist verarbeitet und vertieft sie im Mittelteil. Im Schlußteil werden die Themen des ersten Teils nur wenig verändert wiederaufgenommen. Genauso wie die Sonate sind viele andere Musikwerke aufgebaut.

häufig *frequent*
-s Klavier *piano*
erhalten *to receive*

bestehen + aus *to consist of*
verschiedenartig *different*
-s Stück *piece*
-r Satz (here) *movement*
bezeichnen *to name*
stammen + aus *to originate from*
gewöhnlich *usual*
überschreiben *to write a heading*
meist *usually*
langsam *slow*
gehen *to go, walk*
-r Ausdruck *expression*
-r Tanz *dance*
sprich *pronounced as*

bestimmt *definite*
-s Gesetz *law*
auf'bauen *to construct*

eigentlich *actual, real*
-r Teil *part*
-r Gegensatz *opposition, contrast*
-s Thema *theme*
tief *deep*
verändern *to alter*

auf'nehmen *to take up*
genauso *in the same way*

line 5   erhielt ➜ **R30**
line 7   Zeit, in der ➜ **R114**
lines 14–15 ist . . . überschrieben ➜ **R170, R174**
line 18   ihm folgt ➜ **R96.2, R98, R135.1**
line 35   (genauso) wie ➜ **R163**

Schüler-Brockhaus. Sachwissen von A bis Z (Compact Verlag, Munich, 1980).

Note: Words printed in bold indicate that there is a relevant entry to be found in the **Schüler-Brockhaus**.

Post-reading exercises

1. What is the meaning of 'adagio'?

2. What is the meaning of 'menuett'?

3. Is the last movement of a sonata typically fast or slow?

4. What is said in particular about a sonata's first movement?

5. What constitutes the 'themes' of the first movement?

6. What happens to these themes in the second and final movements?

7. How do the principles of construction for a sonata compare to those for other musical pieces?

12

Two Longer Texts

There are two slightly longer lexicon texts in this chapter, one on Islam and one on human pregnancy. We suggest you do the pre-reading exercises for both texts before choosing one on which to work intensively. There is of course nothing to stop you working through both texts thoroughly.

A: Pre-reading exercises

A1. Spend a few minutes recalling what you know about these two subjects and focusing on the key vocabulary (in English) which you might expect to occur.

A2. Let your eye travel over the text without trying to read it. What features do you notice?

A3. Now quickly scan the text line by line and make a note of any words which you are sure you know the meaning of.

A4. Finally, scan the text quickly once again and make a note of any words which you think you may be able to understand but are not quite sure of.

Now select one of the texts on pages 90–1 and read it intensively.

B: Post-reading exercises

Islam

B1. Questions on the text

1. What is the literal meaning of the word 'Islam'?
2. What are 'Suren' ?
3. What is the 'Mihrab'?
4. Why is Damascus mentioned in this text?
5. What is forbidden inside the mosque?
6. What is forbidden to Muslims?

B2. What do you think the following mean?

1. nach der Lehre (line 9)
2. spätere gesetzliche Bestimmungen (line 17)
3. vor dem Gebet (line 22)
4. Gebetsrichtung (line 29)
5. Vorbeter (line 33)
6. Pilgerfahrt (line 44)
7. sind ihm grundsätzlich untersagt (line 46, see **R96**)

1 **Islam.**—Islam heißt die von dem Araber **Mohammed** am Anfang des 7. Jahrhunderts n.Chr. gestiftete Religion, die besonders in Arabien und ganz Nordafrika,
5 im Iran und in Irak, in der Türkei, in Pakistan und Indonesien verbreitet ist. Der Name bedeutet »Ergebung in den Willen Gottes«, der **Allah** genannt wird. Er hat nach der Lehre des Islams die Welt erschaf-
10 fen und wird sie am Jüngsten Tag richten; von seinem allmächtigen Willen hängt das Schicksal des Menschen ab, diesem Willen soll der Mensch darum ergeben sein.

Das heilige Buch des Islams ist der
15 **Koran**. Er enthält in arabischer Sprache Weissagungen und Predigten Mohammeds und spätere gesetzliche Bestimmungen und ist in **Suren** (Kapitel) gegliedert. Aus ihm wird in der **Moschee**, dem Gebetshaus des
20 Islams, vorgelesen. Die Moschee umfaßt einen Vorhof mit einem Brunnen, an dem sich die Gläubigen vor dem Gebet waschen sollen, ein oder mehrere **Minaretts**—schlanke, hohe Türme, von denen die
25 Gebetszeiten ausgerufen werden—und einen Innenraum, der meist mit Teppichen ausgelegt ist und nicht mit Schuhen betreten werden darf. Eine große Nische (**Mihrab**) gibt die Gebetsrichtung nach
30 **Mekka** in Arabien an, wo sich das Hauptheiligtum des Islams, die **Kaaba**, befindet; oft steht neben dieser Nische ein Pult (**Mimbar**) für den Vorbeter. Darstellungen von Menschen sind verboten. Die älteste
35 große Moschee befindet sich in Damaskus. Der Anhänger des Islams, der **Muslim**, hat bestimmte Pflichten: Er bekennt die Einheit Gottes und daß Mohammed sein Prophet ist. Am Tage soll er fünfmal nach
40 Mekka gewandt beten und am Freitag die Moschee besuchen, Almosen geben und im Monat **Ramadan** tagsüber fasten. Einmal in seinem Leben soll er den **Haddsch**. das ist die Pilgerfahrt nach Mekka, antreten.
45 Alkohol und der Genuß von Schweinefleisch sind ihm grundsätzlich untersagt.

stiften *to found*
verbreiten *to spread*
sich ergeben *to submit, surrender*
-r Wille *will*
-e Lehre *teachings*
erschaffen *to create*
-r Jüngste Tag *day of judgement*
richten *to judge*
-e Macht *power*
ab'hängen + von *to depend on*
-s Schicksal *fate*
darum *therefore*

enthalten *to contain*
-e Weissagung *wise saying*
-e Predigt *sermon*
-s Gesetz *law*
bestimmen *to determine*
gliedern *to divide up*
vor'lesen *to read aloud*
umfassen *to contain, comprise*
-r Hof *courtyard*
-r Brunnen *spring, well*
-r Gläubige *believer*
-s Gebet *prayer*
schlank *thin*
rufen *to call*
meist *often*
-r Teppich *carpet*
aus'legen (*here*) *furnish with*
betreten *to enter*
-e Richtung *direction*
-s Heiligtum *shrine*
-s Pult *desk*
dar'stellen *to represent, depict*
-r Anhänger *follower*
bestimmt *certain, definite*
-e Pflicht *duty*
bekennen *to acknowledge*
sich wenden *to turn*
besuchen *to visit*
Almosen *alms*
tagsüber *during the day*
an'treten *to embark on*
genießen *to enjoy, partake of*
-r Schwein *pig*
grundsätzlich *on principle, absolutely*
untersagen *to prohibit*

Schüler-Brockhaus. Sachwissen von A bis Z (Compact Verlag, Munich, 1980).

Note: Words printed in bold indicate that there is a relevant entry to be found in the **Schüler-Brockhaus**.

Schwangerschaft.—Die Schwangerschaft der Frau ist die Zeit zwischen der **Empfängnis** und der Geburt eines Kindes. —Ebenso wie bei vielen Tieren findet beim Menschen die Befruchtung innerhalb der weiblichen Geschlechtsorgane statt. Falls es beim Geschlechtsakt einem der männlichen Samenfäden gelingt, in die weibliche Eizelle einzudringen, so beginnt damit die Schwangerschaft, die gewöhnlich neun Monate dauert. Die befruchtete Eizelle wandert in die Gebärmutter, wo sie sich in die Schleimhaut einnistet. Im allgemeinen kommen die Eizellen abwechselnd vom rechten oder linken Eierstock. Es kann vorkommen, daß von den beiden Eierstöcken gleichzeitig Eizellen durch die Eileiter zur Gebärmutter wandern. Werden beide befruchtet, so entstehen zweieiige **Zwillinge.** Teilt sich die Eizelle, nachdem der Samenfaden in sie eingedrungen ist, entstehen eineiige Zwillinge.

Das befruchtete, eingenistete Ei wächst durch Zellteilung. Die Nahrung saugt es zunächst aus der Gebärmutterschleimhaut der Umgebung auf. Später entwickelt sich der **Mutterkuchen,** der dem heranwachsenden Lebewesen, das man jetzt **Embryo** nennt, Nahrung zuführt. Der Embryo ist mit dem Mutterkuchen durch die **Nabelschnur** verbunden. In ihr verlaufen die Gefäße, die den Embryo ernähren. Nach 30 Tagen beträgt die Gesamtlänge des Embryos etwa ½ cm. Nach zwei Monaten ist er etwa 4 cm lang. Die einzelnen Körperteile sind zu dieser Zeit schon deutlich zu erkennen. Am Ende des vierten Monats ist der Embryo, der von dieser Zeit an auch **Fötus** genannt wird, etwa 15 cm lang. Die Mutter verspürt die ersten Bewegungen des Kindes. Ihr Leib wölbt sich immer stärker vor. Gegen Ende der Schwangerschaft erreicht das Kind eine Länge von 50–55 cm und ein Gewicht zwischen 3 und 4 kg. Der Abschluß der Schwangerschaft ist die Geburt.

→ Fortpflanzung, Geburt, Geschlecht, Zelle

schwanger *pregnant*
empfangen *to receive*
-e Geburt *birth*
befruchten *to fertilize*
weiblich *female*
-s Geschlecht *sex*
-s Organ *organ*
falls *if*
-r Samenfaden *spermatazoon*
ein'dringen *to penetrate*
-s Ei *egg*
gewöhnlich *usually*
dauern *to last*
-e Gebärmutter *uterus*
-e Schleimhaut *mucous membrane*
im allgemeinen *generally*
ab'wechseln *to alternate*
gleichzeitig *at the same time*
-r Eileiter *Fallopian tube*
-r Zwilling *twin*
teilen *to divide*

wachsen *to grow*
-e Nahrung *nourishment*
auf'saugen *to extract, absorb*
zunächst *to begin with*
-e Umgebung *environment, surroundings*
-s Lebewesen *organism, being*
zu'führen *to deliver to*
-r Mutterkuchen *placenta*
-r Nabel *navel*
-e Schnur *cord*
verbinden *to connect*
verlaufen *to run*
-s Gefäß *vessel*
betragen *to amount to*
etwa *approximately*
einzeln *individual*
-r Teil *part*
deutlich *clear*
erkennen *to recognize*
verspüren *to sense, feel*
bewegen *to move*
-r Leib *(here) abdomen*
sich vor'wölben *to expand, become round*
gegen Ende *towards the end*
ab'schließen *to end, conclude*

Schüler-Brockhaus. Sachwissen von A bis Z (Compact Verlag, Munich, 1980).

Note: Words printed in bold indicate that there is a relevant entry to be found in the **Schüler-Brockhaus**.

B: Post-reading exercises

B3. What do the following words refer to?

(See **R135, R98–100**)

1. er (line 8)
2. sie (line 10)
3. er (line 15)
4. ihm (line 18)
5. sein (line 38)
6. ihm (line 46)

B4. Translate:

1. die von dem Araber Mohammed am Anfang des 7. Jahrhunderts n. Chr. gestiftete Religion. (lines 1–3, see **R115, R117–18**)
2. diesem Willen soll der Mensch darum ergeben sein. (line 12f., see **R69, R96, 138.3**)
3. Aus ihm wird in der Moschee vorgelesen. (lines 18f., see **R10.5**)
4. mit einem Brunnen, an dem sich die Gläubigen vor dem Gebet waschen sollen (lines 21–3, see **R69, R114**)
5. schlanke, hohe Türme, von denen die Gebetszeiten ausgerufen werden. (lines 24–5, see **R114**)

SCHWANGERSCHAFT

B5. Questions on the text

1. Describe the size of the embryo after thirty days.
2. Describe the appearance of the embryo after two months.
3. At what stage in the pregnancy is the embryo 15 cm. long?
4. At what point in the pregnancy is the word 'embryo' used?
5. From what point in the pregnancy is the word 'foetus' used?
6. What do the 'Gefäße' in the 'Nabelschnur' do?

B6. What do you think the following mean?

1. Empfängnis (line 2f.)
2. wandern (line 12)
3. ein'nisten (line 13)
4. Eierstock (line 15)
5. zweieiige Zwillinge (line 19f.)
6. Zellteilung (line 24)
7. Gesamtlänge (line 33)

B7. What do the following words refer to?

(See **R135, R98–100**)

1. sie (line 12)
2. es (line 24)
3. ihr (line 31)

4. er (line 35)
5. Ihr (line 41)
6. damit (line 9, see **R136**)

B8. Translate:

1. Werden beide befruchtet, entstehen zweieiige Zwillinge. (lines 18–20, see **R16**)
2. Teilt sich die Eizelle, nachdem der Samenfaden eingedrungen ist, entstehen eineiige Zwillinge. (lines 20–22, see **R16, R41.2**)
3. Die Nahrung saugt es zunächst aus der Gebärmutterschleimhaut der Umgebung auf. (lines 24–6, see **R5, R19**)
4. Die Körperteile sind deutlich zu erkennen. (line 35ff., see **R78.2**)

13

················

A Social History of Work

The text in this chapter is taken from an essay by the sociologist Iring Fetscher.

A: Pre-reading exercises

This is a fairly long text and the pre-reading exercises have been expanded and broken down into more detailed suggestions, including focusing on parts of the text for close-reading. You should not spend more than the suggested time on each exercise.

A1. Spend one minute thinking about what you understand by 'social history' and in particular what you might expect to find in an essay on the social history of work. What items of vocabulary belong to this field?

A2. Let your eye travel over the text for a few seconds without making any attempt to read it. Note how many paragraphs there are.
    Note: The bold type and italics in this text have been added. They are not part of the original text.

A3. The logical connectors have been printed in bold type in the first two paragraphs and in the final paragraph. Take a few seconds to glance at these.

A4. Negation words have been printed in italics in the first paragraph and the final paragraph. Take a few seconds to glance at these.

A5. Take a minute or so to skim through the text looking briefly at the nouns.

A6. Now skim through the text again, taking a little longer, noticing any words and phrases which you think you recognize. Distinguish between those you are sure you know and those which you think you can guess.

A7. Although you have not been making a conscious effort to read the text so far, take a minute or two now to focus on what you have found out about the text, and in particular on what kind of information it contains.

A8. Now close-read the first sentence of each paragraph and try to use what you have learnt to make a prediction about what each paragraph is about. (Where the first sentence is very long, you can probably stop at a colon (:) or semi-colon (;) without disturbing the meaning.) Once you have worked through the whole text thoroughly, come back to the notes you have made and observe how accurately they predict the meaning of the text as a whole.

Now read the whole text.

Sozialgeschichtliche Entwicklung der Arbeit

1   Seit es Menschen auf der Erde gibt, sind sie gezwungen, die Natur zu verändern, um ihr Leben zu erhalten. Unter günstigen geographischen und klimatischen
5 Bedingungen bleiben diese Veränderungen sehr gering: Früchte müssen gesucht und aufbewahrt werden, Fische und Wild müssen gejagt werden. Schon diese einfachen Tätigkeiten erfordern oft eine
10 komplizierte soziale Organisation und eine Anpassung des einzelnen an die Gruppe, die gemeinsam für den Lebensunterhalt sorgt. **Zwar** waren diese Anstrengungen manchmal groß, **aber**
15 'Arbeit' in dem Sinne, den das Wort für uns hat, waren sie eigentlich *nicht. Ebensowenig* gab es 'Freizeit'.

    Es soll hier **zunächst** ein Beispiel für eine Gesellschaftsform gegeben werden,
20 in der die Menschen praktisch ohne Arbeit zusammenleben. Die Sunis, ein unzivilisierter Stamm von Prärie-Indianern in Neu-Mexiko, leben in einem idealen Klima mit einer Vegetation, die ihnen
25 mühelos liefert, was sie an Nahrung, Kleidung und Wohnung für ihr Leben brauchen. Bei allen ihren Tätigkeiten empfinden sie eine Lust, die man erotisch nennen könnte. Sie fühlen sich in ihrer
30 natürlichen Umgebung völlig zu Hause. Aggressivität, Konkurrenzkampf, Eifersucht und Neid sind ihnen völlig fremd. Sie haben niemals kriegerische Aktionen durchgeführt, da sie Feindschaft und Haß
35 nicht kennen. Ebensowenig unterscheiden sie zwischen Fleiß und Faulheit. Der Preis, den sie für ihre pazifistische und glückliche Natur bezahlen mußten, war ihre historische und kulturelle Stagna-
40 tion.

    Entwickelte Hochkulturen sind hingegen nur auf dem Boden der Sklaverei entstanden; doch sind sie auch wieder untergegangen, wenn sie eine bestimmte
45 Höhe der Produktionstechnik erreicht hatten und das Problem der Organisation der Sklaverei nicht mehr lösen konnten.

-e Geschichte *history*
verändern *to alter*
erhalten *to preserve*
günstig *favourable*
-e Bedingung *condition, circumstance*
gering *slight*
-e Frucht *fruit*
auf'bewahren *to store*
-s Wild *game, wild animals*
jagen *to hunt*
einfach *simple*
-e Tätigkeit *activity*
erfordern *to require, demand*
an'passen (an) *to adapt to*
der einzelne *the individual*
gemeinsam *together*
-r Lebensunterhalt *living*
sorgen für *to see to, take care of*
-e Anstrengung *effort*
ebensowenig *just as little*
-e Freizeit *leisure time*

-s Beispiel *example*
-e Gesellschaft *society*
-r Stamm *tribe*
mühelos *effortless*
liefern *to provide*
-e Nahrung *food*
-e Kleidung *clothing*
-e Wohnung *dwelling, shelter*
brauchen *to need*
empfinden *to feel, sense*
-e Lust *pleasure*
nennen *to call*
-e Umgebung *surroundings, environment*
völlig *completely*
-r Kampf *struggle*
-e Konkurrenz *competition*
-e Eifersucht *jealousy*
-r Neid *envy*
fremd'sein *to be alien to*
durch'führen *to carry out*
-r Feind *enemy*
-r Haß *hatred*
unterscheiden *to distinguish*
-r Fleiß *hard work*
faul *lazy*
-r Preis *price*
bezahlen *to pay*

auf dem Boden *on the back of*
entstehen *to arise, come about*
-e Sklaverei *slavery*
unter'gehen *to decline*
bestimmt *particular*
-e Höhe *height*
-e Technik *technology*
erreichen *to achieve*
lösen *to solve*

Sklavenarbeit war also die erste Form der modernen Arbeit; Arbeit war körperliche Leistung, die mit Mühe und Anstrengung verbunden war, die man quantitativ messen konnte und zu der man gezwungen wurde. Auf der anderen Seite haben sich Tätigkeitsformen entwickelt, die nicht als Arbeit empfunden wurden, die also frei zustandegekommen und nicht mit Zwang und Mühe verbunden waren: diese Tätigkeiten machten Freude und erschafften den betreffenden Personen außerdem ein höheres Sozialprestige. Die Sklavenhalter, die über die Organisation der Arbeit verfügten, konnten sich solche ihnen Spaß und Prestige verschaffenden Tätigkeiten aussuchen und für sich reservieren: religiöses Wissen, Philosophie, Naturwissenschaften, Politik, schließlich auch Literatur und Kunst. Diese Beschäftigungen waren also den Angehörigen der Oberschicht vorbehalten.

Im bürgerlichen Zeitalter ist es das entscheidend Neue, daß Arbeit jetzt *nicht mehr* durch die direkte (sklavische) oder indirekte (feudale) Abhängigkeit von Personen erzwungen wird, **sondern** als frei gilt. Das Bürgertum verherrlicht die Arbeit in der bürgerlichen Eigentumstheorie: **während noch** in der Feudalzeit die ungleiche Verteilung des Eigentums an Individuen und Gruppen einfach als Folge einer von Gott gewollten Rangordnung galt, wurde **jetzt** das Eigentum aus der Arbeit des Individuums abgeleitet: der Bürger erarbeitet sich sein Eigentum und sein Eigentumsrecht. **Doch** mit der zunehmenden Kapitalisierung der bürgerlichen Gesellschaft wurde das naturrechtliche Eigentumsideal durch die Existenz lohnabhängiger Massen desavouiert. Der für Lohn Arbeitende erwirbt **zwar** einen Anspruch auf Bezahlung, **aber** deren Größe hat *nichts* mit dem Wert des von ihm erzeugten Produkts zu tun, das *nicht* er, **sondern** der Arbeitgeber auf den Markt bringt. Ökonomisch gesehen ist die Arbeit des Lohn-

---

körperlich *physical*
-e Leistung *effort, achievement*
messen *to measure*
empfinden als *to see as*
zustande'kommen *to come about*
verbinden *to connect*
-r Zwang *coercion*
-e Freude *joy, happiness*
erschaffen to *obtain, secure*
betreffend *the relevant*
verfügen über *to control, be in charge of*
-r Spaß *enjoyment*
aus'suchen *to select*
-s Wissen *knowledge*
-e Naturwissenschaften *the sciences*
-e Kunst *art*
-e Beschäftigung *activity*
an'gehören *to belong to*
-e Oberschicht *ruling class*
vor'behalten *to keep back, reserve*

bürgerlich *bourgeois*
-s Zeitalter *age, period*
entscheidend *decisive*
abhängig *dependent*
gelten als *to be regarded as*
verherrlichen *to glorify*
-s Eigentum *property*
verteilen *to distribute*
einfach *simply*
-e Folge *consequence*
-r Rang *rank*
-e Ordnung *order*
ab'leiten von *to derive from*
-s Individuum *the individual*
sich etw. erarbeiten *to earn* (s.th)
-s Recht *right, entitlement*
-r Lohn *wage*
-e Masse *mass, crowd*
desavouieren *to repudiate*
erwerben *to acquire*
-r Anspruch auf *claim to*
-e Größe *size*
-r Wert *value*
erzeugen *to produce*
-r Arbeitgeber *employer*

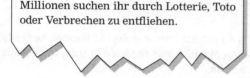

arbeiters *gar **nicht*** 'seine', **sondern** die
des ihn 'Beschäftigenden', sie kann **daher**
100 auch *kaum* jene Befriedigung verschaffen, die noch immer von der bürgerlichen
Moral als selbstverständlich unterstellt
wird. Arbeit wird auch dort, wo der direkte Zwang weggefallen ist—wie in liber-
105 alen bürgerlichen Gesellschaften—noch
immer als 'Zwangsarbeit' empfunden.
Millionen suchen ihr durch Lotterie, Toto
oder Verbrechen zu entfliehen.

beschäftigen *to employ*
befriedigen *to satisfy*
verschaffen *to procure, bring*
-e Moral *moral code*
selbstverständlich *self-evident*
unterstellen *to imply*
weg'fallen *to fall away*
-s Toto *(a form of) lottery*
-s Verbrechen *crime*
entfliehen *to escape from*

Iring Fetscher, **Arbeit und Spiel. Essays zur
Kulturkritik und Sozialphilosophie** (Philipp
Reclam jun., Stuttgart, 1983)

B: Post-reading exercises

B1. What do you think the following mean?

1. eine Anpassung des einzelnen an die Gruppe (line 11 f., see **R175**)
2. praktisch ohne Arbeit zusammenleben (line 20 f., see **R109**)
3. eine Vegetation, die ihnen mühelos liefert, was sie brauchen (lines 24 ff., see **R96, R148**)
4. sich völlig zu Hause fühlen (line 29 f., see R41)
5. Sklavenhalter (line 62, see **R181–2**)
6. solche ihnen Spaß und Prestige verschaffenden Tätigkeiten (line 64 f., see **R96, R115**)
7. waren den Angehörigen der Oberschicht vorbehalten (line 70 f., see **R96, R103.2**)
8. das entscheidend Neue (line 72 f., see **R109, R180**)
9. Folge einer von Gott gewollten Rangordnung (line 82 f., see **R115**)
10. das naturrechtliche Eigentumsrecht wurde desavouiert (lines 88–91 f., see **R75, R181–2**)
11. der für Lohn Arbeitende (line 91, see **R180**)
12. Ökonomisch gesehen (line 96 f., see **R109**)
13. Zwangsarbeit (line 107, see **R181–2**)

B2. Find any 'logical connectors' in the third and fourth paragraphs. (The logical connectors in the rest of the text are printed in bold.)

B3. Find any negation words in the second, third, and fourth paragraphs. (Negation words in the rest of the text are printed in italics.)

B4. Which of the following best describes the Sunis? aggressive, pacifist; forest-dwellers; technologically developed.

B5. What price have the Sunis paid for their idyllic lifestyle?

B6. What is said to have caused the decline of advanced societies in the past?

B7. What is the connection made between lotteries and crime?

B8. Which of the following characterizes the standpoint of the author: Christian, Marxist, Conservative?

14

....

Oskar Schindler

The text in this chapter is an extract from a review of Thomas Keneally's book *Schindler's List*, the German translation of which was reissued in 1994 to coincide with the launch of Steven Spielberg's film version.

A: Pre-reading exercises

Again, the suggested pre-reading exercises in this chapter are fairly detailed. Work quickly through each one:

A1. Spend one minute thinking about what you know about Oskar Schindler, through Keneally's book or Spielberg's film. Briefly list the main items of (English) vocabulary which come to mind.

A2. Let your eye travel over the text quickly, for a few seconds. Make a note of how many paragraphs there are, and of any other features that strike you (e.g. dates, numbers, abbreviations, names of organizations).

A3. Without trying to read the text closely, skim through it looking at the nouns. Make a note of those which you know or which you think you can guess.

A4. Now skim through the text again looking for any other words which you recognize or which you might be able to guess without looking closely at the context.

A5. Skim through the first three paragraphs of the text looking briefly at the logical connectors (printed in bold).
    Note: The logical connectors have not been highlighted in the last three paragraphs.

A6. Now close-read the first sentence of each paragraph and use what you learn to try and predict what each paragraph is about. Once you have worked through the whole text, you can come back to the predictions you have made and see how good they were.
    Note: Some of these sentences are quite long and you can get the main information by stopping before the sentence finishes. As you go through this exercise, think about where these longer sentences can be cut without disturbing the basic information.

Now read the whole text closely.

Schindler verstand es, sich vor dem Militärdienst zu drücken und als Heereslieferant unabkömmlich geschrieben zu werden. Er liebte das Risiko, den schnellen Profit ohne Buchführung und es schien ihm lukrativ, beim großen Aufbruch gen Osten als Kriegsgewinnler mit von der Partie zu sein.

Bereits im September 1939 reiste er im Troß von Wehrmacht, Gestapo und SS nach Polen, übernahm in Krakau die vor dem Konkurs stehenden Rekord-Werke, taufte sie in DEF (Deutsche Email-Fabrik) um und besetzte sie mit polnischen und jüdischen Zwangsarbeitern. In der Krakauer Beckmanns-Rasierklingenfabrik und in vielen anderen Betrieben bekamen die Arbeitssklaven nichts außer Prügel. Schindler **dagegen** behandelte seine mit dem Herstellen von Näpfen, Töpfen und Kübeln beschäftigten Juden und Polen großzügig, zeigte Mitleid auch in kleinen Dingen. Wenn er an Zeichentischen, Pressen oder Schmelzöfen vorbeiging, zündete er sich gewöhnlich eine Zigarette an, legte das ganze Päckchen hin und „vergaß" es wieder einzustecken. Schon für vier Zigaretten konnte man im besetzten Krakau einen ganzen Laib Brot kaufen.

War Schindler ein Widerstandskämpfer? Er kam mit hohen SS-Chargen bestens aus. **Auch** mit Hauptsturmführer Amon Göth, dem Kommandanten des bei Krakau gelegenen KZs Plaszow, der es liebte, vom Balkon seiner Villa mit Blick über das Lager irgendeinen Häftling, der ihm zufällig vor die Flinte kam, zu erschießen. Schindler arrangierte Gelage, machte teure Geschenke, bestach, wen es zu bestechen lohnte.

Gleichzeitig **aber** sorgte er für seine jüdischen Arbeiter, bestand 1942 darauf, daß sie in ein von ihm persönlich eingerichtetes Arbeitslager kamen, **wodurch** sie vor dem Abtransport ins KZ bewahrt blieben. Er verpflegte sie aus eigener Tasche, beschaffte Medikamente, gab das Vermögen, das er mit zwielichtigen

verstehen . . . zu *to know how to*
-r Dienst *service*
sich drücken vor *to avoid*
-s Heer *army*
-r Lieferant *supplier*
unabkömmlich *indispensable*
-s Risiko *risk*
-e Buchführung *accounting*
scheinen *to seem*
-r Aufbruch (here) *attack*
gen = gegen
-r Osten *the east*
-r Gewinnler *profiteer*
mit von der Partie sein *to join in*

bereits *already*
im Troß *as a 'camp-follower'*
übernehmen *to take over*
-r Konkurs *bankruptcy*
um'taufen *rename*
-s Email *enamel*
besetzen *to staff, occupy*
-r Zwangsarbeiter *forced labourer*
-e Rasierklinge *razor blade*
-e Fabrik *factory*
-r Betrieb *factory, business*
nichts außer *nothing but*
-e Prügel (pl.) *beatings*
behandeln *to treat*
her'stellen *to manufacture*
-r Napf *bowl*
-r Topf *pot*
-r Kübel *tub*
beschäftigen (mit) *to occupy (with)*
großzügig *generous*
-s Mitglied *member*
-r Zeichentisch *drawing board*
-r Schmelzofen *smelting oven*
an (+ dat.) vorbei'gehen *to walk past*
an'zünden *to light, ignite*
gewöhnlich *usually*
ein'stecken *to pocket*
-r Laib *loaf*

-r Widerstand *resistance*
kämpfen *to fight*
aus'kommen (mit) *to get on (with)*
gelegen *situated*
KZ *concentration camp*
-r Blick *view*
-s Lager *camp*
-r Häftling *prisoner*
-r Zufall *chance*
-e Flinte *rifle*
erschießen *to shoot dead*
-s Gelage *binge*
-s Geschenk *present*
bestechen *to bribe*
lohnen *to pay, be worth while*
sorgen für *to look after*
bestehen + auf *to insist on*
ein'richten *to set up, equip*
bewahren + vor *to preserve from*
verpflegen *to feed* -e
Tasche *pocket*
beschaffen *to procure*
-s Vermögen *fortune*
zwielichtig *dubious*

Geschäften verdiente, zum Lebenserhalt seiner Schützlinge aus. Die eigentliche Genialität dieses Mannes bestand **jedoch** in seiner atemberaubenden Geistesgegenwart, mit der es ihm immer wieder gelang, Menschenleben zu retten.

Daß er sich ununterbrochen in Lebensgefahr begab, scheint Schindler nicht gestört zu haben, obgleich er dreimal verhaftet wurde. Keneally schreibt, er habe sein Bestes getan, um „zwischen Mythos und Wirklichkeit zu unterscheiden, weil ein Mensch von Oskar Schindlers Ausmaßen ohnehin zur Legendenbildung einlädt."

Keine Legende ist, daß es Schindler 1944 gelang, die Genehmigung für die Verlegung der Produktion in seine Heimatstadt Zwittau im Sudetenland zu bekommen und seine Belegschaft, die von der SS vor dem Rückzug sicherlich ermordet worden wäre, um 400 Juden zu erweitern. Auf Schindlers Evakuierungsliste zu kommen bedeutete Überleben. Schließlich waren 800 Männer und 300 Frauen ausgewählt. Die Männer kamen in Zwittau an, die Frauen jedoch landeten in Auschwitz. Schindler kaufte sie für ein Säckchen Diamanten frei.

In der Einleitung zu seinem Buch behauptet Keneally, einen Roman geschrieben zu haben. Zwar liest sich „Schindlers Liste" nicht schlecht, aber für einen Roman bleibt vieles zu ungestaltet, zu flach, zu schablonenhaft. Es gibt gute Deutsche (Schindler, Madritsch, Titsch), dagegen sind alle Polen glühende Antisemiten, die dazu von Repressalien der Nazis gar nicht betroffen zu sein scheinen. Die Zionisten wiederum erscheinen als eine Art Sekte, wobei die Zersplitterung der jüdischen Bevölkerung in Gruppen und politische Parteien nicht sichtbar wird.

Keneally glorifiziert Schindler nicht. Er versucht auch nicht, in seinem romanhaft aufbereiteten Tatsachenbericht Schindler psychologisch aufzuschlüsseln; todesverachtende Mitmenschlichkeit bleibt letzt-

-s Geschäft *deal*
verdienen *earn*
aus'geben *to spend (money)*
erhalten *to save, preserve*
-r Schützling *protégé(e)*
-e Genialität *ingenuity*
bestehen + in *to consist in*
atemberaubend *breathtaking*
-e Geistesgegenwart *presence of mind*
gelingen (+ dat.) *to succeed*
retten *to rescue*
sich begeben in *to go into*
-e Gefahr *danger*
stören *to disturb*
verhaften *to arrest*
wirklich *real*
unterscheiden *to differentiate*
-s Ausmaß *size, dimension*
ohnehin *anyway, inevitably*
bilden *to form, make*
ein'laden *to invite*

genehmigen *to permit*
verlegen *to transfer*
bekommen *to get, receive*
-e Belegschaft *workforce*
-r Rückzug *withdrawal*
erweitern *to expand*
bedeuten *to mean*
aus'wählen *to choose*
an'kommen *to arrive*

-e Einleitung *introduction*
behaupten *to assert*
-r Roman *novel*
gestalten *to shape, form*
flach *flat*
-e Schablone *cliché*
glühen *to glow*
Repressalien *reprisals*
betreffen *to affect*
wiederum *in turn*
zersplittern *to fragment*
sichtbar *visible*

auf'bereiten *to work up, prepare*
-e Tatsache *fact*
-r Bericht *report*
auf'schlüsseln *to decode*
verachten *to despise*
-r Tod *death*

100 lich unerklärt. Schindler war ein Spieler
und hatte etwas von einem Schwejk, der
es genoß, ein System durcheinanderzu-
bringen. Unter all seiner fröhlichen Sinnlichkeit lag eine Bereitschaft zur Empör-
105 ung über menschliche Roheit, der Wille,
sich nicht unterkriegen zu lassen. Doch
all das, meint Keneally zu Recht, „reicht
wohl nicht aus, die Verbissenheit zu erklären, mit der Schindler die Rettung
110 seiner Häftlinge betrieb".

erklären *to explain*
-r Spieler *gambler*
Schwejk *the Good Soldier Schweik*
genießen *to take pleasure*
-s Durcheinander *chaos*
fröhlich *cheery*
-e Sinnlichkeit *sensuousness*
bereit *prepared, ready*
-e Empörung *indignation*
roh *rough, crude*
-r Wille *the will*
unter'kriegen *to bring someone down*
aus'reichen *to be enough*
verbissen *determined*
betreiben *to carry out*

Janusz Tycner, *Die Zeit*, 4 February 1994

B: Post-reading exercises

B1. Which version of the German is correct?

a. Er liebte den schnellen Profit ohne Buchführung (line 4 f.)
   1. He loved to make a quick profit selling books.
   2. He liked to make a quick profit without keeping accounts.
   3. He liked running his business profitably and by the book.

b. [Schindler] zeigte Mitleid auch in kleinen Dingen (line 22 f.)
   1. He showed no mercy to the little people.
   2. He had sympathy even for the little people.
   3. He showed sympathy even in little things.

c. Er verpflegte sie aus eigener Tasche (line 47 f.)
   1. He looked after his own pocket.
   2. He looked after them out of his own pocket.
   3. He looked after himself from his own pocket.

d. das Vermögen, das er mit zwielichtigen Geschäften verdiente (lines 48–50, see **R110**)
   1. the fortune which earned him his dubious business
   2. the fortune his dubious deals earned him

e. 'Schindlers Liste' liest sich nicht schlecht (cf. lines 81–2, see **R41**)
   1. 'Schindlers List' has been read by a lot of people.
   2. 'Schindlers List' itself reads not badly.
   3. 'Schindlers List' reads quite well.

f. eine Art Sekte (line 90, see **R164**)
   1. an artistic sect
   2. a kind of sect

B2. Reread the last three paragraphs of the text and pick out any logical connectors (see R135–40).

B3. Reread the last three paragraphs of the text and pick out any negation words you can find (see R124–34).

B4. What do you think the following mean?

a. die vor dem Konkurs stehenden Rekord-Werke (line 11f., see **R123**)

   1. the concourse in front of the Rekord Works

   2. the record factory in front of the concourse

   3. the Rekord Works which were facing bankruptcy

b. er bestach, wen es zu bestechen lohnte (line 40f., see **R110**)

   1. he bribed whoever it paid to bribe

   2. he bribed whoever he was paid to bribe

c. ein von ihm persönlich eingerichtetes Arbeitslager (line 44f., see **R109, R123**)

   1. a person invited by him to the work-camp

   2. a work-camp set up by him personally

   3. a work-camp run by someone personally known to him

d. ein Mensch von Oskar Schindlers Ausmaßen lädt zur Legendenbildung ein (cf. lines 62–4, see **R39, R181–2**)

   1. a person of Schindler's stature invites legends.

   2. one of Schindler's dimensions is that he made up lies.

e. Seine Belegschaft wäre sicherlich ermordet worden (cf. lines 69–71, see **R50, R75**)

   1. His workforce certainly had been murdered.

   2. His workforce would surely have been murdered.

   3. His workforce would have been safe from murder.

f. in seinem romanhaft aufbereiteten Tatsachenbericht (line 95–6, see **R109, R123**)

   1. in his novel which is presented as a factual report

   2. in his factual report which is presented as a novel

g. todesverachtende Mitmenschlichkeit (lines 97–8, see **R181–2**)

   1. death-defying comradeship

   2. despised dead comrades

   3. death-defying fellow human beings

B5. Questions on the content

 1. Where did Schindler travel to in 1939?

 2. Where was Beckmann's razor blade factory?

 3. Whom did Schindler employ in his factory?

 4. How did Schindler get on with the SS?

 5. How many Jewish workers did Schindler save from death: 300, 400, 800, or 1100?

 6. Apart from Schindler, who is portrayed as a 'good German' in the book?

 7. Who was Amon Göth?

 8. How many times was Schindler arrested?

 9. How much did a loaf of bread cost in Krakow?

10. Where did Schindler take his factory when he left Krakow?

B6. Which paragraphs in the text are basically biographical, and which contain criticism of Keneally's book?

B7. What criticisms does the reviewer make of Keneally's book as a novel?

*

The German used in this text is quite sophisticated and is of the kind you are likely to encounter in formal documents, books, and the quality press. If you have managed to work through this text, you are probably capable of reading a wide range of German texts on your own with the use of reference works.

You should now be able to read many of the texts in the Text Corpus at the back of this book (with the help of the parallel translations), and this may be a good point to try reading one or two of these texts before proceeding to Chapter 15.

15

Militarism and the 'Little Man' 1871–1914

The text in this chapter is a book review from the quality weekly newspaper *Die Zeit*. The book being reviewed is a study of the war veterans' associations ('Kriegervereine') in Germany in the period between 1871 (the foundation of the German Reich following the wars of unification) and 1914. The German used here is fairly representative of the style and complexity found in non-fiction books and in the quality press.

A: Pre-reading exercises

A1. You may follow the step-by-step pre-reading routines which you have been using so far, or you may wish to vary these routines and perhaps use some other techniques of your own. Either way, make sure that you spend this time on useful pre-reading exercises.
Note: The opening sentence in some of the paragraphs in this text may be too long and complex for an early close-reading. If you cannot extract any useful meaning from them, pick another, shorter, sentence to give you some orientation as to what the paragraph is about. Sometimes the last sentence in a paragraph sums up the whole paragraph.

A2. There are several different words in this text with the meaning 'mentality', i.e. 'way of thinking'. Without reading the text, quickly search the glossary and see how many of these words you can find.

A3. Skim the text for the logical connectors (which are printed in bold).
a. Which of these connectors belong together in logical pairs?
b. Which occur more than once?
(Look at **R138–9** if necessary before you do this. This may help you to see patterns of logical structure within the text.)
Note: The logical connectors in the third paragraph have not been marked.

A4. Skim the text for negation words (which are printed in italics).
Which of these negation words are also part of a 'logical connector'?
(Look at **R138–9** if necessary before you do this.)
Note: The negation words in the third paragraph have not been marked.

Now read the whole text intensively.

Gesinnungsmilitarismus

Zur Kriegsbegeisterung von 1914/Von Wolfram Wette

Thomas Rohrkrämer: *Der Militarismus der „kleinen Leute". Die Kriegervereine im Deutschen Kaiserreich 1871–1914*; Oldenbourg Verlag, München 1990; 301 S., 78,—DM

1 **Je** größer die zeitliche Distanz wird, **desto** rätselhafter erscheint uns das Jahr 1914. Wie konnte es dazu kommen, daß am Beginn des Ersten Weltkrieges *nicht*
5 **nur** Berufsmilitärs, **sondern auch** wehrpflichtige „kleine Leute"—Arbeiter, Bauern und Kleinbürger—in einen Begeisterungstaumel fielen? Erkannten sie *nicht*, daß diese Haltung ihren poli-
10 tischen und materiellen Interessen zuwiderlief? War die angesprochene Stimmungslage ein Produkt der Propaganda, oder resultierte sie aus einer Mentalität, die sich schon in den Jahrzehnten
15 zuvor herausgebildet hatte und die sich jetzt erst richtig entfalten konnte?

Um diese Fragen kreist die in überzeugender Klarheit geschriebene Analyse des Freiburger Historikers Thomas Roh-
20 krämer, in der sozial- und mentalitätsgeschichtliche Ansätze miteinander verknüpft werden. Gegenstand der Untersuchung sind die Kriegervereine im Deutschen Kaiserreich in der Zeit
25 zwischen den Einigungskriegen und dem Beginn des Ersten Weltkrieges. Primär geht es um die Frage, was die „kleinen Leute", die Mitglieder dieser Kriegervereine waren, gedacht und empfunden
30 haben. Es dürfte **in diesem Zusammenhang** der Erwähnung wert sein, daß das Militärgeschichtliche Forschungsamt in Freiburg mit der Übernahme dieser vorzüglichen Dissertation in eine ihrer Pub-
35 likationsreihen erstmals eine Arbeit unterstützt, die der Alltagsgeschichte beziehungsweise einer—noch zu etablie-

-e Gesinnung *mentality, thinking*
begeistern *to enthuse about*
zeitlich *temporal*
rätselhaft *puzzling*
erscheinen *to appear*
-e Militärs (pl.) *soldiers*
-r Beruf *profession*
-e Wehrpflicht *conscription*
-r Bauer *farmer, farm labourer*
-r Kleinbürger *petit-bourgeois (member of the lower middle class)*
-r Taumel *frenzy, whirl*
fallen *to fall*
-e Haltung *attitude*
zuwider'laufen *to run counter to*
ansprechen *to mention*
-e Stimmung *mood, atmosphere*
-s Jahrzehnt *decade*
zuvor *previously*
sich heraus'bilden *to evolve*
entfalten *to unfold*

kreisen + um *to circle around*
überzeugen *to convince*
klar *clear*
-r Ansatz *approach, method*
verknüpfen *to join, link*
-r Gegenstand *subject*
untersuchen *to investigate*
einigen *to unite*
-s Mitglied *member*
empfinden *to feel*
-r Zusammenhang *context*
erwähnen *to mention*
forschen *to research*
-s Amt *office*
übernehmen *to take on, accept*
-e Reihe *series*
unterstützen *to support*
-r Alltag *everyday life*
beziehungsweise *and/or*
etablieren *to establish*

renden—„Militärgeschichte von unten"
zuzurechnen ist.

40 Wer meint, es handle sich bei den
Kriegervereinen jener Zeit um ein eher
exotisches Thema, der sei darauf hinge-
wiesen, daß sie zusammengenommen fast
45 drei Millionen Mitglieder hatten und
damit die größte Massenorganisation des
Kaiserreiches darstellten—größer noch
als Gewerkschaften und SPD—und daß
sie einen kaum zu unterschätzenden
50 Einfluß auf das politische und
gesellschaftliche Leben ausübten. Das
Weltbild der Veteranen in den Kriegervereinen unterschied sich wenig von den
in jener Zeit dominierenden nation-
55 alistischen und militaristischen Überzeugungen. Der Stolz dieser Männer auf die
im Kriege gemeinsam bestandene Gefahr
zielte jedoch, wie der Autor zu belegen
weiß, keineswegs auf eine Neuauflage des
60 Kriegserlebnisses. Charakteristisch für
ihre Gedankenwelt war vielmehr der
merkwürdige Widerspruch, daß sowohl
der Krieg verherrlicht als auch die eigene
Friedfertigkeit betont wurde. Die Frage,
65 ob von ihrer eher diffusen Machtvereh-
rung und ihrem rückwärtsgerichteten
Gesinnungsmilitarismus schon eine direkte Linie zur Kriegsbegeisterung von
1914 gezogen werden könne, verneint
70 Rohkrämer recht eindeutig. Mit anderen
Worten: Die Kriegsveteranen der Eini-
gungskriege waren nicht die Kriegsbegeisterten von 1914.

Bei diesen handelte es sich um eine
75 neue Generation von Kriegervereinsmit-
gliedern, die einer anderen, „modernen"
Variante des Militarismus anhingen.
Aufgrund seiner Analyse des Schrifttums
der Kriegervereine, der Mitgliederbewe-
80 gungen, der sich wandelnden Vereinsaktivitäten sowie des „von oben"
beeinflußten nationalistischen Weltbildes
der „kleinen Leute" kommt der Autor zu
dem Ergebnis, daß um die Jahrhundert-
85 wende herum ein Umschlag des Denkens
stattfand. Die Angehörigen der jüngeren
Generation unter den nationalistisch ein-

zu'rechnen *to count amongst*
hin'weisen + auf *to point out*
zusammengenommen *taken together*
dar'stellen *to represent, be*
-e Gewerkschaft *trade union*
unterschätzen *to underestimate*
-r Einfluß *influence*
aus'üben *to exert, exercise*
-s Weltbild *world-view*
über-zeugen *to convince*
-r Stolz + auf *pride in*
-e Gefahr *danger*
bestehen *to survive*
zielen + auf *to be directed at*
belegen *to demonstrate*
-e Neuauflage *re-run* (lit.: *'new edition'*)
-s Erlebnis *experience*
-e Gedankenwelt *thinking*
merkwürdig *remarkable*
widersprechen *to contradict*
friedfertig *peace-loving*
betonen *to emphasize*
diffus *diffuse*
-e Macht *power*
verehren *to revere*
rückwärts *backwards*
richten *to direct*
eine Linie ziehen *to draw a line*
verneinen *to deny*
eindeutig *clear, emphatic*

an'hängen + dat. *to subscribe to*
aufgrund *based on*
-s Schrifttum *writings*
-e Bewegung *movement*
sich wandeln *to change (gradually)*
-s Ergebnis *result, finding*
-e Wende *turning point*
um'schlagen *to change radically*
-s Denken *thinking*
-r Angehörige *member*
unter *amongst*
eingestellt *-minded*

gestellten Kleinbürgern, Bauern und Arbeitern, die *nicht* als Kriegsveteranen, **sondern** „nur" als Reservisten in die Kriegervereine hinein drängten, waren es nun endgültig leid, aus dem Munde der Veteranen zum hundertsten Male von deren Taten zu hören, die sie einst „zum Manne gemacht" hatten. Sie wollten diese Erfahrung, die dem Gerede der Alten **zufolge** eine Steigerung des Lebensgefühls versprach, selber machen.

Es war die Zeit, in der die Kriegervereine die traditionellen Wege der Vereinsmeierei hinter sich ließen und **dazu** übergingen, paramilitärische Aktivitäten zu entwickeln. So schlug der ältere, eher konservative Gesinnungsmilitarismus in den Kriegervereinen **nunmehr**—im Kontext der imperialistischen Politik Deutschlands seit der Jahrhundertwende—um in eine Haltung mit eindeutig aggressiven Zügen. Da die Stoßrichtung dieses „modernen" Gesinnungsmilitarismus **jedoch** aus politisch-moralischen Gründen nicht offen eingestanden werden konnte, wünschten sich die nationalistisch eingestellten „kleinen Leute" nun einen Angriff der Feinde Deutschlands herbei, um sich in ihm als Teilnehmer eines gerechten „Verteidigungskrieges" bewähren zu können. Die zeitgenössischen Verteidigungs- und Präventivkriegslegenden, die diesen sozialpsychologischen Bedürfnissen Rechnung trugen, erscheinen **so** in einem neuen Licht. In diesem Kontext wird dann auch die Jubelstimmung von 1914 besser verstehbar.

Zum Schluß drängt sich dem Rezensenten ein über die Zeit des Kaiserreichs hinausweisender Gedanke auf: Der Vorgang, daß ein eher rückwärtsgerichteter Militarismus in Zukunftsdenken umschlug, sollte sich zwischen den beiden Weltkriegen—um 1929/30—in durchaus vergleichbaren Formen noch einmal wiederholen. Nach dem Zweiten Weltkrieg, man denke **insbesondere** an die Zeit der 68er-Revolte, nahm die Auseinanderset-

---

endgültig *finally*
leid sein *to be fed up*
-e Tat *deed*
einst *formerly*
-s Gerede *talk*
steigern *to increase*
-s Gefühl *feeling*
versprechen *to promise*
selber *oneself*

Vereinsmeierei *fanatical interest in joining clubs*
hinter sich lasssen *to leave behind*
über'gehen + zu *to go over to*
-r Zug *feature*
-e Stoßrichtung *thrust, direction*
ein'gestehen *to admit*
herbei'wünschen *to wish for something to come along*
an'greifen *to attack*
teil'nehmen *to participate*
gerecht *just(ified)*
verteidigen *to defend*
sich bewähren *to prove oneself*
zeitgenössisch *contemporary*
Rechnung tragen + dat. *to take account of, cater for*
-s Bedürfnis *need*
-r Jubel *jubilation*

auf'drängen + dat. *to force oneself on*
rezensieren *to review*
über . . . hinaus *beyond*
weisen *to point*
-r Vorgang *process*
-e Zukunft *future*
durchaus *absolutely*
vergleichen *to compare*
wiederholen *to repeat*
man denke an *just think of*
-e Auseinandersetzung *debate, argument*

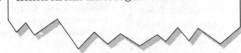

zung der jüngeren Generation mit der ihrer Väter, die 1939 bis 1945 Kriegsteil-
140 nehmer gewesen waren, dann **allerdings** erstmals in diesem Jahrhundert eine gänzlich andere Wendung, indem die militaristischen Denkmuster einer grundsätz-
145 lichen Kritik unterzogen wurden.

-r Vater *father*
erstmals *for the first time*
gänzlich *completely*
-e Wendung *direction*
-s Denkmuster *pattern of thought*
grundsätzlich *thorough, radical*
-e Kritik *criticism*
unterziehen + dat *to subject to*

Die Zeit, 25 January 1991

B: Post-reading exercises

B1. What do you think is meant by the following?

1. Gegenstand der Untersuchung (line 22–3, see **R103**)
2. das Militärische Forschungsamt (line 31–2)
3. eine ihrer Publikationsreihen (line 34–5, see **R98a**)
4. Militärgeschichte von unten (line 38)
5. die Kriegsbegeisterten (line 72–3, see **R101a, R180b**)
6. der Autor kommt zu dem Ergebnis, daß (cf. lines 83–4)
7. dem Gerede der Alten zufolge (line 97, see **R94, R97, R108**)
8. eine Haltung mit eindeutig aggressiven Zügen (lines 109–10f., see **R109**)
9. in durchaus vergleichbaren Formen (lines 133–4 f., see **R109**)

B2. What do you think the underlined word below refers to in its context?

1. Bei <u>diesen</u> (line 74, see **R135c**)
2. <u>deren</u> Taten (line 94, see **R110**)

B3. What do you think the following mean? (see R115)

1. die in überzeugender Klarheit geschriebene Analyse (lines 17–18f.)
2. daß sie einen kaum zu unterschätzenden Einfluß ausübten (cf. lines 48–51ff.)
3. die im Kriege gemeinsam bestandene Gefahr (lines 56–7f.)
4. eine Analyse der sich wandelnden Vereinsaktivitäten (cf. line 78ff.)
5. die nationalistisch eingestellten „kleinen Leute" (lines 114–15)
6. ein über die Zeit des Kaiserreichs hinausweisender Gedanke (lines 128–9)

B4. Select the correct translation for the following:

a. daß sie in einen Begeisterungstaumel fielen (cf. lines 3–8ff., see **R95**)

   1. that they fell in a frenzy of excitement

   2. that they fell into a frenzy of excitement

b. Es dürfte in diesem Zusammenhang der Erwähnung wert sein, daß (lines 30–1f., see **R69**)

   1. In this connection it may be worth mentioning that . . .

   2. In this connection it has to be said that . . .

3. In this connection it was right to mention that . . .

c. eine Arbeit, die der Alltagsgeschichte zuzurechnen ist (lines 35–9, see **R78.2, R96**)

1. a work which adds to the history of everyday life

2. a work which is enriched by the history of everyday life

3. a work which is an example of the history of everyday life

d. sie wünschten sich einen Angriff der Feinde herbei (cf. lines 114–7, see **R40–1**)

1. they wished they could attack their enemies

2. they wished their enemies would attack them

e. Der Vorgang sollte sich um 1929/30 noch einmal wiederholen. (cf. lines 129–35, see **R69**)

1. The process was expected to repeat itself once again around 1929/30.

2. The process was to repeat itself once again around 1929/30.

3. The process was expected to repeat itself once again by 1929/30.

B5. Read through the third paragraph and see if you can pick out any logical connectors (see R135–40).

B6. Read through the third paragraph and see if you can pick out any negation words (see R124–34).

B7. Questions on the content:

1. Which social groups are mentioned as examples of 'kleine Leute'?

2. How many people belonged to veterans' associations in Germany in this period?

3. What was the dominant political mood at this time?

4. Does Rohkrämer's book find a direct link between the veterans of 1871 and the militarism of the younger generation in 1914?

5. Did the veterans of 1871 look forward to another war?

6. What comments does the reviewer make to indicate his view of the quality of this book?

7 What is the 'remarkable contradiction' which Rohkrämer notes about the veterans' associations?

8. What point does Rohkrämer make about the generation of 1968?

9. Does the reviewer make any negative comments about the book?

Many German texts will be easier to read than this one. If you have worked through this text and done most of the post-reading exercises successfully, you should be able to read quite demanding texts with the aid of reference works. You should now be reading the texts in the Corpus on your own, looking at the parallel translations only occasionally.

16

German Emigration to America

This final chapter contains an extract from an article in an academic journal on the causes of German emigration to America in the nineteenth century. The German used here is as complex as you are likely to encounter. In fact, most texts you may want to read will probably be easier than this.

A: Pre-reading exercises

A1. Reading the title

1. What is the German for the United States?
2. If the verb 'to emigrate' is *aus'wandern*, what is the meaning of *Massenauswanderung*?
3. Similarly, what is the meaning of *Wahrnehmung*? (see glossary)
4. Does the article discuss the cause (singular) or the causes (plural) of emigration?
5. Can you now translate the title?

A2. There are several different expressions in this text with the meaning 'emigrate', 'emigration' or 'people who emigrate'. Without reading the text, quickly search the glossary and see how many of these terms you can find.

A3. Now that you have gained an idea of what the article is about, spend a few minutes thinking about what you know about this subject, and about what kind of information you might expect to find in the article. What are the key words in English? (For a suggested solution, see the key.)

A4. Skim the text for words which you recognize immediately, either because (*a*) they look like English words or because (*b*) you have met them before. But beware of 'false friends' (see **R164**).

A5. This text contains several numbers and dates. Skim-read the text, paying attention only to these numbers and dates, and to anything in the immediate context that you recognize. (This may help you to focus on what the article is basically about.)

A6. Skim the text for logical connectors (which are printed in bold).

1. Which of these connectors belong together in logical pairs?
2. Which introduce a contrast of some kind?
3. Which continue and extend the information which has just been provided in the text?

4. Which occur more than once?
(Look at **R138–9** if necessary before you do this.)

A7. Read the first sentence of each of the four paragraphs intensively and write a few words on what you think each of the paragraphs is about. Once you have read the whole article, come back to what you have written and see how accurate your prediction was.

A8. Spend a few moments considering what you have gathered so far about the text. How well do you think you have understood it so far? Make a note of what you are sure of and what you are less sure of.

A9. Imagine you are only reading this article to find out whether the author has said something about a particular aspect, and if so, what. Choose *one* of the following and skim the text until you find the right place to start reading intensively to find out more about:

1. comparisons between Germany and Great Britain (*Großbritannien*). What point does the author make?

2. Friedrich List. What did he do? When?

3. the role of the craftsmen's guild (*die Zunft*). Is it positive or negative in this context?

Now read the whole text intensively.

Die Ursachen der Massenauswanderung in die Vereinigten Staaten — Objektive Zwänge und ihre subjektive Wahrnehmung

Peter Assion

1 Schon im 17. und 18. Jahrhundert sind größere und kleinere Auswanderergruppen von Deutschland nach Nordamerika übergesiedelt, **aber** erst im 19. Jahr-
5 hundert schwoll die transatlantische Migration zur Massenbewegung an mit Auswandererzahlen, die zeitweise pro Jahr in die Hunderttausende gingen und sich bis zum Ersten Weltkrieg auf etwa
10 5,5 Millionen addierten. Die ersten hohen Zahlen wurden in den Jahrzehnten vor der deutschen Reichsgründung 1871 und der ihr nachfolgenden Industrialisierungsphase erreicht. Die Forschung ist sich
15 einig, daß die Massenauswanderung dieser Zeit im Mißverhältnis zwischen Bevölkerungs- und Wirtschaftswachstum ihren Grund hatte und unter dem Druck von Armut und Not im bäuerlich-hand-
20 werklichen Bereich erfolgte. **Nicht mehr** religiöse Gründe oder eine religiös vebrämte Freiheitssuche bestimmten im 19. Jahrhundert den Aufbruch in die Neue Welt, **sondern** Übervölkerung und
25 Pauperismus als Hauptursachen.

Bereits im 18. Jahrhundert war in den deutschen Klein- und Mittelstaaten die Bevölkerung **so** stark angewachsen, **daß** sie—1740 höchstens 18 Millionen zäh-
30 lend—bis 1800 auf 24 Millionen, bis 1856 auf 36 Millionen und bis 1900 auf 56 Millionen anstieg, die Auswanderer schon abgerechnet. Ein ebenso rasches Anwachsen ihrer Bevölkerung hatten **auch andere**
35 europäische Länder zu verzeichnen. **Während aber** in Großbritannien um 1850 nur noch 22 Prozent aller Beschäftigten in der Landwirtschaft tätig waren, galt dies zur gleichen Zeit in Deutschland für siebzig
40 bis achtzig Prozent, ein Anteil, der be-

---

aus'wandern *to emigrate*
-r Zwang *compulsion*
wahr'nehmen *to perceive*

übersiedeln *to resettle*
an'schwellen *to swell*
-e Zahl *number*
zeitweise *occasionally*
-e Reichsgründung *founding of the Reich*
nach'folgen *to follow later*
erreichen *to reach, attain*
-e Forschung *research*
-s Verhältnis *proportion*
-e Wirtschaft *economy*
-s Wachstum *growth*
-r Druck *pressure*
-e Armut *poverty*
-e Not *distress*
bäuerlich *farming (adj)*
handwerklich *artisan (adj)*
-r Bereich *sector, area*
verbrämt *coloured*
bestimmen *to determine*
-r Aufbruch *departure*

an'wachsen *to increase*
zählen *to count*
ab'rechnen *to discount*
rasch *speedy*
etwas zu verzeichnen haben *to record (s.th)*
-r Beschäftigte *employed person*
-e Landwirtschaft *agriculture*
gelten für *to be true of*
gleich *same*
-r Anteil *proportion*

deuteté, daß die Lebensgrundlage nicht ausreichte. Landstrichweise zeigte sich dies in eklatanter Verknappung des Bodens. Wegen unterschiedlicher Rechtsverhältnisse und Vererbungssitten erhielten sich **zwar** profitabel wirtschaftende Betriebe: Vollbauernhöfe in den Anerbengebieten und **zumal** die großen Güter im Norden und Osten Deutschlands. **Um so** kritischer wurde **jedoch** die Lage der dadurch Benachteiligten, der Kleinbauern mit zu geringem Besitz und der auf Tagelohn angewiesenen Landarbeiter und Heuerleute, die sich zum Landproletariat entwickelten. Im Zuge der Bevölkerungsentwicklung wurden **im übrigen** auch bisher ungeteilte Höfe geteilt oder durch Verkäufe verkleinert, **während** dort, wo schon länger die Realteilung des Bodens, das heißt die regelmäßige Aufteilung unter den Erben, üblich war, eine Besitzzersplitterung erfolgte, die immer weniger Betrieben die Mindestgrundlage für eine ausreichende Familienwirtschaft beließ. Für agrarischen Flächenausbau bestand kein Spielraum mehr.

Eine unsichere Überlebenshilfe fanden Kleinbauern und besitzlose Landbewohner zum Teil in der Hausindustrie, vor allem in der Hausweberei im Verlagssystem. Das traditionelle Handwerk bot **hingegen** keinen Ausweg aus der Not im Agrarbereich. Weithin war es eng an die Landwirtschaft gebunden und von der Nachfrage aus dem agrarischen Sektor abhängig, die mit den Wechselfällen der Ernte schwankte und generell unter fehlender Kaufkraft litt. Ländliche Handwerker mit eigenem Ackerbau teilten **außerdem** mit den Bauern auch direkt die Schwierigkeiten, die aus den häufigen Ernteausfällen erwuchsen. **Gleichwohl** blieb nicht aus, daß auf dem Dorf wie in Klein- und Mittelstädten ein Teil des Bevölkerungsüberschusses ins Handwerk drängte. Gemessen an den Verdienstmöglichkeiten hieß dies dann, daß viele Gewerbezweige hoffnungslos überbesetzt

bedeuten	*to mean, signify*
-e Grundlage	*basis, foundation*
aus'reichen	*to suffice*
landstrichweise	*across the land*
sich zeigen	*to show itself*
eklatant	*flagrant*
-e Verknappung	*shortage*
-r Boden	*land*
unterschiedlich	*differing*
-s Verhältnis	*relationship*
-e Sitte	*custom*
vererben	*to inherit*
sich erhalten	*to be preserved*
-r Bauernhof	*farm*
-s Gebiet	*area, territory*
-s Gut (here)	*farm*
-e Lage	*situation*
benachteiligen	*to disadvantage*
-r Bauer	*farmer*
gering	*small, slight* besitzen *to own*
-r Tagelohn	*day wage*
angewiesen auf	*reliant on*
Heuerleute	*casual labourers*
im Zuge	*in the course (of)*
im übrigen	*in addition*
teilen	*to divide* verkaufen *to sell*
während	*whereas*
regelmäßig	*regular*
zersplittern	*to fragment*
erfolgen	*to happen*
Mindest-	*minimum*
aus'bauen	*to extend*
-e Fläche	*area*
bestehen	*to exist*
-r Spielraum	*room for manœuvre*
unsicher	*uncertain*
überleben	*to survive*
-r Bewohner	*inhabitant*
weben	*to weave*
-s Verlagssystem	*syndicate system*
-s Handwerk	*skilled craft*
hingegen	*on the other hand*
bieten	*to offer*
-r Ausweg	*way out*
weithin	*to a large extent*
gebunden an	*tied to* eng *closely*
-e Nachfrage	*demand*
abhängig	*dependent*
-r Wechselfall	*change, vicissitude*
-e Ernte	*harvest*
schwanken	*to vacillate*
leiden unter	*to suffer from*
-e Kaufkraft	*purchasing power*
fehlen	*to be absent*
-e Schwierigkeit	*difficulty*
aus'fallen	*to not happen*
erwachsen aus	*to result from*
aus'bleiben	*to not happen*
gleichwohl	*equally*
-r Überschuß	*surplus*
drängen	*to push* messen *to measure*
verdienen	*to earn*
-r Zweig	*branch*
-s Gewerbe	*business*
besetzen	*to occupy*
-e Hoffnung	*hope*

waren. Der Vermehrung der Meisterbe-
triebe wirkten **zwar** die Zünfte entgegen.
Um so mehr uferte **jedoch** das Gesellen-
wesen mit den Krisensymptomen der lan-
95 gen Wanderjahre und der weiträumigen
Arbeitssuche des verproletarisierenden
Handwerkernachwuchses aus. Wo dann
vor oder nach 1850 die Gewerbefreiheit
100 eingeführt wurde, kam es **entsprechend**
sprunghaft zur Neugründung von Betrieben bei einer Auftragslage, die sich durch
das Aufkommen der Fabriken ab etwa
1860 noch weiter verschlechterte.

105 Gründe zum Auswandern—und zur
politischen Förderung der Auswanderung—gab es **demnach** genug. Und **doch**
lief die Abzugsbewegung nicht gesetzmäßig als Prozeß ab, der jeweils die Ärm-
110 sten aller Stände und Regionen außer
Landes führte. Hemmend wirkten Über-
lebensstrategien, die gerade oft von den
Bedürftigsten angewandt wurden, und
eine—zum Teil kirchlich geförderte—
115 Ergebenheit in die Misere, die **zumal** in
den Unterschichten verhaltensprägend
war. Als Friedrich List (1789–1846) 1817
seine berühmte Befragung württember-
gischer Auswanderer durchführte,
120 zeichnete sich **demgemäß** schon ab, daß
Bevölkerungsgruppen, die noch über ein
gewisses Vermögen verfügten, eher zum
Auswandern bereit waren. Und neuere
Strukturuntersuchungen der Auswander-
125 ung aus Württemberg, aus der Pfalz und
aus Kurhessen bestätigen dies für die fol-
genden Jahrzehnte und machen deutlich,
daß die ersten Migrationswellen stärker
von der Furcht vor Verarmung und kom-
130 mendem Unglück als von tatsächlich
schon erlebter Not ausgelöst wurden.
Dabei hatten die Davonziehenden auch
die politischen Verhältnisse Deutschlands im Blick. Man sah, daß die Regie-
135 rungen nicht fähig waren, den
wirtschaftlichen Niedergang aufzuhalten.
Und man erlebte 1830 bis 1833 und
1848/1849, wie sich mit den Hoffnungen
auf demokratisch freiheitliche Verhält-
140 nisse auch die Erwartungen eines ökono-

---

vermehren *to increase, multiply*
-r Meister (here) *master craftsman*
entgegen'wirken *to counter*
-e Zunft *guild of craftsmen*
aus'ufern *to increase hugely*
-r Geselle *journeyman*
-r Nachwuchs *next generation*
ein'führen *to introduce*
entsprechend *equally*
sprunghaft *rapidly*
-r Auftrag *purchase, order*
auf'kommen *to appear*
etwa *approximately*
schlecht *bad*

fördern *to promote, support*
demnach *accordingly*
genug *enough*
ab'laufen *to proceed (of a process)*
gesetzmäßig *regular*
-r Stand *social class*
außer Landes *abroad*
hemmen *to restrict, limit*
wirken *to have an effect*
bedürftig *needy*
an'wenden *to apply, use*
-e Kirche *church*
sich ergeben *to surrender*
zumal *particularly*
-e Schicht *(social) stratum*
prägen *to shape*
-s Verhalten *behaviour*
berühmt *famous*
befragen *to question*
sich ab'zeichnen *to become apparent*
demgemäß *according (to this)*
verfügen über *to have at one's disposal*
gewiß *certain* (here: *modest*)
bereit *prepared*
eher *sooner, rather*
untersuchen *to investigate*
bestätigen *to confirm*
deutlich *clear*
-e Welle *wave*
-e Furcht *fear*
arm *poor*
-s Unglück *misfortune*
-e Tatsache *fact*
aus'lösen *to trigger off*
davon'ziehen *to move away*
-e Verhält-nisse (pl.) *circumstances*
-r Blick *view*
fähig *capable*
hoffen auf *to hope for*
frei *free*
erwarten *to expect*

mischen Neubeginns zerschlugen, eines Aufschwungs befreit von Adelsrechten und Besitzprivilegien, Steuer- und Abgabepflichten, militärischer Bean-
145 spruchung der Untertanen, behördlicher Willkür usw. Für diejenigen, die sich trotzdem nicht die Aussicht auf bessere Lebensumstände nehmen ließen, wurde die Auswanderung **entsprechend** zum
150 Revolutionsersatz, und nicht zufällig schnellten die Auswandererzahlen gerade nach 1848/1849 gewaltig in die Höhe. Der als unerträglich empfundene Druck wirkte **dabei** als einer jener Steigerun-
155 gsfaktoren, von denen mit Recht gesagt worden ist, daß sie zur allgemeinen Notlage noch hinzukommen mußten, um größere Gruppen zum Emigrationsentschluß zu führen.

zerschlagen *to shatter*
-r Aufschwung *upturn*
-r Adel *nobility*
-e Steuer *tax*
-e Abgabe *levy, tax*
-e Pflicht *obligation*
beanspruchen *to lay claim to*
-r Untertan *subject (of a ruler)*
-e Behörde *official authority*
-e Willkür *whim*
-e Aussicht auf *prospect of*
nehmen *to take*
entsprechend *accordingly*
ersetzen *to substitute, replace*
-r Zufall *coincidence*
schnellen *to move rapidly*
gewaltig *enormously*
ertragen *to bear, endure*
empfinden als *to perceive as*
steigern *to cause to increase*
mit Recht *justifiably*
allgemein *general, universal*
hinzu'kommen *to be added to*
sich entschließen *to decide, resolve*

Zeitschrift für Kulturaustausch 3 (1989), pp. 258–9 (extract)

B: Post-reading exercises

B1. What do you think is meant by the following?

1 Besitzzersplitterung (line 63)?
2 Realteilung des Bodens (line 60f.)?
3 eine religiös verbrämte Freiheitssuche (line 21f.)?
4 militärische Beanspruchung der Untertanen (line 144f.)?
5 der verproletarisierende Handwerkernachwuchs (line 96f.)?
6 What process is described with the words: 'Ein Teil des Bevölkerungsüberschusses drängte ins Handwerk' (line 86ff.)?

B2. Questions on the content

1 How many Germans are said to have emigrated to America by 1914?
2 What was the main cause of emigration in the nineteenth century?
3 What proportion of the working population in Germany was engaged in agriculture around 1850?
4 Which groups were reduced to the status of an agricultural proletariat?
5 Why was the rural population so badly hit by the population trend?
6 What was the cottage industry that helped some smallholders and people owning no property to make a living?
7 Why didn't traditional trades offer a decent living?
8 When was freedom of trade introduced?
9 Is it true that poorer people were often less inclined to emigrate than those still reasonably well off?
10 When do the numbers of those emigrating show the biggest increase?

B3. Once you have worked through the text in this chapter to your satisfaction, try rereading it with the glossary covered up. Note any vocabulary items that you still do not recognize, and then repeat.

This final chapter has focused on a difficult text which would be demanding for many German readers. Many texts will be a lot easier to read than this one. If you have managed to work through this text with some degree of success, you are certainly in a position to tackle quite demanding texts on your own. If you have not done so already, you may like to try reading some of the texts in the Text Corpus near the back of this book, most of which are less challenging than this particular text.

Key to Coursebook Exercises

Chapter 1

1a. Ärger — annoyance, anger, trouble
höflich — polite, courteous
Bühne — stage
verträglich — peaceable, easy-going, amicable
Note: 'vertraglich' (without the UMLAUT) means contractual
Fuß — foot
Maßnahme — measure
rußig — sooty

1b. Leid — Lied — sorrow/grief — song
Reise — Riese — journey/trip/voyage — giant
verschließen — verschleißen — to lock up/close/bolt — to wear out
lieb — Leib — kind/nice/sweet — body
Wiese — Weise — meadow — way/manner/fashion

1c. 1. Ich **spreche** Deutsch, Spanisch und Englisch.
2. In Deutschland **verstehen** viele Leute Englisch.
3. Wir **leben** seit 1993 in Österreich.
4. In vielen anderen Ländern **hört** man diese Sprache.
5. Er **liest** ein Magazin in seiner Muttersprache.
6. Im Sommer **fährt** er nach London.
7. Sie **begrüßt** unsere amerikanischen Freunde.
8. Den Text **übersetze** ich ins Englische.

1d. 1. I **speak**
2. many people **understand**
3. we **live**
4. one **hears**
5. he **reads**
6. he **goes/travels/drives**
7. she **greets**
8. I **translate**

1e. Position I
1. ich — I: SUBJECT
2. in Deutschland — in Germany: ADVERBIAL PHRASE
3. wir — we: SUBJECT

4. in vielen anderen Ländern — in many other countries: ADVERBIAL PHRASE
5. er — he: SUBJECT
6. im Sommer — in summer: ADVERBIAL PHRASE
7. sie — she: SUBJECT
8. den Text — the text: OBJECT

1f. 1. automobile industry
2. problem of interpretation
3. information material
4. computer expert
5. a conference for/of computer experts

Flughafen/restaurant/manager/ausbildung/s/programm = a training programme for airport restaurant managers

CHAPTER 1: Text B
In the Federal Republic of Germany one does not only speak German (= not only German is spoken). Many foreigners live in Germany and they speak, of course, their own mother tongue. One hears e.g. (for example) Turkish, Greek, Spanish, Italian, and Polish. In Germany many people understand and speak English. In the east of the country Russian used to be [*lit.*: was earlier] the main foreign language.

Chapter 2

2a. 1. They load the computer into the car.
They invite the Americans to a party.
They (re)charge the battery.
2. The company dismisses 500 workers.
The company tells 500 workers that there will be a pay increase.
3. She writes a word.
She copies a word.
4. We travel to Berlin.
We depart at 14.30.
5. He comes to Hamburg in summer.
He arrives on 24 July.

2b. **Note:** The use of tenses differs in the two languages.
Read **R37**.
In the following sentences the literal translation is given first. The more common English form then appears in parentheses.

1. In Germany he has spoken (he spoke) German.
2. From 1985 to 1994 he has lived (lived) in Berlin.
3. He has not found (did not find) the information.
4. We have not understood (did not understand) the dialect.
5. I have answered (answered) the letter yesterday.
6. The Americans have produced the prototype.
7. He has not (did not) pronounce the word correctly. (For *ausgesprochen* see **R172**)
8. This group of the population has come (came) to America in the 19th century.
9. The students have travelled (travelled) to Portugal.
10. He has arrived (arrived) yesterday. (For *angekommen* see **R172**)
11. The English people have travelled (travelled) to Spain yesterday.
12. She has not gone (did not go) to the library.

2c.
1. The student wants to learn Portuguese next year.
2. I cannot speak Spanish.
3. In England one ought to speak English.
4. Foreigners cannot understand this dialect.
5. We cannot pronounce this word correctly.
6. One must now test the prototype.
7. In this restaurant one may drink alcohol.
8. But one does not have to drink alcohol.

Note: müssen + nicht **never** means *must not*. It always means *need not/not have to*. See **R69**.

2d.
1. Problem (neuter; das)
2. Kenntnis (feminine; die)
3. Laut (masculine; der)
4. Frage (feminine; die)
5. Computer (masculine; der)
6. Wort (neuter; das)
7. Gruppe (feminine; die)

8. Antwort (feminine; die)
9. Leiter (masculine and feminine) — der Leiter *the leader/manager* / die Leiter *the ladder/steps*
10. Teil (masculine and neuter) — der Teil *the part/section/area* / das Teil *component/spare part*
11. Steuer (feminine and neuter) — die Steuer *tax* / das Steuer *helm/steering wheel*
12. See (masculine and feminine) — der See *the lake* / die See *the sea*

2f.

	PLURAL	SINGULAR
1	Gruppen	**Gruppe**
2	Wörter	**Wort**
3	Mütter	**Mutter**
4	Probleme	**Problem**
5	Millionen	**Million**
6	Bevölkerungen	**Bevölkerung**
7	Computer	**Computer**
8	Bücher	**Buch**
9	Konstruktionen	**Konstruktion**
10	Kenntnisse	**Kenntnis**

Chapter 2: Text B

Last summer we travelled to Eastern Europe. In this part of the world great changes are taking place and one can experience and discover many interesting (things) there. Of course sometimes there are difficulties with the language. But despite the communication problems we have met many nice people there. We made friends with one family in particular. The children of this family want to visit us in England at Easter. They will (see **R37**) arrive in London on the 24th of April.

2e.

	masc.	fem.	neut.	SUBJECT	NON-SUBJECT
1. **diesem** Dialekt	✔				✔
2. **der** Mutter		✔			✔
3. **jenes** Land			✔	✔	✔
4. **einer** Bedeutung		✔			✔
5. **jeder** Student	✔			✔	
6. **dieses** Problems*			✔		✔
7. **manchen** Freund	✔				✔
8. **jenem** Buch			✔		✔
9. **eine** Komposition		✔		✔	✔
10. **dieser** Mensch	✔			✔	

* For **-es . . . -(e)s** see **R104a**.

Chapter 3

3a.

	INFINITIVE
galt	gelten
überflügelte	überflügeln
war	sein
strich	streichen

3b.

		INFINITIVE
1.	sprach	sprechen
2.	verstanden	verstehen
3.	lebten	leben
4.	hörte	hören
5.	las	lesen
6.	fuhr	fahren
7.	begrüßte	begrüßen
8.	übersetzte	übersetzen

3c.
1. *He claimed the opposite.*
   She held her ground in the discussion.
2. *Then new problems arose.*
   After three months the army unconditionally surrendered.
3. *He is interested in modern art.*
4. *They enrolled for a German course.*
5. *She always complains about his dialect.*

3d.

		INFINITIVE
1.	versprach	versprechen
2.	überfuhr	überfahren
3.	verhielten	verhalten
4.	bedachte	bedenken
5.	verhörte	verhören

3e. INFINITIVE

versprechen to promise

überfahren to run over OR to cross over (**Note**: different meaning depending on whether the verb is used as a separable or inseparable verb)

verhalten to hold/stop/behave > see context

bedenken *to consider*

verhören *to interrogate.* But as a reflexive verb: *to mishear* (see **R41.2**)

3f.

		it	he	she	they
1.	er	✔			
2.	sie			✔	
3.	er		✔		
4.	sie			✔	
5.	sie		✔		
6.	es	✔			

3g.

	A	B	C	D	E
1.			✔		
2.				✔	
3.					✔
4.		✔			
5.	✔				

CHAPTER 3: TEXT B
Frederick the Great of Prussia (1740–86) preferred to speak and write in French rather than German. This attitude was (the) prevailing (one) in the eighteenth century at court and among parts of the educated classes—not only in Germany but almost everywhere in Europe. French dominated as the international language. This changed in the course of the nineteenth century. Then France lost its leading political position on the European continent and the importance of German as an international language slowly increased.

Chapter 4

4a.
1. In Österreich spricht man Deutsch.
   Spricht man in Österreich Deutsch?
2. 90 Millionen Menschen sprechen Deutsch als Muttersprache.
   Sprechen 90 Millionen Menschen Deutsch als Muttersprache?
3. Ist Deutsch heute als Wirtschaftssprache wichtig?
   Heute ist Deutsch als Wirtschaftssprache wichtig.
4. Galt Deutsch bis in die dreißiger Jahre als wichtigste Wissenschaftssprache?
   Deutsch galt bis in die dreißiger Jahre als wichtigste Wissenschaftssprache.
5. Die internationale Stellung der deutschen Sprache hat sich sehr verändert.
   Hat sich die internationale Stellung der deutschen Sprache sehr verändert?

4b.
1. Why must one answer this question in the affirmative?
2. Did Albert Einstein formulate this theory? (*lit.*: has formulated)
3. When did he publish this theory/hypothesis?
4. Where does one find German-speaking groups of the population?
5. Is this text available in (an) English translation?
6. Does one also speak German in Switzerland?
7. What did he do last summer? (*Lit.* has done)
8. How does one pronounce this word?
9. Were there many communication problems? (es gibt *there is/are*, es gab *there was/were*)

10. Can you understand this word?

4c. DEPENDENT CLAUSES

1. **Obwohl** er sein Buch schon 1982 **veröffentlichte,**

2. **,weil** er dieses Buch im Original lesen **will.**

3. **,daß** man in Österreich Deutsch **spricht.**

4. **Als** er in Berlin **wohnte,**

5. **Wenn** er diesen Dialekt **spricht,**

In English:

1. Although he already published his book in 1982, I did not know his theory.

2. He has learnt German, because he wants to read this book in the original.

3. I know that one speaks German in Austria.

4. When he was living in Berlin, he learnt German quickly.

5. When(ever)/If he speaks this dialect, I don't understand him.

4d. 1. It is worth the effort to translate this book.

2. Is it important to learn German?

3. It is very difficult/hard to learn this language quickly.

4. In this situation it is easy to meet new people.

5. He intends (has the intention) to read this book in the original.

4e. 1. . . . the dialect which one speaks in the south of Germany/the dialect spoken in the south of Germany

2. . . . the language he did not understand (*lit.*: has not understood)

3. . . . scientists who publish articles

4. . . . the situation which has changed

5. . . . German, which has been deleted from the syllabuses

4f. A. 1. **Hast** du seinen Dialekt verstanden?

2. **Wo spricht** man diese Sprache?

3. **Wenn** man diesen Dialekt nicht **kennt, kann** man das nicht verstehen.

4. Er **will** jetzt in dieses Land reisen **und** diese Sprache lernen.

5. **Weil** er dieses Buch, **das** er auf Englisch gelesen **hat,** jetzt im Original lesen **will, lernt** er diese Sprache.

6. **Obwohl** diese Sprache schwer **ist, hat** er die Absicht, sie schnell **zu lernen.**

B. 1. Yes/No question

2. Question with a question word

3 Dependent clause, main clause

4. Main clause (finite verb is a modal verb and there are two infinitives to go with it linked by the connector **und**)

5. First part of dependent clause,

interrupted by a relative clause, rest of dependent clause, main clause

6. Dependent clause, main clause, zu + infinitive clause

4g. 1. In Austria one speaks German. German is spoken in Austria.

2. He has translated the text into German. The text has been translated into German.

3. When was this theory formulated by Einstein? When did Einstein formulate this theory?

4. By which publisher was (*lit.*: had been) this book published? Which publisher had published this book?

5. This question can now be answered. One can now answer this question.

CHAPTER 4: TEXT B

During the last (i.e. recent) decades numerous (foreign) words were taken over from English (and used) in German-speaking scientific/academic texts. But why should this be a problem? The answer is simple: these words are often not at all adapted to fit in with German spelling, pronunciation or grammar (*lit.*: are not adapted orthographically, phonetically, and grammatically to the German language), but taken over entirely in (their) English form. Such texts which contain many such foreign words are often criticised because (the) communication between scientists/academics and ordinary people (*lit.*: laymen) in Germany is made more difficult because of the (use of) English terms.

Chapter 5

5a. 1A. He is afraid of the exam.

1B. He is afraid of not passing the exam.

2A. She does not think of/bear in mind this fact.

2B. She does not bear in mind that there are many dialects in Austria.

3A. I started the lecture/talk with the explanation of the main points.

3B. I started the lecture by explaining the main points.

4A. We don't believe in his decision to learn German.

4B. We don't believe that he wants to learn German.

5A. He dreamt of a journey to/through Europe.

5B. He dreamt of going on a journey to/through Europe.

6A. He insists on an immediate solution to the problem.

6B. He insists on the problem being solved straight away .

5b. 1. a problem (which is) especially complicated for speakers of a dialect

2. the social situation (which is) unchanged in the West

3. many new theories (which are) interesting for scientists/academics

4. many pronunciation problems (which are) typical for this dialect

5. a question (which is) important for linguists

5c. 1. He is learning German in order to read this text in the original.

2. In order to be able to understand this dialect one must have been living/lived in this country for many years.

3. In order to translate this sentence into English I need a dictionary.

4. He needs time in order to formulate this new theory.

5. In order to achieve this aim he has to work hard.

5d. 1. die früheren Verhältnisse

2. bedeutsamere Theorien

3. ein interessanter Grund

4. kompliziertere Sprachen

5. ein schwieriger Anfang

5e. 1. . . . the theory of which he spoke/the theory he spoke about

2. . . . a possibility of which he did not think/a possibility he did not think of

3. . . . this scientist for whom he translated the text/the scientist he translated the text for

4. . . . his friends with whom he travelled to Eastern Europe/his friends he travelled to Eastern Europe with

5. . . . the country from which they were expelled/the country they were expelled from

5f. 1. He no longer lives in Berlin.

2. Does German no longer have any importance as a language of science?/Is German no longer of importance . . .

3. There are now no longer any communication problems.

4. Is German no longer in the Syllabus? *Lit.*: Is there no longer any German in the Syllabus?

5. Does he no longer work at the university?

CHAPTER 5: TEXT B
This is the Extended Adjective Phrase:

in einer [in vieler Hinsicht so wichtigen] Organisation
in an organization which is so important in many respects

Spanish and Arabic became official languages of the United Nations because they are the official national languages of numerous countries. Because of this privileged status in an organization like the United Nations, which is so important in so many respects, the international position of the languages is strengthened in turn. They then, e.g., play a greater role in the language training of diplomats. In order to determine the rank of German in the hierarchy of official languages one needs to know the number of countries where (*lit.*: in which) German is the official national language.

Chapter 6

6a. The NON-FACTUAL verbs are printed in bold:

1. Der Student **spreche** gut Englisch.
It has been said/I was told that this student speaks English well.

3. Die deutsche Sprache **habe** sich verändert.
It has been said/I was told that the German language has changed.

5. Sie **hätten** diese Sprache nicht verstanden.
It has been said/I was told that they did not understand (*lit.*: **had not understood**) **this language.**

7. Dieser Wissenschaftler **arbeite** auch an diesem Projekt.
It has been said/I was told that this scientist is also working on this project.

9. Das Buch **sei** noch nicht ins Englische übersetzt worden.
It has been said/I was told that the book has not yet been translated into English.

10. Diesen Dialekt **könne** sie nicht verstehen.
It has been said/I was told that she cannot understand this dialect.

6b. Es <u>gebe</u> zwei Hauptgründe dafür, daß Deutsch seine Spitzenstellung als internationale Wissenschaftssprache nicht <u>habe</u> halten können. Erstens <u>seien</u> Deutschland und das wissenschaftlich ebenfalls bedeutsame deutschsprachige Österreich durch den Ersten Weltkrieg ruiniert worden. Deutschland <u>habe</u> nach dem Krieg nicht die Ressourcen gehabt, um die wissenschaftliche Entwicklung weiterhin voranzutreiben. Der zweite, noch einschneidendere Grund <u>sei</u> der Nationalsozialismus gewesen, durch den zahlreiche Wissenschaftler aus Deutschland und Österreich verjagt oder umgebracht worden <u>seien</u> und durch dessen Folgen weitere nach dem Krieg gezwungen gewesen <u>seien</u>, zu emigrieren, weil sie in ihrem zerstörten Land keine Arbeitsmöglichkeit mehr gehabt <u>hätten</u>.

FACTUAL	NON-FACTUAL
es gibt	es gebe
there are	*(it is said that) there are*
, daß . . . . nicht halten konnte	nicht habe halten können
(For Past Tense of NON-FACTUAL see R50)	
that . . . could not hold	*(it is said) that . . . could not hold*
sind ruiniert worden	seien ruiniert worden

have been/were ruined | *(it is said that they) have been/were ruined*
hatte nicht | habe nicht gehabt
had not/did not have | *(it is said Germany) did not have*
war | sei gewesen
was | *(is said to) have been*
, durch den . . . verjagt oder umgebracht wurden | verjagt oder umgebracht worden seien
because of which . . . were forced to leave or were murdered | *(it is said that) because of which . . . were forced to leave or were murdered*
, durch dessen . . . gezwungen waren | gezwungen gewesen seien
as a result of which . . . were forced | *(it is said that) as a result of which . . . have been/were forced*
, weil . . . hatten | gehabt hätten
because . . . had | *(it is said that) because . . . had*

6c.
1. freundlich *friendly*   unfreundlich *unfriendly*
2. Veröffentlichung *publication*   unveröffentlicht *unpublished*
3. schwierig *difficult*
4. Bedeutung *importance, significance*
5. entwickeln *to develop* unterentwickelt *underdeveloped*

CHAPTER 6: Text B
Professor Ammon writes that the role of German as an international language has changed in the course of our century. A [*lit.*: from a] global scientific language has become a business language of regional significance. German functions (now) mainly as a language of business communication between the German-speaking countries and its neighbouring regions. The German-speaking countries are naturally interested in securing the international status of the German language. A strong international position of its language has undeniable advantages for a country: it facilitates (the) communication with other countries and reduces the need for [*lit.*: demands less] foreign language learning at home [*lit.*: in one's own country].

6d.

	MASCULINE	FEMININE	SINGULAR	PLURAL
1. Sprachwissenschaftlerin		✔	✔	
2. Nobelpreisträgerinnen		✔		✔
3. Österreicher	✔		✔	✔
4. Akademikerinnen		✔		✔
5. Verleger	✔		✔	✔

Chapter 7

7a. Please note that these phrases can be rendered in many different ways.
The one given here is just one of many possible ones.

1. We are here dealing with an old problem.
2. Is this a new theory?
3. It is not a question of a communication problem.
4. Do you know what it is about?
5. It can be one thing only.

7b.
1. If he had more time he would read the book.
2. If you were to send him a ticket, he would come next week.
3. She would pass the exam if she learnt/would learn more.
4. If he could carry out this experiment on his own, I would not have to travel to Berlin.
5. If he spoke English he would have good career chances/a good chance of promotion.
6. It would be better if she weren't/would not always be so dominating in the seminar.
7. If he no longer had any opportunity to work he would be forced to emigrate.
8. If these words had been adapted to the German language, one could no longer recognize them as anglicisms.
9. Communication between scientists and non-scientists would be made harder because of these terms.
10. If one wanted to secure the position of the German language one would have to take steps/do something now.

7c.
1. Had he more money then there would not be any problems.
2. If he does not come today perhaps he will come tomorrow.
3. If one is working out the ranking system one must also bear in mind this aspect.
4. If one reads this text in the original, one is surprised by its complexity.
5. If he were here he would explain the problem.

6. Our culture would be poorer, if no foreigners lived/were to live in this country.

7. If this article did not contain so many foreign words, it would be easier to understand it.

8. If she did not know his address we could not make contact.

9. If one observes this development over a longer period of time one reaches a different conclusion.

10. If we were dealing with an international language there would not be this problem.

7d. 1. The article addresses in particular environmentally aware people.

2. Those with a degree in higher education react differently (*lit.*: scientifically-educated people).

3. Unauthorized persons are not allowed to park here.

4. Part-time employees don't get this bonus.

5. This is a great problem for those with behavioural difficulties.

7e. 1. This text is difficult to understand.

2. This text was easy to translate.

3. His colleagues cannot be convinced of the importance of this project.

4. The consequences of this decision could not yet be foreseen at that time (it was not possible to foresee).

CHAPTER 7: TEXT B
My friend would like to learn German and he believes it would be possible to manage it in one summer. If languages could really be learnt that easily one would not have to work hard in school for years. It's true, those with a talent for languages and those who are well motivated certainly manage to acquire a basic knowledge within a short time. But if one wishes to really master a language it often takes years. If he could spend a few months in a German-speaking country and visit a language school there, he would stand a better chance. But that, of course, would cost a lot of money, and he could not afford it at all.

He asked me to help him with his German. (*Lit.*: He has asked me I ought to help him with the learning of German.) Perhaps I could lend him my old text books. But it definitely would be better if he did/were to do a language course (*lit.*: if he would take part in a language course).

Chapter 8

8a. 1. Both languages play an important role in this context too.

2. Here too, the German government finds itself in a certain dilemma.

3. This difference in opinion is also expressed (i.e. becomes clear) here above all.

4. This announcement amazed many nations (countries).

5. Perhaps his plan will be carried out next year.

8b. 2. Here, too, the German government finds itself in a worse dilemma than the other countries.

3. This difference in opinion becomes more clear here than in other countries.

4. This announcement amazed many countries more than expected.

5. Perhaps next year his plan will be carried out earlier than this year.

8c. 1. In diesem Teil der USA wohnen auch [**deutschsprechende**] Bevölkerungsgruppen.
In this part of the USA there also live German-speaking groups of the population.

2. Er liest einen [in englischer Übersetzung **vorliegenden**] Text.
He is reading a text available in an English translation.

3. Der Artikel handelt von den [in diesem Teil der Welt zur Zeit **stattfindenden**] Veränderungen.
The article is about the changes taking place in this part of the world at the moment.

4. Auch dieses [auf französisch **geschriebene** und 1922 **veröffentlichte**] Buch befaßt sich mit diesem Problem.
This book too, written in French and published in 1922, deals with this problem.

5. Er stützt sich auf diese [von ihm falsch **verstandene**] Theorie.
He bases his arguments on this theory which was wrongly understood by him.

6. Dieser [von deutscher Seite oft **kritisierte**] Umstand erschwert die Kommunikation.
This circumstance often criticized by the Germans makes communication more difficult.

7. Er spricht von einer [sich in einem gewissen Dilemma **befindenden**] Regierung.
He is talking of a government which finds itself in a certain dilemma.

8. Sie möchten eine [die weitere Entwicklung der Europäischen Union **belastende**] Situation vermeiden.
They would like to avoid a situation which puts a strain on the further development of the European Union.

9. Der Autor wünscht sich eine [die internationale Stellung der deutschen Sprache **stützende**] Lösung dieses Problems.
The author would like a solution to this problem which would strengthen the international position of the German language.

10. Ich kenne nur eine [vor vielen Jahren schlecht **übersetzte**] Version dieses Buches.
I know only one version of this book, which is a badly translated one from many years ago.

8d. 1. He made this arrangement yesterday./He arranged this yesterday.

2. They are hoping for a quick change of the situation./They are hoping that the situation will quickly change.

3. They have made observations about this development./They have been observing this development.

4. For years he has carried out research in this field./He has been researching in this field for years.

5. The learning of the German language requires much time and patience./Learning (the) German (language) requires much time and patience.

8e. 1. Er will seine Forschungsarbeit bald abschließen und dann schnell veröffentlichen.
He wants to conclude his research (work) soon and then publish [it] quickly.

2. Ich habe seine Theorie gestern zum ersten Mal gehört, aber gleich verstanden.
I heard his theory yesterday for the first time but understood [it] straight away.

3. In diesem Kapitel möchte ich vier Fälle genau beschreiben und dann Schlußfolgerungen ziehen.
In this chapter I would like to describe four cases in detail and then draw the final conclusions.

4. Dieses Wort wird nur in dieser Gegend verwendet und nur von wenigen Leuten richtig ausgesprochen.
This word is only used in this area and [it is] pronounced correctly only by few people.

5. In dieser Zeit wurden viele Wissenschaftler aus dem nationalsozialistischen Deutschland verjagt oder sogar umgebracht.
During this time many scientists/academics were driven out of/expelled from Nazi Germany or even killed.

8f. 1. questions concerning national politics/policies

2. several years of experience

3. this article critical of society

4. a debate about economic policies

5. problems concerning/about educational policies

CHAPTER 8: TEXT B
Germany now has the reputation of being by far the most scientifically advanced country, and rightly so. (Because) from all countries/all over the world students eager to learn go there to carry out further research in all branches of science on German soil. From amongst our students too, the best ones are usually sent to Germany after they have finished their university course (here). Not only in the sciences, but also in commerce and trade, in manufacturing and industry the Germans are now so advanced, that the British government had a study carried out to discover what the causes were. The reports of all those sent to Germany to investigate unanimously agreed that the reason behind this was the progress made in the sciences. All this clearly proves that it is of the greatest advantage to learn the German language.

Quoted from a German language journal, 1898, Japan.

Chapter 9

9a. 1. Either: Next week he is to come here (i.e. he is obliged to).
Or: It is said that next week he will come here.

2. The accused claims to have been at home at the time in question.

3. We intend/want to travel to Austria next year.

4. He does not have to/need not learn German.

5. She is said to have made enquiries already.

6. The essay need not be handed in today.

7. Either: He wants to be (a) millionaire.
Or: He claims to be (a) millionaire.

9b. 1. Many find it difficult to learn languages.

2. If one talks to those who know the country . . .

3. We cannot ask everybody.

4. I have spoken to him with regard to this.

5. Everybody has understood this text.

6. Is this his book or is it mine?

7. She says exactly the same.

8. He told nobody about his plan.

9c.

	A	B
1.	✔	
		✔
2.	✔	
		✔
3.		✔
	✔	
4.	✔	
		✔
5.		✔
	✔	

9d. 1. She followed her husband to Germany. (DATIVE)

2. I trust him completely. (DATIVE)

3. He never joined a political party. (DATIVE)

4. The chairman sincerely thanked all colleagues. (DATIVE)

5. On this day we remember the victims of the catastrophe. (GENITIVE)

6. She now needs his sympathy. (GENITIVE)

7. He explained his theory to the professor. (DATIVE)

8. This behaviour damages their reputation. (DATIVE)

9. Politicians ought to serve the people. (DATIVE)

10. He is accused of murder. (GENITIVE)

9e.
1. This complicated question cannot be answered with a (single) word.

2. The causes could only/were only able to be determined after a thorough investigation.

3. Despite huge efforts this accident could not be prevented.

4. Can an explanation be found at all for this?

5. Which task can be completed more quickly?

9f. This language is easy to learn.

9g.
1. He behaved as if, i.e. it seemed as if, he knew the exact circumstances (**so tun als** *to behave as if*, i.e. *to pretend*)

2. It did not seem as if she had known him before.

3. She speaks the language as perfectly as if it were her mother tongue.

4. She pretended to drop in by chance.

5. One must not interpret this as if he didn't know what he was doing.

9h.

1. Erst <wenn> man eine Fremdsprache lernt, $\boxed{\text{wird}}$ man sich der Eigentümlichkeiten der eigenen Sprache bewußt, <weil> man erst dann in der Lage ist, wirklich Vergleiche **anzustellen**.

The main clause:

$\boxed{\text{wird}}$ man sich der Eigentümlichkeiten der eigenen Sprache bewußt,
one becomes aware of the peculiarities of one's own language

is preceded by a dependent clause explaining when this is the case:

Erst <wenn> man eine Fremdsprache $\boxed{\text{lernt}}$,
only when one is learning a foreign language

and followed by a dependent clause followed by a zu + infinitive clause, both together giving the reason why this is the case:

<weil> man erst dann in der Lage ist, wirklich Vergleiche **anzustellen**.
because only then is one in a position to really make comparisons.

2. <Seit> es ein [seit 1980 geltendes] Gesetz $\boxed{\text{gibt}}$, <das die Gleichbehandlung von Männern und Frauen am Arbeitsplatz $\boxed{\text{sicherstellt}}$, $\boxed{\text{haben}}$ sich die Ausbildungschancen für Mädchen und Frauen deutlich verbessert, <weil> den Frauen seither alle Ausbildungsstätten $\boxed{\text{offenstehen}}$.

The main clause:

$\boxed{\text{haben}}$ sich die Ausbildungschancen für Mädchen und Frauen deutlich verbessert, *the training opportunities for girls and women have significantly improved*

is preceded by two dependent clauses. The first one tells us since when this has been the case:

<Seit> es ein [seit 1980 geltendes] Gesetz $\boxed{\text{gibt}}$,
since there has been a law, valid since 1980 (Note the extended adjectival phrase in brackets)

the second one, a relative clause, gives us more information about the noun 'Gesetz':

<das die Gleichbehandlung von Männern und Frauen am Arbeitsplatz $\boxed{\text{sicherstellt}}$,
which guarantees equal treatment of men and women in the workplace

whilst the last dependent clause gives us the reason why:

<weil> den Frauen seither alle Ausbildungsstätten $\boxed{\text{offenstehen}}$.
because since then all training places have been open to women.

3. <Obwohl> das Abschlußzeugnis der Gymnasien, das sogenannte Reifezeugnis oder Abitur, grundsätzlich alle zum Studium an einer Universität $\boxed{\text{berechtigt}}$, $\boxed{\text{ist}}$ ein Studium genau nach Wunsch nicht immer möglich, <weil> die Zahl der Abiturienten so stark gestiegen $\boxed{\text{ist}}$, <daß> Aufnahmebeschränkungen eingeführt werden $\boxed{\text{mußten}}$, **um** den starken Andrang auf bestimmte populäre Studienfächer **zu regulieren**.

The main clause:

$\boxed{\text{ist}}$ ein Studium genau nach Wunsch nicht immer möglich,
it is not always possible to do exactly the type of course one wants to (lit.: *a course of study exactly according to one's wish(es) is not always possible*)

is preceded by a dependent clause explaining that this is so despite another fact:

<Obwohl> das Abschlußzeugnis der Gymnasien grundsätzlich alle zum Studium an einer Universität $\boxed{\text{berechtigt}}$,
Although the certificate one gets when leaving grammar school in principle entitles everyone to go to a university,

this clause, however, is interrupted by a non-clause insertion giving further information about the certificate:

das sogenannte Reifezeugnis oder Abitur,
the so-called Reifezeugnis *or* Abitur,

The dependent 'weil'-clause following the main clause explains why this is the case:

<weil> die Zahl der Abiturienten so stark gestiegen $\boxed{\text{ist}}$,
because the number of those with 'Abitur' has risen so much

and then in turn is followed by a dependent 'daß'-clause which explains the consequences of this increase:

\<daß\> Aufnahmebeschränkungen eingeführt werden mußten ,
(so much so) that admission restrictions had to be introduced

which then is followed by an 'um . . . zu' + infinitive construction explaining the purpose of this restriction:

um den starken Andrang auf bestimmte populäre Studienfächer **zu regulieren**.
in order to regulate the strong demand for certain popular subject areas.

CHAPTER 9: TEXT B

One hundred years ago it (still) seemed as if one knew exactly when German history began, that is in AD 9 when three Roman legions were defeated in the Teutoburg Forest by Arminius, a prince from a Germanic tribe called the Cheruscans. He was later celebrated as the first German hero and a huge monument was even built for him. But even today one still does not know anything definite about him and can only speculate about it.

But concerning the beginning of German history, one now knows that the matter cannot be presented in such a simple way, because the emergence of the German people was a process which took centuries. The word 'German' probably only appeared during the eighth century and is said to have described at first only the language which was spoken by certain tribes. Not until much later was the term 'German' used for those who spoke this language and finally also transferred to the area where they lived (Germany, *lit.*: German-land).

Chapter 10

Guessing difficult words (10.7)

The missing words in the original English texts are: (1) formerly, (2) domain, (3) mainly, (4) usurped, (5) relegated, (6) fictitious, (7) hereditary. But it is possible to 'read the meaning' of these words without actually predicting the precise word used and without even knowing that this word exists. Other possibilities include:

(1) 'once', 'previously': the missing word contrasts with 'present' in the following clause. It is not even necessary to come up with a word that works precisely in the context. Words like 'before' will get the sense.

(2) 'area', 'field': it is not necessary to predict the word 'domain' here.

(3) There are two possibilities: (i) 'exclusively', 'significantly', 'more'; and (ii) 'partly'. The context makes (i) the more likely reading.

(4) 'used', 'exploited', 'invoked': it is not necessary to come up with 'usurped' to get the general meaning.

(5) 'reduced', 'downgraded': the major clue is the word 'subordinate'.

(6) There is more than one category of meaning possible here: (i) 'dominant', 'all-embracing', 'controlling'; (ii) 'dangerous', 'criminal', 'inhuman'; (iii) 'false', 'bogus', 'misleading'. Of these (ii) and (iii) are more probable because the use of a strongly evaluative (negative) word is suggested by the author's critical attitude towards Nazism.

(7) The sense of this word must be in contrast to the meaning of 'acquired'. While 'learned' and 'taught' are theoretically possible, the context strongly indicates 'inherited', 'handed down', 'in the blood' etc.

Vocabulary test (10.8)

a. language; war; science; century; shadow; population; east; foreigner; communication difficulty; importance.

b. understand; publish; read; live (dwell); discover; arrive; increase; affirm; drive forward; emigrate.

c. important(ly); interesting(ly); European; everywhere; immediate(ly); slow(ly); today; various(ly); economic(ally); again.

Chapter 11

Ancient Rome

1. Romulus and Remus are said to have founded Rome in 753 BC (lines 1 f.).

2. The earliest secure records of ancient Rome date from the fourth century BC (lines 3–5).

3. It extended for a time from England, the Rhine and the Danube in the north to the Sahara in the south, from Portugal in the west to the Euphrates in the east (lines 12–16).

4. Absolute power.

5. The fifth century BC is usually seen as the end of antiquity (lines 22 f.).

6. In AD 395 the Roman Empire split into an eastern and a western empire (lines 23–6).

7. Odoaker was a Germanic warrior and he deposed the last emperor in the western empire (lines 27–9).

Bacteria

1. Bacilli are long and thin (stick-like, line 7).

2. Cocci are spherical (sphere-shaped, line 8).

3. Spirochaea are shaped like spirals (corkscrew-shaped, line 9 f.).

4. Almost everywhere (line 11)

5. They make it fertile (lines 15 f.).

6. Infectious illnesses.

7. They break down food and make it useable for the body.

Inflation

1. From the Latin for 'blowing up' (lines 1–3).

2. Increase in prices; devaluation of savings; the 'flight into material goods' (lines 8–11).

3. Real estate and works of art (lines 13 f.).

4. It increases faster than for other goods (lines 15–17).

5. The 'great inflation' of 1923.

6. 'Creeping Inflation': a slow and gradual increase in prices of about 5 per cent (lines 29 f.).

7. After 1973 many Western countires went far beyond this.

Research and Development

1. die Entwicklung.

2. entwickeln.

3. To offer the right product at the right price and/or to develop and optimize suitable production methods (lines 1–5)

4. They should always be thought of as potential partners in co-operation, together with technical universities and other research institutions (lines 19–23)

5. This is the responsibility of management, not of the R&D team (lines 27–9).

6. Service is to be included in any R&D strategy, together with consultancy and trouble-shooting (lines 24–6).

7. Literally: 'pilot customer'.

The Sonata

1. Slow and full of expression (line 17 f.).

2. A French dance (lines 20 f.)

3. Very fast (line 23).

4. It is in three parts (line 28).

5. Two contrasting musical ideas (lines 29 f.).

6. They are elaborated and deepened in the middle section, and then taken up again with little alteration in the concluding section.

7. They are the same (line 35–6).

Chapter 12

Islam

B1. 1. Submission to the will of God (lines 7 f.)

2. Chapters of the Koran (lines 15–18 f.)

3. A large niche in the mosque which points towards Mecca (lines 28–30).

4. The oldest large mosque is in Damascus (line 34 f.)

5. Wearing footwear; and representations of people (lines 27 f., 33 f.).

6. The consumption of pork and alcohol (lines 45–6).

B2. 1. according to the teachings (of)

2. later legal rulings

3. before prayer/before praying

4. direction in which to pray (literally 'prayer direction')

5. prayer leader

6. pilgrimage

7. are absolutely forbidden him

B3. 1. Allah

2. the world (die Welt)

3. the Koran

4. the Koran

5. God

6. the Muslim

B4. 1. the religion founded at the beginning of the 7th century AD by the Arab Muhammed

2. he has therefore to be submissive to this will

3. it is read aloud from in the mosque

4. with a fountain at which the faithful are to wash themselves before prayer

5. narrow, high towers from which the times for prayer are called out

Schwangerschaft

B5. 1. After thirty days the embryo is about half a centimetre long.

2. After two months it is about 4 cm long.

3. At the end of the fourth month.

4. After the placenta has formed.

5. From the end of the fourth month.

6. They nourish the embryo.

B6. 1. conception

2. to move, travel, migrate

3. to embed

4. ovary

5. literally, 'two-egged (zwei + ei + ig) twins', i.e. twins derived from two different eggs

6. cell division

7. overall length

B7. 1. the fertilized egg cell (die befruchtete Eizelle)

2. the fertilized, embedded egg (das befruchtete, eingenistete Ei)

3. the umbilical cord (die Nabelschnur)

4. the embryo (der Embryo)

5. her (the mother) (die Mutter)

6. with this (= the penetration of the female egg cell by the male spermatazoon)

B8. 1. If both are fertilized, twins from two separate eggs are formed.

2. If the egg cell divides after the spematazoon has penetrated it, twins from the same egg are formed.

3. It extracts nourishment to begin with from the mucous membrane in the immediate vicinity.

4. The parts of the body can clearly be recognized.

Chapter 13

B1. 1. the individual's adaptation to the group

2. to live together practically without work

3. a vegetation that effortlessly provides them with what they need

4. to feel completely at home

5. slave-owners

6. such activities which brought them pleasure and prestige

7. were reserved for members of the upper stratum

8. what is decisively new (the decisively new thing)

9. consequence of a hierarchy willed by God

10. the right to property in natural law was disclaimed

11. the wage-labourer (the person working for a wage)

12. from an economic point of view (seen economically)

13. forced labour

B2. hingegen, doch

also, auf der anderen Seite, außerdem schließlich, also, außerdem,

B3. ohne, un-, -los, niemals, nicht, ebensowenig ('sind ihnen fremd' could also be seen as negation)

nicht mehr

nicht

B4. pacifist

B5. historical and cultural stagnation (lines 36–40)

B6. They were founded on slavery and reached a point of technological development where they could no longer solve the problem of how to organize slavery. (lines 41–7)

B7. They are both ways in which millions of people seek to escape 'enforced labour'. (line 108f.)

B8. Marxist

Chapter 14

B1. a2 He liked to make a quick profit without keeping
accounts.

b3 [Schindler] showed sympathy even in little things.

c2 He looked after them out of his own pocket.

d2 the fortune his dubious deals earned him

e3 'Schindlers List' reads quite well.

f2 a kind of sect

B2. schließlich (line 74); jedoch (76); zwar, . . . aber (81–2); dagegen (86); dazu (87); wiederum (89); wobei (90); letztlich (98–99); doch (106); wohl (108).

B3. keine (65); nicht (82); ungestaltet (83); gar nicht

(88); nicht (92, 94, 95); unerklärt (99); nicht (106, 108).

B4. a3 the Rekord-Works, which were facing bankruptcy

b1 he bribed whoever it paid to bribe

c2 a work-camp set up by him personally

d1 a person of Oskar Schindler's stature invites legends (i.e. is the stuff of legends).

e2 His workforce would surely have been murdered.

f2 in his factual report which is presented as a novel

g1 death-defying comradeship (literally 'death-despising fellow humanity', i.e. a feeling for one's fellow human beings which ignores the danger of being put to death)

B5. 1. Poland (line 11)

2. in Krakow (line 16)

3. Jews and Poles (line 22)

4. extremely well (bestens, line 32)

5. 1100. He enlarged his workforce by 400 (line 71) so that finally it consisted of 800 men and 300 women (line 74).

6. Madritsch and Tietsch (line 85)

7. the commandant of Plaszow concentration camp, situated near Krakow (lines 34 f.)

8. three (line 58)

9. four cigarettes (lines 28 ff.)

10. his home town of Zwittau in the Sudetenland (lines 67–8 ff.)

B6. The first six paragraphs recount Schindler's biography; the last two paragraphs discuss Keneally's book.

B7. It does not read badly, but it is a factual report dressed up as a novel. For a novel, it is too unformed, flat, clichéd. There are stereotypes (good Germans, anti-semitic Poles who are never the object of Nazi atrocities, Jews who are not divided amongst themselves into different groups) (lines 81–99).

Chapter 15

A2. die Gesinnung; die Haltung; die Stimmung; der Ansatz (?); das Weltbild; die Gedankenwelt; das Denken; das Denkmuster. Note also: die Mentalität (lines 13–14); Überzeugungen (55–6); nationalistisch eingestellt (87–8), 114–15

B1. 1. the subject of the study

2. the office or bureau for research into military affairs

3. one of their series of publications

4. military history from the bottom up

5. those people who were excited by the war

6. the author reaches the conclusion that

7. according to the talk of the old men

8. an attitude with clearly aggressive characteristics

9. in absolutely comparable forms, i.e. in very much the same way

B2. 1. 'In the case of these people'—referring to 'die Kriegsbegeisterten'

2. 'their deeds' – referring to the veterans of 1871

B3. 1. the analysis, which is written with convincing (admirable) clarity

2. that they exercised a scarcely to be underestimated influence

3. the danger which they had survived together in the war

4. an analysis of the changing activities of the associations

5. the nationalistically-minded 'little people'

6. a thought that points beyond the time of the Kaiserreich

B4. a2 that they fell into a frenzy of excitement

b1 it may be worth mentioning in this connection that . . .

c3 a work which is an example of the history of everyday life (*lit.*: 'which is to be categorized as . . .')

d2 they wished their enemies would attack them (*lit.*: longed for an attack by their enemies)

e2 the process was to repeat itself once again around 1929/30

B5. wer . . . der (lines 40, 42); damit (46); jedoch (58); vielmehr (61); sowohl . . . als auch (62–3); mit anderen Worten (70–1)

B6. kaum (49); wenig (53); keineswegs (59); nicht (72)

B7. 1. workers, agricultural workers, the bourgeoisie (lower middle classes) (lines 6–7)

2. almost three million

3. nationalistic and militaristic (54–5)

4. no — on the contrary (64–70)

5. no (71–5)

6. 'written with convincing clarity' (17–18); 'excellent' (33–4)

7. on the one hand, they glorified war; on the other they stressed their own peace-loving nature (63–4 ff.)

8. In the 'revolt' of 1968 the debate between the younger generation and the generation of parents (who had fought in the Second World War) took a different direction, in which militaristic attitudes were subjected to thoroughgoing criticism.

9. none

Chapter 16

A1. 1. die Vereinigten Staaten

2. mass emigration

3. perception

4. causes

5. The causes of the mass emigration to the United States: objective forces and their subjective perception

A2. auswandern (die Auswanderung); übersiedeln; der Aufbruch; davonziehen. Note also: die Migration (line 6); das Auswandern (105); außer Landes führen (110f.); die Emigration (158f.).

A3. Reasons for leaving, economic: poverty, social class, property, possessions, recession, depression, proletariat; political: persecution, liberty, democracy, revolution; religious: persecution, faith; actual and perceived poverty, persecution, etc., fear of poverty etc.; industrialization.

A4. For example, in the first paragraph: **(a)** Nordamerika, transatlantische Migration, addierten, Industrialisierungsphase, religiöse, Pauperismus. **(b)** possibly: -gruppen, Ersten Weltkrieg, Zeit, 17. Jahrhundert etc., die Neue Welt. NB the word 'Not' is a false friend.

A6. 1. nicht (mehr) . . . sondern (lines 20, 24); so . . . daß (28); zwar . . . jedoch (46, 51; and 92, 93).

2. aber (line 4); jedoch (51, 93); doch (107); während (35 f., 60).

3. auch (line 34); zumal (49); im übrigen (57 f.); außerdem (82); gleichwohl (84).

4. aber (lines 4, 36); während (35 f., 60); zwar (46, 92); jedoch (51, 93); um so + comparative adjective (51, 93); dabei (132, 154); entsprechend (100, 149)

A9. 1. The percentage of the working population dependent on agriculture was 22% in Britain but 70–80% in the German-speaking regions of Europe (line 36 ff.).

2. He conducted a famous demographic survey of emigrés in 1817 in Württemberg (line 117 f.).

3. Negative. The guilds obstructed an expansion in the number of master craftsmen. (91 f.)

B1. 1. 'fragmentation of property', i.e. parcels of land were getting smaller and smaller.

2. the process by which the available land and property was divided equally amongst all the heirs of the owner.

3. 'a religiously coloured search for freedom', i.e. a quest for a new life which was motivated by religious considerations.

4. 'military demands on the subjects', i.e. compulsory conscription or taxes.

5. 'the proletarianising young generation of craftsmen', i.e. the younger generation of craftsmen were in the process of becoming economically impoverished, part of the proletariat.

6. 'A part of the surplus population tried to get into a trade', i.e. some of those who had no property tried to earn a living by learning a craft skill.

B2.
1. 5.5 million (line 10).

2. Overpopulation and poverty (line 24 f.).

3. Between 70% and 80% (line 39 f.).

4. The small farmers with insufficient property and the agricultural workers and casual workers who depended on waged work (lines 53–6).

5. Because of the fragmentation of ownership: too many people were working unviable parcels of land due to increased demand for farming land and the way ownership was inherited (lines 56–67).

6. Weaving (line 72).

7. They were too dependent on the fate of agriculture (line 75 f.).

8. Around 1850 (line 99).

9. Yes (lines 107 ff.).

10. After 1848/9 (line 152 ff.).

Part II

Reference Section

List of Topics

Word Order

R1 The Three Positions of the Finite Verb

In German there are three kinds of word-order pattern. The FINITE VERB is found in one of three positions, depending on the type of clause. These are:

VERB SECOND

Der Mensch **hat** rund 800 Lebensspannen auf Erden gelebt. [T3:1]
Mankind has lived on earth for about 800 generations.

Watt **baute** die erste Dampfmaschine vor sechs Generationen. [T3:2]
Watt built the first steam engine six generations ago.

Die eigentliche Industrialisierung **begann** vor vier Lebensspannen. [T3:2]
Real industrialisation began four generations ago.

Bis dahin **war** die Gesellschaft statisch. [T3:3]
Until then society was static.

VERB FINAL

obwohl der Mensch rund 800 Lebensspannen auf Erden gelebt **hat**
although mankind has lived for 800 generations on earth

weil Watt die erste Dampfmaschine vor sechs Generationen **baute**
because Watt built the first steam engine six generations ago

da die eigentliche Industrialisierung vor vier Lebensspannen **begann**
because real industrialization began four generations ago.

die Gesellschaft, die bis dahin statisch **war**
society, which until then was static.

VERB INITIAL

War die Gesellschaft bis dahin statisch?
Was society static until then?

War die Gesellschaft bis dahin statisch, . . .
If society was static until then, . . .

R2 Connectors which Do Not Affect Word Order (→R160, R161)

Two or more clauses of the same type can be joined together with **aber/denn/doch/oder/ sondern/und**—without the word order changing:

Die Temperatur verursacht eine Veränderung des Durchmessers,	**aber/denn oder/und**	(sie) verändert auch die Länge [T7:8]
The temperature causes a change in the diameter	*but/for/ or/and*	*(it) also changes the length*
Die Temperatur verursacht keine Veränderung des Durchmessers,	doch sondern	(sie) verändert die Länge

| The temperature causes no change in the diameter | however/ but | (it) changes the length |
| weil die Temperatur eine Veränderung des Durchmessers verursacht *because the temperature causes a change in the diameter* | und oder and or | (weil sie) die Länge verändert *(because it) changes the length* |

(Words in brackets may be left out.)

R3 Verb-Second Clauses

This is the type of clause used for statements. It is the basic form for simple sentences. The finite verb is always the 'second idea' (but not necessarily the second word). English almost always has the order SUBJECT + VERB + OBJECT (SVO), but German allows several variations, including OVS.

Here are possible word orders for the sentence: *'Watt built the first steam engine six generations ago'*:

I	II	III	IV
Vor sechs Generationen	**hat**	Watt die erste Dampfmaschine	**gebaut.**
Watt	**hat**	vor sechs Generationen die erste Dampfmaschine	**gebaut.**
Watt	**hat**	die erste Dampfmaschine vor sechs Generationen	**gebaut.**
Die erste Dampfmaschine	**hat**	Watt vor sechs Generationen	**gebaut.**
Gebaut	**hat**	Watt die erste Dampfmaschine vor sechs Generationen.	

NB: **hat . . . gebaut = baute**, 'built' [T3:2]

There are four basic positions:

I	II III	IV

Vor sechs Generationen **hat** Watt die erste Dampfmaschine **gebaut.**

I.   The subject of the verb does not have to appear in Position I. In fact, any word or phrase can appear as the first idea, except:

II. The FINITE VERB. This is the only fixed point in all the possible word orders. Very often the finite verb is one part of a larger unit, the other part being found at the end of the clause, in

IV. THE VERB COMPLETION. THIS CONTAINS ESSENTIAL INFORMATION WHICH BELONGS WITH THE VERB AND 'COMPLETES' THE MESSAGE. A WHOLE RANGE OF IMPORTANT CONSTRUCTIONS ARE INVOLVED (→R6). Therefore, these two positions need to be read together.

III. THIS PART OF THE CLAUSE CAN CONTAIN A NUMBER OF ITEMS:

The SUBJECT of the verb: When the subject is not the first idea, it usually follows immediately after Position II:

Vor sechs Generationen hat **Watt** die erste Dampfmaschine gebaut.

THE OBJECT(S) of the verb:

Watt hat **die erste Dampfmaschine** gebaut.

ADVERBIALS giving information about how, when, where, etc.:

Watt hat die erste Dampfmaschine **vor sechs Generationen** gebaut.

R4 A Strategy for Reading this Kind of Clause

	I	II III	IV
1.		**hat**	
2.	Vor sechs Generationen		
3.			**gebaut.**
4.		Watt	
5.		die erste Dampfmaschine	

1. Identify the finite verb (Position II).

2. This reveals the extent of the first concept. Everything that comes before the finite verb belongs together in a coherent unit, no matter how many words there are.

3. Add the verb completion (Position IV), *if there is one.*

4. Find the subject of the verb. When it is not the first concept, it is nearly always *straight after the finite verb.*

   NB: The subject is always in the singular when the finite verb is in the singular, and in the plural when the finite verb is in the plural ('Subject–verb-agreement').

5. Look at the remainder of the clause (Position III) to find any remaining information: objects of the verb and/or adverbials.

R5 Position I in a Verb-Second Clause

The subject is not always in Position I. Note the following possibilities for the sentence:

Only after two world wars did people take these appeals seriously. [T2:17]

One possible word order is the English pattern: Subject + verb + object:

I	II	III		IV
Man	hat	diese Appelle	nach zwei Weltkriegen	ernstgenommen.
[S]	[V]	[O]	[ADVERBIAL: 'WHEN?']	[VERB COMPLETION]

But other patterns are also possible:

I	II III	IV
Nach zwei Kriegen	hat man diese Appelle	ernstgenommen.

(It was) **after two wars** *(that) people took these appeals serously.*

The first concept here is an ADVERBIAL.

Diese Appelle	hat man nach zwei Kriegen	ernstgenommen.

These appeals *were taken seriously after two wars. (Lit.: These appeals one took seriously after two wars.)*

The first concept here is the OBJECT OF THE VERB.

Ernstgenommen	hat man diese Appelle nach zwei Kriegen.	

*People **took** these appeals **seriously** after two wars.*

The first concept here is a VERB COMPLETION.

> **Weil es zwei Kriege**
>   **gegeben hatte,**   hat man diese Appelle   ernstgenommen.
> *Because there had been two wars,* *people took these appeals seriously.*

The first concept here is a DEPENDENT CLAUSE (→R142–3)

R6 The Verb and its Completion: Important Patterns

Separable verbs (→R39, R171)

1. Handwerker	**nehmen**	den Platz drei	**ein.**
2. Die Schweiz	**wies**	die höchste Krebsrate in der alten Welt	**aus.**

Compound tenses (→R32)

3. Dieser Kontinent	**hat**	viele Kriegsjahre	**erlebt.**
4. Für alle Bundesregierungen	**ist**	der Ausgleich mit den westlichen Partnern ein Kernpunkt der Außenpolitik	**gewesen.**
5. So	**wird**	man	**feststellen**

Passives (→R74, R75)

6. In ihrer Zeit	**wurde**	die erste Atombombe	**gezündet.**
7. Das Wort Placebo	**wird**	in Amerika seit 200 Jahren	**benutzt.**

Modal verbs (→R63–6)

8. Wir	**müssen**	eine Art Vereinigter Staaten von Europa	**schaffen.**
9. So	**muß**	sein Inneres sehr viel Luftraum	**enthalten.**

'Be/become/appear' + completion

10. Besonders schwierig	**scheint**	die Frage der Kleidung	**zu sein.**
11. Händels Oratorien	**blieben**	dagegen vor allem in England stets	**lebendig.**
12. Mit den Bedingungen	**waren**	sie nicht	**einverstanden.**

Idiomatic phrases with verbs

13. Diese Einrichtungen	**stellen**	die wirtschaftliche Ordnung nicht	**in Frage.**
14. Der Wunsch nach Frieden	**stand**	bei der Gründung der Europäischen Gemeinschaft	**Pate.**

Including verb + verb constructions

15. Die Alten unter uns	**hörten**	vom ersten Flug der Gebrüder Wright	**erzählen.**
16. Gott	**läßt**	ihn sein tröstendes Wort	**hören.**

KEY

1. *Skilled craftsmen **occupy** position three.* [T1:4]
2. *Switzerland **registered** the highest cancer rate in the Old World.* [T16:4]
3. *This continent **has experienced** many years of war.* [T2:2]
4. *For all West German governments reconciliation with their western partners **has been** a core point of West German foreign policy.* [T2:18]
5. *Thus one **will find** that . . .* [T18:3]
6. *In their time the first atomic bomb **was exploded**.* [T3:7]
7. *The word placebo **has been used** in America for 200 years.* [T9:1]
8. *We **must create** a kind of United States of Europe.* [T2:6]
9. *So its inside **has to contain** a great deal of air space.* [T18:11]
10. *The question of dress **appears to be** especially difficult.* [T10a:5]
11. *Handel's oratorios, in contrast, always **remained alive**, especially in England.* [T8:9]
12. *They **were** not **in agreement** with the conditions.* [T15:6]
13. *These institutions do not **call** the economic order **into question**.* [T14:12]
14. *The desire for peace **presided over** the founding of the European Community.* [T2:4]

15. *The old ones amongst us **heard tell** of the first flight of the Wright brothers.* [T3:5]
16. *God **lets** him **hear** His consoling word.* [T6:7]

R7 Word Order in the Verb Completion

German has the reverse of the English order:

Der Durchmesser **kann** sehr genau mit einer Mikro-Schublehre **gemessen werden**. [T7:2]
can   *measured be*
*The diameter **can be measured** very precisely with a micrometer.*

Note the word order: ¹**can** ...   ³**measured**   ²**be**

R8 Finding the Subject

THE SUBJECT DOES NOT HAVE TO COME BEFORE THE VERB.

Since it is not always possible to tell from the form of a noun whether it is the subject of the verb (→**R103**), it is often necessary to rely on the context and common sense. One useful guide is subject–verb agreement (→**R4**):

Neue Finanzierungsmethod<u>en</u> erlaub<u>en</u> die Einführung neuer Verfahren. [T14:3]
              [PLURAL   PLURAL]   SINGULAR

Die Einführung neuer Verfahren **erlaub<u>en</u> neue Finanzierungsmethod<u>en</u>.**
SINGULAR   [PLURAL   PLURAL]

(For plural forms of nouns, →R179; for plural forms of verbs, →R23)

Both these sentences say the same thing, though with a slightly different emphasis. For a similar effect, compare the ACTIVE–PASSIVE relationship in English:

***New methods of finance allow** the introduction of new procedures.* (Active)
*The introduction of new procedures is made possible by **new methods of finance.*** (Passive)

THE SUBJECT NEED NOT BE A NOUN: IT MAY BE A PRONOUN (→R98–100, R135)

Außerdem aber ist **er** noch in gewissem Sinne unser Zeitgenosse. [T11:2]
*Apart from this, however, **he** is still our contemporary in a certain sense.*

Erst nach dem Schrecken zweier Weltkriege nahm **man** diese Appelle ernst. [T1:17]
*Only after the terror of two world wars did **people** take these appeals seriously.*

(man, '*one; people in general*' is always the subject)

or it may be a DEPENDENT CLAUSE (→R146); This will probably not cause any problems when it comes before the main ('verb-second') clause.

Wo ich im Juni bin, ist noch ganz unübersehbar. [T10b:13]
***Where I am in June** is still completely unforeseeable.*

But the reverse order may be difficult for English readers:

Überraschend ist, **daß der unzureichende Zugang zu Forschungsergebnissen keineswegs als Hemmnis angesehen wird.** [T20:11]
*(What is) surprising is **(the fact) that inadequate access to research results is not at all regarded as an obstacle.***

R9 The Remainder of the Clause (Position III)

As well as the subject, this can contain **objects of the verb** and/or <u>adverbials</u>:

I	II	III	IV
Wir	können	**die Wassertemperatur in einem Glas** <u>mittels eines Thermometers</u>	messen. [T7:12]

*We can measure **the water temperature in a glass** <u>using a thermometer</u>.*

R10 Variations on the Basic Pattern of Verb-second Clauses

1. FINDING THE SUBJECT WHEN THERE IS A REFLEXIVE VERB (→R40, R163, R168)

usually with the reflexive 'sich'. Note the pattern.

Auch in Mitteleuropa setzt sich **die industrielle Revolution** durch. [T14:1]
*In Central Europe, too, **the industrial revolution** establishes itself.*

2. FINDING THE SUBJECT WHEN THERE IS A DELAYED SUBJECT

The subject can be placed near the end of the clause, for stylistic reasons.

So sagte schon 1946 (ein Jahr nach dem Ende des Zweiten Weltkriegs) **der bedeutende britische Premierminister Winston Churchill.** [T2:9]
*This is what **the great British Prime Minister Winston Churchill** said as early as 1946, one year after the end of the Second World War.*

In gleicher Weise kann sich in der Psychologie **das Verhalten** ändern. [T7:14]
*In the same way, **behaviour** can change in psychology.*

3. VERBS WITH TWO OBJECTS (→R84)

Letztes Jahr hat **mir** die Universität **den Doktorgrad** verliehen. [T10a:1]
*Last year the university awarded **me a doctorate.***

4. TOKEN SUBJECT 'ES'

A slot-filler. The real subject comes after the verb.

Es leben **Menschen**, die . . . [T12:2]
*There are **people** (living) who . . .*

Es fehlt nicht **der Hinweis**, daß . . . [T20:16]
*There are **signs** that . . . (Literally: The **indication** is not lacking that . . .)*

This kind of construction is often found in PASSIVE sentences (→R79.3 and .4)

Es wurde **viel** erreicht. [T2:19] = **Viel** wurde erreicht.
***A lot** has been achieved.*

5. SUBJECTLESS CLAUSES

These are found in passive sentences (→R79). Basically, **es** has been left out:

So wird behauptet.
This is what is asserted. (Lit.: Thus is asserted)

Im Nürnberger Bereich wird auf die Überlegenheit der USA verwiesen. [T20:6]
In the Nuremberg area the superiority of the USA is pointed to.

6. THE VERB COMPLETION (POSITIONS II + IV)

Position IV is sometimes not literally at the end of the clause.

Das Thermometer **kann** kälter **sein** als das Wasser. [T7:13]
*The thermometer **can be** colder than the water.*

Sometimes the verb completion (Position IV) is brought forward from the end of the clause, though it still does not conform to English word order:

Den breitesten Raum in Dovers Buch **nimmt** ein Prozeß gegen den Athener Timarchos **ein**, aus dem Jahr 346 v. Chr. in Athen. [T15:3]

This kind of structure is found in COMPARATIVES (as above, →R107) and in long sentences, especially where the verb completion would otherwise come after a long list.

7. INDIRECT REPORTS (→R54–6)

Ich erklärte den Medizinern, ich **sei** der päpstliche Legat. [T10b:8]
*I explained to the medics that I **was** the Papal Legate.*

Firmen geben an, sie **hätten** einen technologischen Nachholbedarf. [T20:5]
*Firms report that they **have** a technology deficit.*

A 'verb-second' word order is found in this kind of clause. The NON-FACTUAL form of the verb (→R47) is enough to characterize whole sentences as a report of someone else's words:

Auffallend ist, . . . daß die Unternehmen . . . den Eindruck vermitteln, daß große Anstrengungen gemacht werden, den Rückstand aufzuholen. Vielfach **sei** er bereits aufgeholt worden. [T20:8–9]

8. W-QUESTIONS (E.G. WITH 'WER?', 'WAS?', 'WARUM?', 'WIE?', 'WANN?', ETC.)

Warum **brauchen** wir Europa? *Why do we **need** Europe?*

Note how INDIRECT QUESTIONS have a verb-final word order (→R12):

Die Leute haben vergessen, warum wir Europa **brauchen**.
*People have forgotten why we **need** Europe.*

Warum wir Europa **brauchen**, ist ja offenkundig.
*Why we **need** Europe is really quite obvious.*

9. WISHES

Gott **segne** dieses Haus. *God **bless** this house.*

(Comparatively rare, with the verb in a non-factual form (→R61))

R11 Verb-Final Clauses

This is the word order found in DEPENDENT CLAUSES of various kinds. The three main kinds are:

CLAUSES INTRODUCED BY A CONJUNCTION (→R12)

daß dies ein rechter Trugschluß **ist** [T19:3]
that this is a complete fallacy

RELATIVE CLAUSES: (→R13)

Bundestagsabgeordneten, **die** im Westen auf Platz 19 **kommen** [T1:8]
members of the Bundestag, who come in 19th place . . .

INFINITIVE CLAUSES: (→R14)

es ist nie **möglich**, den genauen Durchmesser **zu bestimmen** [T7:5]
it is never possible to determine the exact diameter

R12 Clauses Introduced by a Conjunction

See **R143** for a list of CONJUNCTIONS which send the finite verb to the end of the clause.

Das Automobil **wurde** zur Alltäglichkeit.

Sie haben erlebt, **wie** das Automobil zur Alltäglichkeit **wurde**. [T3:6]

*They experienced **how** the automobile became an everyday phenomenon*

Eine Kampagne für Milchabstinenz **setzte** in aller Welt **ein**.

ehe eine Kampagne für Milchabstinenz in aller Welt **einsetzte** [T16:8]

***before** a campaign for milk abstinence started all over the world*

R13 Relative Clauses (→R110–13, 147)

Die Bundestagsabgeordneten **kommen** im Westen auf Platz 19.

Nicht viel besser geht es
den Bundestagsabgeordneten, **die** im Westen auf Platz 19 **kommen**. [T1:8]

*It's not much better for
MPs in the Bundestag,*   ***who come** in 19th place in the West.*

R14 Infinitive Clauses (→R149)

Often found in constructions like *(im)possible to, intend to,* etc.

Es ist nie **möglich**, den genauen Durchmesser **zu bestimmen**. [T7:5]
*It is never **possible to determine** the exact diameter.*

NOTE THE CONSTRUCTION 'um (. . .) zu', 'in order to' (→R151):

Um eine gute Schätzung **zu erhalten**, werden verschiedene Messungen
zusammengenommen. [T7:4]
In order to get *a good estimate, different measurements are taken together.*

R15 Variations in the Basic Pattern of Verb-Final Clauses

1. GENERAL COMMANDS AND INSTRUCTIONS

Gerät mit Taste 4 **einschalten**. [T23:1] **Switch on** *the machine with knob* 4.

The infinitive of the verb is at the end of the clause, often with an exclamation mark.

2. IF ONLY . . .

Wenn das Licht doch besser **wäre**! *If only the light* **were** *better*.

The verb is in a non-factual form (➔R48), often with an exclamation mark.

3. POSITION OF SICH (REFLEXIVE VERBS) (➔R10.1)

Unternehmen, die **sich** nicht zur Spitzenstellung **bekennen**, . . . [T20:10]
firms which do not **regard themselves** *as being in the top group* . . .

Note how **sich** tends to stay near the front of the clause while the verb itself appears at the end.

4. VERB IS NOT LITERALLY IN 'FINAL' POSITION:

Wenn das Thermometer kälter **ist** als das Wasser, . . . [T7:13]
If the thermometer **is colder** *than the water* . . .

The verb can be brought forward, especially where there is a comparison (example above) or a long and involved sentence. But the verb is still not in second position!

5. WORD ORDER IN THE VERB COMPLETION:

wodurch der Zylinder nicht **gedreht werden kann** [T17:5]
                                    turned   be   can
(because of which *the cylinder* **cannot be turned)**

The order is the reverse of the English order. The only exception to this is found when there is a MODAL VERB in the past tense (➔R67):

wodurch der Zylinder nicht **hat gedreht werden können**
because of which the cylinder **could** *not* **be turned**

This word order is common in expressions of the kind 'would have/could have' (➔R51.3).

R16 Verb-Initial Clauses

The most difficult to recognize is the 'IF'-CLAUSE WITHOUT 'IF'

Kann ein Körper mehr Flüssigkeit verdrängen . . ., so . . . [T18:7]
If a body **can** *displace more liquid* . . ., *then* . . .

The meaning is exactly the same as:

Wenn ein Körper mehr Flüssigkeit verdrängen **kann** . . .,

This is an alternative to a clause beginning with **wenn**. Here are some examples from the Text Corpus, rewritten with verb-initial word order: The first example shows that a similar structure exists in English.

Würden wir in einer Dorfstraße eine Verkehrssignalanlage aufstellen, . . . [cf T19:1]
Were *we to put up traffic lights in a village street* . . . .

Ist das Thermometer kälter als das Wasser, ... [T7:13]
If the thermometer **is** *colder than the water* . . .

Often, the IF-CLAUSE expresses an unreal condition: the verb is then in a non-factual (also called 'subjunctive') form (→R47–8):

Wäre das Thermometer kälter als das Wasser, . . .
Were the thermometer colder than the water, . . . /
If the thermometer were colder than the water, . . .

R17 Other Verb-Initial Clauses

1. YES/NO QUESTIONS

Brauchen wir Europa?
Do we need Europe?

2. DIRECT COMMANDS

Lesen Sie bitte weiter!
Please read on.

3. WISHES (RARE; ANTIQUATED STYLE)

Möge der Kaiser noch lange leben!
May the Kaiser live for a long time!

'IF ONLY' wishes are often characterized by the presence of **doch** or **nur**:

Wäre das Wasser **doch** wärmer!
If only the water were warmer!

R18 Summary: The Three Types of Clause and What Each Can Express

VERB-SECOND:

If a clause has the finite verb in second position, it can be:

- A STATEMENT:

  Die Firmen haben einen technologischen Nachholbedarf.
  The companies have a technological deficit.

- AN INDIRECT REPORT:

  Die Firmen geben an, sie hätten einen technologischen Nachholbedarf.
  The companies report that they have a technological deficit.

- A W-QUESTION:

  Welche Firmen haben einen technologischen Nachholbedarf?
  Which companies have a technological deficit?

- A WISH OR INVOCATION:

  Gott verhüte es!
  God forbid!

VERB-FINAL:

If a clause has the finite verb in final position, it can be:

- a dependent clause:

  . . . Firmen, die einen technologischen Nachholbedarf haben, . . .
  Companies which have a technological deficit . . .

■ (INCLUDING INDIRECT STATEMENTS):

> Firmen geben zu, daß sie einen technologischen Nachholbedarf haben.
> *Companies concede that they have a technological deficit.*

■ A GENERAL INSTRUCTION OR COMMAND:

> Gerät mit Taste 4 einschalten!
> *Switch on the apparatus with switch number 4.*

VERB-INITIAL:

If a clause has the finite verb in first position, it can be:

■ A YES/NO QUESTION:

> Haben die Deutschen einen technologischen Nachholbedarf?
> *Do the Germans have a technological deficit?*

■ A DIRECT COMMAND OR INSTRUCTION:

> Bedenken Sie den technologischen Nachholbedarf!
> *Remember the technological deficit.*

■ AN 'IF' CLAUSE WITHOUT THE 'IF':

> Haben wir einen technologischen Nachholbedarf, so/ dann . . .
> *If we have a technological deficit, then . . .*

■ 'IF ONLY . . .':

> Hätten wir nur keinen technologischen Nachholbedarf!
> *If only we didn't have a technological deficit.*

R19 Summary: The First Position in a 'Verb-Second' Clause: What it Can Contain:

THE SUBJECT OF THE VERB:

1. **Dies** geht aus einer Umfrage hervor. [T1:2]
2. **Handwerker** nehmen bei den Ostdeutschen sogar den Platz drei ein. [T1:4]

A TOKEN SUBJECT:

3. **Es** wird in unserer Gesellschaft **die Täuschung** aufrechterhalten. [T19:2]

AN ADVERBIAL:

4. **Erst nach dem Schrecken zweier Weltkriege** nahm man diese Appelle ernst. [T2:17]
5. **Anders** verhält es sich bei der Bewertung des Hausfrauenberufs [T1:5]
6. **Bis dahin** war die Gesellschaft statisch. [T3:3]
7. **Vor einigen Jahren** hat eine neue Epoche in der Geschichte begonnen. [T5:8]
8. **Dadurch** steigt ihre Leistung. [T7:17]
9. **Wie von einem Erdbeben** wurde die Öffentlichkeit aufgeschreckt. [T16:1]

AN OBJECT OF THE VERB:

10. **Den Talar** leiht man Ihnen sicher von der Universität. [T10b:5]
11. **Den Ideologen** ist vorzuwerfen, daß . . . [T19:8]
12. **Keines besonderen Fachwissens** bedarf es in den meisten Fällen. [T16:15]
13. **In das natürliche Geschehen** greifen die übernatürlichen Mächte ein. [T6:6]
14. **Am Krebs** erkranken die meisten Menschen erst im fortgeschrittenen Alter. [T16:9]
15. **Auf ihn** wirkt eine entgegengesetzte Kraft. [T18:5]

A VERB COMPLETION:

16. **Beklagt** wird hier insbesondere die Abhängigkeit der Deutschen von . . . [T20:7]

AN ADJECTIVE OR COMPLEMENT OF THE SUBJECT:

17. **Einig** sind sich Ost und West über die Berufsgruppe mit dem geringsten Ansehen. [T1:7]
18. **Nicht viel besser** geht es den Bundestagsabgeordneten. [T1:8]
19. **Besonders schwierig** scheint die Frage der Kleidung zu sein. [T10a:5]

A DEPENDENT CLAUSE:

20. **Seitdem der Mensch existiert**, gibt es Musik. [T5:2]
21. **Wo ich im Juni bin**, ist noch ganz unübersehbar. [T10b:14]

KEY:

1. *This* is clear from a public opinion survey.
2. *Skilled craftsmen* even occupy third position with the East Germans.
3. *There is the illusion* maintained in our society.
4. *Only after two wars* did people take these appeals seriously.
5. The situation is *different* when it comes to putting a value on the profession of housewife.
6. *Until then,* society was static.
7. *A few years ago* a new epoch in history began.
8. *Because of this,* their performance improves.
9. The public were shaken *as if by an earthquake.*
10. They will certainly lend you *the gown* from the university.
11. One can accuse *the ideologists of* . . . (**vorwerfen** + DATIVE, →R93, R84)
12. It needed *no special expertise* in most cases. (**bedürfen** + GENITIVE, →R93, R84)
13. The supernatural forces intervene *in the natural events.* (**eingreifen** + in →R175, R84)
14. Most people fall ill *with cancer* only at an advanced age. (**erkranken** + an →R175, R84)
15. An opposing force operates *on it.* (**wirken** + auf →R175, R84)
16. *What is complained about* here is especially the Germans' dependency on . . .
17. East and West Germans are *united* about the professional group with the least respect.
18. The MPs in the Bundestag do *not* fare *much better.*
19. The question of dress seems *especially difficult.*
20. *Since man has existed* there has been music.
21. *Where I am in June* is still completely unforeseeable.

R20 The Verb and its Completion

VERB SECOND

I	II	III	IV
SEPARABLE VERBS			
Die Schweiz	**wies**	die höchste Krebsrate	**aus.**
COMPOUND TENSES			
Dieser Kontinent	**hat**	viele Kriegsjahre	**erlebt**
So	**wird**	man	**feststellen.**
Für die Regierung	**ist**	das ein Kernpunkt der Außenpolitik	**gewesen.**
PASSIVES			
In ihrer Zeit	**wurde**	die erste Atombombe	**gezündet.**
Das Wort Placebo	**wird**	in Amerika seit 200 Jahren	**benutzt.**
MODAL VERBS			
Wir	**müssen**	eine Art Vereinigter Staaten von Europa	**schaffen.**
'BE', 'BECOME', 'APPEAR TO' + COMPLETION			
Besonders schwierig	**scheint**	die Frage der Kleidung	**zu sein.**
Mit den Bedingungen	**waren**	sie nicht	**einverstanden.**
IDIOMATIC PHRASES WITH VERBS (INCLUDING VERB + VERB CONSTRUCTIONS)			
Diese Einrichtungen	**stellen**	die wirtschaftliche Ordnung nicht	**in Frage**
Die Alten unter uns	**hörten**	vom ersten Flug der Gebrüder Wright	**erzählen.**

VERB FINAL

obwohl die Schweiz die höchste Krebsrate **auswies,**

dieser Kontinent, *der* viele Kriegsjahre **erlebt hat,**
ob man so **feststellen wird**
weil das für die Regierung ein Kernpunkt der Außenpolitik **gewesen ist**

wenn in ihrer Zeit die erste Atombombe **gezündet wurde**
daß das Wort Placebo in Amerika seit 200 Jahren **benutzt wird**

warum wir eine Art Vereinigter Staaten von Europa **schaffen müssen**

die Frage der Kleidung, *die* besonders schwierig **zu sein scheint**
da sie mit den Bedingungen nicht **einverstanden waren**

weil diese Einrichtungen die wirtschaftliche Ordnung nicht **in Frage stellen**

als die Alten unter uns vom ersten Flug der Gebrüder Wright **erzählen hörten**

VERB INITIAL

'IF-CLAUSE WITHOUT IF'

Stellten diese Einrichtungen die wirtschaftliche Ordnung **in Frage,** (. . .
[dann/so] kann man sagen . . .)
If these institutions did challenge the economic order, (. . . [then] one can say . . .)

YES-NO QUESTION

Stellten diese Einrichtungen die wirtschaftliche Ordnung **in Frage?**
Haben diese Einrichtungen die wirtschaftliche Ordnung **in Frage gestellt?**

INSTRUCTION

Stellen Sie die wirtschaftliche Ordnung **in Frage!**

Verbs
(Factual Expressions)

R21 Stems and Endings

Verbs consist of a STEM + ENDING.

The INFINITIVE form (the basic verb form given in the dictionary) consists of

STEM + **(e)n**, e.g.

lern**en**	*to learn*
komm**en**	*to come*
find**en**	*to find*
arbeit**en**	*to work*
wachs**en**	*to grow*
handel**n**	*to act/trade*
tu**n**	*to do*
versicher**n**	*to insure/assure*

R22 Definition of 'Finite Verb'

Verb forms can change according to whether the subject of the verb is SINGULAR or PLURAL, and whether the verb itself is PRESENT or PAST TENSE. Such forms are then referred to as FINITE VERBS. Changes may occur in the ending and/or the stem.

In English, too, these factors can affect the form of the verb: *they sing – he sings – he sang*

R23 Overview of the Six Tenses

There are six TENSES (i.e. time-forms, such as present, past, etc.) in German. Four of these are so-called COMPOUND TENSES which require AUXILIARY VERBS (e.g. *have, will*).

Here, for example, are the most important forms for the verb **lernen** *(to learn)*:

	SINGULAR	PLURAL
PRESENT TENSE	der Student lernt *the student learns*	viele Studenten lern**en** *many students learn*
SIMPLE PAST TENSE 'Imperfect'	der Student lern**te** *the student learnt*	viele Studenten lern**ten** *many students learnt*
COMPOUND TENSES		
COMPOUND PAST I 'Perfect'	**hat . . . gelernt** *has learnt*	**haben . . . gelernt** *have learnt*

COMPOUND PAST II	**hatte . . . gelernt**	**hatten . . . gelernt**
'Pluperfect'	*had learnt*	*had learnt*
FUTURE I	**wird . . . lernen**	**werden . . . lernen**
	will learn	*will learn*
FUTURE II	**wird . . . gelernt haben**	**werden . . . gelernt haben**
'Future Perfect'	*will have learnt*	*will have learnt*

See **R32** and **R3** for the WORD ORDER in compound tenses.

R24 The Verb and its Subject

The SUBJECT of a verb is typically either a NOUN or a PRONOUN

in the SINGULAR e.g.:	**der Student** lernt	**er** lernt
	the student learns	*he learns*
or PLURAL	**die Studenten** lernen	**sie** lernen
	the students learn	*they learn*

When the subject is a noun the verb has the so-called 3rd-PERSON forms (see below).

R25 The Subject Forms of Pronouns

Here are the SUBJECT forms of the PRONOUNS:

SINGULAR	1st PERSON	**ich**	*I*
	2nd	**du**	familiar form, singular:*you*
	3rd	**er/sie/es**	*he/she/it*
		man	*one.* Also used with the meaning *you/they/we/people in general*
PLURAL	1st PERSON	**wir**	*we*
	2nd	**ihr**	familiar form, plural:*you*
	3rd	**sie**	*they*
	2nd	**Sie**	formal *you*, used for both singular and plural

German has a formal and a familiar form of address. In written German the familiar forms (**du** and **ihr**) tend to be quite rare.

ich, du, er, man, wir: These pronouns are always the SUBJECT of the particular clause they are found in.

sie, es, ihr, sie, Sie: These pronouns, as well as being subject forms, have other functions too, see **R98**.
For **es** also see **R163**.

R26 Weak, Strong, Mixed, Irregular Verbs

In German and in English, there are four basic patterns for forming tenses:

WEAK   Verbs in this group follow a completely regular pattern of endings and no changes occur in the stem itself. (In English e.g.: *learn/learnt/has learnt*)

STRONG   Various changes occur in the stem and endings do <u>not</u> follow a regular pattern. (In English e.g.: *sing/sang/has sung*)

MIXED   Various changes occur in the stem, but endings do follow a regular pattern. (In English e.g.: *bring/ brought/has brought*)

IRREGULAR These verbs follow no particular pattern at all. (In English e.g.: *is/was/ has been*)

See also **R35**.

Common forms of STRONG and MIXED verbs as well as those of IRREGULAR verbs (→**R28– R31**) are given in **R46**. See also **R169** on how to look up these forms in the dictionary.

R27 The Present Tense: Weak Verbs

			sagen *to say*	**warten** *to wait*	**gehen** *to go*
ich		e	sag**e**	wart**e**	geh**e**
du		st	sag**st**	wart**est**	geh**st**
er, sie, es, man ⎱ SINGULAR NOUN ⎰	INFINITIVE STEM	t	sag**t**	wart**et***	geh**t**
wir		en	sag**en**	wart**en**	geh**en**
ihr		t	sag**t**	wart**et**	geh**t**
sie, Sie ⎱ PLURAL NOUN ⎰		en	sag**en**	wart**en**	geh**en**

*To ease pronunciation an additional e is sometimes put in between stem and ending or, alternatively, omitted.   e.g.   sie arbeitet   infinitive:arbeiten   *to work*
er atmet   infinitive:atmen   *to breathe*
ich sammle   infinitive:sammeln   *to collect*

R28 The Present Tense: Strong Verbs

Some strong verbs follow the present tense pattern given in **R27** (e.g. **gehen**), but others have an irregular stem form in the 2nd and 3rd person singular. These verbs are listed in **R46**. Also see **R169** on how to look up these forms in the dictionary.

			tragen	lesen	helfen
			to carry	*to read*	*to help*
			trage	lese	helfe
du		st	trägst	liest	hilfst
er, sie, es, man	CHANGED	t	trägt	liest	hilft
SINGULAR NOUN	STEM				
	FORM		tragen	lesen	helfen
			tragt	lest	helft
			tragen	lesen	helfen

The only verb that does not conform to either of the two patterns above is **wissen** *(to know)*: the singular form has no ending: ich, er, sie, es, man **weiß**.

Note: There are different patterns for AUXILIARY VERBS (**→R31**) and MODAL VERBS (**→R66**).

R29 The Simple Past Tense: Weak and Mixed Verbs

			sagen	kennen	denken
			to say	*to know*	*to think*
ich		te	sagte	kannte	dachte
du		test	sagtest	kanntest	dachtest
er, sie, es, man,⎫	INFINITIVE	te	sagte	kannte	dachte
SINGULAR NOUN ⎭	or				
wir	PAST	ten	sagten	kannten	dachten
ihr	STEM	tet	sagtet	kanntet	dachtet
sie, Sie ⎫		ten	sagten	kannten	dachten
PLURAL NOUN ⎭					

Note:

- **t** can be part of the stem. e.g.: **warten** *to wait*. Thus a **ten**-ending does not always mean the verb is in the past tense. The past tense of **warten**: er **wartete**, sie **warteten**.

- In some grammars the SIMPLE PAST TENSE is called IMPERFECT or PRETERITE.

R30 The Simple Past Tense: Strong Verbs

The same PAST STEM form throughout, but **no ending** in the 1st and 3rd person singular.

			tragen	lesen	helfen
			to carry	*to read*	*to help*
ich			trug	las	half
du		st	trugst	lasest	halfst
er, sie, es, man,⎫			trug	las	half
SINGULAR NOUN ⎭	PAST				
wir	STEM	en	trugen	lasen	halfen
ihr		t	trugt	last	halft
sie, Sie ⎫		en	trugen	lasen	halfen
PLURAL NOUN ⎭					

Note:

- **ich** and **er/sie/es/man** forms consist of the verb stem only.
- Thus strong singular past tense forms are difficult to recognize as verbs.
  e.g.: **lud,**   **verlor,**   **belief,**   **trat,**   **aß**   etc.
  Infinitive: laden,   verlieren,   belaufen,   treten,   essen
            to load,   *lose,*   *amount [to],*   *step/kick,*   *eat*
- Plural forms of strong verbs in the past tense can easily be mistaken for present tense forms. See **R44 Note 2.**

  Strong and mixed verb forms are listed in **R46**. See also **R169** on how to look up these forms in the dictionary.

R31 haben sein werden

These verbs may be used

a. as full verbs in their own right, (**haben** means *to have*, **sein** means *to be*, **werden** means *to become*)

b. as AUXILIARY VERBS in COMPOUND TENSES (→**R32**) or the PASSIVE (→**R74–5**).

	haben	sein	werden
PRESENT TENSE			
ich	habe	bin	werde
du	hast	bist	wirst
er, sie, es, man } SINGULAR NOUN	hat	ist	wird
wir	haben	sind	werden
ihr	habt	seid	werdet
sie, Sie } PLURAL NOUN	haben	sind	werden
SIMPLE PAST TENSE			
ich	hatte	war	wurde
du	hattest	warst	wurdest
er, sie, es, man } SINGULAR NOUN	hatte	war	wurde
wir	hatten	waren	wurden
ihr	hattet	wart	wurdet
sie, Sie } PLURAL NOUN	hatten	waren	wurden

PAST PARTICIPLES (→**R34**)

gehabt	gewesen	geworden
had	*been*	*become*
		worden (→**R75** and **R79.1**)
		been

R32 Overview of Compound Tenses

For word order also see **R3** and **R6**.

COMPOUND PAST I	Sie **haben** das Buch wahrscheinlich **gelesen**.	
COMPOUND PAST II	**hatten**	**gelesen**.
	*They probably **have (had)***	***read** the book.*
COMPOUND PAST I	Sie **sind** aus der Emigration **zurückgekehrt**. [T13:4]	
COMPOUND PAST II	**waren**	**zurückgekehrt**.
	*They **have [had] returned from** emigration.*	

Note: Where English uses '**have**' as an auxiliary some German verbs use **haben** and some use **sein**.

FUTURE I	Es **wird** die Temperatur leicht **senken**. [T7:13]	
FUTURE II	**wird**	**gesenkt haben**.
	*It **will lower (will have lowered)** slightly the temperature.*	

R33 The Compound Past

Some German verbs use **haben** (➔**R31**) as an auxiliary:

		AUXILIARY		PAST PRINCIPLE
COMPOUND PAST I	Der Mensch	**hat** rund 800 Lebensspannen auf Erden	**gelebt** [T3:1]	
COMPOUND PAST II		**hatte**	**gelebt**.	
	*Man **has (had) lived** on earth for about 800 generations.*			

and some verbs use **sein** (➔**R31**):

		AUXILIARY	PAST PRINCIPLE
COMPOUND PAST I	Er	**ist** mit dem Bus aus London	**gekommen**.
COMPOUND PAST II		**war**	**gekommen**.
	*He **has (had) come** by bus from London.*		

COMPOUND PAST TENSES are formed by a finite AUXILIARY VERB + the PAST PARTICIPLE (*lived* and *come* in the above examples) of the main information-carrying verb. The auxiliary is either **haben** or **sein** (➔**R31**). Here are the third-person forms:

COMPOUND PAST I	**hat/ist/haben/sind**	+ PAST PARTICIPLE
Auxiliary in the PRESENT TENSE	*has/have*	(for forms ➔**R34**)
COMPOUND PAST II	**hatte/war/hatten/waren**	+ PAST PARTICIPLE
Auxiliary in the PAST TENSE	*had*	

Note: Since there is only <u>one</u> auxiliary used in English, both **haben** and **sein** forms read as a form of *to have*.

For the word order of compound tenses see **R3** and **R6**. Also note the word order in dependent clauses, e.g.

weil der Mensch rund 800 Lebensspannen auf Erden **gelebt hat**.
*because man **has lived** on earth for about 800 generations.*

R34 Past Participle Forms

There are several patterns:

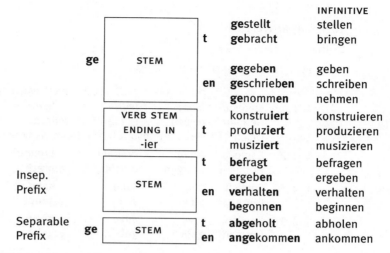

				INFINITIVE
ge	STEM	t	**ge**stell**t**	stellen
			gebrach**t**	bringen
		en	**ge**geb**en**	geben
			geschrieb**en**	schreiben
			genomm**en**	nehmen
	VERB STEM ENDING IN -ier	t	konstru**iert**	konstruieren
			produz**iert**	produzieren
			musiz**iert**	musizieren
Insep. Prefix	STEM	t	**be**frag**t**	befragen
		en	**er**geb**en**	ergeben
			verhalt**en**	verhalten
			begonn**en**	beginnen
Separable Prefix	**ge** STEM	t	**ab**ge**holt**	abholen
		en	**an**ge**kommen**	ankommen

Note:

■ The stem may be:

the INFINITIVE stem	ge**stell**t, be**frag**t, ge**geb**en, ver**halt**en
the PAST TENSE stem	ge**brach**t, ge**schrieb**en
a new PAST PARTICIPLE stem	ge**nom**men (Infinitive: nehmen)
	be**gonn**en (Infinitive: beginnen)

■ For a list of INSEPARABLE PREFIXES (e.g.: be-, er-, ver-) and SEPARABLE PREFIXES (e.g.: ab-, ein-, vor-) see **R174**. For separable prefixes also see **R39**.

■ Past participles of verbs with inseparable prefixes can look like infinitives. See above, e.g. **ergeben, verhalten**.

■ Past participles of verbs with inseparable prefixes and verbs with a stem ending in **-ier** can look like present tense, 3rd person singular forms, e.g.

man	**erwartet**	*one expects*
man hat . . . **erwartet**		*one has expected*
man	**produziert**	*one produces*
man hat . . . **produziert**		*one has produced*

See the table in **R46** and consult **R170** for how to look up past participle forms in the dictionary. See **R39** and **R172** for past participles of verbs with SEPARABLE PREFIXES. See **R67** for past participles of MODAL VERBS.

R35 Verb Patterns in German and English

Compare the patterns verbs may follow. Some verbs follow the same pattern in both English and German:

1: the INFINITIVE STEM

2: the PAST TENSE STEM

3: a new PAST PARTICIPLE STEM

		INFINITIVE	PAST STEM	PAST PARTICIPLE
1 1 1	English:	*learn*	*learnt*	*learnt*
	German:	**lern**en	**lern**te	ge**lern**t

(Such 111 verbs are also referred to as WEAK verbs.)

		INFINITIVE	PAST STEM	PAST PARTICIPLE
1 2 2	English:	*bring*	*brought*	*brought*
	German:	**bring**en	**brach**te	ge**brach**t
1 2 3	English:	*sing*	*sang*	*sung*
	German:	**sing**en	**sang**	ge**sung**en
1 2 1	English:	*give*	*gave*	*given*
	German:	**geb**en	**gab**	ge**geb**en

However, not all verbs follow the same patterns in both languages:

1 2 2	English:	*find*	*found*	*found*
1 2 3	German:	**find**en	**fand**	ge**fund**en
1 2 2	English:	*sell*	*sold*	*sold*
1 1 1	German:	**verkauf**en	**verkauf**te	**verkauf**t (weak)
1 2 3	English:	*write*	*wrote*	*written*
1 2 2	German:	**schreib**en	**schrieb**	ge**schrieb**en
1 1 1	English:	*call*	*called*	*called* (weak)
1 2 1	German:	**ruf**en	**rief**	ge**ruf**en

R36 The Future Tense

	AUXILIARY		INFINITIVE
FUTURE I	Es **wird** die Temperatur leicht		**senken.** [T7:13]

		PAST PARTICIPLE	
FUTURE II	**wird**	**gesenkt**	**haben.**

*It **will lower (will have lowered)** the temperature slightly.*

FUTURE I is formed by a finite present tense form of the AUXILIARY **werden** (→R31) + the INFINITIVE of the main information-carrying verb.

Here are the third person forms:

> **wird**/**werden** + INFINITIVE
> *will*/*shall*   + *INFINITIVE*

In FUTURE II (a rare form) **werden** is combined with the PAST PARTICIPLE of the main information-carrying verb + **haben** or **sein**.

> **wird**/**werden** + PAST PARTICIPLE haben/sein
> *will*/*shall have* + *PAST PARTICIPLE*

Note: The main use of this construction is to express an assumption, e.g.

> Es **wird** die Temperatur **gesenkt haben**.
> *It is assumed that it has lowered the temperature.*

→**R3** and **R6** for the word order of compound tenses.

Note the word order in dependent clauses, e,g.

> e.g.: weil es die Temperatur **senken wird**.
> *because it **will lower** the temperature.*

Note: werden also has other functions. See **R163**.

R37 The Use of Tenses: Differences between English and German

Unlike English, German has only **one** verb form for each person in each tense. Special nuances, which in English are expressed by the use of the continuous form (*she is working*) or emphatic form (*she did work*) can be rendered in German by the use of ADVERBS, e.g.

> Ich las **gerade** als er kam.   *I was [just] reading when he came.*
> Schließlich schrieb ich den Brief **doch**.   *In the end I did write the letter.*
> Er hat ihn **wirklich** getroffen.   *He did [really] meet him.*

Even without the adverb, the verb may be emphatic or have a 'continuous' meaning. e.g.: Ich las, als er kam. *I was reading when he came.*

Thus a single German form may correspond to several English ones, e.g.

$$
\text{sie sagt} \begin{cases} \textit{she says} \\ \textit{she is saying} \\ \textit{she does say} \end{cases} \quad \text{sie sagte} \begin{cases} \textit{she said} \\ \textit{she was saying} \\ \textit{she did say} \end{cases} \quad \text{sie hat gesagt} \begin{cases} \textit{she has said} \\ \textit{she has been saying} \\ \textit{she said} \\ \textit{she did say} \\ \textit{she was saying} \end{cases}
$$

$$
\text{sie hatte gesagt} \begin{cases} \textit{she had said} \\ \textit{she had been saying} \end{cases} \quad \text{sie wird sagen} \begin{cases} \textit{she will say} \\ \textit{she will be saying} \end{cases}
$$

Be guided by the context.

R38 The Use of Tenses (II)

There are also some differences in the use of tenses (the most important ones are listed below) which necessitate a flexible approach in the interpretation of tenses. Note that it is necessary to attribute the appropriate English tense **according to context**.

The following gives the main areas in which German usage differs from English:

The PRESENT TENSE may be used to describe

a. events in the immediate/foreseeable future, e.g.

> Ich **lese** den Bericht später.
> *I **shall read** the report later.*

Sie **fährt** übernächstes Jahr nach England.
*She **will go** to England the year after next.*

b. events which began in the past but last up to the present, e.g.

Er **arbeitet** seit zwanzig Jahren an diesem Projekt.
*He **has been working** on the project for twenty years.*

Note that here **seit** (*for, since*) is usually used.

Unlike in English, the SIMPLE PAST and COMPOUND PAST I frequently overlap. Often the compound past I is used when an overall view/a summary of events is given in the introduction and/or final part of an account. The remainder of the text is written in the simple past tense, e.g.

Wie andere Industrieländer **hat** die Bundesrepublik Deutschland ihren politischen Weg im Zeichen des 'demokratischen Klassenkampfes' **begonnen**. So **nannte** damals der amerikanische Sozialwissenschaftler S. M. Lipset die zivilisierte, parlamentarisch verfaßte Auseinandersetzung zwischen 'bürgerlichen' und 'Arbeiterparteien', die sozusagen das letzte Überbleibsel des Kampfes der frühkapitalistischen Klassen **war**.

*Like other industrialized countries, the Federal Republic **began** (lit.: **has begun**) its political path under the auspices of the 'democratic class war'. That is what the American sociologist S. M. Lipset **called** the civilized dispute within the parliamentary framework between the 'bourgeois' and the 'workers'' parties which in a way **was** the last remnant of the early capitalist class war.*

The FUTURE TENSE may be used to express the attitude of the speaker towards the event described, such as the desirability that something should happen, e.g.

Besser als vom kirchlichen 'Amt' **wird** man in präziser biblischer Redeweise vom kirchlichen 'Dienst' **sprechen**.

Instead of a Church 'office' it is preferable to talk (lit.: one will better talk) in precise biblical style of ecclesiastical 'service'.

R39 Separable Verbs

FINITE VERB   PREFIX
Victor Hugo **kündigte** 1851 die Vereinigten Staaten von Europa **an**.   [T2:13]
kündigen means *to hand in one's notice, to dismiss, to discontinue*.
But **an**kündigen means *to announce, to herald*.
Victor Hugo prophesied (lit. *heralded*) in 1851 the United States of Europe.

A SEPARABLE PREFIX can be added to almost any basic verb in German, thus giving it a new meaning, e.g.

halten	*to hold*
anhalten	*to stop*
aushalten	*to endure*
vorhalten	*to reproach*
etc.	

A list of the most common prefixes is given in **R174**.

See **R171** on how to look up separable verbs in the dictionary.

Note:

■ It is in the present tense and the simple past tense that the prefix is separated from the verb and appears at the end of the clause. **→R6**

■ As prefixes of separable verbs vary in length it can be difficult to recognize them as prefixes (e.g. **an, zu, durch, auseinander, entgegen, gegenüber, zugrunde** etc.). As a matter of routine, check the end of the clause for any word that may be a separable prefix.

In the PAST PARTICIPLE (**→R34**) of separable verbs the **ge-** is enclosed between prefix and stem. In the compound past I the above sentence reads:

> Victor Hugo **hat** 1851 die Vereinigten Staaten von Europa **ange̲kündigt**.

Past participle forms of verbs ending in **-ieren** (**→R34**) with a separable prefix have no **ge-**, e.g.

> Sie hat zum Schluß auch **mitmusiziert**.
>   (musiz**ieren**   *to play a musical instrument;*
>   **mit**musiz**ieren**   *to join others playing a musical instrument*)
> *In the end she also joined in (in the music-making).*

In INFINITIVE constructions with **zu** (**→R154**) **zu** is enclosed between prefix and stem, e.g.

> , um das Konzert an**zu**kündigen.
> *, in order to announce the concert*

Very occasionally you may come across a word which looks like the prefix of a separable verb but in fact isn't, e.g.

> Mit der Industrialisierung verändert sich die soziale Landschaft von Grund **auf**. [T14:5]
>   (The fixed phrase **von Grund auf** means *entirely, completely*)
> *With the onset of industrialization, the social landscape changed completely.*

Here are a few others:

> **von Anfang an**   *right from the beginning*
> **von alters her**   *from time immemorial*
> **bis in die Nacht hinein** *till late at night*

R40 Verbs with a Reflexive Pronoun

> In der Mitte **befindet** **si̲ch** die Erde. [T6:3]
>   (**sich befinden** means *to be, to be situated/located*)
> *In the middle is the earth.*
> Diese Zahl hat **si̲ch** nur unwesentlich **verändert**. [T13:2]
>   (**sich verändern** means *to change*)
> *This figure has changed only insignificantly.*

A great number of German verbs are used with a REFLEXIVE PRONOUN.

REFLEXIVE PRONOUNS

ich	**mich/mir**	*myself*
du	**dich/dir**	*yourself*
er, sie, es, man	**sich**	*himself, herself, itself, oneself*
wir	**uns**	*ourselves*
ihr	**euch**	*yourselves*
sie, Sie	**sich**	*themselves, yourselves*

Some verbs always have a reflexive pronoun as an integral part of the phrase, e.g.

sich ereignen	*to happen*
sich entschließen	*to decide*
sich begnügen	*to be content/satisfied*

Many other verbs can be used either with or without a reflexive pronoun, e.g.

ändern	*to change (something)*
sich ändern	*to change [lit. itself]*
zeigen	*to show (something)*
sich zeigen	*to appear*
durchsetzen	*to push through (something, e.g. a plan)*
sich durchsetzen	*to assert oneself, to be successful*

Note that the meaning of these verbs may change if they have a reflexive pronoun, e.g.

Der Betrieb beschäftigt 350 Leute.
  (beschäftigen *to employ*)
*The company employs **350** people.*
Bach beschäftigte sich nie mit dieser Form. [T8:4]
  (**sich beschäftigen mit** *to 'occupy' oneself with*)
Bach never dealt with/used/occupied himself with this form.

R41 Three Possibilities

If **sich** or any of the other REFLEXIVE PRONOUNS given above appear be prepared for three possibilities:

1. The German reflexive pronoun may sometimes have an equivalent in English e.g.

   Er distanzierte **sich** von den anderen. [T15:7]
   *He dissociated **himself** from the others.*

2. More frequently, however, the corresponding English phrase will not be a reflexive one, e.g.

   Deshalb verschlechterte **sich** die Situation.
     (**sich verschlechtern** *to worsen [itself]*)
   Therefore the situation worsened.

Here **sich** has no equivalent meaning of its own in English.

It is, however, crucial to recognize the reflexive pronoun as an indicator of the German reflexive form, since a verb used reflexively may have a different meaning from the non-reflexive form of the same verb, e.g.

Der Richter verhörte den Zeugen.
  (verhören *to question/examine/interrogate*)
The judge examined/questioned the witness.

Der Richter verhörte **sich**.
(**sich verhören** *to mishear, to hear wrongly*)
The judge misheard.

Note, however, that only **sich** is a distinct reflexive form. All other reflexive pronouns also have other functions (**→R98**), e.g.

Wir bemühen **uns**, das Problem zu lösen.
(**sich bemühen** *to endeavour, to try hard*)
We are trying hard to solve the problem.

BUT:

Er bemüht **uns** nie mit Kleinigkeiten.
(**jemanden bemühen** *to trouble, bother someone*)
*He never bothers **us** with details.*

If you are not sure whether a pronoun is a reflexive one, check in the dictionary whether a reflexive meaning is given for the verb in question and if that meaning fits the context.

→R168 on how to look up reflexive verbs in the dictionary.

3. Occasionally the meaning of **sich/uns/euch** is: *each other, one another*, e.g.

Planung und Freiheit schließen **sich** aus. [T19:2]
*Planning and freedom **exclude each other**.*

Thus the meaning of **sich** can be ambiguous, e.g.

Sie beschuldigten **sich**.

could mean: *They accused **themselves**.*
or: *They accused **each other**.*

Be guided by the context!

If the word **gegenseitig** appears in combination with **sich** the meaning is always *each other, one another*, e.g.

Sie beschuldigten **sich gegenseitig**.   *They accused each other.*

→R78.3 for **lassen + sich** and REFLEXIVE VERBS with a passive meaning.

In main clauses **sich** usually follows the finite verb. Note the word order in dependent clauses:

  , weil das Metall **sich** bei höherer Temperatur ausdehnt, [T7:7]
or: , weil **sich** das Metall bei höherer Temperatur ausdehnt,
or: , weil das Metall bei höherer Temperatur **sich** ausdehnt,
  , because the metal expands at a higher temperature,

R42 Verb Idioms with 'es'

Some verbs can be used in combination with the impersonal pronoun **es**. The meaning of such constructions usually differs from the original meaning of the verb. It is given in the dictionary under the entry for the verb.

es gibt keinen größeren Feind [T16:18]
There is no bigger enemy

geben means *to give*. But **es gibt** means *there is/are*.

The noun which is used with **es gibt** is in the ACCUSATIVE (→**R97**)

> **Es handelt sich** hier **um** eine absichtliche Suggestion. [T9:5]
> *This is an intended suggestion.*

handeln means to *act, to trade*. But **es handelt sich um** means *something is about/is a question/matter of something*. Lit.: *Here it is a matter of an intended suggestion.*

> Hier **geht es um** dasselbe Prinzip.
> *Here we are dealing with the same principle.*

gehen means *to go*. But **es geht um** means *it is about, it concerns*

Lit.: *Here it concerns the same principle.*

→**R175** for constructions consisting of VERB + PREPOSITION.

Note that these phrases are used in all tense forms, e.g.

> Damals **gab es** nur Dorfstraßen.
> *At that time there were only village streets.*
> Seitdem **hat es** Veränderungen **gegeben**.
> *Since then there have been changes.*

Note:

1. Sometimes **es** is omitted, e.g.

> **es** ist ihm klar, daß . . .
> or: ihm ist klar, daß . . .
> *it is clear to him that*
> Obwohl ihm dabei klar sein muß, daß . . . [T21:6]
> Lit.: *Although to him must be clear that . . .*
> *Although it must be clear to him that . . .*

> **es** fällt uns nicht schwer [T16:14] could read:
> uns fällt nicht schwer
> (schwerfallen *to be difficult*)
> Lit.: *to us is not difficult. It is not difficult for us*

For PASSIVE constructions with an omitted **es** →**R79.3**.

2. Sometimes **es** is a kind of token subject →**R10.4**:

> **es** wird die Täuschung aufrechterhalten, [T19:2]
> has the same meaning as:
> die Täuschung wird aufrechterhalten
> *the deception is maintained*

In some of these constructions the 'real subject' for the English reader appears as a dative pronoun →**R98**:

> **es** fällt **uns** schwer [T16:14]
> (**schwerfallen** *to be difficult*)
> *it is difficult **for us***
> *we find it difficult*
> **es** gelingt **uns**
> (**gelingen** *to succeed*)
> *we succeed*

For other functions of **es** also see **R163**.

R43 The present participle

The PRESENT PARTICIPLE in German is formed by adding **-d** to the infinitive of the verb, e.g.

> lernen**d**
> denken**d**

The present participle is used in certain phrases described in **R157** and in EXTENDED ADJECTIVE PHRASES. (→**R115–116**).

R44 Summary: Spotting the Finite Verb

FACTUAL forms only. For NON-FACTUAL forms see **R62**.

Scan the sentence for words in FINITE VERB POSITION (→**R1**) with the following

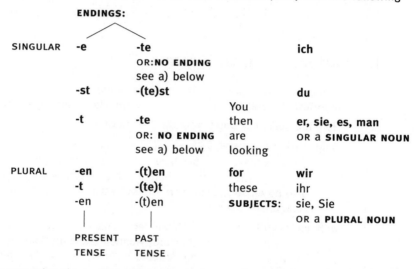

	ENDINGS:			
SINGULAR	**-e**	**-te** OR:**NO ENDING** see a) below		**ich**
	-st	**-(te)st**		**du**
	-t	**-te** OR: **NO ENDING** see a) below	You then are looking	**er, sie, es, man** OR a **SINGULAR NOUN**
PLURAL	**-en**	**-(t)en**	for	**wir**
	-t	**-(te)t**	these	ihr
	-en	**-(t)en**	**SUBJECTS:**	sie, Sie OR a **PLURAL NOUN**
	PRESENT TENSE	PAST TENSE		

When scanning the sentence note the presence of any of these pronouns: **ich, du, er, man, wir**. Whenever they appear they are the SUBJECT of the clause and as such determine the verb ending.

SINGULAR SUBJECT ←——→ SINGULAR VERB
PLURAL SUBJECT ←——→ PLURAL VERB

sie, es, ihr, Sie can be either the SUBJECT or an OBJECT (→**R98**.) Check their position within the clause (→**R4**), e.g.

> . . . damit wird **sie** es besser machen. [T7:16]
> . . . and so **she** will do **it** better.

If **es** appears in subject position you may be dealing with a VERB IDIOM with es. (→**R42**)

If there is no subject pronoun in the clause, the subject will be a SINGULAR NOUN or a PLURAL NOUN and the verb will have the appropriate endings as given in the table above.

Note that very occasionally there are words which might be mistaken for verbs since they end in the same letters. e.g. **zuletzt** *(in the end, last)*, **zunächst** *(first)*, **hingegen** *(however)*, etc.

If none of the above endings is present you may be dealing with

a. strong singular past tense forms, i.e. verb forms WITHOUT ENDING. e.g.: las, zog, half, bog, hieß, drang, lag, bat, trug, schien (→R30)

b. an AUXILIARY VERB (→R31) or a MODAL VERB (→R66) FAMILIARIZE YOURSELF WITH THESE FORMS.

Note:

1. Verb STEMS vary considerably in length, e.g.

    tut *(does)*, **gratulier**t *(congratulates)*

2. Strong plural forms in the simple past tense can be mistaken for present tense forms, e.g.

| SIMPLE PAST TENSE | kamen | lasen | warfen | hoben | liehen | rieten |
| PRESENT TENSE | kommen | lesen | werfen | heben | leihen | raten |

3. **sein** as well as **haben** is used as an auxiliary to form the compound past tense (→R33).

R45 Interpreting verb forms

It is important to interpret the verb forms correctly. In cases where verb endings are **identical** the presence of a pronoun in the clause identifies the personal form.

Here are some examples from the Text Corpus:

zeigt [T19:7] (infinitive: zeigen) could be a second person (informal) plural *(you show)*, but in context it is obviously 3rd person singular, because there is no pronoun **ihr** present in the sentence. Therefore it definitely is 3rd person singular. Since there is also no **er, sie, es,** or **man**, the subject is a noun: dieser Vergleich zei**g**t *(this comparison shows)*.

wohnen [T14:8] (infinitive: wohnen) 'en' signals infinitive or if in finite position (→R1) 1st or 3rd person plural. In [14:8] **wohnen** takes up finite position, but there is no pronoun. Therefore: die Arbeiter wohn**en** *(the workers live)*.

wächst [T14:2] (infinitive: wach**s**en) '**s**' is part of the verb stem and, of course, there is no pronoun **du**. The subject is therefore a singular noun: die Schwerindustrie. Therefore: die Schwerindustrie wäch**st** *(the heavy industry grows)*.

sagte [T2:9] (infinitive: sagen) '**te**' is 1st or 3rd person singular, but there is no **ich**. Therefore the subject is 3rd person singular. Since there is also no 3rd person pronoun, the subject has to be a noun: der Premierminister sag**te** *(the prime minister said)*.

dachte [T10b:8] (infinitive: **d**enken) Here there is an **ich**. ich dach**te** *(I thought)*. This is a mixed verb.

folgten [T2:15] (infinitive: folgen) No **wir**, therefore 3rd person plural: Neue Kriege fol**gten** *(New wars followed)*.

kam [T16:8] (infinitive: kommen) No ending, therefore 1st or 3rd person singular. There is, however, no **ich**, therefore: der Einfall kam *(the idea came)*.

nahm [T2:17] (infinitive: **n**ehmen) There is the pronoun **man**: man nahm *(one took)*.

erfand [T3:2] (infinitive: erfinden) No ending, therefore 1st or 3rd person singular. There is, however, no **ich**, therefore 3rd person singular: Gutenberg erfand *(Gutenberg invented)*. See **R174** for PREFIXES like **er-**.

gaben [T4:2] (infinitive: **geben**) 1st or 3rd person plural. But there is no **wir**, therefore it must be 3rd person. At a first glance, however, you cannot tell whether this is a past or present tense. You need to consult the table in **R46** or your dictionary to find the infinitive (**geben**): diese Erfindungen gaben *(these inventions gave)*.

R46 List of Strong, Mixed, and Irregular Verbs

Most verbs are listed here, but for very rare and outdated forms consult the List of Strong, Mixed, and Irregular Verbs in your dictionary.

Note that only the basic verb, i.e. without prefixes, is given. See **R169** and **R174** for how to look up verbs with prefixes.

INFINITIVE →R21	PRESENT TENSE FACTUAL →R28 3rd person singular	SIMPLE PAST TENSE FACTUAL →R29 and →R30 3rd person singular	SUBJUNCTIVE II NON-FACTUAL →R48 3rd person singular	PAST PARTICIPLE
befehlen	befiehlt	befahl	befähle/beföhle	befohlen
beginnen	beginnt	begann	begänne	begonnen
beißen	beißt	biß	bisse	gebissen
bergen	birgt	barg	bärge	geborgen
bersten	birst	barst	bärste	geborsten
bewegen	bewegt	bewog	bewöge	bewogen
biegen	biegt	bog	böge	gebogen
bieten	bietet	bot	böte	geboten
binden	bindet	band	bände	gebunden
bitten	bittet	bat	bäte	gebeten
blasen	bläst	blies	bliese	geblasen
bleiben	bleibt	blieb	bliebe	geblieben
braten	brät	briet	briete	gebraten
brechen	bricht	brach	bräche	gebrochen
brennen	brennt	brannte	brennte	gebrannt
bringen	bringt	brachte	brächte	gebracht
denken	denkt	dachte	dächte	gedacht
dingen	dingt	dang	dänge/dingte	gedungen
dreschen	drischt	drosch	drösche	gedroschen
dringen	dringt	drang	dränge	gedrungen
dürfen	darf	durfte	dürfte	gedurft
empfangen	empfängt	empfing	empfinge	empfangen
empfehlen	empfiehlt	empfahl	empfähle/empföhle	empfohlen
empfinden	empfindet	empfand	empfände	empfunden
essen	ißt	aß	äße	gegessen
fahren	fährt	fuhr	führe	gefahren
fallen	fällt	fiel	fiele	gefallen
fangen	fängt	fing	finge	gefangen
fechten	ficht	focht	föchte	gefochten
finden	findet	fand	fände	gefunden
flechten	flicht	flocht	flöchte	geflochten
fliegen	fliegt	flog	flöge	geflogen

INFINITIVE	PRESENT TENSE FACTUAL	SIMPLE PAST TENSE FACTUAL	SUBJUNCTIVE II NON-FACTUAL	PAST PARTICIPLE
→R21	→R28	→R29 and →R30	→R48	
	3rd person singular	3rd person singular	3rd person singular	
fliehen	flieht	floh	flöhe	geflohen
fließen	fließt	floß	flösse	geflossen
fressen	frißt	fraß	fräße	gefressen
frieren	friert	fror	fröre	gefroren
gären	gärt	gor	göre	gegoren
gebären	gebiert	gebar	gebäre	geboren
geben	gibt	gab	gäbe	gegeben
gedeihen	gedeiht	gedieh	gediehe	gediehen
gehen	geht	ging	ginge	gegangen
gelingen	gelingt	gelang	gelänge	gelungen
gelten	gilt	galt	gälte/gölte	gegolten
genesen	genest	genas	genäse	genesen
genießen	genießt	genoß	genösse	genossen
geschehen	geschieht	geschah	geschähe	geschehen
gewinnen	gewinnt	gewann	gewänne	gewonnen
gießen	gießt	goß	gösse	gegossen
gleichen	gleicht	glich	gliche	geglichen
gleiten	gleitet	glitt	glitte	geglitten
glimmen	glimmt	glomm	glömme	geglommen
graben	gräbt	grub	grübe	gegraben
greifen	greift	griff	griffe	gegriffen
haben	hat	hatte	hätte	gehabt
halten	hält	hielt	hielte	gehalten
hängen	hängt	hing	hinge	gehangen
heben	hebt	hob	höbe/hübe	gehoben
heißen	heißt	hieß	hieße	geheißen
helfen	hilft	half	hülfe/hälfe	geholfen
kennen	kennt	kannte	kennte	gekannt
klimmen	klimmt	klomm	klömme	geklommen
klingen	klingt	klang	klänge	geklungen
kneifen	kneift	kniff	kniffe	gekniffen
kommen	kommt	kam	käme	gekommen
können	kann	konnte	könnte	gekonnt
kriechen	kriecht	kroch	kröche	gekrochen
küren	kürt	kor	köre	gekürt/gekoren
laden	lädt	lud	lüde	geladen
lassen	läßt	ließ	ließe	gelassen
laufen	läuft	lief	liefe	gelaufen
leiden	leidet	litt	litte	gelitten
leihen	leiht	lieh	liehe	geliehen
lesen	liest	las	läse	gelesen
liegen	liegt	lag	läge	gelegen
löschen	lischt	losch	lösche	geloschen
lügen	lügt	log	löge	gelogen
meiden	meidet	mied	miede	gemieden
melken	melkt/milkt	molk	mölke	gemolken
messen	mißt	maß	mäße	gemessen
mißlingen	mißlingt	mißlang	mißlänge	mißlungen

INFINITIVE →R21	PRESENT TENSE FACTUAL →R28 3rd person singular	SIMPLE PAST TENSE FACTUAL →R29 and →R30 3rd person singular	SUBJUNCTIVE II NON-FACTUAL →R48 3rd person singular	PAST PARTICIPLE
mögen	mag	mochte	möchte	gemocht
müssen	muß	mußte	müßte	gemußt
nehmen	nimmt	nahm	nähme	genommen
nennen	nennt	nannte	nennte	genannt
pfeifen	pfeift	pfiff	pfiffe	gepfiffen
preisen	preist	pries	priese	gepriesen
quellen	quillt	quoll	quölle	gequollen
raten	rät	riet	riete	geraten
reiben	reibt	rieb	riebe	gerieben
reißen	reißt	riß	risse	gerissen
reiten	reitet	ritt	ritte	geritten
rennen	rennt	rannte	rennte	gerannt
riechen	riecht	roch	röche	gerochen
ringen	ringt	rang	ränge	gerungen
rinnen	rinnt	rann	ränne	geronnen
rufen	ruft	rief	riefe	gerufen
saufen	säuft	soff	söffe	gesoffen
saugen	saugt	sog	söge	gesogen
schaffen	schafft	schuf	schüfe	geschaffen
scheiden	scheidet	schied	schiede	geschieden
scheinen	scheint	schien	schiene	geschienen
scheißen	scheißt	schiß	schisse	geschissen
schelten	schilt	schalt	schölte	gescholten
scheren	schert	schor	schöre	geschoren
schieben	schiebt	schob	schöbe	geschoben
schießen	schießt	schoß	schösse	geschossen
schlafen	schläft	schlief	schliefe	geschlafen
schlagen	schlägt	schlug	schlüge	geschlagen
schleichen	schleicht	schlich	schliche	geschlichen
schleifen	schleift	schliff	schliffe	geschliffen
schleißen	schleißt	schliß	schlisse	geschlissen
schließen	schließt	schloß	schlösse	geschlossen
schlingen	schlingt	schlang	schlänge	geschlungen
schmeißen	schmeißt	schmiß	schmisse	geschmissen
schmelzen	schmilzt	schmolz	schmölze	geschmolzen
schneiden	schneidet	schnitt	schnitte	geschnitten
schrecken	schrickt	schrak	schräke	geschrocken
schreiben	schreibt	schrieb	schriebe	geschrieben
schreien	schreit	schrie	schrie	geschrieen
schreiten	schreitet	schritt	schritte	geschritten
schweigen	schweigt	schwieg	schwiege	geschwiegen
schwellen	schwillt	schwoll	schwölle	geschwollen
schwimmen	schwimmt	schwamm	schwömme	geschwommen
schwinden	schwindet	schwand	schwände	geschwunden
schwingen	schwingt	schwang	schwänge	geschwungen
schwören	schwört	schwor	schwüre	geschworen
sehen	sieht	sah	sähe	gesehen
sein	ist	war	wäre	gewesen
senden	sendet	sandte	sendete	gesendet/gesandt
singen	singt	sang	sänge	gesungen

INFINITIVE	PRESENT TENSE FACTUAL	SIMPLE PAST TENSE FACTUAL	SUBJUNCTIVE II NON-FACTUAL	PAST PARTICIPLE
→R21	→R28	→R29 and →R30	→R48	
	3rd person singular	3rd person singular	3rd person singular	
sinken	sinkt	sank	sänke	gesunken
sinnen	sinnt	sann	sänne	gesonnen
sitzen	sitzt	saß	säße	gesessen
sollen	soll	sollte	sollte	gesollt
spinnen	spinnt	spann	spänne/spönne	gesponnen
sprechen	spricht	sprach	spräche	gesprochen
sprießen	sprießt	sproß	sprösse	gesprossen
springen	springt	sprang	spränge	gesprungen
stechen	sticht	stach	stäche	gestochen
stecken	steckt	stak	steckte/stäke	gesteckt
stehen	steht	stand	stände/stünde	gestanden
stehlen	stiehlt	stahl	stähle	gestohlen
steigen	steigt	stieg	stiege	gestiegen
sterben	stirbt	starb	stürbe	gestorben
stieben	stiebt	stob	stöbe	gestoben
stinken	stinkt	stank	stänke	gestunken
stoßen	stößt	stieß	stieße	gestoßen
streichen	streicht	strich	striche	gestrichen
streiten	streitet	stritt	stritte	gestritten
tragen	trägt	trug	trüge	getragen
treffen	trifft	traf	träfe	getroffen
treiben	treibt	trieb	triebe	getrieben
treten	tritt	trat	träte	getreten
triefen	trieft	troff	tröffe	getrieft/getroffen
trinken	trinkt	trank	tränke	getrunken
trügen	trügt	trog	tröge	getrogen
tun	tut	tat	täte	getan
verderben	verdirbt	verdarb	verdürbe	verdorben
verdrießen	verdrießt	verdroß	verdrösse	verdrossen
vergessen	vergißt	vergaß	vergäße	vergessen
verlieren	verliert	verlor	verlöre	verloren
verzeihen	verzeiht	verzieh	verziehe	verziehen
wachsen	wächst	wuchs	wüchse	gewachsen
wägen	wägt	wog	wöge	gewogen
waschen	wäscht	wusch	wüsche	gewaschen
weben	webt	wob	wöbe	gewoben
weichen	weicht	wich	wiche	gewichen
weisen	weist	wies	wiese	gewiesen
wenden	wendet	wandte	wendete	gewandt
werben	wirbt	warb	würbe	geworben
werden	wird	wurde/ward	würde	geworden/worden
werfen	wirft	warf	würfe	geworfen
wiegen	wiegt	wog	wöge	gewogen
winden	windet	wand	wände	gewunden
wissen	weiß	wußte	wüßte	gewußt
wollen	will	wollte	wollte	gewollt
wringen	wringt	wrang	wränge	gewrungen
ziehen	zieht	zog	zöge	gezogen
zwingen	zwingt	zwang	zwänge	gezwungen

Verbs (Non-Factual Expressions)

R47 Non-Factual Statements

The verb forms given in **R27–42** are used for factual statements. This chapter deals with the verb forms used when the writer wants to make a hypothetical statement or to show that he or she is simply passing on someone else's words:

FACTUAL

> Dies **ist** eine unnötige Einschränkung.
> *This is an unnecessary restriction.*

NON-FACTUAL

> (Jemand behauptet,) dies **sei** eine unnötige Einschränkung.
> *(Someone claims that) this is an unnecessary restriction.*
>
> (Jemand behauptete,) dies **sei** eine unnötige Einschränkung.
> *(Someone claimed that) this is/was an unnecessary restriction.*
>
> Dies **wäre** eine unnötige Einschränkung. [**T19:4**]
> Dies **würde** eine unnötige Einschränkung **sein**.
> *This would be an unnecessary restriction.*

The various 'non-factual' forms of verbs can be put to a number of uses and for some of these uses, practice varies from one writer to another. Accordingly, this section is divided into two main parts: forms and uses. It is important first to be able to recognize the non-factual forms, and then to know the ways in which these forms are used in particular situations.

R48 Non-Factual Forms

Note how minor changes in the form of the verb can signal a fundamental change in its meaning.

	FACTUAL		NON-FACTUAL		
	Present	Past	Subjunctive I	Subjunctive II	würde-Phrase
(man)	**gibt**	**gab**	**gebe**	**gäbe**	**würde geben**

Note:

1. Subjunctive II and würde-phrase are identical in meaning.

2. Some grammars refer to 'present subjunctive' for subjunctive I, and 'imperfect subjunctive' for subjunctive II. This is misleading because e.g. 'gäbe' is NOT the past tense of 'gebe'.

3. In written German, non-factual forms are found mostly in the 3rd person (the form

found with **er/sie/es, man,** or a noun as the subject), although the same form is used for the third person singular and the 1st person singular (**ich**). Note the following pattern of differences between 'factual' and 'non-factual' forms:

	FACTUAL		NON-FACTUAL		
	PRESENT	PAST	SUBJ. I	SUBJ. II (=)	würde-phrase
(man)	ist	war	sei	wäre	würde sein
(man)	hat	hatte	habe	hätte	würde haben
(man)	wird	wurde	werde	würde	würde werden

WEAK VERBS (→R26)

	STEM + t	STEM + te	STEM + e	STEM + te	
(man)	macht	machte	mache	machte	würde machen
(man)	lernt	lernte	lerne	lernte	würde lernen

STRONG VERBS (→26)

	STEM + t	PAST STEM	STEM + e	PAST STEM [+¨] + e	
(man)	kommt	kam	komme	käme	würde kommen
(man)	geht	ging	gehe	ginge	würde gehen
(man)	bringt	brachte	bringe	brächte	würde bringen

MODAL VERBS (→R66)

(man)	darf	durfte	dürfe	dürfte	würde dürfen
(man)	kann	konnte	könne	könnte	würde können
(man)	mag	mochte	möge	möchte	würde mögen
(man)	muß	mußte	müsse	müßte	würde müssen
(man)	soll	sollte	solle	sollte	würde sollen
(man)	will	wollte	wolle	wollte	würde wollen

The above table shows only the **er/sie/es** forms. Here are some examples of a complete set of non-factual forms:

Singular:	ich		sei	wäre	ginge	würde . . .
	du		sei**est**	wär**est**	ging**est**	würd**est** . . .
	er/sie/es/man etc.		sei	wäre	ginge	würde . . .
Plural:	wir		sei**en**	wär**en**	ging**en**	würd**en** . . .
	ihr		sei**et**	wär**et**	ging**et**	würd**et** . . .
	sie		sei**en**	wär**en**	ging**en**	würd**en** . . .
Formal 'you':	Sie		sei**en**	wär**en**	ging**en**	würd**en** . . .

The following are examples of non-factual forms:

SUBJUNCTIVE I: er habe; du habest; es komme; man lerne; ihr habet

SUBJUNCTIVE II: ich käme; es ginge; du möchtest; wir könnten; ihr hättet

R49 Identical forms (Importance of Context)

Weak verbs do not have a distinctive form in subjunctive II:

	FACTUAL		NON-FACTUAL		
	PRESENT	PAST	SUBJ. I	SUBJ. II (=)	würde-phrase
(man)	macht	**machte**	mache	**machte**	würde machen
(man)	lernt	**lernte**	lerne	**lernte**	würde lernen
(man)	stellt	**stellte**	stelle	**stellte**	würde stellen

Note: The highlighted forms are exactly the same for the factual past tense and the non-factual subjunctive II. On the rare occasions when these forms are used 'non-factually', it is the context which makes this obvious, e.g.

Wir **stellten** Verkehrssignale auf, wenn . . .

In this example, 'stellten . . . auf' could mean 'did put up' or 'would put up'. It is best to assume such verb forms are factual unless the context suggests otherwise. It is non-factual if there is a non-factual verb form in the accompanying clause.

Compare: Wir **stellten** Verkehrssignale auf, wenn es nötig **wäre**. [T19: 4]
We would install traffic lights if it were necessary.

and: Wir **stellten** Verkehrssignale auf, wenn es nötig **war**.
We installed traffic lights when it was necessary.

R50 Past Tenses

None of the non-factual verb forms given in **R48–9** is a past tense. Never read a form such as **käme** or **wäre** *on its own* as a past tense: it **always** refers to the present or the future. The past tense forms are fairly easy to recognize:

VERB	FACTUAL	NON-FACTUAL		würde-phrase
	PAST TENSES	SUBJ. I	SUBJ. II	
kommen	kam OR	**sei** gekommen	**wäre** gekommen	würde
	ist gekommen			gekommen sein
geben	gab OR	**habe** gegeben	**hätte** gegeben	würde
	hat gegeben			gegeben haben

It needs to be understood that **wäre gekommen** is not a past tense of **sei gekommen**, and **hätte gegeben** is not a past tense of **habe gegeben**. These forms are used for different purposes (→**R52**).

R51 Non-Factual Forms of Modal Verbs

These have already been set out (→**R48**). There are three points to note.

1. The forms **wollte** and **sollte** may be factual or non-factual:

| (man) soll | **sollte** | solle | **sollte** | würde sollen |
| (man) will | **wollte** | wolle | **wollte** | würde wollen |

See the guidance on reading identical forms, above (→**R49**).

2. The subjunctive II forms of the other modal verbs differ from the factual past tense only in having an umlaut. Note how a slight change in form produces a significant change in meaning:

könnte	*could (possibly)*	müßte	*would have to*	dürfte	*may well*
konnte	*could (was able to)*	mußte	*had to*	durfte	*was allowed to*

The modal verbs have a wide and unpredictable range of meanings. See **R69**.

3. 'WOULD HAVE', 'COULD HAVE', 'SHOULD HAVE' . . .

Es **hätte** keine deutlichere Korrelation **geben können**. [T16:7]
There could not have been a clearer correlation.

. . ., weil es keine deutlichere Korrelation **hätte geben können**.
. . ., because there could not have been a clearer correlation.

Note the distinctive word order (compare the 'normal' word order, ➔**R1**).

R52 Uses and Forms of Non-Factual verbs

The following sections (**R53–61**) are organized according to the uses which the non-factual forms have. Here is an overview:

	USE	FORM INVOLVED
R53	CONDITIONAL STATEMENTS	mainly subjunctive II
R54–6	INDIRECT REPORTS	both subjunctive I and II
R57	'LET IT BE'	mainly subjunctive I
R58	INSTRUCTIONS	subjunctive I
R59	'als ob' ('as if')	mainly subjunctive II
R60	'damit' ('so that')	mainly subjunctive I
R61	WISHES	both subjunctive I and II

R53 Conditional Statements (mainly subjunctive II)

■ Some express what *would* (have) happen(ed) if . . .

Ein Krieg **könnte** in Europa ausbrechen. [T2:3]
A war could break out in Europe.

Ich **wäre** Ihnen dankbar, wenn . . . [T10a:9]
I would be grateful to you if . . .

The würde-phrase carries exactly the same meaning:

Wir **würden** Verkehrssignale **aufstellen**, wenn . . . [T19:4]
We would instal traffic lights if . . .

. . . wenn Europa sein Erbe **verwalten würde**, dann . . . [T2: 5]
. . . if Europe were to look after its inheritance, then . . .

Note that an 'if-clause' can begin with the verb in German (➔**R16**):

(Und) **wäre** es nichts [T22:5]
(Even) if it were nothing.

Conditonals occur in questions, too:

> **Hätte** es eine deutlichere Korrelation geben können? [T16:7]
> *Could there have been a clearer correlation?*

■ 'IF ONLY . . .': Often the conditional expresses an unfulfilled wish:

> **Hätte** es nur diesen furchtbaren Krieg nicht gegeben, dann . . .
> *If only there hadn't been this terrible war, then . . .*
> Wären die Alliierten doch nur einen Tag früher gekommen, so . . .
> *If only the Allies had come one day earlier, then . . .*

Often these statements contain 'nur' and/or 'doch', and the linked clause often begins with 'dann' or 'so'.

R54 Indirect reports (both subjunctive I and II)

> Compare: Milch **kann** krebserregend sein.
> *Milk can/may be carcinogenic.*

> and: **a.** Der Verdacht . . . , daß Milch krebserregend sein **kann**.
> Der Verdacht . . . , Milch **kann** krebserregend sein.
> **b1.** Der Verdacht . . . , Milch **könne** krebserregend sein. [T16:1]
> **b2.** Der Verdacht . . . , Milch **könnte** krebserregend sein.

A writer reporting someone else's assertion, belief, suspicion, etc that 'milk can be carcinogenic' can choose between:

a. the 'factual' form of the verb (here, **kann**). This tends to imply that the writer accepts the statement s/he is reporting as true or likely.

b. a 'non-factual' form of the verb. There is a potential difference between the two non-factual forms here:

> **b1.** Subjunctive I (**könne**) marks the statement in a neutral way as coming not from the writer but from another source.

> **b2.** Subjunctive II (**könnte**) emphasizes the speculative nature of the reported remark and may signal that the writer is sceptical about the truth of the statement she or he is reporting.

However, this potential difference in nuance is not observed by some writers, who use subjunctive II indiscriminately for all indirect reporting. Be wary about jumping to conclusions about the writer's own standpoint, especially when s/he uses subjunctive II everywhere.

Note that these non-factual verbs are in Position II (➔**R3**).

R55 Indirect Reports Introduced by Verbs or Nouns

■ Reports may be introduced by verbs of saying or thinking:

> Der Verdacht **wurde geäußert**, . . . [T16:1] *The suspicion was voiced (that) . . .*
> Diese Firmen **geben an**, . . . [T20:5] *These companies report (that) . . .*

■ But they can also be introduced by nouns such as **Bericht** (*report*), **Gedanke** (*thought*), **Behauptung** (*assertion*), **Gerücht** (*rumour*):

> Der **Verdacht**, Milch **könne** . . .
> *The suspicion (that) . . .*

> Die **Annahme**, ein Tonstück **müsse** Vorstellungen erwecken, . . . [T21:2]
> *The assumption that music has to awaken ideas . . .*

> Die **Auffassung**, die deutsche Wirtschaft **habe** das Weltniveau verloren, . . .
> *The view that German industry has lost its world class . . .*

R56 Indirect Reports with No Introductory Verb or Noun

> Churchill wollte 1946 eine Art Vereinigter Staaten von Europa schaffen. Der Weg dahin **sei** einfach. [T2:7]
> *Churchill wanted to create a kind of United States of Europe in 1946. (He said that) the path to this goal was simple.*

> Seine Gegner drehten den Spieß um. Er **dürfe** das Amt nicht ausüben, weil . . . [T15:9]
> *His opponents turned the tables. (They said that) he was not allowed to hold this office because . . .*

R57 'Let it Be' (mainly subjunctive I)

> Dies **sei** durch einen Vergleich veranschaulicht. [T19:3]
> *Let this be illustrated by a comparison.*

> ABC **sei** ein gleichschenkiges Dreieck.
> *Let ABC be an isosceles triangle.*

R58 Instructions (subjunctive I)

> Man **nehme** drei Eier.
> *Take three eggs.*

R59 'als ob' and 'als' ('as if') (mainly subjunctive II)

> Die Ideologen tun so, als ob sie die Möglichkeit **hätten**, . . . [T19:8]
> *The ideologues are acting as if they had the possibility of . . .*

Where 'als' is used in this sense, the word order is:

> Die Ideologen tun so, als **hätten** sie die Möglichkeit, . . . [T19:8]

Note the idiom **so tun, als ob** . . .: *to pretend that . . ., act as if.*

R60 damit (*in order that*) (mainly factual forms, but also subjunctive I and II)

(For other uses of **damit** see **R163**)

> Die Musik muß umgewandelt werden, damit der Mensch sie hören **kann**.
> or: Die Musik muß umgewandelt werden, damit der Mensch sie hören **könne**.
> *Music has to be transformed so that people can hear it.* [T5:6]

R61 Wishes (both subjunctive I and II)

> Wäre er doch am Leben!
> *If only he were alive!*
>
> Lange möge er leben!
> *Long may he live!*

R62 Non-Factual Verbs: Summary

The possibility that there is a 'non-factual' verb which affects the meaning of the text should be considered when:

1. THE VERB ENDS IN -E INSTEAD OF -T, AND THE PRONOUN **ich** is not in the context,
   or: the verb is **sei, wäre, hätte, würde**,
   or: one of these verbs is in a neighbouring clause.

2. there is a verb of speaking or thinking introducing the clause (e.g. **behaupten**).

3. there is a noun implying a report is being introduced (e.g. **Behauptung**).

4. THERE IS AN 'IF-CLAUSE' BEGINNING WITH **wenn** or **wenn auch** (or the clause begins with a verb but there is no question mark at the end).

Take care to recognize minor changes in the verb form—especially the presence or absence of an umlaut. Once a 'non-factual' verb has been identified, look carefully at the whole context before interpreting it.

Modal Verbs

R63 The Six Modal Verbs

There are six MODAL VERBS in German:

dürfen können mögen müssen sollen wollen

e.g.:

Die Studenten **dürfen** Krakehl **machen**. [T10b:10]
*The students **are allowed** to **make** a noise.*

Sie **können** die Musik **hören**. [T5:6]
*They **can hear** the music.*

Das **mag** mit der Wiedervereinigung **zusammenhängen**. [T1:9]
*This **may be connected/have something to do** with the reunification.*

Wir **müssen** die Freiheit **planen**. [T19:1]
*We **must plan** (for) freedom.*

Timarchos **sollte** der Hauptankläger **sein**. [T15:8]
*Timarchos **was supposed** to **be** the main prosecutor.*

Sie **wollten** ihn vor Gericht **stellen**. [T15:6]
*They **wanted** to **take** him to court.*

Modal verbs modify other verbs which appear in the infinitive form in position IV (→R6). A modal verb can convey for example that one has permission, or the ability, the wish or intention to do something, that there is a possibility or that one is under some obligation to carry out a particular action. What the particular action is, however, is stated by the verb in the infinitive form.

R64 If the 'verb in the infinitive' (→R63) is **haben** or **sein** it may be preceded by a verb in the past participle form, e.g.

Das **mag** ihre Entscheidung **beeinflußt haben**.
*This **may have influenced** their/her decision.*

Er **muß** gestern morgen **angekommen sein**.
*He **must have arrived** yesterday morning.*

Note that in these cases the modal verbs express an assumption or speculation (→R69).

R65 In colloquial German the 'verb in the infinitive' (→R63) may not be expressed but understood from the context, e.g.

Haben Sie Dr. X auch eingeladen? Ja, aber er **kann** nicht ( ).
*Did you invite Dr. X too? Yes, but he **cannot** (come).*

In a few idiomatic phrases the 'verb in the infinitive' is never expressed, e.g.

Er **muß** nach Hause.
*He **must [go]** home.*

R66 Modal Verbs: Forms

Forms predominant in written German are printed in bold.

	dürfen	können	mögen	müssen	sollen	wollen
FACTUAL						
PRESENT TENSE						
ich; er, sie, es, man	**darf**	**kann**	**mag**	**muß/muss**	**soll**	**will**
du	darfst	kannst	magst	mußt	sollst	willst
				(→R191)		
wir; sie; Sie	**dürfen**	**können**	**mögen**	**müssen**	**sollen**	**wollen**
ihr	dürft	könnt	mögt	müßt	sollt	wollt

Note: Modal verbs do not end in **-t** in the present tense singular.

	dürfen	können	mögen	müssen	sollen	wollen
SIMPLE PAST TENSE						
ich; er, sie, es, man	**durfte**	**konnte**	**mochte**	**mußte**	**sollte**	**wollte**
du	durftest	konntest	mochtest	mußtest	solltest	wolltest
				(→R191)		
wir; sie, Sie	**durften**	**konnten**	**mochten**	**mußten**	**sollten**	**wollten**
ihr	durftet	konntet	mochtet	mußtet	solltet	wolltet

NON-FACTUAL (→R48)

	dürfen	können	mögen	müssen	sollen	wollen
SUBJUNCTIVE I						
ich; er, sie, es, man	**dürfe**	**könne**	**möge**	**müsse**	**solle**	**wolle**
du	dürfest	könnest	mögest	müssest	sollest	wollest
wir; sie, Sie	*as present tense factual*					
ihr	dürfet	könnet	möget	müsset	sollet	wollet
SUBJUNCTIVE II						
ich; es, sie, es, man	**dürfte**	**könnte**	**möchte**	**müßte**	*as past tense*	
du	dürftest	könntest	möchtest	müßtest	*factual*	
wir; sie, Sie	**dürften**	**könnten**	**möchten**	**müßten**	*as past tense*	
ihr	dürftet	könntet	möchtet	müßtet	*factual*	

Note:

■ **sollte/n, wollte/n**: Simple past tense factual forms and subjunctive II forms are identical. Check the context to find out if you are dealing with a FACTUAL or NON-FACTUAL form. (→R49)

■ **Umlaut + e/te/ten** signals NON-FACTUAL in modal verbs.

R67 Compound Tenses of Modal Verbs

Er	**hat**	die Musik	hören	können.	*He*	*has been able to hear the music.*
	hatte		hören	können.		*had been able to hear*
	wird		hören	können		*will be able to hear*

Note that a 'double infinitive' may indicate a compound past tense as well as the future. Check which auxiliary verb is used.

MAIN CLAUSE:

	II	IV	
COMPOUND PAST I	PRESENT TENSE of **haben**	VERB	INFINITIVE
COMPOUND PAST II	PAST TENSE of **haben**	in the	of the
FUTURE I	PRESENT TENSE of **werden**	INFINITIVE	MODAL VERB

DEPENDENT CLAUSE:

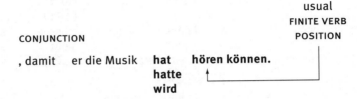

		usual FINITE VERB POSITION
CONJUNCTION		
, damit	er die Musik	**hat** **hören können.** **hatte** **wird**

| so that he | **has been able to hear** **had been able to hear** **will be able to hear** | the music |

Note the exceptional word order (→**R15.5**) It is found only where a modal verb is used in a compound tense.

Modal verbs in phrases without a 'verb in the infinitive' (→**R63**) form their past participles with **ge—t**, e.g.

Er hat es so **ge**wollt. (Lit.: *He wanted it thus. He asked for it.*)

R68 Modal Verbs: Two Different Patterns/Two Different Meanings

You have to distinguish between

1. The compound past of the modal verb: (haben + INFINITIVE + MODAL 'INFINITIVE')

   Er **hat** diese schwierige Aufgabe nicht allein **lösen können.**
   *He **has** not **been able/was not able to solve** this difficult problem on his own.*

2. The compound past of the 'verb in the infinitive': (MODAL + PAST PARTICIPLE + haben/sein)

   Er **kann** diese schwierige Aufgabe nicht allein **gelöst haben.**
   *He cannot **have solved** this difficult problem on his own.*
   i.e. it is not possible that he has solved it on his own.

   Er **muß** heute **angekommen sein.**
   *He **must have arrived** today.*

The same principle applies to the non-factual (→**R48** and **R51.3**):

> Er **hätte** Sie auf der Durchreise **besuchen können.** [T10a:11]
> *He **could have visited** you on his way through (but didn't)*
> *i.e. **it would have been possible to.***

> Er **könnte** ihn auf der Durchreise **besucht haben.**
> *He **might have visited** him on his way through*
> *(i.e. **it's possible that he has**).*

> Er **könnte** heute **angekommen sein.**
> *He **could/might have arrived** today (i.e. **it is possible**)*

R69 Meanings of Modal Verbs

As well as the main meanings listed below there are idiomatic usages of modal verbs. Consult the dictionary.

	PERMISSION AUTHORITY	ABILITY KNOWLEDGE	WISH INTENTION INCLINATION FREE WILL	POSSIBILITY OPPORTUNITY	ASSUMPTION SPECULATION	OBLIGATION (MORAL) DUTY NECESSITY
dürfen darf durfte/n	to be allowed/ permitted to 'may'					
+ nicht	'must/may not'					'must not'
dürfte/n				may well, is probably, should could, might, ought to		
können kann **konnte/n**	'can' to have the right / power to	'can' to be able to to know / understand how to, to be skilled in		'can', 'may' to be in a position to		
könnte/n				'could'	'could', 'might'	
mögen mag mochte/n			to like/desire to to want/wish to to be inclined to	'may'	'may'	
möge/n			'may'			'should'
möchte/n			'would like to'	'would', 'might'		
müssen muß mußte/n					'must'	to have to 'must' to be obliged to, to need to
+ nicht						'need not' not to have to

	PERMISSION AUTHORITY	ABILITY KNOWLEDGE	WISH INTENTION INCLINATION FREE WILL	POSSIBILITY OPPORTUNITY	ASSUMPTION SPECULATION	OBLIGATION (MORAL) DUTY NECESSITY
müßte/n					'should'	'would have to' should/ought to
sollen soll sollte/n					to be said to	to be supposed to, to be obliged to, to have to 'is to', 'shall'
sollte/n						'should', 'ought to' 'was to'
wollen will wollte/n			to wish/want/ desire to to like to, to intend to, to be about to, 'will', 'is willing'		to claim to	

Note:

■ For subjunctive forms see **R48**. Note the umlaut in these forms: dürfte/n, könnte/n, möge/n, möchte/n, müßte/n

■ **müssen + nicht** <u>never</u> means *must not*.

■ **vermag/vermögen/vermochte/n + zu** is sometimes used as an alternative for kann/ können/konnte(n)

■ **braucht/brauchen/brauchte/n + <u>nicht</u>** is an alternative for muß/müssen/mußte(n) + <u>nicht</u>

R70 Each modal verb has a number of meanings and the whole context has to be taken into account before deciding on the appropriate one.

Note:

■ one modal verb can have several meanings.
Read the table in **R69** horizontally.

■ the same meaning may be expressed by several modal verbs.
Read the table in **R69** vertically.

For example, **können/kann/konnte/könnte/n** can express:

PERMISSION	Die Studenten **können** Krakehl machen. [T10b:9]
	*The Students **are allowed/have the right** to make a noise.*
ABILITY	Der Mensch **kann** die Musik hören. [T5:6]
	*Man **can/is able to** hear the music.*
	Statistik **kann** nicht alles beweisen. [T16:14]
	*Statistics **cannot/are** not **able to** prove everything.*
POSSIBILITY	
OPPORTUNITY	Das Proletariat **kann** nur in England studiert werden. [T3:4]
	*The proletariat **can** only be studied in England (it is possible).*
	Wir **konnten** die Mondlandung ansehen. [T3:5]
	*We **were in a position** to watch the landing on the moon.*
	4 Millionen Einwohner **könnten** Wohlstand genießen. [T2:5]
	*4 million inhabitants **could/might** (i.e. have the opportunity to) enjoy prosperity.*
ASSUMPTION	
SPECULATION	. . . ., ob wieder ein Krieg ausbrechen **könnte**. [T2:3]
	*. . ... whether a war **might** break out again.*

The same meaning may be expressed by more than one modal verb, e.g.

permission/authority can be expressed both by **dürfen/darf durfte** and **können/kann konnte**, e.g.

> Die Studenten **dürfen** Krakehl machen. [T10b:10]
>   (**können** might be used instead of **dürfen**)
> Die Studenten **können** Krakehl machen.
> *The students **are allowed to** make a noise.*

R71 Modal Verbs: Summary

1. Modal verbs are used with another verb in the infinitive form to convey whether the action described by the 'verb in the infinitive' is permitted, necessary, possible etc, e.g.

	MODAL VERB		INFINITIVE	
Sie	**darf**	das Buch	**lesen.**	*She **is allowed to read** the book.*
Sie	**kann**	das Buch	**lesen.**	*She **can read** the book.*
Sie	**möchte**	das Buch	**lesen.**	*She **would like to read** the book.*
Sie	**muß**	das Buch	**lesen.**	*She **has to read** the book.*
Sie	**will**	das Buch	**lesen.**	*She **wants to read** the book.*

2. In German modal verbs can be found in all these tense forms, e.g.

PRESENT TENSE	Sie **will** das Buch lesen.	***wants** to read*
PAST TENSE	Sie **wollte** das Buch lesen.	⎫
COMPOUND PAST I	Sie **hat** das Buch lesen **wollen.**	⎬ ***wanted** to read*
COMPOUND PAST II	Sie **hatte** das Buch lesen **wollen.**	⎭ (→R37)
FUTURE I	Sie **wird** das Buch lesen **wollen.**	***will want** to read*

3. Note the forms for the compound past and future (➔**R67**), e.g.

Sie **hat** das Buch   **lesen wollen.**
Sie **hatte** das Buch **lesen wollen.**
Sie **wird** das Buch **lesen wollen.**

4. Note the exceptional word order in dependent clauses (➔**R67** and **R15.5**), e.g.

. . . , daß sie das Buch <u>**hat**</u> **lesen wollen.**

5. Note the difference in meaning between

hat . . . . . . **lösen können** (*could/was able to solve*)
kann . . . . **gelöst haben** (*it is possible that . . . has solved*)
(➔**R68**)

6. Modal verbs have a very wide range of meaning (➔**R69**) and all of them are also used in various idiomatic phrases. Consult the dictionary and be guided by the context.

Passives

R72 A Variety of Equivalent Constructions

The same meaning can be expressed through a number of different constructions:

> Das Durchmesser **wird** mit einer Mikro-Schublehre **gemessen.** [T7:2]
> *The diameter is (being) measured with a micrometer.*

> Der Durchmesser **läßt sich** mit einer Mikro-Schublehre **messen.**
> *The diameter can be measured with a micrometer.*

> Der Durchmesser **ist** mit einer Mikro-Schublehre **zu messen.**
> *The diameter is to be measured with a micrometer.*

> **Man** kann den Durchmesser mit einer Mikro-Schublehre messen.
> *One can measure the diameter with a micrometer.*

R73 Active and Passive Sentences

The relationship between active and passive sentences should be clear from the following:

> Ein Statistiker hatte **den Verdacht** geäußert, . . . [T16:1]
> *A statistician had voiced the suspicion . . .*

> Diese Firmen nennen **andere Gründe.** [T20:13]
> *These firms mention other reasons.*

> Einige Leute erhalten **die Täuschung** aufrecht, . . . [T19:2]
> *Some people maintain the illusion . . .*

> | ACTIVE: |
> | --- |
> | Someone **does** something |

> **Der Verdacht** wurde (von einem Statistiker) geäußert, . . .
> *The suspicion was voiced (by a statistician) . . .*

> **Andere Gründe** werden (von diesen Firmen) genannt.
> *Other reasons are mentioned (by these firms).*

> **Die Täuschung** wird (von einigen Leuten) aufrechterhalten, . . .
> *The illusion is maintained (by some people) . . .*

> | PASSIVE: |
> | --- |
> | Something **is done** (by someone) |

Using the passive gives the writer the option to leave the 'doer of the deed' unmentioned—either because this is obvious from the context, or because the doer is not known, or because the writer does not want to give this information:

> In ihrer Zeit wurde die erste Atombombe gezündet,
>   der erste Elektronenrechner gebaut,
>   die Doppel-Helix enträtselt. [T3:7]
> *In their time, the first atomic bomb was exploded, the first electronic calculator built, the double helix unravelled.*

R74 Using 'werden'

Das Durchmesser **wird** mit einer Mikro-Schublehre **gemessen**. [T7: 12]
The diameter is (being) measured with a micrometer.

Die internationale Spitzenstellung **wird** von Stuttgarter Unternehmen **bestimmt**.
The international standard is (being) dictated by Stuttgart companies.

Der Kleinbetrieb **wird** von dem Großbetrieb **bedrängt**.
The small firm is (being) threatened by the large firm.

The combination of a form of **werden** + a past participle (**→R34**) is the distinguishing feature of the passive in German. This construction must not be confused with other constructions using **werden** (**→R163** 'Problem Words'), notably the future tense (**→R36**). Note, however, that the form **worden** is **only** ever found in passive constructions.

R75 Tense Forms of 'werden'

is	Der Kleinbetrieb	**wird**	von dem Großbetrieb	**bedrängt.**
was		**wurde**		**bedrängt.**
has been		**ist**		**bedrängt worden.**
had been		**war**		**bedrängt worden.**
will be		**wird**		**bedrängt (werden*).**

* This is often omitted when the context clearly refers to the future:

Der Kleinbetrieb wird in Zukunft immer mehr von dem Großbetrieb bedrängt.
The small firm will be increasingly threatened in the future by the large firm.

Note the pattern in a verb-final clause (**→R12**):

... zeigt, daß der Kleinbetrieb von dem Großbetrieb **bedrängt wird.**
... *shows that ...* **bedrängt wurde.**
bedrängt worden ist.
bedrängt worden war.
bedrängt (werden*) wird.

R76 'von' and 'durch'

von and **durch** are both used where English uses *by.*

durch generally denotes an instrument or a process rather than an agent, i.e. it often has the sense *because of, by means of, using:*

Die Messungen werden **von einem Ingenieur** vorgenommen.
The measurements are made by an engineer.

Die Messungen werden **durch diese Bedingungen** beeinflußt. [T7:6]
The measurements are influenced by these conditions.

R77 Various Meanings of 'von'

In a passive sentence, **von** is likely to mean *by*, but it can of course have other meanings, depending on the context:

> Die Frau von diesem Mann wurde gesehen.
> *The wife **of** this man was seen.*

> Die Frau wurde von diesem Mann gesehen.
> *The woman was seen **by** this man.*

> Die Frau wurde von ihrem Kind getrennt.
> *The woman was separated **from** her child.*

R78 Related Constructions with a Passive Meaning (→R72)

1. **man** (*one, people in general, someone . . .*) is a very common alternative to the 'werden'-passive. **man** is **always** the subject of its clause:

   > **man** sagt
   > *it is said/ they say/people say*
   > So wird **man** feststellen, daß . . . [T18:3]
   > *Thus it will be found that . . .*

2. **ist zu + INFINITIVE** ('is to be done') is frequently used with an adverbial, e.g. **leicht** (*easily*):

   > Das Problem **ist** leicht **zu** erkennen.
   > *The problem is easily recognized.*

   Where there is no adverbial, the sense is either 'can be done' or 'must be done':

   > Das Problem **ist zu** lösen.
   > *The problem must be/can be solved.*

   With a negative, the sense is usually 'cannot be done':

   > Das Problem **ist nicht zu** lösen.
   > *The problem cannot be solved.*

   > Gewisse Andeutungen **sind nicht zu** übersehen. [T20:4]
   > *Certain indications cannot be overlooked.*

   > Die Entstehung der Musik **ist nicht** von der Entstehung der Menschheit **zu** trennen. [T5:1]
   > *The origins of music cannot be separated from the origins of mankind.*

3. **sich + INFINITIVE + lassen** ('allow itself to be done'). This is also usually found with an adverbial:

   > Diese Schrift **läßt sich** schwer entziffern.
   > *This writing is hard to decipher.*

   > Es **läßt sich** zeigen, daß . . .
   > *It can be shown that . . .*

4. **Reflexive Verbs** sometimes *translate* into an English passive:

   > In Europa **zeigte sich** ähnlich Alarmierendes. [T16:3]
   > *In Europe similarly alarming things were to be seen.*

5. **'-bar'** is a suffix corresponding to English '-able/-ible' (→R186)

> Er ist dreh**bar** gelagert. [T17:2]
> *It is rotatably mounted.*

> Das ist nicht mach**bar**.
> *That is not doable/It can't be done.*

6. **OVS Word Order** in German (**Object-verb-subject** →R5, R19) starts with the 'done to' rather than the 'doer', and so is like the passive in some ways. It is often a good idea to translate a German OVS sentence into an English PASSIVE:

OBJECT	VERB	SUBJECT
Diese Lücken	**schließen**	die ersten drei Artikel des Grundgesetzes.
These gaps	*are closed by*	*the first three articles of the Basic Law.*

R79 Other Points to Note

1. **'worden' vs. 'geworden'**

> es ist jetzt dunkel **geworden**   *it has got dark now*
> es ist jetzt bestätigt **worden**   *it has been confirmed now*

worden is always part of a passive construction.
geworden is never part of a passive construction.

2. **'wird gemacht' vs. 'ist gemacht'**

> Der Bericht **wird/wurde** geschrieben.   *The report is/was (being) written.*
> Der Bericht **ist/war** geschrieben.   *The report is/was written.*

German can distinguish between the PROCESS of an action and the RESULTING STATE when the action has been completed.

> **werden** + past participle   expresses PROCESS
> **sein** + past participle   expresses RESULTING STATE.

When it is used with **sein**, the past participle is often more like an adjective:

> Er **ist** drehbar im Gehäuse **gelagert**. [T17:2]
> *It is rotatably mounted in the housing.*

> Die Annahme **ist** so weit **verbreitet** . . . [T21:2]
> *The assumption is so widespread . . .*

This last example illustrates the tendency for some frequently used past participles to acquire specialized meanings as adjectives in their own right (→R170).

3. **'Subjectless' (Impersonal) Passives**

> **Es wird** im Ausland von einem deutschen 'Wirtschaftswunder' **gesprochen**.
> Im Ausland **wird** von einem deutschen 'Wirtschaftswunder' **gesprochen**.
> *There is talk abroad of a German 'economic miracle'.*

The **es** in first position here is a 'token subject' (→R10.4). When the first position is occupied by another element, e.g. an adverbial, this **es** disappears:

> Im Nürnberger Bereich **wird** auf die Überlegenheit der USA **verwiesen**. [T20:6]
> *In the Nuremberg area they point to the superiority of the USA.*

This construction is of course also found in verb-final clauses:

> Keineswegs, wie oft behauptet wird, . . .
> *By no means, as is often asserted, . . .*

Compare this structure with one where the subject is there but not in first position:

> Beklagt wird hier insbesondere **die Abhängigkeit der Deutschen** . . . [T20:7]
> *What is complained about here is above all the dependency of the Germans . . .*

4. Verbs dictating the Dative or Genitive (→**R93**, **R84**)

Only accusative objects of a verb can be turned into passives using **werden** and the pattern shown in **R73**. A verb which dictates one of the other cases forms a passive with a 'Token' **es**:

I	II		
es	wurde	ihm geholfen	
ihm	wurde	geholfen	*he was helped*
			(helfen + DATIVE)
es	wurde	der Opfer gedacht	
der Opfer	wurde	gedacht	*the victims were commemorated*
			(gedenken + GENITIVE)

This means that the impersonal form of **werden** is **always** in the singular. Compare:

> Der Opfer wurde gedacht   *The victims were commemorated*
> Die Opfer wurden entschädigt.   *The victims were compensated.*
>   (entschädigen + ACCUSATIVE)

Examples from the Text Corpus:

> Den Ideologen ist vorzuwerfen, daß . . . [T19:8]
> *The ideologues are to be rebuked for . . .*
> Im ersten Versuch wird ihr erlaubt, sich zu üben. [T7:16]
> *In the first experiment she is allowed to practise.*

R80 Summary: How to Recognize the Passive and its Related Constructions

- The first task is to learn to recognize all the different constructions using **werden** (→**R163**).
- Familiarize yourself with the other constructions which can have a similar force.
- Note that past participles can be used as adjectives with specialized meanings (→**R170**).
- Remember that not all past participles are formed using 'ge-' (→**R34**).
- Note that 'von' in a passive sentence usually indicates the doer of the action, but may occasionally have another sense.

Core Sentences

R81 The Verb and its Complements

Sections **R81–9** look at how the basic structure of a sentence is shaped by the verb. A CORE SENTENCE is composed of a verb and a small number of other items (e.g. Nouns) which need to be present to make a simple sentence. These other items are the verb's COMPLEMENTS. Learning how to read the 'core sentence' is a useful aid to comprehension, especially in longer sentences. The following abreviations are used:

[S] Subject	[prep] Preposition
[V] Verb	[Vprep] Verb + Preposition phrase
[O] Object	

Put fairly crudely, verbs tell us about events and processes ('What happened?'), and their complements tell us who or what was involved in the event ('Who did it?', 'Who to?'). The sentence:

Watt built the first steam engine six generations ago. [T3:2]

contains the verb 'built'. The core sentence is:

*Someone **built** something.*

In other words, once we have identified the verb, it is logical to ask '*Who did the building?*' and '*What did they build?*'

There is also a further, additional piece of information:

six generations ago

Starting with the verb as the most important item, we can represent this as:

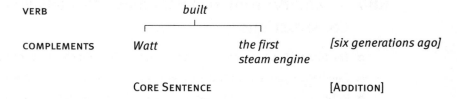

This is a useful strategy for sorting out the basic information structure of longer sentences, though it is important to remember that *in context* the most important piece of information in the sentence is often not found in the 'core' structure at all. (For example, the above sentence as an answer to the question '***When** did the industrial revolution begin?*')

R82 Important Points to Note

In thinking about the ways in which verbs can be used in English as well as German, it may be useful to note the following points.

1. **A verb can have more than one core pattern**

SV   *A new age **began**.*
SVO *The judge **began** his summing up.*

This is quite common. A particular verb can occur in more than one pattern.

2. **'Missing' complements**

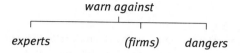

'*experts warn (firms) against dangers*'

Some complements can be omitted, when the meaning is obvious from the context:

Experts warn the firms against these dangers.
Experts warn against these dangers.

3. **Verb + preposition phrases: [Vprep] (e.g. 'belong to')**

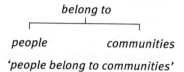

'*people belong to communities*'

There are many verbs (*belong to, rely on, insist on, suffer from, complain about* etc.) which are always used with a particular preposition, which is part of the core sentence.

4, **Modal verbs** are not part of a core sentence. They modify the basic proposition. Compare the following two sentences:

Es **kommt zu** Kommunikationssssschwierigkeiten.
It leads to difficulties in communication.

Es kann **zu** Kommunikationssssschwierigkeiten **kommen**.
It can lead to difficulties in communication.

So for the purposes of finding the core sentence, they have the same structure:

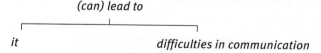

A more complex example:

Nach der Meinung von Emnid **mag** das schlechte Ergebnis für die Parlamentarier im Osten **mit** der Enttäuschung über die wirtschaftliche Situation nach der Wiedervereinigung **zusammenhängen**. [T1:9]
*In the opinion of Emnid the poor result for the parliamentarians in the East **may be connected with** disappointment over the economic situation following reunification.*

The core structure of this sentence is:

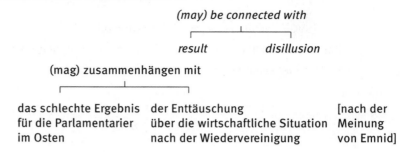

das schlechte Ergebnis	der Enttäuschung	[nach der
für die Parlamentarier	über die wirtschaftliche Situation	Meinung
im Osten	nach der Wiedervereinigung	von Emnid]

Note how important it is to see **zusammenhängen + mit** as a unit (*be connected with*). (→**R175** on finding verb + preposition phrases in the dictionary.)

R83 The Main Core Patterns in English

Core	Sentence Example
SV	*A new age **began**.*
SVO	*The temperature **causes** a change.*
S[Vprep]O	*A few people **belong to** Jewish communities.*
SVOO	*The university **awarded** him a degree./*
	The university awarded a degree to him.
S[Vprep]OO	*Experts **warn** the firms **against** over-optimism.*
SV[prepO]	*The earth **is situated** in the middle.*
	*Most Jews **came** from Eastern Europe.*
SV=S	*Europe's history **is** a history of wars.*

R84 The Main Core Patterns in German

German has the same core sentence types, except that the objects of the verb appear in a non-subject CASE, usually the accusative (Oacc) and/or the dative (Odat) Case. The CASE SYSTEM is explained in **R90–4**.

Core Sentence	Example
SV	Ein neues Zeitalter **begann**. [T2:7]
	A new age began.
SVOacc	Die Temperatur **verursacht** eine Veränderung. [T7:8]
	The temperature causes a change.
SVOdat	Wenige Menschen **gehören** den jüdischen Gemeinden **an**. [T13:2]
	Not many people belong to the Jewish communiities.
SVOgen	Es **bedarf** keines Fachwissens. [T16:15]
	It does not require any specialist knowledge.
S[Vprep]Oacc	Die übernatürlichen Kräfte **greifen in** das natürliche Geschehen **ein**. [T6:6]
	The supernatural powers intervene in the natural world.

S[Vprep]Odat	Es **basierte auf** einer Statistik. [T16:2]
	It was based on a statistic.
SVOaccOdat	Die Universität **verleiht** ihm den Doktorgrad. [T10A:1]
	The university is awarding him a doctorate.
S[Vprep]OaccOdat	Sie **warnen** die Firmen **vor** der Überbewertung. [T20:15]
	They warn firms against overestimation.
SV[prepO]: loc	Die Erde **befindet sich** in der Mitte. [T6:3]
	The earth is situated in the middle.
SV[prepO]: dir	Die Mehrzahl der Juden **kam** aus Osteuropa. [T13:3]
	The majority of Jews came from Eastern Europe.
SV = S	Europas Geschichte **ist** eine Geschichte von Kriegen. [T2:1]
	Europe's history is a history of wars.

R85 Differences Between German and English

German verbs generally behave like their English equivalents, but occasionally there are differences between the two languages. Some of these are systematic and predictable. Note the following two core sentence patterns:

1. English   *The length of the steel rod **changes**.*
   German   Die Länge der Stahlstange **verändert sich**.

German literally says: '*The length **changes** itself'* — using a REFLEXIVE form (➔R40):

   SVO   Die Hitze **ändert** die Länge. (*The heat changes the length.*)
   SVO(reflex)   Die Länge **ändert sich**. (*The length changes.*)

2. English   *Only a few people **belong to** Jewish communities.*
   German   Nur wenige Menschen **gehören** jüdischen Gemeinden **an**.

These look like different patterns, but the difference is only superficial. The verb **angehören** always takes a dative object (SVOdat). See 'Focus on the Dative', ➔R96.

Other instances are 'one-off' — not really systematic and so not really predictable. Check your dictionary to see how it handles the following:

German	diskriminieren	Er **diskriminiert** mich.	SVOacc
English	*discriminate against*	*He **discriminates against** me.*	S[Vprep]O
German	resignieren	Er resignierte.	SV
English	*resign oneself*	*He gave up.*	SVreflexive

Note: **Er resignierte** does **not** mean *He resigned*. (➔R164 for 'False Friends')

R86 Clause Complements

It is not just nouns and pronouns that act as complements in core sentences. Clauses can also complement a verb:

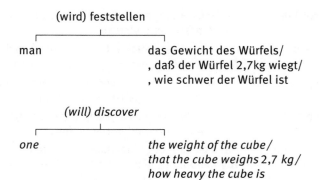

This gives several possible ways of shaping a sentence containing the verb **feststellen**:

Man wird das Gewicht des Würfels feststellen.
Man wird feststellen, daß der Würfel 2,7kg wiegt. [T18:3]
Man wird feststellen, wie schwer der Würfel ist.

Note that the same meaning can be expressed in different ways:

Das verursacht eine Veränderung des Durchmessers. [T7:8]
That causes a change in the diameter.

Das verursacht, daß sich der Durchmesser verändert.
That causes the diameter to change.

R87 Superfluous *es*

Sie haben **es** erlebt, **daß das Automobil zur Alltäglichkeit wurde**. [T3:6]
They experienced the automobile becoming an everyday phenomenon.

English readers can ignore this **es** which simply anticipates the clause complement.

R88 Verb + Preposition Phrases

Er **warnt** die Firmen **davor, daß** sie die Ergebnisse überbewerten.
It warns the firms against over-estimating the results.

Note the pattern with verbs where the clause complement is linked into the core sentence, with **da-** before the preposition, e.g.

davor, **daß** . . .
davor, . . . **zu** . . . (→**R155**)

The following three sentences all say the same thing:

Er **warnt** die Firmen **vor** der Überbewertung der Ergebnisse. [T20:15]
Er **warnt** die Firmen **davor, daß** sie die Ergebnisse überbewerten.

Er **warnt** die Firmen **davor,** die Ergebnisse **über**zubewerten.
It warns the firms against over-estimating the results.

i.e.

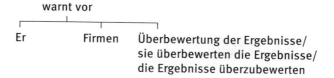

warnt vor

Er   Firmen   Überbewertung der Ergebnisse/
sie überbewerten die Ergebnisse/
die Ergebnisse überzubewerten

Similarly, the following two sentences have the same basic pattern:

Der Verdacht **basierte auf** einer Statistik.
The suspicion was based on a statistic.

Der Verdacht **basierte darauf, daß** die Rate in Minnesota hoch war. [T16:2]
The suspicion was based on the fact that the rate in Minnesota was high.

basierte auf

Verdacht   einer Statistik/
'Die Rate in Minnesota ist hoch'

R89 Summary: Reading a 'Core Sentence'

Starting with the verb, it is possible to construct the core sentence. For longer and more complex sentences, this is a useful strategy for building up the sense of the whole. You should be guided by the meaning of the verb and by what you know about the common core sentence patterns in German. In doing so, watch out for the following points:

- Core sentence patterns in German are often, but not always, like those for the equivalent verb in English. Take special note of the patterns which are peculiar to German (➔R85).

- The same basic information can be expressed in two or more different ways within the same core sentence pattern (➔R86).

- The existence of prepositional verbs like **warnen + vor** (*warn against*) and **zusammenhängen + mit** (*be connected with*) needs to be stressed. In long and complex sentences, the verb and the preposition it is tied to may be some distance apart (➔R88).

- Constructing the core sentence is often just a basic technique for building up the sense of a complex sentence. Quite often the most important information contained in the sentence is found *outside* the core (➔R81).

Nouns and Pronouns

R90 The Case System

The concept of CASE is often difficult for English learners, because English has virtually no case system. However, case distinctions exist in the English pronouns, and they mark the difference between subject and non-subject in a sentence:

SUBJECT	*I*	*he*	*she*	*we*	*they*
NON-SUBJECT	*me*	*him*	*her*	*us*	*them*

So English has e.g. **She** likes **me** and **I** like **her.**
She went to the party with **me.**

Even then, not all English pronouns mark the difference: *you* and *it* are used for both subject and non-subject ('*I like you and you like me*'). So the 'system' is not perfect.

The above examples illustrate the two occasions when case distinctions are made:

1. when there is an object of the verb:

I	*like*	**her**
She	*likes*	**me**
SUBJECT		OBJECT

2. when the pronoun (and, in German, the noun) is part of a prepositional phrase:
    with **me**, after **her**, before **us**, beside **him**, from **them** . . .

Case distinctions are marked much more regularly in German, though in German, too, the system is not 'perfect'.

R91 Case and Gender in German

All German nouns have a grammatical GENDER, i.e. they belong to one of three groups. These are sometimes called MASCULINE ('**der**'), FEMININE ('**die**'), and NEUTER ('**das**'). Gender does not necessarily have anything to do with masculineness or feminineness:

der Dialekt	*the dialect*
die Sprache	*the language*
das Wörterbuch	*the dictionary*

Two points to note:

1. **All gender distinctions disappear in the plural:**

die Dialekte	*the dialects*
die Sprachen	*the languages*
die Wörterbücher	*the dictionaries*

2. **The gender of a noun is not really marked on the noun itself** but rather on a special class of words which come before the noun, e.g.

the	**der** Dialekt	**die** Sprache	**das** Wörterbuch
a	**ein** Dialekt	**eine** Sprache	**ein** Wörterbuch
this	**dieser** Dialekt	**diese** Sprache	**dieses** Wörterbuch
that	**jener** Dialekt	**jene** Sprache	**jenes** Wörterbuch
every	**jeder** Dialekt	**jede** Sprache	**jedes** Wörterbuch
my	**mein** Dialekt	**meine** Sprache	**mein** Wörterbuch

These words are called DETERMINERS, and they carry the case markings in German. (For a full list see **R97**.)

The gender of a German noun is fixed—it never changes. The case form changes depending on whether the noun is the subject of the verb or is performing some other role in the sentence.

R92 Three Non-Subject Cases

All the forms given so far are for the subject case, the NOMINATIVE. There are three non-subject cases: ACCUSATIVE, DATIVE, and GENITIVE. The case distinctions are marked mainly by changes in the form of the determiner, e.g.

SUBJECT	NOMINATIVE	**Dieser** Dialekt ist schwer.
		This dialect is difficult.

	ACCUSATIVE	Viele Leute sprechen **diesen** Dialekt.
		Many people speak this dialect.
NON-SUBJECT	DATIVE	Ich habe keine Probleme mit **diesem** Dialekt.
		I have no problems with this dialect.
	GENITIVE	Die Laute **dieses** Dialekts sind so schön.
		The sounds of this dialect are so beautiful.

Time expressions such as **eines Tages** *one day* are in the form of a phrase in the genitive, while expressions of length or duration are in the accusative:

Die Ausstellung war **einen Monat** in Stuttgart.
The exhibition was in Stuttgart for a month.

However, which case a noun appears in is usually dictated by either the verb (➔**R93**) or a preposition (➔**R94**).

In fact, verbs and prepositions dictating the genitive case are not very common. The main use of the genitive is to indicate possession:

die Laute **dieses Dialekts**	*the sounds of this dialect*
die Bewertung **dieses Berufs**	*the evaluation of this profession*
die Zahl **der Opfer**	*the number of victims*

Note that '**der**' and '**das**' nouns add an '-s' or an '-es' in the genitive singular.

The most important non-subject cases are thus the accusative and the dative. The dative, in particular, has a wide range of uses and is found in a wide range of contexts. A special section (➔**R96**) is devoted to recognizing datives.

R93 Verbs Dictate Case

Individual verbs dictate which case the noun or pronoun should appear in.

1. INTRANSITIVE VERBS

Some verbs can form a complete sentence without having an object:

> Sie schlief.   *She slept.*
> Er arbeitet.   *He is working.*

The basic sentence consists only of a subject and a verb. Where there is an equation of some kind being made (two things being or remaining the same), two nominatives are used in German:

> **Er** bleibt **der junge Mann**, den wir 1967 kennengelernt haben.
> *He remains the young man we got to know in 1967.*

2. VERBS DICTATING THE ACCUSATIVE

> Ich verstehe **ihn** nicht/**diesen** Dialekt nicht.
> *I don't understand him/this dialect.*

Most verbs with an object take the accusative case.

3. VERBS DICTATING THE DATIVE

> Die Firmen glauben **den Statistiken** nicht.
> *The companies do not believe the statistics.*

A number of fairly common verbs have the object in the dative. Thus it is possible to have the same person or thing referred to by a different form in the same sentence:

> Ich kenne **sie** seit Jahren und glaube **ihr** gerne.
> *I have known _her_ for years and readily believe _her_.*

It is worth learning the most common verbs which dictate the dative. See the list in **R96.2**.

4. VERBS DICTATING BOTH ACCUSATIVE AND DATIVE

These are verbs which have two objects. Compare:

> he bought **the dog**
> he bought **a bone**
> he bought **the dog a bone**

English does not distinguish between a DIRECT OBJECT (what was bought) and an INDIRECT OBJECT (who for). In German, the direct object is accusative, and the indirect object is dative:

> *he bought the dog a bone.*
> er kaufte **dem Hund** einen **Knochen.**

This pattern is found with verbs of telling, showing, giving, etc., e.g.

> Die schönen Laute geben ***diesem*** Dialekt ein**en** besonder**en** Charakter.
> *The beautiful sounds give this dialect a special character.*

A NOTE ON WORD ORDER:

Er kaufte dem Hund den Knochen.	(dative noun + accusative noun)
Er kaufte ihn dem Hund.	(pronoun + noun)
Er kaufte ihm den Knochen.	(pronoun + noun)
Er kaufte ihn ihm.	(accusative pronoun + dative pronoun)

Sometimes the dative object will come before the accusative object, and sometimes after it, depending on the combination of nouns and pronouns involved. The typical word orders are shown above.

5. VERBS DICTATING THE GENITIVE

These are rare and are found only in restricted, formal contexts, e.g.

> **bedürfen** (*to require, be in need of*)
> Dieser Tatbestand bedarf **einer** Erklärung.
> *This state of affairs requires an explanation.*

> **gedenken** (*to commemorate*)
> Wir gedenken **der** Opfer des Krieges.
> *We commemorate the victims of the war.*

R94 Prepositions Dictate Case

All prepositions dictate a non-subject case, i.e. nouns in phrases beginning with a preposition must be in the accusative or dative or genitive.

1. ABBREVIATIONS

Combinations of preposition + determiner are often abbreviated:

Dative	**an dem** is reduced to **am**	
	Similarly: **im, beim, zum, zur, hinterm**	
Accusative	**an das** is reduced to **ans**	
	Similarly: **ins, hinters, aufs, durchs, fürs** and so on.	

2. PREPOSITIONS DICTATING THE ACCUSATIVE

e.g.
für eine Übergangszeit	*for a transitional period*
durch einen Vergleich	*by means of a comparison*
um diese Zeit	*at about this time*
um die Hälfte	*by half*

The main prepositions which always dictate the accusative are:

bis	*until*
durch	*through/by means of*
entlang*	*along*
für	*for*
gegen	*against*
ohne	*without*
um	*around, about, the difference by which*
wider	*against*

***entlang** comes after the noun:
die Grenze **entlang**   *along the border*

and so, occasionally, does **über**:
die ganzen 50er Jahre **über**   *throughout the entire fifties*

3. PREPOSITIONS DICTATING THE DATIVE

e.g. **nach** der Wiedervereinigung *after the reunification*
      seit meiner Kindheit   *since my childhood*

The main prepositions which **always** dictate the dative are:

ab	*from, beginning with*
aus	*out of, from*
außer	*except, apart from*
bei	*at, by, near*
gegenüber*	*opposite, across from; compared with*
gemäß*	*in accordance with; according to*
mit	*with*
laut	*according to*
nach*	*towards; according to*
seit	*since*
von	*from; of; by*
zu	*to, towards*
zufolge*	*according to*

*These prepositions can come after the noun:
dieser Umfrage **nach**   *according to this survey*

4. PREPOSITIONS DICTATING THE GENITIVE

e.g. mittels **eines** Thermometers *by means of a thermometer*
      während **der** Adenauerzeit   *during the Adenauer period*

Some of these prepositions can also be used with the dative. The meaning does not change:

wegen **des** schlechten Ergebnisses   *because of the poor result*
wegen **dem** schlechten Ergebnis   *because of the poor result*

The main prepostions which dictate the genitive are:

angesichts	*in the face of*
anstatt	*instead of*
außerhalb	*outside of*
diesseits	*this side of*
innerhalb	*inside of*
jenseits	*on the far side of*
mittels	*by means of*
oberhalb	*on top of*
statt	*instead of*
trotz*	*in spite of*
unterhalb	*underneath*
während*	*during*
wegen*	*because of*

*These prepositions may also dictate the dative, with the same meaning.

R95 Prepositions Dictating either the Accusative or the Dative

The full list is:

an	*on/onto* [vertical plane]
auf	*on/onto* [flat plane]
hinter	*behind*
in	*in/into*
neben	*next to*
über*	*over/above/*about*
unter	*under*
vor	*before/in front of*
zwischen	*(in) between*

*In the sense of *about,* **über** always takes the accusative:
Alle reden über das/übers Wetter.
Everyone is talking about the weather.

These prepositions deserve special attention since they are the only group where the same preposition can dictate more than one case. There is a subtle difference in meaning:

Dative implies no change of location: the action takes place in one and the same place.

Accusative implies a change of location: the action moves from one location to another.

e.g.:

Die Chefin **ist am** Telefon.	*The boss is on the phone.*
Sie **kommt ans** Telefon.	*She is coming to the phone.*
Der Gewinn **ist unter dem** Mittelwert.	*Profit is below the mean average.*
Der Gewinn **fällt unter den** Mittelwert.	*Profit falls below the mean average.*

Usually, there is a 'static' verb with the dative construction, and a verb of movement with the accusative construction, but this is not always so. Note the difference between:

a. Der Bus fährt **vor dem** Bahnhof ab.
The bus departs from in front of the station.
b. Der Bus fährt **vor den** Bahnhof.
The bus drives in front of the station.

In **a**, the bus *remains* in front of the station for the duration of the action (departing). In **b**, the bus *ends up* in front of the station.

R96 Focus on the Dative

1. A basic function of the dative is to express relationships which in English are often expressed using *to* and *from*.

For example, words such as **nahe** (*near to*), **fern** (*far from*), and **ähnlich** (*similar to*), are likely to be used with a dative in German:

> Wir sind **dem Krieg nahe**.
> *We are close to war.*

> Europa war **dem Krieg** stets **näher** als **dem Frieden**.
> *Europe has always been closer to war than to peace.*

This is also true wherever 'nahe' and 'fern' are part of a verb:

> I   II   III   IV
> Diese Leute **stehen** **den Primitiven** sehr **nahe**. [T12:2]
> *These people are very close to the primitives.*

Note how important it is to recognize the link between Position II and Position IV (→**R6**). This identifies the verb in the above example as:

> **nahestehen**:   *to be close to/be closely connected with*

Generally, a good command of the word order as summarized in **R18–20** will make recognizing these dative constructions much easier. Compare:

> Ihre Minister haben **ihr** den Rücktritt <u>nahegelegt</u>.
> *Her ministers suggested resignation to her.*

> Der Gedanke lag **ihm** <u>fern</u>.
> *The idea was far from his mind.*

> Diese Stadt ist **meiner Stadt** <u>ähnlich</u>.
> *This town is similar to my town.*

> Eine Großstadt des Jahres 1886 war **einer Metropole** des Jahres 86 n. Chr. <u>ähnlicher</u> als **einer heutigen Großstadt**. [T3:4]
> *A metropolis of the year 1886 resembled a city from the year AD 86 more than it resembled a modern city.*

Some verbs obviously have a 'to' or a 'from' implied in their meaning:

> Dieses Gemälde <u>gehört</u> **der** Stadt.
> *This painting <u>belongs to</u> the town.*

> Man kann **diesem Brief** nichts <u>entnehmen</u>.
> *One can <u>deduce</u> nothing <u>from</u> this letter.*

Some verbs are formed with a preposition that dictates the dative, and often these verbs take the dative too. For example, separable verbs with **entgegen** (*opposite to, opposed to, towards*) as a prefix:

Diese Kraft ist **der Schwerkraft** <u>entgegen</u>gesetzt. [T18:5]
This force is <u>opposed to</u> the force of gravity.
   (**entgegensetzen** literally means '*to set against, to oppose*')

Diese Kunstform kommt **dem Auffassungsvermögen** <u>entgegen</u>. [T21:3]
This art form accommodates one's ability to comprehend.
   (**entgegenkommen** literally means '*to come towards, to meet*')

Other verbs may be harder for an English reader to recognize:

Der Regierung <u>fehlt</u> die Mehrheit.
The government <u>lacks</u> a majority.
   (Lit.: *A majority is missing to/from the government.*)

Das Projekt <u>gelang</u> **ihr** nicht.
She was not successful in her project.
   (Lit.: *The project did not <u>succeed</u> to her;*
   gelingen (*to succeed*) is an impersonal verb) cf.

= Es gelang **ihr** nicht, das Projekt zu beenden. (→**R42**)

2. Some verbs do not obviously fit into the categories of 'dativeness' described here, and
   are best learnt separately. Here is a **list of common verbs** which dictate the dative:

antworten	*to answer someone*
befehlen	*to order someone*
begegnen	*to meet, bump into (by chance), occur*
bei'treten	*to join, become a member of an organization*
danken	*to thank*
dienen	*to serve*
drohen	*to threaten*
entsprechen	*to correspond to, be in accord with*
gehören	*to belong to*
gelingen	*to succeed (impersonal verb)*
gelten	*to apply to, be true of, be true of*
glauben	*to believe*
folgen	*to follow*
gleichen	*to be the same as, to amount to*
gratulieren	*to congratulate*
helfen	*to help*
kündigen	*to give notice to quit*
mißtrauen	*to distrust*
schaden	*to damage*
schmeicheln	*to flatter*
trauen	*to trust, have faith in*
unterliegen	*to be subject to*
vertrauen	*to trust, have faith in*
vor'beugen	*to anticipate, avoid, prevent*
widersprechen	*to contradict*
widerstehen	*to resist*

R97 The Case Forms of Determiners: Overview

Note: This table shows masculine ('der') and neuter ('das') forms next to each other in order to point out where these two patterns coincide.

CASE	MASCULINE	NEUTER	FEMININE	PLURAL*	MAIN FUNCTIONS
NORMINATIVE	der dieser	das dieses	die diese ein keine	die diese — keine	■ SUBJECT ■ with **sein** (*to be*) **werden** (*to become*) **bleiben** (*to remain*) →**R93.1**
	ein kein				
ACCUSATIVE	den diesen einen keinen	das dieses ein kein			■ OBJECT →**R93.2** ■ can indicate *duration of time, definite time,* distance *covered,* direction up/down, *a* measurement →R92 ■ with these PREPOSITIONS: bis, durch, entlang, für, gegen, ohne, um, wider. →**R94.2**
DATIVE	dem diesem einem keinem		der dieser einer keiner	den diesen — keinen	■ These PREPOSITIONS dictate EITHER the ACCUSATIVE OR the DATIVE →**R95**: an, auf, hinter, in, neben, über, unter, vor, zwischen
				[NOUN+(e)n]	■ OBJECT →**R93.3** ■ with these PREPOSITIONS aus, außer, bei, gemäß, laut, mit, nach, seit, zu, von, entsprechend etc. →**R94.3**
GENITIVE	des dieses eines keines [NOUN+(e)s]**			der dieser — keiner	■ To link two Nouns, e.g. to show POSSESSION. →**R92** ■ OBJECT →**R93.5** ■ shows *indefinite time* →**R92** ■ with these PREPOSITIONS: (an)statt, außerhalb, bezüglich, infolge, innerhalb, mittels, trotz, während, wegen, etc. →**R94.3**

* No gender distinction in the plural. →**R91.1**
** Some masculine nouns do not add -es. →**R101**

all- (*all*), **jen-** (*that, those*), **jed-** (*each, every*), **welch-** (*which*), **manch-** (*many, many a*), **solch-** (*such, such a*) are declined like **dieser**.

mein (*my*), **unser** (*our*), **sein** (*his, its*), **ihr** (*her, their*), **dein, euer, Ihr** (*your*) are declined like **kein**.

Note: Prepositions are often joined together with the determiner:
an dem = **am**, bei dem = **beim**, von dem = **vom**, zu dem = **zum**, in das = **ins** etc. →**R94.1**

R98 The Case Forms of Personal Pronouns (→R25)

CASE		SINGULAR	PLURAL	MAIN FUNCTIONS

NOMINATIVE	1st person
	2nd person
	(familiar)
	3rd person
		ich
		du
		
		er
		sie
		es
		man
			wir
			ihr
			
			sie
				■ SUBJECT
				
				■ with **sein** (to be)
				   werden (to become)
				   bleiben (to remain)
				→R93.1

	2nd person (formal)	Sie	Sie	

ACCUSATIVE	1st person
	2nd person
	(familiar)
	3rd person
		mich
		dich
		
		ihn
		sie
		es
		einen
			uns
			euch
			
			sie
				■ OBJECT →R93.2
				■ with these PREPOSITIONS:
				   bis, durch, entlang, für, gegen,
				   ohne, um, wider →R94.2

	2nd person (formal)	Sie	Sie	

DATIVE	1st person
	2nd person
	(familiar)
	3rd person
		mir
		dir
		
		ihm
		ihr
		ihm
		einem
			uns
			euch
			
			ihnen
				■ These PREPOSTIONS dictate
				either the ACCUSATIVE
				or the DATIVE →R95:
				an, auf, hinter, in, neben, über
				unter, vor, zwischen
				
				■ OBJECT →R93.3
				■ with these PREPOSITIONS:
				   aus, außer, bei, gemäß,
				   laut, mit, nach, seit, zu, von,
				   entsprechend etc. →R94.3

	2nd person (formal)	Ihnen	Ihnen	

GENITIVE[1]	1st person
	2nd person
	(familiar)
	3rd person
		meiner
		deiner
		
		seiner[4]
		ihrer[4]
		seiner[4]
		—
			unser
			euer
			
			ihrer[4]
				■ OBJECT →R92
				■ with these PREPOSITIONS:
				   (an)statt[2], außerhalb, bezüglich,
				   infolge, innerhalb,
				   mittels, trotz[2], während[2],
				   wegen[2,3], etc. →R94.3

	2nd person (formal)	Ihrer	Ihrer	

[1] These pronouns in the GENITIVE form occur rarely in modern German.
[2] With these prepositions you may also find the DATIVE forms.
[3] Special forms are used with this preposition: **meinetwegen, deinetwegen, seinetwegen, ihretwegen, unseretwegen, euretwegen**. The same applies to '-willen' and '-halben', e.g.: **seinetwillen, seinethalben**.
[4] **dessen/deren/derer** are also used instead (→R99).

R99 The Case Forms of Pronouns/Determiners (→R135)

Note: This table shows masculine ('der') and neuter ('das') forms next to each other in order to point out where these two patterns coincide.

Most DETERMINERS are also used as PRONOUNS and in most instances they then have the same CASE forms as the DETERMINERS (→R97). The following table therefore lists the differences only. The table also contains DETERMINERS/PRONOUNS not listed in R97 for reasons of space.

CASE	SINGULAR			PLURAL	MAIN FUNCTIONS
	MASCULINE	NEUTER	FEMININE		
NOMINATIVE	einer keiner[1] derjenige[2] derselbe[3]	ein(e)s kein(e)s[1] dasjenige[2] dasselbe[3]	diejenige[2] dieselbe[3]	diejenigen[2] dieselben[3]	■ SUBJECT ■ with **sein** (*to be*) **werden** (*to become*) **bleiben** (*to remain*) →R93.1
ACCUSATIVE	denjenigen[2] denselben[3]	ein(e)s kein(e)s[1] dasjenige[2] dasselbe[3]	diejenige[2] dieselbe[3]	diejenigen[2] dieselben[3]	■ OBJECT →R93.2 ■ with these PREPOSITIONS: bis, durch, entlang, für, gegen, ohne, um, wider →R94.2
					■ These PREPOSITIONS dictate *either* the ACCUSATIVE *or* the DATIVE →R95: an, auf, hinter, in, neben, über, unter, vor, zwischen
DATIVE	demjenigen[2] demselben[3]		derjenigen[2] derselben[3]	denen denjenigen[2] denselben[3]	■ OBJECT →R93.3 ■ with these PREPOSITIONS: aus, außer, bei, gemäß, laut, mit, nach, seit, zu, von, entsprechend etc. →R94.3
GENITIVE	dessen desjenigen[2] desselben[3]		deren derjenigen[2] derselben[3]	deren/derer derjenigen[2] derselben[3]	■ OBJECT →R92 with these PREPOSITIONS: (an)statt, außerhalb, bezüglich, infolge, innerhalb, mittels, trotz, während, wegen, etc. →R94.3

[1] The same form for **mein-, dein-, sein-, ihr-, unser-, eu(e)r-**

[2] Note that both parts of the word are declined, the first part like a determiner, the second like an adjective (→R108). It corresponds to English *that which, s/he who*, etc.

[3] Here, too, both parts of the word are declined as described in 2. It corresponds to English *the same*.

R100 The Case Forms of Interrogative Pronouns 'wer' (who), 'was' (what)

CASE		MAIN FUNCTIONS
NOMINATIVE	wer was	■ SUBJECT ■ with **sein** (*to be*) 　　**werden** (*to become*) 　　**bleiben** (*to remain*)
ACCUSATIVE	wen was[2]	■ OBJECT　→R93.2 ■ for example with these PREPOSITIONS: durch, für,[1] gegen, um, wider →R94.2
DATIVE	wem was[2]	■ These PREPOSITIONS dictate *either* the ACCUSATIVE *or* the DATIVE →R95: an, auf, hinter, in, neben, über, unter, vor, zwischen ■ OBJECT　→R93.3 ■ for example with these PREPOSITIONS: bei, laut, mit, nach, zu, von, etc. →R94.3
GENITIVE	wessen	■ OBJECT　→R92 ■ for example with these PREPOSITIONS: infolge, mittels, etc. →R94.3

[1] **für was** means *for what/what for*
But **was für** means *what kind of, what sort of*
[2] Instead of the preposition followed by **was** you will often find **wo(r) + Preposition**, e.g. **wofür, wogegen, womit, woran**, etc. →R136.2

R101 Nouns Which Have an Ending Added

These are of three kinds:

1. Nouns which have been derived from adjectives retain their usual adjective endings (→**R108**) and begin with a capital letter. See also R180 on looking these up in the dictionary.

2. Some masculine nouns add '-(e)n' in **all** the non-subject cases and in the plural. They include all masculine nouns ending in **-ent** or **-ant** (e.g. **Student, Intendant**). Some other common masculine nouns have this pattern (e.g. **Mensch**). In the dictionary these are usually indicated as follows:

Produzent, -en, -en der (masc.), *manufacturer, producer*
      └── SHOWS THE PLURAL
     └─────── SHOWS THE GENITIVE SINGULAR

Note that the non-subject singular form of these nouns is the same as the plural:

des Produzenten	*of the producer*
dieses Produzenten	*of this producer*
die Produzenten	*the producers*
diese Produzenten	*these producers*

The full list of forms for these nouns is as follows:

	der Produzent (manufacturer)	der Mensch (human being)	der Photograph (photographer)
NOM.	der Produzent	Mensch	Photograph
ACC.	den Produzenten	Menschen	Photographen
DAT.	dem Produzenten	Menschen	Photographen
GEN.	des Produzenten	Menschen	Photographen
PLURAL (all cases)	Produzenten	Menschen	Photographen

Other nouns that decline like **der Mensch** include:

der Junge	*boy*	der Chirurg	*surgeon*
der Neffe	*nephew*	der Nachbar	*neighbour*
der Franzose	*Frenchman*	der Russe	*Russian (male)*

3. A small number of masculine nouns basically follow the pattern in (2) except that the genitive singular ends in '-ens'. In the dictionary these may appear as:

Gedanke, -ns, -n der (masc.) *thought, idea*

The full forms of these nouns are as follows:

NOM.	der Gedanke
ACC.	den Gedanken
DAT.	dem Gedanken
GEN.	des Gedankens
PLURAL	Gedanken

Other nouns that follow this pattern include:

der Name   *name*
der Friede   *peace*
der Glaube   *faith*
der Wille   *will(power)*

and one neuter noun: das Herz *heart*

R102 Interpreting the Signals about Case

It can be seen from the list given in **R97** that there are just six different forms of the DETERMINER ('**der/die/das**') to cover sixteen different case/gender combinations. Note the following points:

1. The form of the determiner distinguishes between subject and non-subject only for masculine (**der**) nouns, and even then only in the singular. For neuter (**das**) nouns and feminine (**die**) nouns, and for all plurals, there is no way of distinguishing between nominative and accusative case just by looking at the determiner on its own.

2. The form of the determiner follows the same pattern in the dative and genitive singular for masculine and neuter nouns.

Interpreting the case of a noun correctly comes partly from knowing what the case markers can signal, and partly from reading the sentence as a whole, using information provided by the context, mainly:

   a. other clues about subjects and objects contained elsewhere in the sentence (→**R8**),

   b. common sense! Your knowledge of the meaning so far, predictions about what you expect the text to say, knowledge about the world, etc.

R103 Subject or Non-Subject?

1. **None** of the determiner forms is **always** found with the subject:

der das die
dieser dieses diese   } can be the subject, but they can
jeder jedes jede etc.   } also have other functions

der
jeder   } for example, can be (1) the subject, (2) a genitive singular, (3)
dieser   } a dative singular, (4) a genitive plural:

  1   2   3   4
Der Abbau   **der** Mauer   in **der** Nähe   **der** Häuser.
The taking down of the wall in the vicinity of the houses.

1   der Abbau   Nominative case   Subject
2   der Mauer   Genitive case of   '*of the*
                feminine noun   *wall*'
                '**die Mauer**'

| 3 | der Nähe | Dative case of feminine noun 'die Nähe', dictated by the preposition 'in' (→R94) | *'in the vicinity'* |
| 4 | der Häuser | Genitive plural of neuter noun 'das Haus' | *'of the houses'* |

dieses jedes jenes, etc. can be (1) the subject, (2) an accusative singular, (3) a genitive singular:

    1   2   3

Jedes Buch   **dieses** Autors nimmt   **jenes** Thema auf.

Every book of this author takes up that theme.

1	Jedes Buch	Nominative case	Subject
2	dieses Autors	Genitive singular of masculine noun 'der Autor'	*'of this author'*
3	jenes Thema	Accusative singular of neuter noun 'das Thema', dictated by the verb 'aufnehmen' (→R93)	*'that theme'*

Note that the sequence **dieses** [NOUN]**(e)s** is a genitive singular:

jedes Buches   *of every book*
jenes Themas   *of that topic*

But note also that it is important to recognize when the final 's' on a noun is part of the noun itself:

dieses Ereignis   *this event*
dieses Ereignisses   *of this event*

Mistaking 'der', 'das', or 'die' for the subject tends to be a problem only where the German sentence has the object in first position, as in the following examples (the subject is underlined):

Das Denkmal entdeckte <u>er</u> . . .	*He discovered the monument . . .*
Die Macht haben <u>die Minister</u> . . .	*The ministers have the power . . .*
Die Eltern sucht <u>man</u> sich nicht aus.	*One does not choose one's parents . . .*
Dieser Regierung fehlt <u>die Mehrheit</u> . . .	*This government lacks a majority . . .*

    (The verb **fehlen** dictates the dative case, →R93, R96)

Jener Opfer gedenken <u>wir</u> . . .   *We commemorate those victims . . .*

    (The verb **gedenken** dictates the genitive case, →R93)

2. Some determiner forms are **never** found with the subject:

des	Nouns following these are
den diesen jeden jenen, etc.	**never** the subject
dem diesem jedem jenem, etc.	

3. **es gibt** ('there is/ there are') **always** dictates the accusative, but for English readers this accusative is the 'logical' subject:

es gab ein**en** Aufschwung   *there was an upturn*

R104 Interpreting Case Endings Added to Nouns

Note the following patterns:

1. das Funktionieren **des Markts/des Marktes** *the functioning of the market*

In the genitive singular, most **'der'** and **'das'** nouns add '-s' or '-es'.

Be careful not to read these as plurals.

2. in den meisten Fäll**en**   *in most cases*
   (die meisten Fälle   *most cases*)
  den staunenden Mediziner**n**   *to the astonished medics*
   (die staunenden Mediziner   *the astonished medics*)

In the dative plural, most nouns add '-n' or '-en' to the plural form (unless the plural already ends in '-n' or '-en', or it ends in '-s').

The repeated '-n' on the endings of all the words in the noun phrase makes dative plurals relatively easy to spot.

3. im Zug**e** der Westintegration   *in the course of western integration*
  an einem warmen Tag**e**   *on a warm day*

In the dative singular, masculine and neuter nouns sometimes add '-e'.
Be careful not to read these as plurals.

R105 Interpreting Nouns which Have an Ending Added →R101

Interpeting these forms correctly depends on recognizing whether they are part of a structure which dictates the accusative, or one that dictates the dative.

These forms are accusative singular in contexts like:

durch **diesen Produzenten/Abgeordneten**
'through/ by means of this manufacturer/delegate'
  Because **durch** always dictates the accusative (→**R94**)

den Produzenten/Abgeordneten finden
'to find the manufacturer/delegate'
  Because **finden** always dictates the accusative (→**R93**)

an **den Produzenten/Abgeordneten** schicken
'to send (something) to the manufacturer/delegate'
  Because **an** dictates the accusative when it signals a change of location (→**R95**).

These forms are dative plural in contexts like:

mit **diesen Produzenten/Abgeordneten**
'with these manufacturers/delegates'
  Because **mit** always dictates the dative (→**R94**)

den Produzenten/Abgeordneten danken
'*to thank the manufacturers/delegates*'
   Because **danken** always dictates the dative (→**R93**)

an **den Produzenten/Abgeordneten** liegen
'*to be caused by the manufacturers/delegates*'
   Because **an** dictates the dative when it signals no change of location (→**R95**).
   Here, **liegen an** + dative means '*to lie with/be because of*'.

Adjective Constructions

R106 Simple Phrases

German adjectives have an ending added to them when they are part of the noun phrase, i.e. when they immediately precede the noun they describe. (This is part of the case/gender system →**R91**.) The ending changes depending on the function of the noun it precedes, but it does not affect the meaning of the adjective. In the following examples, the adjective is in bold, and the adjective ending is underlined:

Dieses Ergebnis ist **positiv**. [T20:15]   *This result is positive.*
Diese Ergebnisse sind **positiv**.   *These results are positive.*
Positiv sind diese Ergebnisse.   *These results are positive.*
(Here the adjective is not part of the noun phrase.)

Das **positive** Ergebnis ist . . .   *The positive result is . . .*
Ein **positives** Ergebnis ist . . .   A/One positive result is . . .
Diese **positiven** Ergebnisse sind . . .   *These positive results are . . .*
Positive Ergebnisse sind . . .   *Positive results are . . .*
(Here the adjective is inside the noun phrase.)

The adjective endings used are:

-e   -en   -em   -es   -er

A complete table of adjective endings is given in **R108**.

R107 Comparative and Superlative Forms

Note: Adjective endings are underlined throughout this section.

1. COMPARATIVE FORMS add '-er' to the adjective, and sometimes add an umlaut to the adjective:

   groß *great*   größer *greater*
   gering *small*   geringer *smaller*

   eine geringe durchschnittliche Dichte
   a low average density

   Holz besitzt eine geringere Dichte als Wasser. [T18:10]
   Wood has a lower density than water.

Because '-er' is used **both** as an adjective ending **and** as a marker of comparison, special care needs to be taken to recognize comparative forms of adjectives. The umlaut over an 'a', 'o', or 'u' is often an important signal of comparison.

Note that the comparative form can sometimes convey the sense of *'fairly'*:

eine **älter**e Maschine	*a fairly old machine*
ein **größer**es Haus	*quite a large house*

It is important to be able to recognize comparative forms and to distinguish them from the adjective ending '-er'. Compare:

ein **wichtig**er Faktor	i.e. dieser Faktor ist **wichtig**	*an important factor*
ein **wichtiger**er Faktor	i.e. dieser Faktor ist **wichtiger**	*a more/fairly important factor*
ein **groß**er Fehler	i.e. der Fehler ist **groß**	*a big mistake*
ein **größer**er Fehler	i.e. der Fehler ist **größer**	*a bigger/fairly big mistake*

die Interessen **weit**er Kreise des Bürgertums [T14:17]
the interests of broad sections of the middle classes

die Interessen **weiter**er Kreise des Bürgertums
the interests of broader/fairly broad sections of the middle classes

immer + a comparative form means *'more and more'*:

immer älter	*older and older*
die Interessen immer weiterer Kreise	*the interests of ever broader sections*

2. SUPERLATIVE FORMS (-st-) add '-(e)st' to the adjective, and sometimes add an umlaut to the adjective:

groß *great*	am größten	*the greatest (of all)*
gering *small*	am geringsten	*the smallest (of all)*

der schnell**ste** Zug   *the fastest train*

die **größt**en Fehler   *the biggest mistakes*

(Note how -**ß** + **st** becomes simply -**ßt**)

Dieser Zug fährt **am schnellsten**.   *This train travels the fastest.*

R108 Table of Adjective Endings

Note: In this section, masculine ('der') and neuter ('das') forms are shown next to each other in order to point out where these two patterns coincide.

Endings are added to adjectives when they come immediately before the noun they describe. Adjective endings never change the meaning of the adjective. Instead, they help to give information about the case and gender (➜**R91**) of the noun. The particular ending which is added depends on whether there is a determiner (➜**R91, 97**) before the adjective and, if so, what kind of determiner.

There are THREE patterns:

1. **dieser gute Wein** *this good wine*

When one of the determiners shown below precedes the adjective, the pattern of adjective endings is as follows:

	MASC.	NEUT.	FEM.	PLURAL	
after any case form of					
der/das/die	-e	-e	-e	-en	NOM.
dieser/dieses/diese					
jener/jenes/jene	-en	-e	-e	-en	ACC.
jeder/jedes/jede					
mancher/manches/manche	-en	-en	-en	-en	DAT.
solcher/solches/solche					
welcher/welches/welche	-en	-en	-en	-en	GEN.

e.g.

das schlechte Ergebnis [T1:9]
(nominative, singular, neuter)

der erste Elektronenrechner [T3:7]
(nominative, singular, masculine)

der bedeutende britische Premierminister [T2:9]
(nominative, singular, masculine)

Ende des zweiten Weltkriegs [T2:9]
(genitive, singular, masculine)

mit den westlichen Partnern [T2:18]
(dative, plural)

einer heutigen Großstadt [T3:4]
(dative, singular, feminine)

2. **ein guter Wein** *a good wine*

When the determiner is one of the following, a slightly different pattern of adjective endings is found:

	MASC.	NEUT.	FEM.	PLURAL	
after any case form of					
ein/eine	-er	-es	-e	-en	NOM.
kein/keine					
mein/meine	-en	-es	-e	-en	ACC.
sein/seine					
dein/deine	-en	-en	-en	-en	DAT.
unser/unsere					
ihr/ihre	-en	-en	-en	-en	GEN.

and all other possessive adjectives

e.g.

sein gemeinsames Erbe [T2:5]
(accusative, singular, neuter)

seine beweglichen Lettern [T3:2]
(accusative, plural)

3. **guter Wein** *good wine*

When there is **no determiner** preceding the adjective, there is just a sequence of adjective + noun. The endings on the adjective then generally imitate those of the definite article (der/das/die):

MASC.	NEUT.	FEM.	PLURAL	
-er	-es	-e	-en	NOM.
-en	-es	-e	-en	ACC.
-em	-em	-er	-er	DAT.
-en	-en	-er	-er	GEN.

This pattern is also found after numbers and **viele** '*many*',

e.g.   europäische Politiker [T2:3]

(nominative, plural)

zwei europäische Politiker

(nominative, plural)

viele europäische Politiker

(nominative, plural)

neue Kriege [T2:15]

(nominative, plural)

Kernpunkt deutscher Außenpolitik [T2:18]

(genitive, singular, feminine)

guter Wein

(nominative, singular, masculine)

Note that in the genitive singular for masculine and neuter, the adjective ending does not follow the **der/das/die** pattern when the genitive is marked by an '-s' on the end of the noun (➔**R92**):

der Preis guten Weins *the price of good wine*

(genitive, singular, masculine)

4. Any sequences involving adjective endings which do not conform to one of the three patterns shown here must belong to a different kind of construction, such as a RELATIVE CLAUSE (➔**R110, R113**):

die Frage, die britische Premierminister seit Jahren intensiv beschäftigt

the question which has occupied British prime ministers intensively for years

die Frage, der britische Premierminister seit Jahren viel Aufmerksamkeit schenken

the question to which British prime ministers have given much attention for years

die Flutwelle, die ganze Städte und Dörfer zerstört hat

the tidal wave which has destroyed whole towns and villages

or an EXTENDED ADJECTIVAL PHRASE (➔**R119g, h**)

die Frage der britische Premierminister seit Jahren intensiv beschäftigenden europäischen Integration

the question of European integration which has occupied British prime ministers intensively for years

die <u>ganze Städte</u> und Dörfer zerstörende Flutwelle
the whole-towns-and-villages-destroying tidal wave

Note how important it is to recognize these larger structures.

R109 Adjective or Adverb?

Compare: Diese Ergebnisse sind **eindeutig**.
These results are clear.

and: Diese Ergebnisse sind **eindeutig positiv**. [T20:15]
These results are clearly positive.

Also: eine **traditionell starke** Industrie
a traditionally strong industry
(i.e. it has always been strong in the past)

and: eine **traditionelle, starke** Industrie
a traditional, strong industry
(the industry is of the kind one would expect, and it is strong)

In English, adverbs usually have a different form from adjectives (*traditional: traditionally*). In German, most adjectives can also function as adverbs without any change in form. They simply appear in a different place in the sentence:

eine **geräuschlose** Revolution
a silent revolution

Diese Revolution ging **geräuschlos** vor sich. [T4:3]
This revolution happened silently.

R110 Relative Clauses (→R13, R147, R148)

die Ergebnisse, **die überraschend gut ausgefallen sind**, . . .
*the results, **which have turned out surprisingly well**, . . .*

In German, relative clauses are always introduced by a relative pronoun, have verb-final word order, and are marked off from other clauses by commas. The forms of the relative pronoun are identical to those of the definite article **der/das/die** (→**R97**), **except** for the following:

	der das	die	PLURAL
DATIVE			**denen**
GENITIVE	**dessen**	**deren**	**deren**

Note: The masculine ('der') and neuter ('das') forms are shown next to each other here to show where these two patterns coincide.

Note that **welcher** (➔R97) and wer (➔R100) can also be used as relative pronouns:

die Ergebnisse, **welche** überraschend gut ausgefallen sind, . . .

the results, which have turned out surprisingly well, . . .

Am meisten verdient, **wer** am meisten arbeitet.

i.e. Am meisten verdient derjenige, der am meisten arbeitet.

Whoever does the most work earns the most.

The relative pronoun has the same gender as the word it refers back to, but it does not have to have the same case as the word it refers back to:

			GENDER ⟵		
1	. . . Faktor . . . ,	**der**	hier sehr wichtig ist.	NOM.
2		**den**	man nicht unterschätzen darf.	ACC.
3		**dem**	man keine Bedeutung beimißt.	DAT.
4		**dessen**	Relevanz er nicht versteht.	GEN.
		CASE ⟶		

Translations:
1 . . . *factor which is very important here.*
2 . . . *factor which one must not underestimate.*
3 . . . *factor to which one accords no significance.*
4 . . . *factor whose relevance he does not understand.*

R111 The Relative Clause as a Downgraded Sentence

It is useful to see the relative clause as a sentence in its own right which has been 'downgraded' and inserted in another, dominant sentence. In the examples in **R110** the 'downgraded' sentences are:

(Dieser Faktor ist hier sehr wichtig.) ('Faktor' is NOM.)

This factor is very important here.

(Man darf diesen Faktor nicht unterschätzen.) ('Faktor' is ACC.)

One must not underestimate this factor.

(Man mißt diesem Faktor keine Bedeutung bei.) ('Faktor' is DAT.)

One does not attribute any importance to this factor.

(Ich verstehe die Relevanz dieses Faktors nicht.) ('Faktor' is GEN.)

I do not understand the relevance of this factor.

R112 Matching the Relative Clause to the Preceding Clause

In the example below, any clause on the left can be combined with any clause on the right. The subject of each clause is printed in bold.

NOM.	1929 begann **die Wirtschaftskrise,**	**die** die Deutschen sehr hart traf.
	Then came the recession	*which hit the Germans very badly.*
		(The recession hit the Germans)
ACC.	**Das** verursachte eine Wirtschaftskrise,	die **die Deutschen** nur kaum durchstanden.
	That caused a recession	*which the Germans only barely survived.*
		(The Germans barely survived the recession.)
DAT.	**Es** geschah nach der Wirtschaftskrise,	der **die Situation in Amerika** zugrunde lag.
	It happened after the recession	*for which the situation in America was responsible.*
		(The situation in America underlay the recession.)
GEN.	Das war **der Beginn** der Wirtschaftskrise,	deren **Folgen** für Europa furchtbar waren.
	That was the beginning of the recession	*whose consequences were terrible for Europe.*
		(The consequences of the recession were terrible for Europe.)

The clauses on the left have the word **Wirtschaftskrise** (gender: **die**) in each of the four cases. The clauses on the right have the relative pronoun in each of the four cases. Note how the case of the relative pronoun is not determined by the case of **Wirtschaftskrise** in the clause on the left, but by the role the word **Wirtschaftskrise** plays in the downgraded sentence on the right. So it is possible to have, e.g.

Das verursachte eine Wirtschaftskrise, deren Folgen für Europa furchtbar waren.
That caused an economic crisis whose consequences were terrible for Europe.
(Die Folgen der Wirtschaftskrise waren für Europa furchtbar.)

R113 Finding the Subject in a Relative Clause

This can be a problem for beginning readers. The relative pronoun may be in any case, and the first noun in a relative clause is not necessarily the subject of the clause. One useful tip is to look for SUBJECT–VERB AGREEMENT (→R8). The subject and verb are printed in bold in the following examples:

die deutschen Juden, die **die Nazi-Herrschaft** vernichten **wollte**, . . .
the German Jews, who the Nazi regime wanted to annihilate, . . .
(die Nazi-Herrschaft wollte die deutschen Juden vernichten.)

die deutschen Juden, **die** die Nazi-Herrschaft überlebt **haben,** . . . [T13:4]
the German Jews who survived the Nazi regime . . .
(Diese deutschen Juden haben die Nazi-Herrschaft überlebt.)

Otherwise, it is simply a matter of constructing the most plausible reading. What makes best sense? What would you expect the writer to be saying at this point? In context it is very rare to have two equally plausible readings. For instance, the sequence:

Die deutschen Juden, die die Konzentrationslager überlebt haben, . . .

could have two different readings:

1. The German Jews who have outlived the concentration camps . . .
2. The German Jews who(m) the concentration camps have outlived. ..

But in most contexts, the first of these would be the only plausible reading.

R114 Relative Clauses Introduced by a Preposition

Die Firma, **in der** sie arbeitet, . . .
The company in which she works . . .
(Sie arbeitet **in der Firma**.)

An example from the corpus:

Messungen werden durch die Bedingungen, **unter denen** sie durchgeführt werden, beeinflußt. [T7:6]
*Measurements are influenced by the conditions **under which** they are carried out.*
(Messungen werden **unter diesen Bedingungen** durchgeführt.)

R115 Extended Adjectival Phrases: Structure

diese **schwierige** Konstruktion!
. . . **verdammt schwierige** . . .
. . . **für Ausländer ganz schwierige** . . .
. . . **für Ausländer kaum zu begreifende** . . .
. . . **den ausländischen Leser oft verwirrende** . . .
. . . **von den Deutschen in ihren Schriften sehr oft benutzte** . . .

*this **difficult** construction!*
damned difficult
for foreigners very difficult
for foreigners hardly to be comprehended
often confusing the foreign reader
by the Germans in their written documents very often used

Again, it is useful to think of this construction as a former sentence which has been downgraded and incorporated in a more complex sentence. Thus the sequence:

. . . die durch Demontage des Oberteils zugängliche Sicherung [T23:13] can be read as follows:

	1			2
. . . die		3		Sicherung
	durch Demontage des Oberteils zugängliche			
. . . the				fuse
	by dismantling of the upper part accessible			

Compare English constructions such as *a never-to-be-forgotten experience*. In German, however, this kind of extended adjectival phrase is a common feature of formal texts across all subject-areas, and can be quite difficult for the unskilled reader to process. English readers are usually aware of a 'break' in the 'natural' sequence of words. In the example above, . . . **die durch** . . . [. . . *the through/by* . . .] is such a break.

Extended adjectival phrases can be very long and are often a cause of difficulty even for quite competent readers, because the longer phrases usually have a word order which is not possible in English.

In order to read this construction properly, the reader needs to establish the connection between 1 and 2—in the example above, this is **die Sicherung**, *the fuse*. The problem is that these words can be some distance apart, and you need to be sensitive to the context and the overall sense when scanning the text for the noun in position 2. In the above example, the first noun with the gender **'die'** is **Demontage**, but this is not the noun that belongs with **die** in position 1.

Everything between 1 and 2 is an adjective (a rather long and complex one). This means that the final word in the sequence carries an adjective ending (➜**R108**). Compare:

The extended sequence is unusual in English, which uses relative clauses to express the adjectival content:

> **in ihren Abmessungen nicht normgemäße** Dias [T23:8]
>
> lit.: *in their dimensions not standard slides*
>
> i.e. *slides which are not standard (in their) size*

Occasionally, however, the German word order goes straight into English:

> **unsachgemäß gerahmte** Dias [T23:8]
>
> *incorrectly framed slides*

R116 Extended Adjectival Phrases with a Present Participle

Extended adjective phrases often contain a present participle of a verb (➜**R43**). This ends in **-end** + an adjective ending (➜**R9**). There are two main kinds:

1. PRESENT PARTICIPLE on its own

This can be used with transitive and intransitive verbs (➜**R168**), and has a generally ACTIVE meaning:

der **nach dem Krieg einsetzende** Aufschwung
the after the war beginning boom
i.e. the boom which begins/began after the war

auf Statistik beruhende Aussagen [T16:17]
on statistics resting statements
i.e. statements based on statistics

ein **mich zutiefst bewegender** Gedanke
a thought which moves me deeply

eine **den Erfolg dieses Projekts gefährdende** Entwicklung
a development threatening the success of this project

2. 'zu' + PRESENT PARTICIPLE

With transitive verbs, this produces a PASSIVE meaning (→R78.2):

das **zu prüfende** Medikament [T9:10]
the to be tested medicine
i.e. the medicine (which is/was) to be tested

die **nur allzuleicht zu durchschauende** Armut [T21:7]
the only all too easy to see through poverty
i.e. the poverty which is/was only too plain to see

With intransitive verbs, the meaning is gained simply from the verb:

der **noch anzukommende** Zug
the still-to-arrive train

Damals gab es noch kein Zeichen von dem **bald einzusetzenden** Aufschwung.
At that time there was still no sign of the soon-to-begin upturn . . .

R117 Extended Adjectival Phrases with a Past Participle

The past participle of transitive verbs generally has a PASSIVE meaning:

ein **von den Humanisten geprägter** Begriff [T11:6]
a by the humanists coined term
i.e. a term coined by the humanists

eine **für den Patienten unvorhergesehene** Suggestion [T9:5]
a for-the-patient-unanticipated suggestion
i.e. a suggestion not anticipated by the patient

However, the past participle of intransitive verbs merely indicates a past action:

der **gerade angekommene** Zug
the just-having-arrived train
i.e. the train which has just arrived

Note that in the extended phrase, these participles of the verb have no tense.
Unsachgemäß gerahmt, like *incorrectly framed*, could refer to present, past, or future (*is/was/had been/will be incorrectly framed*).

R118 Word Order within the Extended Phrase

Note the tendency for participles to occur at the end of an extended phrase:

        1   3   2

eine Gemeinschaft der **der Massenvernichtung <u>entronnenen</u>** Juden [T13:5]
a community of from-mass-extermination-having-escaped Jews
i.e. *a community of Jews who escaped mass extermination*

Compare the sentence:

Diese Juden **sind/waren** der Massenvernichtung **entronnen**.

Simple adjectives too (i.e. not derived from verbs) tend to show up in 'final' position within the phrase:

in ihren Abmessungen nicht normgemäße Dias [T23:8]
slides which are not standard (in their) size

For this reason it is usually a good idea to look first at the end of the adjectival part (3) before going to the beginning and reading the remainder in the usual 'left-to-right' sequence:

        1   3   2

die pilzförmigen, **senkrecht zur Achse angeordneten** Stifte [T17:3]
the mushroom-shaped pins
arranged
vertically to the axis
i.e. *the mushroom-shaped pins (which are) arranged vertically to the axis*

R119 Characteristic Sequences

Some sequences are harder to recognize than others at first: a–d are relatively easy to spot because the 'break' is fairly obvious, and in a–c the word order makes reasonably acceptable English. Where there is a 'break' in the word order, this is marked here by a vertical line:

a. ein | **noch zu besprechender** Punkt
   a still-to-be-discussed point

b. ein | **häufig falsch verstandener** Prozeß
   a frequently wrongly understood process

c. der Typus des | **nach innen gerichteten** Musikers
   the type of the introverted (lit.: turned inward) musician

d. die | **der Situation angepaßten** Maßnahmen
   the measures (which are/were . . .) adapted to the situation

e and f are more difficult as they have no introductory word in position 1, so the onset of the sequence is not characterized by a 'break':

e. **nicht zu übersehende** Andeutungen
   not-to-be-ignored indications

f. **auf Statistik beruhende** Aussagen
statements based on statistiics

In g and h the 'break' between 1 and 2 is not at first obvious. It reads like a 'natural' sequence and is only likely to be spotted if you are focusing on the context rather than the immediate words in the sequence:

g. die | **Städte und Dörfer zerstörende** Flutwelle
the whole-towns-and-villages-destroying tidal wave

Here, the sequence is actually **die Flutwelle,** but on a first reading it could be taken to be **die Städte.**

h. die | **ausländischen Autoherstellern günstigen** Bedingungen
the for-foreign-car-manufacturers-favourable conditions

Here, the sequence might be taken to be *the foreign car-manufacturers* (**die ausländischen Autohersteller**—without the dative plural **-n**), but is actually **die (günstigen) Bedingungen**, with the adjectival phrase answering the question: *'Favourable—who to?'*

R120 Combination with Simple Adjectives

It is possible to have a simple adjective together with an extended one. The simple adjective can be to the right or to the left of the extended phrase:

1. **Simple adjective to the left:**

die pilzförmigen,   Stifte [T17:3]
        senkrecht zur Achse angeordneten

Here, the sequence SIMPLE ADJECTIVE + EXTENDED ADJECTIVE is relatively easy to spot, since it is marked by a comma.

2. **Simple adjective to the right:**

eine Gemeinschaft der   osteuropäischen Juden [T13:5]
        der Massenvernichtung entronnenen

The sequence EXTENDED ADJECTIVE + SIMPLE ADJECTIVE is not always demarcated by a comma.

R121 Multiple Phrases

Note the following example, in which there are several extended adjectival phrases:

eine Gemeinschaft der   osteuropäischen Juden.
        der Massenvernichtung entronnenen,
        zufällig überlebenden,
        ungewollt in der Bundesrepublik gestrandeten   [T13:5]

a community of   *East European Jews.*
                                    from-mass-annihilation-having-escaped,
                                    by-chance-surviving,
                                    unwanted-in-the-Federal Republic-stranded

A community of East European Jews who escaped from mass annihilation, surviving
by chance, and stranded unwanted in the Federal Republic

R122 Phrases inside Phrases

This is fairly rare, but it is possible that one extended phrase is embedded within another.
Note how the linear sequence can be broken down into different 'levels':

die wegen ihrer für den Handelsverkehr sehr günstigen Lage blühende Stadt.
the because-of-its-for-trade-very-advantageous-position-flourishing town.

die   Stadt
the   *town*

                                                                            blühende
                                                                            flourishing

            wegen ihrer   Lage
            because of its   *position*

                                    sehr günstigen
                                    very favourable

            für den Handelsverkehr
            for trade

The town, which flourished because of its very favourable position for trade, . . .

R123 Summary: Reading an Extended Phrase

When readers 'lose the thread' of a sentence, one of the likely reasons is that they have
failed to recognize this construction. The following procedure is recommended as a guide
to recognizing and understanding such phrases:

1. Be sensitive to what seem like 'breaks' in the 'natural' (i.e English!) word order
   (→R119).

2. Look carefully to establish what noun belongs with the word at which the 'break'
   occurs. Make the connection between positions 1 and 2 (→R115).

3. Treat all the words in between as a complex adjective, describing some attribute of the
   noun in position 2.

4. In reading the adjectival part (3), it is often useful to read the word at the end before
   returning to the start and reading it 'left to right'.

5. For comprehension purposes, it may be useful to interpret the adjectival part as a
   relative clause, since this is much more likely to produce idiomatic English.

Negation

R124 nicht *(not)*

nicht can negate the verb or another part of the clause. Wherever it appears in the clause it always means **not**, e.g.

> Er kennt dieses Buch **nicht**.
> *He does **not** know this book.*
>
> Das ist **nicht** nötig. [T10b:3]
> *This is **not** necessary.*
>
> Statistik kann **nicht** alles beweisen. [T16:14]
> *Statistics cannot prove everything.*
>
> Das Tonstück ist von den Leuten **nicht** verstanden worden. [T21:2]
> *The piece has **not** been understood by the people.*
>
> Es kann **nicht** genau gemessen werden. [T7:10]
> *It cannot be measured exactly.*
>
> , da die Voraussetzungen **nicht** immer die gleichen sind. [T7: 10]
> *, because the prerequisites are **not** always the same.*

R125 kein *(no, not a, not any)*

kein negates the noun which follows. It is a determiner and is inflected like **ein** (→R97), e.g.

> Er kennt **kein** Buch von diesem Autor.
> *He knows **no** book by this author.*
> *He does **not** know any book by this author.*
>
> Sie brauchen **keine** Rede zu halten. [T10b:1]
> Lit.: *You need make **no** speech. You need **not** make a speech.*
>
> Es gibt **keinen** größeren Feind . . . [T16:18]
> *There is **no** greater enemy . . .*

R126 nicht/kein in Fixed Phrases

Both **nicht** and **kein** are used in combination with other words in fixed phrases. In such combinations the meaning may differ from the meaning of the individual words. Consult the dictionary.

1. **nicht mehr/kein + NOUN mehr**
   mehr means *more*. But **nicht/kein** . . . **mehr** means *no longer*, e.g.

   > Diese Probleme sind ohne sorgfältige Analyse **nicht mehr** zu ordnen.
   > *These problems can **no longer** be worked out without careful analysis.* [T19:9]
   >
   > Das ist **kein** Problem **mehr**.
   > *This is **no longer** a problem.*

2. **nicht einmal**

   einmal means *once*; **nicht einmal** means *not once*, but also *not even*, e.g.

   > **Nicht einmal** 10% der Befragten stimmten zu.
   > ***Not even*** 10% *of those questioned agreed.*

3. **noch nicht**

   noch means *still*, but **noch nicht** means *not [yet]*, e.g.

   > Und das war **noch nicht** alles. [T16:5]
   > *And that was **not [yet]** all.*

4. **nicht ein +** NOUN

   not a single + *NOUN*, e.g

   > **Nicht eine** Frage hat er beantwortet.
   > *He did **not** answer **a single** question.*

5. **bis heute/jetzt nicht**

   not to this day/not yet (do NOT read this as '*not until now*'), e.g.

   > Wir haben den Zweck dieses Werkzeuges **bis heute nicht** feststellen können.
   > *We have **not** been able **to this day** to find out the purpose of this tool.*

6. **nicht zuletzt**

   zuletzt means *last, in the end*; **nicht zuletzt** means *not last* but also *not least*, e.g.

   > Der Bau neuer Verkehrswege verändert das Aussehen der Städte und **nicht zuletzt** das Landschaftsbild.
   > *The building of the new highways changes the appearance of the cities and **not least** the landscape.*

7. **kein +** NUMBER [+ NOUN]

   not even/fewer than + NUMBER [+ NOUN], e.g.

   > **Keine zwanzig Studenten** kamen zu seiner Vorlesung.
   > ***Fewer than twenty students*** *came to his lecture.*

8. **noch kein +** NUMBER [+ NOUN]

   not + NUMBER [+ NOUN *(yet)*], e.g.

   > Sie war **noch keine drei Tage** da, als . . .
   > *She had **not** been there **three days yet** when . . .*

9. **kein noch so +** ADJECTIVE + NOUN

   no + NOUN, *however* + ADJECTIVE, e.g.

   > **Kein noch so kluger Mann**, der nicht ab und zu Fehler macht.
   > *[There is] **no man, however clever**, who does not make a mistake every now and then.*

For **kein/ein →R97**.

R127 Negation Pronouns

1. **keiner/keine/keines** and **niemand** can be used as pronouns with the meaning *nobody, no-one, not anybody, none, not any*, etc.

   Note: these forms are inflected, e.g.

Keiner/Niemand kann behaupten, daß . . .
No one/Nobody can claim that . . .

Er hat es **niemandem/keinem** gesagt.
*He told **no one/nobody**. OR: He did **not** tell **anyone/anybody**.*

2. **nichts** *(nothing)*, e.g.

Leute, die **nichts** lernen wollen. [T22:1]
*People who want to learn **nothing/do not** want to learn **anything**.*

But note:

■ **nichts außer** *(nothing but)* is not really a negation. It can be replaced by **nur** *(only)*.

■ Do not mix up **nichts** and **nicht**:

Er trinkt **nicht**. *(He does **not** drink. [alcohol])*
Er trinkt **nichts**. *(He drinks **nothing**. OR: He is **not** drinking **anything**.)*

R128 Other Negation Words

1. **ebensowenig** literally means *just as little*. Often it can be read as *neither*. But sometimes it has to be interpreted much more loosely according to context, e.g.

Als Wissenschaftler war er nicht besonders begabt. **Ebensowenig** hat er als Dozent überzeugt.
*He was not very gifted as a scientist. **Neither** was he convincing as a lecturer.*

2. **kaum** *(hardly, scarcely)*, e.g.

Ein Unterschied zwischen Vergangenheit und Gegenwart existierte **kaum**. [T3:3]
*There was **hardly** a difference between past and present.*

3. **keinesfalls/auf keinen Fall**
under no circumstances/not under any circumstances, e.g.

Das darf **keinesfalls** veröffentlicht werden.
*This must **not** be published **under any circumstances**.*

4. **keineswegs** *(not at all, by no means, in no way)*, e.g.

Die Antwort auf diese Frage ist **keineswegs** ausgemacht.
*The answer to this question is **by no means** certain.*

mitnichten is an old form with the same meaning as **keineswegs**.

5. **nie/niemals/noch nie/nimmer** *(never)*, e.g.

Es ist **nie** möglich. [T7:5]
*It is **never** possible.*

6. **nirgends/nirgendwo** *(nowhere, not anywhere)*, e.g.

Ich konnte das Buch **nirgends** finden.
*I could find the book **nowhere**. I could **not** find the book **anywhere**.*

7. **ohne (** *(without)*, e.g.

. . . **ohne** bewußte, sorgfältige Analyse [T19:9]
. . . ***without*** *conscious, careful analysis*

But note: **ohnehin** *(inevitably, in any case)* is not a negative.

8. **ohne daß** *(without that/without . . . ing)*, e.g.

..., **ohne daß** es einen ersichtlichen Grund gibt. [T19:5]
..., *without* there *being* an obvious reason.

R129 Words which Indicate the Presence of a Negation

1. **sondern** *(but)* is used instead of 'aber' after a negation, e.g.

   Ich werde das Buch nicht kaufen, **sondern** ausleihen.
   *I shall not buy the book, **but** borrow it.*

   Er ist kein Kind mehr, **sondern** ein Erwachsener.
   *He is no longer a child, **but** an adult.*

   Er hat ihn nicht über-, **sondern** unterschätzt.
   *He did not overestimate, **but** underestimate him.*

   →**R181.3** for COMPOUND WORDS with the same base component.

2. **weder . . . .noch . . . [noch . . .]** *(neither . . . nor . . . [nor. . .])*, e.g.

   Weder der Hinweis auf Fehlleistungen . . . **noch** die irreführende Identifizierung . . . [T19:10]
   ***Neither** pointing out the failures . . . **nor** the misleading identification . . .*

3. **dafür aber** *(but [instead])*, e.g.

   Aufgabe A hat er **nicht** gemacht, **dafür aber** Aufgabe C.
   *He did **not** answer question A, **but** he did question C [**instead**].*

4. **im Gegenteil** *(on the contrary)*, e.g.

   Er löste das Problem nicht. **Im Gegenteil**, er komplizierte die Sache.
   *He did not solve the problem. **On the contrary** he complicated the matter.*

5. **gar/überhaupt** *(at all)*. These two words can be used to intensify a negation, e.g.

   Und wir kommen **überhaupt** nicht mehr durch. [T19:6]
   *And we no longer get through **at all**.*

   Ich konnte es **gar** nirgends finden.
   *I could not find it anywhere **at all**.*

R130 Negation Suffix: -los;
Negation Prefixes: un-, a-, des-, in-, miß-

(See also **R184–6** for WORD FORMATION)

arbeits**los**	*unemployed*
schuld**los**	*free from blame, innocent*
unzureichend	*insufficient* [T20:11]
menschen**unwürdig**	inhumane/beneath human dignity [T14:8]

   →**R181** for COMPOUND WORDS

asozial	*antisocial*
Desinteresse	*lack of interest*
instabil	*unstable*
Mißverständnis	*misunderstanding*
mißachten	*to disregard*

R131 Negation Words as Part of Compounds

Negation words can occasionally be used as integral parts of COMPOUND WORDS (→R181), e.g.

das **Nicht**erreichen [T20:14]	*the non-achievement*
das **Nie**dagewesene	*the unprecedented; lit.: never-been-here*
zweifels**ohne**	*without doubt, undoubtedly*

R132 Verbs with a Negative Meaning

Note that some verbs have a negative meaning, e.g. **fehlen** *(to be lacking, missing).*

Den Deutschen **fehlten** nach dem Krieg die nötigen Ressourcen.
*The necessary resources **were not available** to the Germans after the war.*

This verb can be difficult to translate because it is a so-called DATIVE verb. Also see **R96**.

ausbleiben   *fail to appear/materialize*
Die Antwort **blieb aus**.   *There was no reply.*

For idiomatic usage of negation words consult the dictionary!

R133 Double Negation

This roughly corresponds to the English usage.

1. Two negatives = A positive statement, e.g.

Denn es **fehlt** auch **nicht** der Hinweis, daß . . . [T20:16]
(es fehlt means *there is a lack of, there is no . . ., . . . is missing*)
Lit.: *Also the indication is **not missing** that (i.e. it is there).*
Also because the indication is there that

Sie sprach mit **niemandem**, der das noch **nicht** gehört hatte.
*She spoke to **no one** who had **not** yet heard it.*
Everybody she spoke to had heard it.

2. Negation word + word with negative meaning = Limited positive meaning, e.g.

Nicht unwillig stimmte er zu.
Lit.: ***Not un**willingly he agreed.*
Quite willingly he agreed.

Note, however, that in older texts (mainly pre-nineteenth-century) a double negative may mean an intensified negative, e.g.

. . . das der Bapst noch **nie keyn** mal hat mit schrifft odder vornunft widderlegt eynen, der widder yhn geredt . . . hatt, . . . (Luther, 1520)
(**nie** means *never*, **keyn mal (keinmal)** means *never once*)
*. . . that the pope **never, not** even once, through the Scriptures or through reasoning, proved anyone wrong who has spoken against him . . .*

R134 Rhetorical Negation (in Questions and Exclamations)

Der Vortrag war interessant, **nicht wahr**?
*The lecture was interesting, **wasn't it?**/**Wasn't** the lecture interesting!*
Was der **nicht alles** weiß!
The things he knows!

Text Features

Text consists of individual sentences which form a coherent and continuous whole. The following sections focus on features which belong to the text rather than to individual sentences. Being able to recognize them helps to promote fluent reading because they help to signal the way the meaning of the text as a whole is being developed. Of course, some of these features can also serve to link parts of a sentence, but they are listed here because they are important for reading 'beyond the sentence'.

R135 Pro-Words

These are words which refer back to some other word or words earlier in the text. The main kinds of 'PRO-WORD' are pronouns and words like **so, dieser/e/es** and **solcher/e/es**.

1. PRONOUNS usually refer back to a noun. For pronoun forms, see **R98–100**.

> **Die Temperatur** verursacht eine Veränderung des Durchmessers der Stahlstange. **Sie** verändert auch die Länge. [T7:8]

> **Der Sozialismus** zieht radikale Konsequenzen und ruft zum Umsturz des kapitalistischen Systems auf. In Karl Marx findet **er seinen** führenden Theoretiker. [T14:13–14]

German pronouns are part of the case and gender system (see **R90–1**):

> The GENDER of the pronoun must be the same as the gender of the noun to which it refers.

> The CASE of the pronoun does not have to be the same as the case of the noun to which it refers.

The noun referred to may be further back in the text than is usual in English. It is likely that non-subject forms and possessive forms will be harder to recognize:

> In **Bach und Händel** fand das Barockzeitalter **seine** Krönung. So unterschiedlich wie **ihr** Lebenslauf ist auch **ihr** Lebenswerk. [T8:1]

Here, **seine** refers back to **das Barockzeitalter** (*its*); while **ihr** refers back to Bach and Händel (*their*).

> Nehmen wir an, die Fähigkeit einer **Person**, arithmetische Probleme zu lösen, werde durch Zeitmessungen ermittelt. Im ersten Versuch wird ihr erlaubt, sich zu üben; damit wird **sie** es in **ihrem** nächsten Versuch sehr wahrscheinlich besser machen. [T7:15–16]

Here, three words refer back to the feminine noun **die Person** (*person*):

> **ihr wird erlaubt . . .**: *this person is allowed . . .* (The verb **erlauben** dictates the dative case →**R93, R96**).
> **sie**: *he* or *she* (nominative case).
> **in ihrem nächsten Versuch**: *in this person's next attempt* (possessive, dative because of the preposition **in** →**R194**).

Further examples:

> Mittelalter: ein von den Humanisten geprägter Begriff für die Zeit zwischen dem Verfall der Antike und **ihrer** Wiedergeburt (Renaissance). [T11:6]

> Die Arbeiter wohnen in oft menschenunwürdigen Behausungen. **Ihr** Verdienst liegt meistens an der Grenze des Existenzminimums. [T14:8–9]

dessen and **deren** can sometimes be used in place of possessive pronouns:

> Neben einem wohlhabenden Industriebürgertum entsteht ein ständig wachsendes **Industrieproletariat**. Mit sinkenden Reallöhnen verschlechtert sich **dessen** Situation zunehmend. [T14:6–7; also T9:2]

2. **so** often refers back to a concept expressed earlier in a verb or in a clause:

> „'Wir müssen eine Art Vereinigter Staaten von Europa schaffen . . .'. **So** sagte der bedeutende britische Premierminister Winston Churchill. [T2:6–9; also see T10b:4, T12:3]

3. **dieser (diese, dieses); jener (jene, jenes)** can be used in the sense 'the latter' and 'the former' respectively.

> Das Barockzeitalter fand seine Krönung in **Bach** und **Händel**. Dieser stellte den seines Lebens in den dienst der Oper, **jener** beschäftigte sich nie mit dieser Form. [T8:1–4]

4. **mancher (manche, manches); solcher (solche, solches)** can refer back to nouns earlier in the text:

> Es gibt einige **Probleme**. Für **manche** gibt es keine einfache Lösung.
> *There are many problems. For many/some of them there is no simple solution.*

R136 da PREP, WO PREP, hier PREP (→R163)

All these constructions refer back to something mentioned earlier. German usage here is like antiquated English words such as *thereafter, whereafter,* and *hereafter*.

> Je älter also man wird, desto größer ist die Wahrscheinlichkeit, daß er am Krebs stirbt. **Darin** lag die Lösung. [T16:10–11]

> Das Kernland der industriellen Revolution ist Preußen, das ein immer stärkeres wirtschaftliches Gewicht innerhalb Deutschlands gewinnt. **Damit** wird zugleich auch seine politische Stellung gestärkt. [T14:15–16]

The constructions involved are:

1. **da + (r) + a preposition** (e.g. dabei, darin, dadurch)
2. **wo + (r) + a preposition** (e.g. wobei, worin, wodurch)
3. **hier + a preposition** (e.g. hierbei, hierin, hierdurch)

Here are three examples using the same preposition:

1. Zur Schematisierung seines Gegenstandes teilt der Historiker das bisherige Geschehen in zusammenhängende Zeitabschnitte ein. **Dabei** wurde es seit dem 17. Jahrhundert üblich, die Weltgeschichte in Vorgeschichte, Alte, Mittlere und Neuere Geschichte zu gliedern. [T11:1–2]

2. Von keiner Kunst verlangt man Ähnliches, sondern begnügt sich mit den Wirkungen

ihres Materials, **wobei** allerdings in den anderen Künsten das Stoffliche dem beschränkten Auffassungsvermögen des geistigen Mittelstandes von selbst entgegenkommt. [T21:3]

3. Beide Mittel, das Placebo und das Originalmittel, werden verordnet, um den suggestiven und den chemischen Anteil eines Medikaments auseinanderzuhalten. Es handelt sich **hierbei** um eine absichtliche, für den Patienten dagegen unvorhergesehene Suggestion. [T9:4–5]

For other examples, see T2:8, 10b:10, 16:16 (**dazu**); T7:16, 8:8, 9:2 (**damit**); T10a:4 (**dabei**), T7:17 (**dadurch**), T8:9 (**daraus**).

Note that daPREP can also point forward to an item later in the same sentence. This is a usage that is quite different from English (→**R88**, **R155**).

Note that while **daPREP** and **hierPREP** can refer back to a previous sentence, **woPREP** usually refers back to the content of the previous clause:

Weil die Oberstifte nach unten gedrückt werden, sperren sie die Trennlinie zwischen Zylinder und Gehäuse, **wodurch** der Zylinder nicht gedreht werden kann. [T17:5]

R137 'Missing' Words and Parts of Words

Often, words or parts of words are missed out in order to avoid needlessly repeating them.

1. The missing item may be part of a word. Note the hyphen:

Dieser Kontinent hat mehr Kriegs- als Friedensjahre erlebt. [T2:2]
(i.e mehr Kriegs**jahre** als Friedensjahre)

Informationsverzerrungen oder -verluste
(i.e Informationsverzerrungen oder **Informations**verluste)
distortions or loss of information

2. The missing item may be part of a noun construction. The gap left by the 'missing' item is shown by ø. The word which it would have repeated is boxed:

Hätte es eine deutlichere ø als diese einfach bestätigte ⟨ Korrelation ⟩ geben können? [T16:7]

ein Tonstück müsse ⟨ Vorstellungen ⟩ irgendwelcher Art erwecken, und wenn solche ø ausbleiben . . . [T21:2]

This can lead to two determiners appearing one after the other:

Ihre ⟨ Bewohner ⟩ erreichten ein höheres Alter als die ø der anderen Länder. [T16:12]
(i.e. 'than those ø of the other countries')

. . . sodaß seine durchschnittliche ⟨ Dichte ⟩ geringer wird als die ø des Wassers. [T18:11]
(i.e 'than that ø of water')

Where there are several nouns or noun phrases in a sentence care must sometimes be taken to interpret the 'missing' item or items correctly:

Die Geschichte der arbeitenden Klasse in England beginnt ⟨ mit der Erfindung ⟩ der Dampfmaschine und ø ø ø der Maschinen zur Verarbeitung der Baumwolle. [T4:1]

Here the sequence is not **mit der Maschinen**, but **mit der Erfindung der Maschinen**.

The missing item may be a preposition:

die Kunde ⌐von⌐ seiner Kunst, ø ⌐seiner⌐ Religion und ø ø Lebensanschauung [T12:1]

(Note that both **von** and **seiner** are 'missing' in the second half of this phrase.)

3. The missing item may be part of the verb and its completion. The pattern is sometimes like that found in English:

In ihrer Zeit ⌐ wurde ⌐ die erste Atombombe gezündet, ø der erste Elektronenrechner gebaut, ø die Doppelhelix enträtselt. [T3:7]

But often the pattern is unlike English, especially where there is a verb-final word order (→**R11**):

. . . Kriege, die ganze Städte ø, halbe Völker ⌐vernichteten⌐ . [T2:1]

Auch der Arzt weiß nicht, welches das zu prüfende Medikament ø und welches das Leerpräparat ⌐ist⌐ . [T9:10]

(For a more complicated example, see T15:10.)

Note the double omission in:

Der Zylinder ⌐kann⌐ gedreht ø, das Schloß also ø geöffnet ⌐werden⌐ . [T17:7]

In high or affected style, the finite verb in a verb-final construction may be omitted:

Den Menschen der Vorzeit kennen wir in den Entwicklungsstadien, die er durchlaufen ⌐hat⌐ , durch die unbelebten Denkmäler und Geräte, die er uns hinterlasssen ø. [T12:1]

(The 'missing' word here is **hat**.)

R138 Logical Connectors: single words and phrases

These are words or phrases which help to develop and connect the ideas in a text in a way that makes clear how they relate to each other, e.g. by adding further information of the same kind, by adding a note of contrast, or by explaining where something has come from or what it has led to.

They are listed here under headings which give an approximate guide to their meaning in a text:

1. 'HOWEVER', etc.

The following signal some kind of contrast or opposition to what has been said before, sometimes challenging what has been said earlier:

aber	*but, however*
andererseits	*on the other hand* [T5:10]
dagegen	*against that, on the other hand* [T8:9, 9:4, 10b:2, 18:10]
dennoch	*however, but, nevertheless* [T20:4]
doch	*however, but, nevertheless* [T5:3, 9:7]
eher (als)	*rather (than)*
gleichwohl	*yet, nevertheless*
hingegen	*against that, on the other hand*
im Gegenteil	*on the contrary*
immerhin	*nevertheless*
indes	*however*
jedoch	*however, but, nevertheless* [T22:4]
nunmehr (nun)	*(not x but) actually (y)* [T17:6]
trotzdem	*nevertheless* [T20:10]
vielmehr	*(not x but) actually (y)*
während	*whereas* (see **R163**; T1:3, 1:4, 19:8]

e.g.   Alle diese Einrichtungen stellen die bestehende Ordnung nicht in Frage. Der Sozialismus **dagegen** zieht radikale Konsequenzen. [T14:12–13]

2. 'IN ADDITION' etc.

The following extend the current line of thought by adding a new idea. They can all be used with the meaning 'in addition':

außerdem	[T12:2, 14:17]
darüber hinaus	*over and above that*
dazu	[T11:2, 14:15]
hinzu	
mehr noch	
noch	
sowie	*as well as*
zudem	[T22:3]

e.g.   Andere Gründe werden genannt: die mangelnde Auslastung neuer Anlagen ebenso wie das Fehlen qualifizierter Arbeitskräfte. **Darüber hinaus** nannten viele Unternehmen den „Mangel an Kapital" als Hemmnis. [T20:13–14]

3. 'THEREFORE' etc.

The following show that there is a relationship of cause and effect:

also	*therefore*
aus diesem Grund	*for this reason*
daher	*therefore* [T9:4, 17:1]
darum	*for this reason* [T4:3]
deshalb	*therefore*
denn	*for, because* [T2:16, 20:16, 22:3]
so daß	*with the result that* (also see 4 below)

e.g.   England ist **darum** das klassische Land für die Entwicklung des Proletariats. [T4:3]

4. 'IN ORDER THAT' (to express purpose):

damit   *in order that*

e.g.   Die Musik der Atome muß umgewandelt werden, **damit** der Mensch sie hören kann. [T5:6]

Note the difference in meaning between **damit** and **so daß** (above). Note also the different uses of **damit**. Compare the examples in **R136**.

5. 'CORRESPONDINGLY' etc.

The following show that there is a commensurate relationship between the current sentence and an earlier sentence, i.e. that one thing corresponds to or equates to another:

dementsprechend	*accordingly* (also as two words, T22:3)
demnach	*accordingly* [T11:3]
demgemäß	*accordingly*
demzufolge	*accordingly*
ebenfalls	*also, equally*
ebenso	(+ Adjective or adverb) *equally, just as* [T20:13, 22:5]
entsprechend	(as an adjective, or followed by an adjective or adverb) *corresponding-ly*
in gleicher Weise	*in the same way* (see T7:14]
um so	(+ Comparative adjective or adverb) *all the -er*
wiederum	*in its/their etc. turn* (showing a similarity between two consequences or events)

e.g. Zur Schematisierung seines Gegenstandes teilt der Historiker das bisherige Geschehen in zusammenhängende Zeitabschnitte ein. Dabei wurde es üblich, . . . die Begriffe Neueste Geschichte und Zeitgeschichte zu verwenden. **Demnach** stellt sich eine schematische Gliederung der abendländischen Geschichte folgendermaßen dar: [T11:1–3]

6. 'ADMITTEDLY', 'INDEED' etc.

The following add a concessionary note:

allerdings	*admittedly, indeed* [T20:10, 21:3]
immerhin	*all the same, indeed* [T21:7]
schon	*admittedly, indeed* (also see **R163**)
zugegebenermaßen	*admittedly*

e.g. Selbst Schopenhauer . . . verliert sich. Obwohl ihm dabei klar sein muß, daß die Sprache der Welt . . . verlorengeht. Aber **immerhin** ist er berechtigt . . . [T21:5–7]

7. 'IN OTHER WORDS'/'TO SUM UP'

The following spell out or explain what has just been said:

also	*that is to say* [T11:6, 16:2, 18:5] (also see **R158.2**)
das heißt (d. h.)	*that is to say* [T9:4]
kurzum	*in short* [T19:1]
mit anderen Worten (m. a. W.)	*in other words*
nämlich	*you see, in other words* [T10b: 6]
zusammenfassend	*in conclusion, briefly*

e.g. In den US-Staaten Minnesota und Wisconsin, in Gegenden **also**, in denen viel Milch konsumiert wurde . . . [T16:2]

8. 'IN PARTICULAR'

The following help a writer to pick out a particular aspect from what has been said and to give it a particular prominence:

gerade	*even, especially*
besonders	*especially* [T16:17]
insbesondere	*especially* [T20:7]
selbst	*even* [see **R163**; T21:5]
sogar	*even* [T1:4]
vor allem	*above all* [T2:3, 14:2]
zumal	*especially*

e.g.   Im Nürnberger Bereich wird vielfach auf die Überlegenheit der USA und Japan verwiesen. Beklagt wird hier **insbesondere** die Abhängigkeit der Deutschen von Vorlieferungen aus diesen Ländern. [T20:6–7]

9. 'APART FROM THAT'

The following all mean 'apart from that', 'otherwise':

ansonsten
außerdem (also see 2 above)
im übrigen
davon abgesehen
sonst

10. 'FOR EXAMPLE'

zum Beispiel
etwa (see **R163**; T20:8)

e.g.   der zeitweilig vorhandene Rückstand **etwa** bei der Aufwendung der Mikroelektronik [T20:8]

11. 'IN THIS WAY, LIKE THIS'

auf diese Weise
so (also see **R135.2**)

12. 'UNLIKE'

anders (als)	*differently*
im Gegensatz zu	*in contrast to*
zum Unterschied von	*unlike*

13. 'THEN AND NOW'

Any combination of the following can be used to contrast the past with the present:

THEN	NOW
damals (noch)	**heute**
früher	**heutzutage**
in jener Zeit (noch)	**jetzt**
(noch) im 17. Jahrhundert	

R139 Logical Connectors: Paired Words and Sequences

1. Paired Words

The following are logical pairs of words which may be separated in a text and can appear in different sentences:

zwar . . ., aber	*indeed, . . . but*
zwar . . ., doch	[T16:14]
zwar . . ., jedoch	*it is true . . ., however*
je . . ., desto (je . . . je)	*the . . ., the . . . (as in: 'the more, the better')*
nicht . . ., sondern	*not [x] but [y]* [cf T9:10]
nicht nur . . ., sondern (auch)	*not only [x], but also [y]*
nicht mehr . . ., sondern	*no longer [x], but [y]*
einerseits . . ., andererseits	
auf der einen Seite . . ., auf der anderen (Seite)	*on the one hand . . . on the other*
entweder . . . oder	*either . . . or* [T12:1]
weder . . . noch	*neither . . . nor* [T19:10]
sowohl . . . als auch	*both . . . and*
die einen . . ., die anderen	*some . . ., others* [T21:4]
wer . . ., der . . .	*whoever . . .*
so (adjective or verb) . . ., daß	*so . . . that (e.g. 'so big that'; in such a way that . . .*

e.g.: **Je** älter man wird, **desto** größer ist die Wahrscheinlichkeit, daß er am Krebs stirbt. [cf. T16:10]

2. Sequences

Any combination of the following signals that several things are being enumerated in a text:

FIRST OF ALL	THEN/NEXT	FINALLY
erstens *first*	**zweitens** *second*	
	drittens *third*	
	viertens *fourth* (etc.)	
zunächst *to begin with*	**dann** *then*	**abschließend** *in conclusion*
		schließlich *finally*
zuallererst *first of all*	**anschließend** *next*	**zum Schluß** *in conclusion*
	ferner *further*	**zusammenfassend** *in conclusion*

[T15:2, 22:1]

R140 'Superfluous' Words (→R138, R139)

German has a number of 'modal particles', words which can be used to express the author's personal attitude towards what he or she is saying and which also address the reader and try to engage the reader more directly in what is being said. Although these words are more characteristic of spoken German, they are also found in written German, especially in argumentative or evaluative texts. (Many of the words listed in **R138–9** have a similar function.)

For beginning readers who insist on finding the meaning of every word, these modal particles can retard or disrupt reading of a text. For comprehension and translation purposes, they can often be disregarded. The commonest such words are:

auch denn doch eben eigentlich einmal gar ja jedenfalls noch schließlich schon sicher wohl

e.g. So war es jedenfalls in Glasgow (T10b:5)
Well anyway, that's how it was in Glasgow.

These words can also occur together in combinations, e.g. **eben ja noch**.

Note that most of these words can also be used as 'regular' words with a 'straight' dictionary meaning: and that **auch** and **denn** can also connect clauses (→**R2, R160, R163**). Most of these words can have several meanings, e.g.

doch	can also mean *however* or express dissent (→**R138.1**)
eben	can also mean *even, level* (→**R163**)
eigentlich	can also mean *actual, real*
einmal	can also mean *once*
gar	can also intensify a negative (**gar nicht** *not at all*)
ja	can also mean *yes*
noch	can also mean *still* or *yet* (noch nicht *not yet*) (→**R138.2**)
schließlich	can also mean *in conclusion, finally*
schon	can also mean *already* (→**R138.6, R163**)
sicher	can also mean *safe, secure, certain*
wohl	can also mean *well* (→**R163**)

With experience, it should be possible to see from the context whether these words are being used as 'modals' or in their straight 'dictionary' sense. Here are some examples:

'Modal' Use	'Regular' Use
Er durfte nicht **einmal** mehr in der Volksversammlung sprechen. [T15:10]	Man kann das **einmal** machen, aber beim zweiten Mal . . . *You can do that once. But the second time . . .*
Die Engländerinnen überlebten die japanischen Frauen **gar** um zwölf Jahre [T16:13]	Das ist **gar** kein Problem. *That is no problem at all*
Man tritt **wohl** im Frack an? [T10a:6]	Ihm war nicht **wohl** bei der Sache. *He was not happy with the matter.*
Den Talar leiht man Ihnen **sicher** von der Universität [T10b:4]	Es ist nicht **sicher**, ob das stimmt . . . *It is not certain whether that is true . . .*
Das man heutzutage **ja** wirklich nötig [T10b:11] *We really need that these days (of course)*	Ja, wirklich. *Yes indeed*

Complex Sentences

R141 Expanding Clauses

Any clause may be expanded by adding any number of DEPENDENT CLAUSES and CONSTRUCTIONS, e.g.

> **Der Student lernt Deutsch.**
>
> *The student is learning German.*
>
> **Der Student lernt Deutsch**, weil er das Buch im Original lesen will.
>
> *The student is learning German, because he wants to read the book in the original (version).*
>
> Weil der Student das Buch im Original lesen will, **lernt er Deutsch.**
>
> *Because the student wants to read the book in the original (version), he is learning German.*
>
> **Der Student**, der das Buch im Original lesen will, **lernt Deutsch.**
>
> *The student who wants to read the book in the original (version) is learning German.*

DEPENDENT CLAUSES and CONSTRUCTIONS may

precede ⟶ the MAIN CLAUSE ⟵ follow

e.g. Der Student lernt Deutsch.

↑

be inserted in

The different types of dependent clauses and constructions are given below.

R142 Dependent Clauses introduced by a Conjunction

CONJUNCTION	FINITE VERB
, **daß** sie trotzdem Probleme	**haben.** [T20:10]
*that they nevertheless **have** problems*	

The finite verb appears in FINAL position (➔**R1** and **R12**) and the clause is always separated from the main clause by a COMMA.

R143 Common Conjunctions

als (*when, as*)	**indem** (*while, as, by [. . . ing]*)	**während** (*while, whereas*)
bevor (*before*)	**je . . . [desto]** (*the . . . er, the . . . er*) See note below for example.	**wann** (*when*)
bis (*until, till*)	**nachdem** (*after*)	**warum** (*why*)
da (*as, since*)	**ob** (*if, whether*)	**weil** (*because*)
damit (*so that, in order for*)	**obwohl** (*although*) **obgleich** (*although*)	**wenn** (*if, in case/ when*)
daß or **dass** (*that*) (→R191)	**seit** (*since*) **seitdem** (*since*)	**wie** (*as, like; how*)
ehe (*before*)	**so . . . auch** (*however*) See note below for example.	**wo** (*where*)
falls (*if, in case*)	**solange** (*as long as*)	

Note:

- **als, da, damit, während, wie** also have other functions. →**R163**

- **wann, warum, wie, wo** are used in indirect questions. →**R10.8**
  e.g. Ich weiß nicht, **wo** er wohnt. *I don't know **where** he lives.*

- **Je** älter also jemand wird, **desto** größer ist die Wahrscheinlichkeit . . . [T16:10]
  *The older someone gets, **the** greater is the probability . . .*

- **So** schnell er **auch** arbeitet, ... *However fast he works* . . . . . .

Consult the dictionary for less frequently occurring conjunctions and for rarer meanings of those given above.

R144 Positions Dependent Clauses introduced by a Conjunction

These may be found:

1. following the main clause, e.g.
   Der Durchmesser ist an einem warmen Tag größer,
   weil das Metall sich **ausdehnt**.   [T7:7]
   The diameter is greater on a warm day
   ***because** the metal expands.*

2. preceding the main clause, e.g.
   Damit ein eisernes Schiff **schwimmt**,   [T18:11]
   muß sein Inneres sehr viel Luftraum enthalten.
   In order for an iron ship to float, it(s inner space) must contain a lot of airspace.

When a dependent clause or construction precedes the main clause
it constitutes the FIRST CONCEPT of the main clause. (→**R5**)

Note the characteristic . . . FINITE VERB, FINITE VERB . . . pattern, e.g.

I	II	III	IV
CONJUNCTION	**FINITE VERB,**	**FINITE VERB**	
Damit ein Schiff	**schwimmt,**	**muß**	es Luftraum enthalten

When an 'if'-clause with or without **wenn** (→**R16**) precedes the main clause **so** or **dann** (then) are often found preceding the finite verb of the main clause, e.g.

I	II		
Taucht man ihn aber in Wasser,	**so**	wiegt er nur 1,7 kg.	[T18:3]
Wenn wir . . . aufstellen würden,	**dann**	wäre dies . . .	[T19:4]

*If one immerses it in water, **then** it only weighs 1.7 kg.*
*If we were to put up . . . ., **then** this would be . . . .*

3. inserted within a main clause, e.g.

Der Gedanke, **obwohl** es eigentlich kein neuer **war**, erschreckte sie sehr.
The idea, although it was not a new one, scared her very much.
Sie warf den Brief, **nachdem** sie ihn gelesen **hatte**, in den Papierkorb.
She threw the letter in the waste paper basket, after she had read it.

Note: The insertion of a dependent clause within a main clause does not alter the word order of the main clause.

R145 Occasionally a CONJUNCTION may be preceded by words such as **aber** (but), **eben** (exactly, precisely), **gerade** (especially), **auch** (also), **doch** (but), e.g.

Eben weil das Metall sich ausdehnt, muß es noch einmal gemessen werden.
*(It is) **precisely** because the metal expands, (that) it has to be measured again.*

Such preceding words may give additional emphasis, link the dependent clause closer to preceding clauses or simply function as 'fillers'.

R146 Note that a dependent clause can be the SUBJECT of the main clause (→**R86**), e.g.

SUBJECT
Daß dies ein Trugschluß **ist,** sei durch einen Vergleich veranschaulicht. [T19:3]
That this is a fallacy can be shown by a comparison.

R147 Relative Clauses

→**R110** for the function of relative clauses and forms of RELATIVE PRONOUNS, e.g.

	RELATIVE PRONOUN	FINITE VERB
. . . Entwicklungsstadien,	**die** er durchlaufen	**hat** [T12:1]
. . . stages of development	*which* he has passed through	

In a relative clause the finite verb appears in FINAL position (→**R1** and **R12**) and the clause is always separated by a COMMA from the noun or clause it refers to.

A relative pronoun may be preceded by a PREPOSITION (For lists of prepositions see **R94** and **R95**), e.g.

	PREPOSITION		
Menschen,	**von**	**denen** wir **glauben**	[T12:2]
people	*of*	*whom we believe*	

R148 When RELATIVE CLAUSES relate to individual words or phrases in the previous clause they can be found in almost any position within or following the main clause, e.g.

Nach diesem Prinzip wird jeder Körper, **der** in eine Flüssigkeit getaucht wird, leichter. [T18:2]
*According to this principle, any body **which** is immersed in a fluid becomes lighter.*

Ein Würfel aus Holz, **der** etwa 0,8 kg wiegt, taucht nicht tief ins Wasser ein. [T18:8]
*A wooden cube **which** weighs about 0.8 kg, does not sink deep into the water.*

Es entsteht ein Industrieproletariat, **das** sich aus Handwerkern und Landarbeitern rekrutiert. [T14:6]
*An industrial proletariat arises **which** is recruited mainly from manual and agricultural workers.*

When a RELATIVE CLAUSE relates to the whole previous clause it follows the clause it relates to, e.g.

Seine Reaktion war durchaus positiv, **was** sie sehr überraschte.
*His reaction was quite positive, **which** rather surprised her.*

R149 zu + Infinitive Clauses

e.g.

	(comma)		ZU +	INFINITIVE
Es ist nicht möglich	, den genauen Durchmesser	**zu**		**bestimmen.** [T7:5]
*It is not possible **to***	*determine the exact diameter.*			

The ZU + INFINITIVE is always in final position within this 'INFINITIVE CLAUSE'.

An INFINITIVE construction with **zu** (e.g. Er beabsichtigt **zu arbeiten**. *He intends **to work**.*) which contains further information (even if it is just one additional word, e.g. Er beabsichtigt, **jetzt zu arbeiten**: *He intends **to work now***) was traditionally separated from the rest of the clause by a comma. However, the Spelling Reform of 1996 (→**R191**) abolished this rule. You will, of course, find the comma in older texts.

Note:

- **zu** has many functions other than in connection with INFINITIVE CLAUSES. →**R163**
- For **ist . . . zu** + INFINITIVE (see **R78.2**).

R150 Note the position of ZU + INFINITIVE in the following example where two long infinitive clauses are linked by **und**.

Es wurde üblich, in den geschichtlichen Lehrbüchern die Weltgeschichte in Vorgeschichte, Alte, Mittlere und Neuere Geschichte **zu gliedern und** seit 1945 dazu auch die Begriffe Neueste Geschichte und Zeitgeschichte **zu verwenden**. [T11:2]

*In historical text books it has become usual **to divide** the history of the world into Prehistory, Ancient History, Medieval and Modern History **and** also, since 1945, **to use** the terms (Most) Recent History and Contemporary History.*

R151 Introduced zu + Infinitive Clauses

ZU + INFINITIVE CLAUSES may be introduced by one of these words:

um (*in order to*), **ohne** (*without . . . ing*), **(an)statt** (*instead of . . . ing*), e.g.

Um eine gute Schätzung **zu erhalten**, werden verschiedene Messungen zusammengenommen. [T7:4]
In order to get a good estimate, several readings are taken together.

Sie beantworteten seine Fragen, **ohne** lange **zu überlegen**.
*They answered his questions **without thinking** about it for long.*

Anstatt den Bericht **zu lesen**, legte sie ihn zu den Akten.
Instead of reading the report she filed it away.

If **um/ohne/(an)statt** introduce a ZU + INFINITIVE CLAUSE they appear at the beginning of the sentence or immediately after the comma if there is one.

um/ohne/(an)statt may occasionally be preceded by words such as aber (*but*), eben (*exactly, precisely*), gerade (*especially*), auch (*also*), doch (*but*), e.g.

Doch um die Situation **zu verstehen**, muß man erst . . .
But in order to understand the situation, one first has to . . .

R152 Occasionally, **um/ohne/(an)statt** (despite appearing at the beginning of a sentence or straight after a comma) are *not* part of a ZU + INFINITIVE construction, e.g.

Er beabsichtigte, **ohne** Pause zu arbeiten.
*He intended to work **without** (a) break.*

If **um/ohne/(an)statt** appear somewhere else within the clause they are never part of a zu + INFINITIVE construction, e.g.

Sie hatten die Möglichkeit, die Straßenkreuzung **ohne** Verkehrsanlage zu ordnen. [T19:8]
*They had the opportunity to regulate the traffic **without** traffic signals.*

Sie beabsichtigten, die Preise **um** 10% zu reduzieren.
*They intended to reduce the prices **by** 10%.*

R153 ZU + INFINITIVE CLAUSES can be found preceding or following other clauses (see examples above) or, occasionally, inserted within a clause, e.g.

Ihre Absicht, das Experiment **zu beenden**, ist leider nicht durchführbar.
*Her intention, (that is) **to complete/finish** the experiment, is unfortunately not feasible.*

R154 For zu + SEPARABLE VERB see **R39** and **R173**, e.g.

Um dieser Kritik **zuvorzukommen,** möchte ich betonen, . . .
In order to anticipate this criticism, I would like to emphasize . . .

R155 da(+r) + PREPOSITION (e.g.: daraus, darauf, dabei, dafür, dagegen etc.) preceding DEPENDENT CLAUSES (→R136, R163, R88)

Dependent clauses introduced by **daß** or zu + INFINITIVE clauses can complete NOUN + PREPOSITION or VERB + PREPOSITION PHRASES, e.g.

Sie lassen keinen Zweifel daran, daß sie Probleme haben. [T20:10]
(Zweifel an (NOUN + PREPOSITION) *doubts about*)
They leave no doubt that they have problems.

Sie sollen sich darauf beschränken, bessere Lebensbedingungen zu schaffen.
(sich beschränken auf (VERB + PREPOSITION) *to confine oneself to*)
They should confine themselves to creating better living conditions.

If the information which completes the message of the phrase (e.g. above: to confine oneself to what? doubts about what?) is given in a subsequent daß-clause or zu + INFINITIVE clause, **da(+r)** precedes the preposition, e.g.

Er **wartet auf** das Testergebnis.
(**warten auf** (VERB + PREPOSITION) *to wait for*)
He is waiting for the test result.

Er **wartet darauf**, das Testergebnis **zu sehen**.
He is waiting to see the test result.

Er **wartet darauf, daß** das Testergebnis veröffentlicht wird.
He is waiting for the test result to be published.

Note, however, that da(+r) + PREP words also have other functions. **→R163**

R156 Anticipatory 'es'

Er hat **es** abgelehnt, den Bericht zu lesen.
Lit.: *He declined it, to read the report. He declined to read the report.*

Like da + PREP, **es** is sometimes used to anticipate a zu + INFINITIVE clause or occasionally also a daß-clause. (**→R87**)

→R163 for other functions of es.

R157 Phrases using Participles

Das Grundgesetz für die Bundesrepublik Deutschland, im Jahre 1949 **geschaffen**, sollte . . .

OR: **geschaffen** im Jahre 1949,

*The Basic Law for the Federal Republic of Germany, **created** in 1949, was meant to . . .*

Der Durchmesser, von der hohen Temperatur **verändert**, muß nochmals gemessen werden.
*The diameter, **changed** by the high temperature, has to be measured again.*

Die Situation sofort **überblickend**, handelte er unverzüglich.
***Grasping** the situation straight away, he acted at once.*

Such phrases can be separated by commas from the rest of the clause. The PARTICIPLES (PAST PARTICIPLES ➔**R34**, PRESENT PARTICIPLES ➔**R43**) appear either at the end or, less frequently, at the beginning of the phrase. They can precede, follow, or be inserted within a clause.

There are also a number of short phrases with **wie** which can appear anywhere within a clause. e.g. **wie gesagt** (*as mentioned*, *said before*), **wie erwartet** (*as expected*), **wie vermutet** (*as suspected*).

R158 Other Non-Clause Insertions

1. Noun phrases in apposition, i.e. where a noun describes a preceding noun more closely (e.g. his professor, the eminent scholar) are usually separated by commas from the rest of the clause, e.g.

   Die Schweiz, **das Land mit dem höchsten Milchverbrauch**, wies die höchste Krebsrate auf. [T16: 4]
   *Switzerland, **the country with the highest milk consumption**, showed the highest cancer rate.*

   In den fünfziger Jahren, **der Zeit der politischen Reaktion**, schafft die wirtschaftliche Entwicklung eine völlig neue Situation. [T14:1]
   *In the 1850s, **a period of political reaction**, economic development created an entirely new situation.*

2. Other phrases which give further information or examples, e.g.

   In Neu-England und in den US-Staaten Minnesota und Wisconsin, **in Gegenden also**, in denen viel Milch produziert und konsumiert wurde, . . . [T16:2].
   *In New England and in the US states of Minnesota and Wisconsin, **that is in areas** in which a lot of milk was produced and consumed, . . .*

Such phrases may contain words like **also** (*thus, therefore, so, i.e.*), **auch** (*also*), **außer** (*except*), **zum Beispiel** (*for example*).

R159 The 'Layered' Structure of a Complex Sentence

A COMPLEX SENTENCE can be broken down to show the way the different clauses relate to each other, e.g.

1. [T19:7]

Dieser Vergleich
$\boxed{\textbf{zeigt}}$ uns,
  └──→ ⟨daß⟩es
       möglich $\boxed{\textbf{ist}}$,
          └──→ einfache gesellschaftliche
               Probleme dem ungeregelten
               Spiel der Kräfte
               zu überlassen, ──────────────┐

  ┌──→ ⟨daß⟩ aber mit zunehmender
  │   Komplexität die Planung
  │   unvermeidbar $\boxed{\textbf{ist}}$,
  │   └──→ ⟨wenn⟩ nicht das
  │   Chaos herrschen
  │ $\boxed{\textbf{soll}}$.

Level 1: MAIN CLAUSE

Level 2: Two **daß**-CLAUSES both dependent on the MAIN CLAUSE (→R142)

Level 3: One ZU + INFINITIVE CLAUSE (→R149) dependent on the first **daß**-CLAUSE, and a DEPENDENT CLAUSE introduced by **wenn** dependent on the second **daß**-CLAUSE

This comparison shows us that it is possible to leave simple social problems to the unregulated interplay of forces; that, however, with increasing complexity planning becomes unavoidable if chaos is not to prevail.

Conventions used in this section:

1    $\boxed{\text{finite verb}}$

2   ⟨conjunction⟩

3   ⟨relative pronoun

4   ZU + INFINITIVE CONSTRUCTION

2. [T21: 1]

1 Es $\boxed{\textbf{gibt}}$ relativ wenig Menschen,

2   ⟨**die** imstande $\boxed{\textbf{sind}}$,

3   rein musikalisch **zu verstehen,**

4   ⟨**was** Musik zu sagen $\boxed{\textbf{hat}}$.

Level 1: MAIN CLAUSE

Level 2: RELATIVE CLAUSE (→R147) dependent on MAIN CLAUSE

Level 3: **zu** + INFINITIVE CLAUSE dependent on the Level 2 RELATIVE CLAUSE

Level 4: RELATIVE CLAUSE dependent on the Level 3 INFINITIVE CLAUSE

There are comparatively few people who are able to understand in a purely musical way what music has to say.

Note that, in theory at least, there is no limit to the number of levels!

3. Further DEPENDENT CLAUSES need not just be added on, but may appear inside the clause they depend on, e.g. [T21:5]:

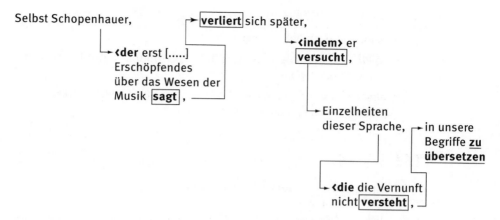

Level 1: MAIN CLAUSE interrupted by the first DEPENDENT CLAUSE on Level 2.

Level 2: A RELATIVE CLAUSE and a DEPENDENT CLAUSE introduced by **indem**, both dependent on the MAIN CLAUSE, **a.** dependent on 'Schopenhauer'
b. dependent on 'verliert sich später'

Level 3: A ZU + INFINITIVE CLAUSE, dependent on the DEPENDENT CLAUSE on Level 2, interrupted by

Level 4: A RELATIVE CLAUSE, dependent on the ZU + INFINITIVE CLAUSE in Level 3.

Literally: *Even Schopenhauer, who at first said exhaustive things about the nature of music, loses (his way) later when he tries to translate details of this language which reason does not comprehend into our terminology.*

(For an idiomatic translation see T21:5)

R160 Connectors (→R2)

CONNECTORS link elements of the same kind at the same level. These elements can be larger units (such as MAIN CLAUSES, DEPENDENT CLAUSES, ZU + INFINITIVE CLAUSES) or simply words or phrases of the same type. Here are the most common ones:

aber	*but*
denn	*for*
doch	*but, but still*
entweder . . . oder	*either . . . or*
oder	*or*
sondern	*but*
sowie	*as well as*
sowohl . . . als/wie [auch]	*. . . as well as*
und	*and*
weder . . . noch	*neither . . . nor*

Note:

- **denn** and **doch** link clauses only.

- **sowie** links words and phrases only. This word can also function as a CONJUNCTION
  (→**R143**) (*as soon as*).

- **aber** can also appear in mid-clause position: (cf. English *however*) Die Studenten **aber**...
  [T10b:10] Taucht man ihn **aber**... [T18:3].

R161 1. It is important to recognize which two elements are linked by a connector. Compare

the different functions of the connectors in the following sentence:

The first **und** in Level 1 links **Straße** and **Haus**, the second one links two MAIN CLAUSES
which share the same subject **wir**. The **und** in Level 2 links **Jahre** and **Ereignisse**. In Level 3
und links two DEPENDENT CLAUSES. Note that the conjunction **als ob** is not repeated for
the second clause.

*We immediately recognized the street and also the house and were amazed that after all
the years and events everything still looked as if no time had passed and (as if) we were
still living in the year 1960.*

2. Connectors are sometimes found at the beginning of a sentence linking it to
   information given in preceding sentences, e.g.

> **Und** das war noch nicht alles. [T16:5]
> *And that was not yet all.*

> **Denn** es fehlt auch nicht der Hinweis, daß... [T20:16]
> *Because the indication is there, that...*

Occasionally connectors appear preceding CONJUNCTIONS (→**R2**) or introducing zu +
INFINITIVE CLAUSES, e.g.

> ..., **und** wenn sie ausbleiben [T21:2]
> ...., *and if they fail to emerge/appear*

In such cases the connector usually links one sentence to another sentence beginning
with a dependent clause or construction, e.g. [T7:2]:

SENTENCE I		SENTENCE II
Der Durchmesser einer Stahlstange kann sehr genau mit einer Mikro-Schublehre gemessen werden,	**aber**	weicht eine Messung leicht von der anderen ab.
		wenn von einer Stahlstange verschiedene Messungen gemacht werden,

*The diameter of a steel rod can be measured very accurately with a micro-slide gauge, **but** if several measurements are taken each measurement diverges slightly from the others.*

R162 Reading Complex Sentences: Procedure

If a sentence contains more than one FINITE VERB (➔R22) you are dealing with a COMPLEX SENTENCE and the relations between the MAIN CLAUSE and the DEPENDENT CLAUSE (➔R141) have to be worked out.

When working out the **structure** of a complex sentence keep in mind that the structural core of each complex sentence is the MAIN CLAUSE, which can be arrived at by eliminating all clearly identifiable DEPENDENT CLAUSES and NON-CLAUSE INSERTIONS (➔R142, R147, R149, R151, R157, R158).

Only after working out the basic structure of the complete sentence, i.e. after establishing which clause links up with which other clause, which clause is dependent on which other clause etc., start looking at the exact meaning of the individual clauses and units within the sentence.

Working out the core meaning of the main clause first may give you a first idea of 'what the sentence is about' or at least it will give you a starting point to decide in which order to tackle any dependent clauses.

The steps needed to tackle a COMPLEX SENTENCE are:

1. Establish the extent of the sentence. Usually a semicolon can be treated as a full stop. A colon, as well as indicating the beginning of a quotation/direct speech/a list/ an example, may sometimes be used instead of a full stop. (e.g. T21:10). Question marks and exclamation marks may indicate the end of the whole sentence. Alternatively they may indicate only the end of a clause within a clause, e.g. in a quotation. Note that in the latter case the word following the punctuation mark will begin with a small letter.

2. Now scan the sentence for FINITE VERBS, CONJUNCTIONS, RELATIVE PRONOUNS, ZU + INFINITIVES. Use some kind of marker system to clearly identify these key elements in the sentence, e.g.

   FINITE VERBS

   ‹CONJUNCTIONS›

   ‹RELATIVE PRONOUNS

   ZU + INFINITIVES (with or without an introductory **um/ohne/(an)statt**)

Work from the beginning of the sentence to each COMMA and/or CONNECTOR. Disregard those commas and connectors which clearly 'only' separate/link individual units within a list of words or word groups, e.g. adjectives: [T19:9]: . . . bewußte, sorgfältige (Note same endings! →R106) or nouns: [T14:10] Konsumgenossenschaften, Krankenversicherungen und Darlehenskassen, [T20:5] Eisen-, Blech- und Metallindustrie (→R181.3).

3. Check if each $\left\{ \begin{array}{c} \text{DEPENDENT} \\ \text{RELATIVE} \\ \text{ZU + INFINITIVE} \end{array} \right\}$ CLAUSE IS COMPLETE,

i.e. if both characteristic elements are present.

., ⟨CONJUNCTION⟩. . . . . . .　　. . . . . |FINITE VERB| , .

, ⟨RELATIVE PRONOUN . . . . |FINITE VERB| , .

[.,] (um/ohne/(an)statt) . . . . ZU + INFINITIVE [,.]

If not, the clause has been interrupted by another clause or construction dependent on the first subordinate clause. Check where further on in the sentence the 'rest' of the first subordinate clause appears.

4. Thus, by 'eliminating' all clearly identifiable dependent clauses, you have established the position/extent of the main clause. (Indicators: FINITE VERB in II (→R3) or FINITE VERB, FINITE VERB pattern (→R144.2). Note that the main clause may be positioned anywhere within the complex sentence.

Make sure that you have spotted the whole of the main clause. Check for elements of VERB COMPLETION (→R6).

5. Identify any NON-CLAUSE INSERTIONS (→R158). Double-check that they are in fact NON-CLAUSE INSERTIONS and not the continuation of an interrupted main clause.

If you now wish to practise analysing complex sentences go to the Further Exercises Section (E47 to E51).

Problem Words

R163 Words with Multiple Functions/Meanings

This is a list in alphabetical order of words which often cause problems to the reader because of their multiple functions and/or meanings. Letters in bold draw attention to features (e.g. position within the clause, words which always appear together with a specific problem word, etc.) which help to distinguish between the different functions and meanings.

Note: This list is not exhaustive. Consult the dictionary for further meanings.

als

- *than* (in comparisons)
  —**er als**

  Der Durchmesser ist an einem warmen Tag größ**er als** an einem kalten Tag. [T7:7]
  greater than

  Wenn das Thermometer kält**er** ist **als** das Wasser. [T7:13] (**→R15.4**)
  colder than

- *when, as*
  A/als . . . FINITE VERB (**→R143**)

  . . . , **als** der Verdacht geäußert **wurde** [T16:1]
  when the suspicion was voiced

- *as if*
  . . . , [**so**] . . . , **als ob** . . .
  . . . , [**so**] . . . , **als** + VERB IN THE SUBJUNCTIVE (**→R59** and **R48**)

  . . . , **so als ob** sie drin sein **müßten**. [T21:10]
  as if they had to be there

  Frequently there is no **ob**. The following sentence has exactly the same meaning as the one above:

  . . . , **so als müßten** sie drin sein.

- *as* ('in the capacity/role of')
  . . . **als** (ADJECTIVE) NOUN. . .

  , die **als Kind** davon hörten [T3:5]
  who as children (lit.: *as a child*) *heard about it*

- *as* (part of a phrase)
  e.g. **gelten als** *to be regarded as*

  Die Welt **gilt als** in drei Stockwerke gegliedert.
  The world is regarded/seen as being divided into three levels.

auch

■ *also, too*

Die gleichen Probleme treten **auch** in psychologischen Experimenten auf.
*The same problems appear, **too**, in psychological experiments.* [T7:9]

Andererseits glaube ich **auch,** daß . . . [T5:10]
*On the other hand I **also** believe, that* . . .

The German word **also** NEVER means *also* but *so, therefore, thus, well.*

See list of FALSE FRIENDS in **R164**.

■ *even*
  . . . A/**auch wenn** . . .
  . . . VERB IN THE SUBJUNCTIVE (→R48) . . . **auch** . . .
  . . . W/**wenn auch** . . .

Auch wenn diese Voraussetzung zutreffend ist [T12:4]
***Even** if this premise applies*

und **wäre** das **auch** der Fall . . .
*and **even** if this were the case* . . .

Wenn auch unter Schmerzen und Schuldgefühlen [T13:6]
***Even** if it was painful and done with a sense of guilt*

da

■ *as, since* (Conjunction →R143)
  . . . , . **d/Da** . . . FINITE VERB, .
  As a conjunction **da** appears at the beginning of a sentence or clause.

  . . . , **da** die Voraussetzungen nicht immer die gleichen sind [T7:10]
  ***since** the preconditions are not always the same*

■ *then*

Da aber drehten die Gesandten den Spieß um. [T15:9]
*But **then** the delegates turned the tables.*
da with the meaning 'then' has no fixed position.

Aber **da** drehten die Gesandten den Spieß um.
Aber die Gesandten drehten **da** den Spieß um.

■ *here, there*

, daß es **da** und dort Schwachstellen gibt. [T20:4]
*that **here** and there there are weak points*

da + (r) + PREPOSITION

daran, daraus, dabei, dadurch, dafür, dagegen, darin (abbreviated: drin), damit, darüber (drüber), davon, dazu, etc.

■ **da + (r) +** PREP can refer back to something mentioned earlier (→R136).

Ich bin bei allen Universitätsanlässen **darin** herumgelaufen. [T10b:6]
*At all university functions I ran around **in it**. (i.e. the gown)*

- **da + (r) + PREP** can point forward to the following clause. The PREPOSITION is part of a larger phrase. (→R155, R88)

... **da + (r) + PREP** (. . .), **daß** . . .
... **da + (r) + PREP** (. . .), . . . **zu** INFINITIVE

Ich bin **davon** überzeugt, daß . . . OR: Ich bin überzeugt **davon**, daß . . .
  von is part of a VERB + PREPOSITION phrase:
überzeugt sein von *to be convinced of*

Thus the above sentences literally read:

I am convinced of it that . . . (I am convinced that)

- **da + (r) + PREP** can have a special meaning, different from that of the PREPOSITION. e.g.: **dabei, dafür, dagegen, damit.** Consult the dictionary.

Händels Oratorien blieben **dagegen** vor allem in England lebendig. [T8:9]
*Händels oratorios **on the other hand** continued to stay alive especially in England.*

dann (not to be confused with **denn** below)

- *then* (under these circumstances)

Sind Sie im Juni in Bonn? **Dann** könnte ich Sie dort besuchen. [T10a:10/11]
*Will you be in Bonn this June? **Then** (in that case) I could visit you there.*

- *then* (sequence of events)

Zuerst fährt er nach Berlin und **dann** nach Bonn.
*First he'll travel to Berlin and **then** to Bonn.*

- *if . . . then*

. . . , . w/Wenn . . . VERB (often in the SUBJUNCTIVE), **dann**
. . . , . VERB in the SUBJUNCTIVE . . . , **dann**

Wenn wir dort eine Signalanlage aufstellen würden, **dann wäre** dies eine unnötige Einschränkung unserer Freiheit. [T19:4]

This sentence could also read:

Würden wir dort eine Signalanlage aufstellen, **dann** . . .
*If we were/Were we to put up a signalling system **then** this would be an unnecessary limitation of our freedom. (→R144.2)*

denn

- *because, for* (Connectors →R160 and R2)
. . . , . d/Denn . . .

Denn sie impliziert, daß . . . [T22:3]
Because it implies that . . .

- **denn** appears in a number of fixed phrases. Consult your dictionary. Examples from the Text Corpus:

. . . , geschweige **denn** . . . [T15:10]
  let alone . . ./not to mention

wenn schon, **denn** schon [T10b:7]
in for a penny, in for a pound

eben

■ *precisely, exactly, that is to say*
[T16:2] could read:

In Neu-England und in den US-Staaten Minnesota und Wisconsin, in Gegenden **eben**, in denen viel Milch produziert wird, . . .
. . . that is to say in areas where . . .

■ *just as*
. . . **eben so** . . . , **wie**

. . . wird dir alsdann **eben so** natürlich sein, **wie** . . . [T22:5]
will then be just as natural for you as

erst

■ *first*
erst + ADJECTIVE ENDING (→R106)

die **erste** Atombombe [T3:7]
the first atomic bomb

unter den **ersten** zehn [T1:4]
amongst the first ten

■ *for the first time, only then/now, not until then*

Am Krebs erkranken die meisten Menschen **erst** im fortgeschrittenen Alter.
It is not until an advanced age that most people contract cancer. [T16:9]

Erst nach dem Schrecken zweier Weltkriege nahm man die Appelle ernst.
It was only after the horrors of two world wars that the appeals were taken seriously. [T2:17]

es

■ *it* (Pronoun →R98)

Wenn das Thermometer kälter ist als das Wasser, wird **es** die Temperatur des Wassers leicht senken, sobald **es** in das Glas getaucht wird. [T7:13]
If the thermometer is colder than the water it will slightly lower the temperature of the water as soon as it is immersed in the glass.

Ich habe **es** getan. [T10b:6]
Lit.: I have done it. I did it.

■ **es** appears in a number of fixed phrases. (→R42) They are listed in dictionaries under the verb. Note that these phrases appear in all tense forms. Here are some of the most frequent phrases:

es gibt
there is/there are

es gab/es hat gegeben
there was/there were

es wird . . . geben
there will be

Es gibt nur Dorfstraßen. [T19:8]
***There are** only village streets.*

es handelt sich um
to be about something, to concern s.th., it is a matter of, one is dealing with

Es handelt sich hierbei **um** eine absichtliche Suggestion.
*Here **one is dealing with/this is** an intentional suggestion.*

es geht um
it is about/it concerns

Es ging um die Friedensbedingungen. [T15:5]
***It concerned** the conditions for peace.*

Wie geht es Ihnen/Dir/Euch?
How are you ?

es geht mir/uns gut
I am/We are well

Wie geht es Ihnen und Ihrer Familie? [T10a:12]
***How are you** and your family?*

es bedarf
there is a need for

Es bedarf in den meisten Fällen keines besonderen Fachwissens.
*In most cases **there is no need** for specialist knowledge. [T16:15]*

es heißt, daß . . .
es heißt, . . . + verb in the SUBJUNCTIVE (→R48)
it is said that

einer Region, von der **es** oft **hieß**, sie **habe** den Anschluß verpaßt.
*a region, of which it **was** often **said** that it had fallen behind. [T20:2]*

es fehlt (an) . . .
there is a lack of, s.th. is missing

Es fehlt auch nicht der Hinweis, daß . . . [T20:16]
*Lit.: Also the indication **is** not **missing**. The indication is there that . . .*

■ **es** as a token subject acting as a 'slot-filler' (→R42.2)

Und **es** wurde viel erreicht. [T2:19]
And much was achieved.

The real subject here is **viel** *much*. Thus the sentence could also read:

Und viel wurde erreicht.

Es leben Menschen, von denen wir glauben, daß . . . [T12:2] Menschen leben, . . .
There are people living/People are living, of whom we believe that . . .

■ There are also colloquial fixed phrases with **sich** which rarely occur in written German, e.g.

Hier arbeitet **es** sich gut.   *You can work well here.*

Consult your dictionary!

etwa not to be confused with etwas (see below)

■ *approximately, roughly*

ein Würfel, der **etwa** 0,8 kg wiegt [T18:8]
*a cube, which weighs **approximately** 0.8 kg.*

■ *for instance, for example, such as*

Die Quellen sind Meinungen in Geschichtsbüchern, philosophischen Schriften und in Komödien (**etwa** in den Dialogen Platons und in den Bühnenstücken des Aristophanes) [T15:2]
*The sources are opinions in history books, philosophical writings and in comedies (**such as** the dialogues of Plato and in the plays of Aristophanes)*

etwas

■ *something*

und dazu wurde **etwas** in unverständlichem Latein gemurmelt [T10b:9]
*and at the same time **something** in unintelligible Latin was murmured*

■ *some, any*

Sie hat ihm **etwas** Geld gegeben.
*She gave him **some** money.*

■ *somewhat, a little*

Er ist wahrscheinlich **etwas** zu schnell gefahren.
*He probably drove **a little** too fast.*

lassen, läßt, ließ, gelassen

■ *leave, let, allow*

Allerdings **lassen** die Unternehmen keinen Zweifel daran, daß . . . [T20:10]
*However, the companies **leave** no doubt that . . .*

Gott kann ihn himmlische Gesichte schauen **lassen**. [T6:7]
*God can **let** him see heavenly visions.*

■ **lassen** + **sich** + INFINITIVE (→R78.3)
can be + PAST PARTICIPLE

[T19:9] could read:

Die Probleme **lassen sich** ohne sorgfältige Analyse nicht mehr **ordnen**.
*The problems **can** no longer **be solved** without careful analysis.*

■ **lassen** + INFINITIVE
to get somebody to do something for you

Er **läßt** die Operation von seinem Assistenten **durchführen**.

*He **gets** his assistant **to do** the operation.*

schon

■ *already, as early as*

Solche Versuche wurden **schon** 1843 durchgeführt. [T9:6]
*Such experiments were carried out **as early as 1843**.*

■ Sie sind dieser Ehre ja **schon** früher teilhaftig geworden. [T10a:2]
I know you had this honour bestowed on you earlier.

Note how 'schon' has no equivalent word in the English translation. It merely adds emphasis to 'früher'. →R140

■ **schon** is used in a number of idiomatic phrases. Consult your dictionary.

Wenn **schon**, denn schon. [T10b:7]
In for a penny, in for a pound.

selbst

- *itself, oneself* etc. (referring to the preceding word)

Die Meßvorrichtung **selbst** kann einen Einfluß auf das Gemessene haben.
*The measuring device **itself** can have an influence on what is being measured.* [T7:11]

- **selber** is sometimes used instead of **selbst**:

Der Doktorierungsakt **selber** ist überaus feierlich. [T10b:9]
*The ceremony (of bestowing the doctorate) **itself** is exceedingly solemn.*

- *even* (referring to the following word)

Selbst Schopenhauer, der . . . [T21:5]
***Even** Schopenhauer, who . . .*

sich (→R40)

- A reflexive pronoun (→**R40**) with an equivalent in English:
  itself, herself, himself, oneself, themselves

Demosthenes, der **sich** von den anderen distanziert hatte, [T15:7]
*Demosthenes, who had dissociated **himself** from the others,*

Muß man **sich** ein Doktor-Kostüm erstehen? [T10a:7]
*Does one have to buy a gown (lit.: a doctor's costume) for **oneself**?*

- No equivalent in the English reading. The dictionary lists these reflexive phrases under a separate heading in the verb entry.

In gleicher Weise kann **sich** das Verhalten ändern. [T7:14]
  (**sich** verändern *to change*)
In the same way behaviour can change.

Mit sinkenden Reallöhnen verschlechtert **sich** die Situation. [T14:7]
  (**sich** verschlechtern *to get worse, to deteriorate*)
With sinking real wages the situation got worse.

- **sich** as part of a fixed phrase (often with **es**)

Anders verhält es **sich** beim Hausfrauenberuf. [T1:5]
  (es verhält **sich** anders *it is different*)
It is different with regard to the job of housewife.

- *each other, one another*

Planung und Freiheit schließen **sich** aus. [T19:2]
*Planning and freedom exclude **each other**/are **mutually** exclusive.*

so

- *thus, like this, that way*

So sagte der britische Premierminister. [T2:9]
***Thus** spoke the British Prime Minister.*

So war es in Glasgow. [T10b:4]
*It was **like this** in Glasgow.*
***That's** how it was in Glasgow.*

■ *if . . . then* (See also **dann**)
. . . , . **w/Wenn** . . . VERB (often in the SUBJUNCTIVE →**R47**) **so** . . .
. . . , . **VERB** (often in the SUBJUNCTIVE) . . . , **so**

Wenn diese Voraussetzung **zutreffend ist, so** . . . [T12:4]
If this premiss applies, then . . .

Kann ein Körper mehr Flüssigkeit **verdrängen, so** . . . [T18:7]
If a body can displace more fluid, then . . .

Note the VERB INITIAL position (→**R16** and **R144.2**)

■ **(eben) so . . . wie/bis**
(just) as . . . as/until

So unterschiedlich **wie** ihr Lebenslauf . . . [T8:2]
As different as their lives . . .

das wird dir dann **eben so** natürlich sein, **wie** [T22:5]
*this will then be **just as** natural for you **as***

Ein Würfel taucht **so** weit ins Wasser ein, **bis** er [T18:8]
*A cube sinks **(as far)** into the water **until***

■ **so, als [ob]**
as if

daß sie **so** tun, **als ob** . . . [T19:8]
*that they behave, **as if***

■ *the (e.g. bigger) the (better)*
um so ADJECTIVE + **-er, je** ADJECTIVE + **-er**

diese Umwälzung, die **um so** gewaltiger war, **je** geräuschloser . . . [T4:3]
*this revolutionary change which was **the more** fundamental, **the** quieter . . .*

■ **, so daß . . .**
so that . . . ., with the result that

. . . , **so daß** seine Dichte geringer wird [T18:11]
*. . . **so that** its density becomes less*

■ **so** followed immediately by an ADJECTIVE/ADVERB means *so*

Das ist **so** angemessen.
*This is **so** suitable.*

■ **so ein** + ADJECTIVE ENDING
such a

so eine Spitzenstellung
such a top position

■ **so** is sometimes used as a filler and can be omitted in the English reading.

so im täglichen Umgange [T22:1]
in one's everyday contacts

um

- **., U/um . . . zu + INFINITIVE (→R151)**
  in order to + INFINITIVE

  Um Schäden am Projektor **zu vermeiden,** [T23:9]
  In order to avoid damage to the projector

  Note the pattern for separable verbs (→R39):

  um in internationale Spitzenstellung vor**zu**dringen. [T20:11]
  in order to penetrate to international front rank.

- **. . . um**
  PREFIX OF SEPARABLE VERB (→R39)

  Da aber drehten die Gesandten den Spieß **um.** [T15:9]
  (den Spieß **um**drehen *to turn the tables*)
  But then the delegates turned the tables.

- **. . . um** (Determiner + ADJECTIVE +) NOUN . . .
  A PREPOSITION. Consult the dictionary for meanings.

  Die Engländerinnen überlebten die japanischen Frauen **um** 12 Jahre.
  *The English women survived the Japanese women **by** 12 years.* [T16:13]

  Das Bemühen **um** die Einigung Europas [T2:18]
  *The endeavour to unite Europe (lit.: **for** the unification)*

- A PREPOSITION which is part of a VERB + PREPOSITION phrase

  Darf ich Sie **um** eine Auskunft bitten? [T10a:1]
  (bitten **um** *to ask for*)
  May I ask you for some information?

  Such prepositional verbs are listed in the dictionary under the entry for the verb.

- **. . . es . . . (sich) . . .. um** + (DETERMINER + ADJECTIVE +) NOUN
  A verb construction with **es** (→R42)
  es geht **um**/es handelt sich **um** *to be about*

  Im Prozeß gegen Timarchos ging **es** allein **um** den letzten Punkt. [T15:11]
  The case against T was solely about the last point.

- **. . . um** + GENITIVE **willen**
  for the sake of

  um des Friedens **willen**
  for the sake of peace

während

- **., W/während . . . FINITE VERB**
  (as a CONJUNCTION →R143) *while/whereas*

  Während die Hausfrau im Westen den zehnten Platz einnimmt, [T1:6]
  While in the west the housewife occupies the tenth position,

  . . ., **während** sie in Wirklichkeit nichts anderes tun, als . . . [T19:8]
  *. . ., **whereas** in reality they do nothing other than . . .*

- **während** (DETERMINER + ADJECTIVE +) NOUN
  (as a Preposition) *during*

  während dieser Zeit   *during* this time

wenn

. , W/wenn . . . FINITE VERB (Conjunction →R143)

- *if*

  Wenn diese Voraussetzung zutreffend ist, [T12:4]
  If this premiss applies,

  Note: **wenn** can be preceded by **aber** (→R161.2):

  , **aber wenn** verschiedene Messungen gemacht werden, [T7:2]
  , but if several measurements are taken,

  Note: the verb may be in the SUBJUNCTIVE. (→R48)

  Wenn wir eine Signalanlage aufstellen **würden**, [T19:4]
  If we were to put up a signalling system,

- *when, whenever*

  Sie müssen lächeln, **wenn** Sie erwähnt werden. [T10b:2]
  You must smile when you are being mentioned.

werden, wird, wurde/n, würde/n, ge/worden (→R31)

- PASSIVE AUXILIARY (→R74):
  is/are, has/have been, were, would be
  form of **werden** + PAST PARTICIPLE

  Das **wurde** in vielen Mythen **beschrieben**. [T5:7]
  This was described in many myths.

- FUTURE AUXILIARY (→R36): *will/shall*
  form of **werden** + INFINITIVE
  [T10b:13] could read:

  Wo ich im Juni **sein werde**, ist unübersehbar.
  Where I shall be in June cannot be foreseen.

- A verb in its own right with the meaning
  to become
  form of **werden** (NO PAST PARTICIPLE/INFINITIVE)

  Das Automobil **wurde** zur Alltäglichkeit. [T3:6]
  The car became an everyday thing.

wie

- *like, as, alike*

  Im Westen **wie** im Osten Deutschlands [T1:1]
  In the West and East of Germany alike

  Wie von einem Erdbeben wurde die Öffentlichkeit aufgeschreckt [T16:1]
  The public was shaken as if (lit.: like) by an earthquake

- so . . . wie
  as . . . as

  So unterschiedlich **wie** ihr Lebenslauf [T9:2]
  as different as their lives

■ **. , W/wie . . .** FINITE VERB
as (Conjunction →R143)

. . . , **wie** die Völkerkunde sie lehrt. [T12:4]
as anthropology teaches it

■ *how?* (in questions)

Wie geht es Ihnen? [T10a:12]
How are you?

wohl

■ *probably, possibly, no doubt*

Daraus erklärt es sich **wohl** . . . [T8:9]
*This **probably** explains . . .*

■ *perhaps*

die Andeutung, daß es **wohl** zweierlei Existenz geben möge [T22:3]
*the hint, that there might **perhaps** be two forms of existence*

■ *well, fine, happy*

Bei uns steht es **wohl.** [T10a:13]
*Here things/we are **well/fine.***

zwar

■ **. . . zwar . . . , (doch/aber) . . .** (→R139)
it's true

Statistik kann **zwar** nicht alles beweisen, **doch** . . . [T16:14]
***It's true** statistics cannot prove everything, **but** . . .*

■ **. . . und zwar . . .**
in fact, actually, that is to say
[T1:3] could read:

Handwerker nehmen den Platz drei ein, **und zwar** gleich hinter dem Arzt und Zahnarzt.
*Skilled manual workers are in third place, **in fact** immediately behind the doctor and dentist.*

zu

■ **. . . zu/zum/zur** (DETERMINER + ADJECTIVE +) NOUN
A PREPOSITION: *to, at, for, with* (For further meanings check the dictionary.)

Deutschland war auf dem Wege **zu einem modernen Industriestaat.**
*Germany was on its way **to** (becoming) **a modern industrial state.** [T14:4]*

zu jener Zeit [T16:6]
at that time

Man wird es Ihnen nachher **zum** Kauf anbieten. [T10b:6]
*Afterwards it will be offered to you **for** sale.*

Maschinen **zur** Verarbeitung der Baumwolle [T4:1]
*machines **for** processing cotton*

■ Part of a VERB + PREPOSITION phrase.
Check the meaning under the entry for the verb, e.g. **gehören zu** *to belong to.*

Sie **gehört** nicht **zu** den beliebtesten zehn. [T1:6]
*She does not **belong** to the ten most popular ones.*

■ Part of a NOUN + **zu** phrase

der **Anstoß zu** einer Revolution [T4:2]
*the **impetus to** (start/bring about) a revolution*

■ Part of a phrase, e.g. **berechtigt sein zu** *to be entitled to*

Er ist **berechtigt zu** solchem Verhalten.
*He **is entitled** to such a conduct.*

■ . , . . . **zu** + INFINITIVE . ,
. , . . . PREFIX**ZU**INFINITIVE (➜**R39**)
***to** + INFINITIVE* (➜**R149**)

Aber es ist nie möglich, den genauen Durchmesser **zu bestimmen**. [T7:5]
*But it is never possible **to determine** the exact diameter.*

. . . , das Wesen der Welt **darzustellen**. [T21:7]
*. . . **to show** the nature of the world.*

■ . . . **ist, sind, war/en** . . . **zu** INFINITIVE (➜**R78.2**)
. . . **ist, sind, war/en** . . . PREFIX**ZU**INFINITIVE
*. . . **is, are, was to be, can be** + PAST PARTICIPLE*

Die Entstehung der Musik **ist** nicht von der Entstehung der Menschheit **zu trennen**. [T5:1]
*The genesis of music **cannot be separated** from the genesis of mankind.*

Die Probleme der Gesellschaft **sind** nicht mehr **zu ordnen**. [T19:9]
*The problems of society **can** no longer **be solved**.*

Die Sicherung **ist** vom Fachmann **auszuwechseln**. [T23:13]
*The fuse **is to be changed** by an expert.*

■ . . . VERB . . . **zu** INFINITIVE
Check the verb entry for the meaning, e.g.

Besonders schwierig **scheint** diese Frage **zu sein**.
*This question **appears to be** especially difficult.*

■ . . . **zu** . . . **end**ENDING + NOUN
EXTENDED ADJECTIVE PHRASE (➜**R116**)

ein Medikament, das mit einem **zu** prüf**end**en Mittel gleich sein soll. [T9:4]
*a medicine which is to be identical with the substance **to be examined**.*

■ . . . **zu** ADJECTIVE/ADVERB
too

. . . **zu** hoch
*. . . **too** high*

■ . . . **von** . . . **bis zu**(r/m)
*. . . **from** . . . **until***

von 1500 **bis zur** Französischen Revolution [T11:7]
***from** 1500 **until** the French Revolution*

R164 'False Friends'

There are many so-called *international* words which have the same meaning in both German and English, e.g. Industrie/industry, Philosophie/philosophy, international/international, intelligent/intelligent etc.

However, there is also a large group of words which have the same or a similar form in both German and English but their meaning may (or then again in a particular context may not!) differ in the two languages. Such words are usually called FALSE FRIENDS. The following alphabetical list gives you an idea of the kind of problem you are dealing with. Note that only a small number of these words can be given here. So if you come across a new word which looks the same as or is similar to an English word do be cautious and consult your dictionary!

absolvieren	Only in the specific theological context does this word mean *to absolve*. Its usual German meaning is *to complete, to take*. Letztes Jahr absolvierte er einen Deutschkurs. *Last year he did (took/completed) a German course.*
adäquat	In German this usually means *suitable, valid* rather than *adequate* or *sufficient*.
Akademiker/in	Means *somebody who has a degree*, not an *academic* in the English sense.
aktuell	Means *topical, current, relevant*.
also	Has a meaning completely different from the English *also*. It means *so, therefore, then, well*.
Art	Never means *art*, but *kind, sort, type, way*. diese Art Problem *this sort of problem*
bekommen	Always means *to get*, never *to become*.
brav	In modern German always means *well behaved, good, honest*. In old texts however it may mean *brave*.
checken	This can have the same meaning as in English but colloquially it also means *to understand*. Er hat das nicht gecheckt. *He did not understand this./He did not check it.*
Christ	As well as *Christ* this also means *Christian*. The famous theologian Hans Küng's book 'Warum ich Christ bin' therefore does, of course, mean 'Why I am a Christian'.
Etikett	means *label*, though there is also the word **Etikette** *etiquette*.
eventuell	Never means *eventually*, but *possible, possibly, perhaps*.
fatal	Very often means *embarrassing, awkward*, but it can also have the same meaning as in English, i.e. *fatal, fateful, dire*.
feudal	As a historical/political term this word has the same meaning as the English word *feudal*. In colloquial German, however, it means *plush, posh*.

Fraktion	Only in a scientific context does this word mean *fraction*. As a political term it means (*coalition*) *party*. In Austrian German it also means *district*.
Garage	In German this word only describes the place where you leave your car at night/park it; it is not a repair workshop.
genial	This word means something completely different in German: *brilliant*, *inspired*, *ingenious*.
Gift	This word also has two completely different meanings in the two languages. The sign 'gift shop' or stickers like 'This is a gift from the United States' may cause amusement/consternation since in German this word means *poison*, *venom*, *toxic substance*.
Gymnasium	In texts referring to antiquity this word means the same as in English. Outside this context however, it means *grammar school/high school*.
Hochschule	This word always means *university*, *college*, *institute of higher education*.
Hose	In German this word always means *trousers*.
human	In German this word means *humane*, *considerate*, *decent*.
Instanz	The meaning in German is (*judicial/legal*) *authority*, *court*, *court case*, *trial*.
isoliert	Can mean *isolated*, but it can also mean *insulated*.
Jalousie	This has nothing to do with jealousy! In German this means (*venetian*) *blind*.
Justiz	The German meaning of this word is *the courts* and *the judiciary* but not as in English *justice* or *judge*.
Kapazität	This can mean *capacity* as in English, but it also means *expert/authority on*.
Kaution	In German this means *bail*, *security*, *deposit*.
Konfession	The German meaning is *religious denomination*.
konsequent	This does not mean *consequent* but *consistent*.
Lokal	Unlike in English this is not just the local pub, but a word for any *pub*, *inn*, or *restaurant*.
Lust	This word can mean (*sexual*) *lust*, but much more common meanings are *pleasure*, *joy*, *desire*, *inclination*. There is a series of books published with titles like **Lust auf Musik, Lust auf Philosophie** (*Enjoying Music/Philosophy*).
Marmelade	In German this means any kind of *jam*.
Mist	In German this word means *dung*, *manure*, *animal droppings*, also *rubbish*, *nonsense*.
Note	This word can mean (*musical*) *note* or (*bank*) *note*. But it also means *mark*, as in *exam mark*.

Notiz	This means *note* as in **Notizblock** *notepad*. It can also mean newspaper item. However, when used together with the verb 'nehmen' *to take*, it has the same meaning as in English: *to take notice*.
ordinär	This can mean *ordinary*, but it is also used with the meaning *vulgar*.
Paragraph	means §, and always refers to a section in a <u>legal</u> text only.
Plane	This has none of the English meanings. In German it is simply a *tarpaulin, canopy, awning*.
Police	In German this has nothing to do with *the police*. Instead it means *insurance policy*.
prägnant	This word does not mean *pregnant*. The German meaning is *concise, succinct, terse*.
Promotion	This can mean *promotion* as in *promoting a product*. It also means *doctorate*!
Prospekt	In German this word usually means *brochure, leaflet, pamphlet*.
Provision	This does not mean *provision*, but *commission*.
Rate	This can mean *rate*, but it also means *instalment*.
Regal	In German this word has nothing to do with *royalty*. It usually simply means *shelf*. As a legal term, however, it does mean *regale*, and as a music term it is either also a *regal* or it means *vox humana*.
Rente	This word has nothing to do with *rent*. In German it means *(old age) pension* or *annuity*.
restlos	This does not mean *restless*, but *complete* or *total*.
resümieren	The German meaning is not *to resume*, but *to summarize*.
Schnake	If you are bitten by this animal there is no need to panic. This word does not mean *snake* but *gnat, midge*.
sensibel	A person thus described may be far from being *sensible*. In German the word means *(over) sensitive*.
spenden	The German meaning is not *to spend*, but *to donate, to give (to charities)*.
Stipendium	In German this word means *scholarship, grant*.
Store	In German these are *net curtains*, in Swiss-German *shutters*.
Tablett	This means *tray*. The German word for *tablet/pill* is **Tablette**.
Terminus	Here again the meaning is completely different in the two languages. In German it means *(technical/specialized) term*.
Zirkel	This word can mean *circle*. But it also means *a pair of compasses*.

R165 Cognate Words in English and German (→R164)

The fact that German and English are historically related languages means that there are a great many words which are found in both languages either with an identical form or with slightly different, but recognizable forms. Generally speaking, focusing on the consonants rather than the vowels will help you to spot cognate words, for instance the relationship between German **Meister** and English *master*. There are three main categories:

1. Words which have the same or very similar spelling in both languages, and the same or a similar meaning. Many of these are of Latin or Greek origin:

   in *in*; flexibel *flexible*; kompatibel *compatible*; total *total*; absolut *absolute*; Land *land*; Hand *hand*; Form *form*; Familie *family*; Computer *computer*; Garage *garage*; Institut *institute*; Parlament *parliament*; Disziplin *discipline*; Organisation *organization*; organisch *organic*; Orchester *orchestra*; Firma *firm*; populär *popular*; Popularität *popularity*; Popmusik *pop music*; Allianz *alliance*; Differenz *difference*; Hyperinflation *hyperinflation*; Hybride *hybrid*; Nitrat *nitrate*; Psychopathologie *psychopathology*; Sozialismus *socialism*; Nationalismus *nationalism*; (occasionally the German word ending in **-ismus** differs slightly: Totalitarismus *totalitarianism*; Zynismus *cynicism*).

2. Words which sound alike in the two languages but are spelt differently:

   Haus *house*; braun *brown*; faul *foul*; Schauer (*rain*) *shower*; Eis *ice*; Preis *price/prize*; fein *fine*; jung *young*; Bier *beer*; schier *sheer*; hier *here*.

3. Words which are related historically but which are now spelt differently.

   The following table shows the common patterns where differences in spelling between English and German are related. The changes affect individual consonants or clusters of consonants.

GERMAN SPELLING	ENGLISH SPELLING	EXAMPLES
pf, f, ff	p	Pfennig *penny*; Pfund *pound*; Pfad *path*; hüpfen *hop*; tief *deep*; Hilfe *help*; Affe *ape*
f	v	fünf *five*; zwölf *twelve*; Ofen *oven*
t, tt	d/th	tief *deep*; Bart *beard*; kalt *cold*; unter *under*; tausend *thousand*; Vater *father*; Wetter *weather*
v	f	vier *four*; Vater *father*; voll *full*
-b	-f/v	halb *half*; Kalb *calf*; sieben *seven*; eben *even*; über *over*
d	th	daß *that*; Bad *bath*; Pfad *path*; Ding *thing*
k	c/ch	kalt *cold*; Katze *cat*; Kirche *church*; Kind *child*
-s, ss, ß	-t	dies/das *this/that*; was *what*; beißen *bite*; biß *bit*; Wasser *water*; schießen *shoot*; Schuß *shot*

GERMAN SPELLING	ENGLISH SPELLING	EXAMPLES
z, tz	t	zehn *ten*; Zunge *tongue*; zu *to/too*; sitzen *sit*; setzen *set*; Sitz *seat*; Satz *set* of; Katze *cat*
zw	tw	zwei *two*; zwölf *twelve*; Zwilling *twin*; zwischen *between*
-ch(t)	-gh(t)	acht *eight*; Nacht *night*; Fracht *freight*; Tochter *daughter*; leicht *light*; hoch *high*; lachen *laugh*
-ch	-k	Buch *book*; Koch *cook*; sprechen *speak*; brechen *break*; Woche *week*
-chs	-x	Ochs *ox*; Achse *axis/axle*; Fuchs *fox*; Büchse *box*; Buchsbaum *boxtree*
j	y/i	Joga *yoga*; Jahr *year*; jung *young*; Jalta *Yalta*; Jota *iota*; jambisch *iambic*; Jod *iodine*
-g	-y	sagen *say*; Tag *day*; lausig *lousy*

4. Limits to the usefulness of cognates

While the similarities between the languages outlined above are very helpful when reading German texts, it is important to realize that these are only guidelines. Three points need to be noted:

(i) The best guide to the precise meaning of a German word is always its context. Even when the cognate words have broadly the same meaning in English and German, they often have a slighty different range of senses in which they can be used. Note, for example, the following senses of words from the above list:

die Differenz: *quantitative difference*; *disagreement* (contrasting with der Unterschied: *qualitative difference*)
das Fieber: *high temperature*; *fever*
der Satz: *sentence*; *set of something*
unter: *under*; *amongst*
faul: *lazy*; *foul, rotten*
leicht: *easy*; *light*

(ii) The meanings of some cognates are now only remotely related. For example:

German word	English cognate	Meaning of German word
Volk	*folk*	a people
fechten	*to fight*	to fence, duel
heben	*to heave*	to lift, raise
prüfen	*to proof/to prove*	to test
Zwist	*twist*	quarrel, dispute, feud
Opfer	*offer*	victim, sacrifice

(iii) Some German words look like cognates of English words but are 'false friends', i.e. they mean something entirely different (→R164).

Using the Dictionary

R166 Selecting a Dictionary

A good dictionary

- gives gender (→**R178** and **R91**) and plural forms (→**R179**) of nouns
- contains a list of strong/mixed/irregular verb forms (→**R26**), (usually at the back of the dictionary or between the German/English and English/German section) and also lists common irregular forms in the main part of the dictionary.
- indicates if a verb is transitive, intransitive or reflexive, separable or inseparable (→**R168, R171, R169, R174 Note 1**)
- has an introductory chapter which explains the special features of the dictionary or at least has a detailed list of the symbols and abbreviations used
- has a list of abbreviations (e.g. BRD, EDV, SPD) or lists them alphabetically in the main part
- lists words which are frequently used as prefixes and gives the meaning of words which change their basic meaning when used as components in compounds (→**R181**).
  e.g. **Haupt** means *head*, but **Haupt-** in a compound means *main, principal, chief*. Check if meanings are given for
  e.g. **Grund-, Fach-, fehl-, ur-, Sonder-, fort-, hinein-, dazu-**.
- lists common suffixes (→**R186**). Check if the dictionary lists
  e.g. **-bar, -chen, -fach, -gut, -haft, -haltig, -los, -mäßig, -weise, -werk, -zeug**.
- clearly indicates if a verb changes its meaning if it is
  1. used together with a preposition (→**R175**). Check if for example meanings are given for
     halten + preposition (**halten . . . auf, halten . . . für, halten . . . zu**, etc.)
  2. used with a noun (→**R176**). Check for example: etwas in Aussicht stellen.

R167 Getting to know your Dictionary

The symbols and abbreviations used in dictionaries and the way the entries are organized vary greatly from one dictionary to another. In order to use the dictionary efficiently it is important to familiarize yourself with the particular system used. Consult the appropriate introductory chapter or list.

Make use of the various subheadings and sections given for most entries. Many dictionaries, for example, indicate in which field a particular word is used. e.g. (Maths), (Tech.), (Eccl.), etc.

If a particular word cannot be found or if the meaning found does not fit the context, it may be because the spelling is not correct. Check UMLAUTS (the two dots on a, o, u → ä, ö, ü), vowel combinations (especially ie–ei). Don't ignore capitals as noun indicators, e.g.

Lieder *songs*	Kuchen *cake*	zahlen *to pay*
leider *unfortunately*	Küchen *kitchens*	zählen *to count*
		Zahlen *numbers*

liegen *to lie*	fallen *to fall*
legen *to lay, to put*	fällen *to fell*

Note that **ä, ö, ü** are usually listed after a, o, u. The letter **ß** is treated as ss.

Also allow for the effects of the Spelling Reform introduced in 1996. **→R191**

R168 Looking up Verbs

The meaning of one and the same verb can vary according to how it is used, i.e. which COMPLEMENTS it has. (**→R81–4**)

Take for example the verb **trauen**.

1.	Er **traut** sich nicht.	He does not **dare.**
2.	Er **traut** das Paar nicht.	He does not **marry** the couple.
3.	Er **traut** ihm nicht.	He does not **trust** him.

In the first sentence the verb is used with the reflexive pronoun 'sich' (**→R40**). In the second sentence there is an accusative object (**→R93.2**). In the third sentence trauen is complemented by the dative pronoun 'ihm' (**→R93.3, R98**).

A verb which dictates the accusative case for its object is called a transitive verb. The dictionary entry for **trauen** therefore will look something like this:

trauen	(reflexive)	*to dare*
	(transitive)	*to marry*
	(intransitive + dative)	*to trust*

Check your dictionary to find out which abbreviations are used to indicate reflexive, transitive and intransitive verbs.

Here is a dictionary entry for the verb **erinnern**. Compare it with the entry in your dictionary.

erinnern	(transitive)	*to remind somebody of something*
	(reflexive)	*to recall or recollect something*
	(intransitive)	**~ an**: *to be reminiscent of, to call to mind* (For VERBS + PREPOSITIONS **→R175**)

Note: Many dictionaries use **~** or **-** to represent the headword whenever it occurs in an unchanged form within an entry.

Always consult the context to decide on the meaning of the verb.

Only the infinitive form of verbs (**→R21**) is usually given in the main part of the dictionary. Some larger dictionaries, though, also list finite forms of common strong or irregular verbs.

R169 Looking up Finite Verbs

When looking up a strong, mixed or irregular finite verb (→**R26, R46, R28, R30**) start by locating the verb in its alphabetical place in the LIST OF STRONG, MIXED AND IRREGULAR VERBS given in **R46** or in your own dictionary (usually at the back), taking into account any possible vowel and consonant changes. Then move horizontally along the line to the infinitive form, which is the form listed in the main part of the dictionary.

Examples from a LIST OF STRONG, MIXED, AND IRREGULAR VERBS.

INFINITIVE	PRESENT TENSE FACTUAL	SIMPLE PAST TENSE FACTUAL	SUBJUNCTIVE II NON-FACTUAL	PAST PARTICIPLE
bringen *(to bring)*	bringt	brachte	brächte	gebracht
geben *(to give)*	gibt	gab	gäbe	gegeben
nehmen *(to take)*	nimmt	nahm	nähme	genommen

(Note that your dictionary may be using a different set of grammatical terms.)

e.g. **brachten** Simple past tense, plural, of **bringen**
gibt   3rd person singular, present tense, of **geben**
nähme   Non-factual, singular, of **nehmen**

There are only two verbs where the first letter in the stem differs in the various personal forms:

essen *(to eat)*	ißt	aß	äße	gegessen
sein *(to be)*	ist	war	wäre	gewesen

For a complete list of forms for the verb **sein** *(to be)* →**R31**.

In the case of compound verbs, i.e. verbs with PREFIXES, usually only the basic form of the verb (without the prefix) is listed (List of PREFIXES →**R174**). If this basic form of a verb cannot be found in the LIST OF STRONG AND IRREGULAR VERBS it may be a weak verb (→**R26**) which is listed in the main part of the dictionary, or it may belong to a small group of verbs where the prefix has become an integral part of the verb and must not be split off when looking for the verb in the LIST OF STRONG, MIXED AND IRREGULAR VERBS.

e.g. | PAST TENSE, SINGULAR | INFINITIVE |
|---|---|
| begann | beginnen |
| empfahl | empfehlen |
| geschah | geschehen |
| mißlang | mißlingen |
| verlor | verlieren |

R170 Looking up Past Participles

The procedure for finding the infinitive depends on the type of past participle you are dealing with (→R34).

■ ge STEM t

1. Check if the STEM form + en is listed in the main part of the dictionary.
   e.g. ge**stell**t   **stellen** *(to put)*

2. If not, find the stem form in the Past Participle column in the LIST OF STRONG, MIXED, AND IRREGULAR VERBS. Alternatively, look in the Past Tense column for forms beginning with the first letter/s of the stem.
   e.g. ge**brach**t   Past Tense: **brachte**   Infinitive: **bringen** *(to bring)*

■ ge STEM en

These past participle forms are all listed in the LIST OF STRONG, MIXED, AND IRREGULAR VERBS.

e.g. **gegeben**   Infinitive: **geben** *(to give)*
      geschrieben Infinitive: **schreiben** *(to write)*
      geholfen   Infinitive: **helfen** *(to help)*

■ PREFIX STEM en / t

Some of these past participle forms are either completely identical with their infinitive forms or they have identical stem forms.

e.g. **verraten**   Infinitive: **verraten** *(to betray)*
      entschuldigt   Infinitive: **entschuldigen** *(to excuse)*

All others with a strong or irregular stem form are given in the LIST OF STRONG, MIXED, AND IRREGULAR VERBS, either in their entirety

e.g. **begonnen**   Infinitive: **beginnen** *(to begin)*

or as the past participle of the verb without the prefix (→R174).

e.g. **verholfen** [PAST PARTICIPLE listed: **geholfen**. INFINITIVE: **helfen**]
      Infinitive **verhelfen**

      entnommen [PAST PARTICIPLE listed: **genommen**. INFINITIVE: **nehmen**]
      Infinitive **entnehmen**

■ STEM ending in **ier** t

To get the infinitive form simply replace the **-t** by **-en**.

e.g. konstru**ier**t   Infinitive: konstru**ieren** *(to construct)*

When looking up PAST PARTICIPLES also note:

■ A small number of the verbs with **ge-** as an integral part of their stem have a **-t** as past participle ending. Thus **ge- -t** can be the past participle form of a verb with a stem beginning in **ge-** as well as the much more frequently occurring past participle of a weak verb. If in doubt check the meaning of both forms to see which fits the context.

1. Das Buch hat ihm **gehört.**

   gehören *to belong to*   PAST PARTICIPLE: **gehör-t**
   The book (has) belonged to him.

2. Er hat die Nachrichten **gehört.**

   hören *to hear, to listen to*   PAST PARTICIPLE: **ge-hör-t**
   He has heard/listened to the news.

■ Adjectives which are derived from verbs can look like past participles. In the dictionary they are listed as adjectives.

  e.g.   Ich war **gefaßt.**   *I was calm.*

         Er war **angesehen.**   *He was respected.*

R171 Looking up Separable Verbs (→R39)

The meaning of a verb may change completely depending on which PREFIX (→**R174**) is attached to the basic verb.

  e.g. **geben** (without any PREFIX) *to give*

abgeben *to hand in, to give away*
   Sie **gibt** den Aufsatz **ab.**
   She hands in the essay.

angeben *to boast; to state, to declare*

   Er **gibt** dauernd **an.**
   He is always boasting.

aufgeben *to give up; to check in; to post*
   Sie **gibt** ihre Arbeit nicht **auf.**
   She does not give up her job.

ausgeben *to spend; to distribute*
   Er **gibt** viel Geld **aus.**
   He spends a lot of money.

eingeben *to feed (computer); to submit*
   Ich **gebe** alle Daten **ein.**
   I feed in all the data.

hergeben *to hand over*
   Sie **gibt** das Bild nicht **her.**
   She does not hand over the picture.

mitgeben *to give something to take with one*

   Sie **gibt** ihm das Buch **mit.**
   She gives him the book to take away with him.

nachgeben *to give in; to give way to*

   Er **gibt** ihrem Drängen **nach.**
   He gives in to their requests.

vorgeben *to pretend*
   Sie **gibt vor,** ihn zu kennen.
   She pretends to know him.

zugeben *to admit; to add; to acknowledge*
   Er **gibt** den Fehler **zu.**
   He admits the mistake.

To get the infinitive (i.e. the dictionary) form of a separable verb, the prefix has to be re-attached after the infinitive of the verb has been found, e.g.

gibt ......   **ab**

gibt > INFINITIVE: geben   **geben**   **abgeben**

R172 Looking up Past Participle forms of Separable Verbs

Detach prefix, then as in **R170**. When the infinitive has been found re-attach the prefix before looking up the meaning, e.g.

ab **gegeben**
gegeben > INFINITIVE: **geben abgeben**

R173 The Infinitive with zu of Separable Verbs

If a separable verb is used in an infinitive construction with **zu** (➔R149) or in the form of a present participle in an extended adjectival construction (➔R116) the **zu** goes between the PREFIX and the STEM of the verb. The **zu** simply has to be omitted when looking for the infinitive form, e.g.

,um es nächste Woche **abzugeben.**

abgeben to hand in

in order to hand it in next week.

eine nicht **vorauszusehende** Komplikation

voraus[zu]sehen[de] (➔R43) **voraussehen** to foresee

a complication not to be foreseen, an unforeseeable complication.

If two **zu**'s are found in an infinitive construction, one is a verb PREFIX (**zu-, dazu-, herzu-, hinzu-**), e.g.

, um nicht **zuzuhören.**

zuhören to listen

in order not to listen

R174 List of Verb Prefixes

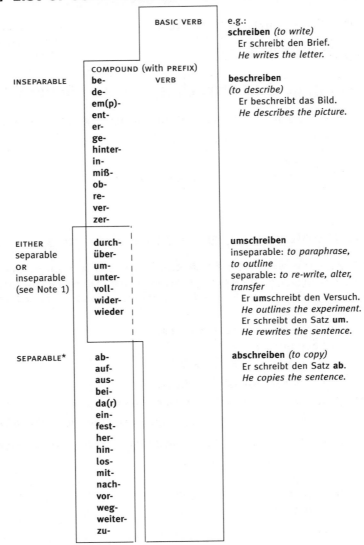

		e.g.:
	BASIC VERB	**schreiben** *(to write)*
		Er schreibt den Brief.
		He writes the letter.

INSEPARABLE — COMPOUND (with PREFIX) VERB

be-
de-
em(p)-
ent-
er-
ge-
hinter-
in-
miß-
ob-
re-
ver-
zer-

beschreiben
(to describe)
Er beschreibt das Bild.
He describes the picture.

EITHER
separable
OR
inseparable
(see Note 1)

durch-
über-
um-
unter-
voll-
wider-
wieder

umschreiben
inseparable: *to paraphrase, to outline*
separable: *to re-write, alter, transfer*
Er **um**schreibt den Versuch.
He outlines the experiment.
Er schreibt den Satz **um**.
He rewrites the sentence.

SEPARABLE*

ab-
auf-
aus-
bei-
da(r)-
ein-
fest-
her-
hin-
los-
mit-
nach-
vor-
weg-
weiter-
zu-

abschreiben *(to copy)*
Er schreibt den Satz **ab**.
He copies the sentence.

* The list of **SEPARABLE** PREFIXES is not complete. Only the most common ones are given.

Note 1: Verbs which can be SEPARABLE or INSEPARABLE with a difference in meaning are listed separately in good dictionaries. The forms of these verbs are distinct for all tenses. The INFINITIVE forms without **zu**, however, are identical. Here only the context will help in deciding which of the two forms you are dealing with, e.g.

Er **umschreibt** seine Theorie.   *He **outlines** his theory.*

Er **schreibt** seine Theorie **um**.   *He **rewrites** his theory.*

BUT: Morgen wird er seine Theorie **umschreiben**.

*Tomorrow he will **outline** his theory.*

OR: *Tomorrow he will **rewrite** his theory.*

R175 Verb + Preposition Phrases

A combination of a particular verb + a particular preposition may form an idiomatic unit, the meaning of which should be found in the dictionary entry for the verb, e.g.

halten *to hold; to keep; to stop*

> Wir halten den Dieb. Ich halte den Hund.
> *We stop the thief.* *I hold the dog.*

BUT: **halten . . . für**   *to take somebody to be something,*
    to take somebody for something.

> Wir **halten** ihn **für** einen Dieb.
> *We take him to be a thief.*

halten . . . zu *to stick to or stand by somebody*

> Wir **halten** trotzdem **zu** ihm.
> *We nevertheless stand by him.*

Note how the following sentence can be interpreted in two different ways depending on whether we read the verb as **halten** or **halten für**.

> Ich **halte** den Hund **für** meinen Freund.
> *I take the dog to be my friend.*

But if **halten** and **für** do not form an idiomatic unit:

> Ich **halte** den Hund für meinen Freund.

the meaning is:

> *I am holding the dog for my friend.*

Often only the context makes it clear which of the two structures is present!

> Ich **halte** den Hund für meinen Freund, damit das Tier nicht wegläuft.
> *. . ., so that the animal does not run away.*

Note how your dictionary lists e.g. **halten** (a) . . . (b) . . . (c) ~ **für** . . . (d) ~ **zu** . . .

Note that the two elements of the phrase (VERB + PREPOSITION) need not occur next to one another in the text. If the preposition appears before the verb it is particularly difficult to recognize it as part of such a phrase, e.g.

> **Für** einen Dieb **halten** wir ihn nicht.
> *We do not consider him to be a thief.*

R176 Verb + (Preposition) + Noun Phrases

Verbs like **halten** *(to hold)*, **treffen** *(to meet)*, **kommen** *(to come)*, **bringen** *(to bring)*, etc. can be used in VERB + (PREPOSITION) + NOUN combinations. As in the VERB + PREPOSITION (**→R175**) phrases, the verb can acquire a different meaning. The new meaning is often closely linked to the meaning of the noun used in the phrase and is usually listed in the entry for the noun.

Ausschau halten nach *to look out for*

Wir **halten Ausschau nach** ihm. *We look out for him.*

eine Rede halten *to make or give a speech*

Muß man **eine Rede halten**? *Must one give a speech?* [T10a:4]

eine Anordnung treffen *to give an order.* Anordnung *order*

Er **trifft eine Anordnung.** *He gives an order.*

zur Durchführung kommen *to come into force, be implemented.* Durchführung *implementation, carrying out*

Wird das Gesetz bald **zur Durchführung kommen**? *Will the law soon come into force?*

in Wut bringen *to infuriate.* Wut *rage, fury*

Ihre Behauptung **brachte** ihn **in Wut.** *Her statement infuriated him.*

Since dictionary entries for these verbs can be voluminous, it may be quicker to first check the entry for the particular noun used in the phrase, e.g.

Ausschau: ~ halten nach . . .

Rede: eine ~ halten

R177 Verb + Prefix vs. Verb + Preposition

Before looking up any combination of VERB + PREFIX or VERB + PREPOSITION, work out which of the two forms you are dealing with since the meanings can differ considerably. Check the word order: If the PREPOSITION/PREFIX appears in Position IV (→R3 and R6), then you are dealing with a separable verb. If it is found in Position III or in Position I it is a VERB + PREPOSITION phrase (→R175), e.g.

	I	II III	IV

VERB + PREFIX (SEPARABLE VERB)

aufhalten *to stop, to halt*

Diese Maßnahme **hielt** die Entwicklung nicht **auf.**
This measure did not stop the development.

VERB + PREPOSITION

halten . . . auf

to attach importance to something

Er **hielt** viel **auf** ihre Meinung.

Auf ihre Meinung **hielt** er viel.

He attached great importance to their opinion.

Because the VERB and the PREPOSITION or the VERB and the NOUN which goes with it need not appear next to one another in the sentence it can be difficult to recognize them as being part of the same phrase. It is therefore best, when looking up a verb, to develop a routine of keeping an eye open for phrases listed in the verb entry which include prepositions appearing in the clause, e.g.

Er freut sich auf das Konzert.

(Look up: **freuen** (reflexive) *to be glad/pleased.*

Then check if there is a phrase given which includes **auf**:

sich auf etwas freuen *to look forward to.)*

The sentence therefore does NOT read: *He is pleased about the concert,* BUT *He is looking forward to the concert.*

R178 Looking up Nouns

Usually three abbreviations are found after the NOUN, e.g.

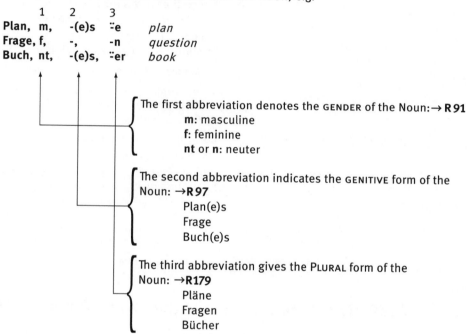

	1	2	3	
Plan,	m,	-(e)s	̈e	*plan*
Frage,	f,	-,	-n	*question*
Buch,	nt,	-(e)s,	̈er	*book*

The first abbreviation denotes the GENDER of the Noun: → **R 91**
  m: masculine
  f: feminine
  nt or **n**: neuter

The second abbreviation indicates the GENITIVE form of the Noun: →**R 97**
  Plan(e)s
  Frage
  Buch(e)s

The third abbreviation gives the PLURAL form of the Noun: →**R179**
  Pläne
  Fragen
  Bücher

R179 Plural Forms of Nouns

Nouns are listed in the singular form. Therefore plural endings and/or UMLAUTS have to be omitted from any plural form as it appears in a text, before looking up the noun in its alphabetical place in the dictionary.

The following are **PLURAL** indicators:

-e/ ̈e

For example:

die Tag**e** *(days)* — der Tag
After final s in the singular:
die Ergebni**sse** *(results)* — das Ergebnis
die Vorg**ä**ng**e** *(events)* — der Vorgang

-er/ ̈er	die Lied**er** *(songs)* — das Lied
	With an umlaut if the stem vowel is: **a, o, u,**:
	die Bücher *(books)* — das Buch
-(e)n	Most feminine nouns.
	die Frag**en** *(questions)* — die Frage.
	Exclusively feminine noun endings:
	-heit, -ion, -keit, -schaft, -tät, -ung.
	die Freund<u>schaft</u>**en** *(friendships)* — die Freundschaft
	A final **-a, -um, -on, -us** is replaced by **-en** in the plural.
	die Them**en** *(subjects, topics)* — das Them**a**
	die Individu**en** *(individuals)* — das Individu**um**
-	No plural ending added to the singular form.
	die Lehrer *(teachers)* — der Lehrer
..	No ending but umlaut added.
	die Mütter (mothers) — die Mutter
-ien	Die Mineral**ien** *(minerals)* — das Mineral
-s	Mainly words 'recently' adopted from other languages:
	die Test**s** *(tests)* — der Test
	die Radio**s** *(radios)* – das Radio
	Not to be mixed up with GENITIVE 's' (➜**R97** + **R104.1**)!
	e.g.: **des** Professors
Rare plural forms	of foreign words are usually listed in their entirety.
	die Anti-Biotika — das Anti-Biotikum
	*die Appendi**zes** — der Appendix*

Note: The above umlauts/endings do not always denote plurals. They may simply be part of the singular form, e.g. the following are all singular!

Träne, Frage, Wagen, Meister *(tear, question, car, master)*

R180 Nouns Derived from Other Word Types (➜R184)

These nouns may have to be looked up under the original word form.

1. Nouns derived from VERBS:

INFINITIVES, e.g.

bis zum **Einsetzen** schriftlicher Quellen [T11:4]

(einsetzen *to start, to begin*)

Until the beginning of written sources

PRESENT PARTICIPLES, e.g.

Das **Zutreffende** bitte unterstreichen.

(zutreffend > zutreffen to *apply to, be applicable*)

Underline that which is applicable.

PAST PARTICIPLE, e.g.

Das **Gesagte** trifft hier nicht zu.

(gesagt > sagen *to say*)

What has been said does not apply here.

2. Nouns derived from ADJECTIVES, e.g.

>bereits **Bekanntes** in neuem Licht zu sehen [T12:4]
>
>>(bekannt *(well) known)*
>
>*to see what is already well known in a new light*
>
>Das Überleben des **Stärkeren** . . .
>
>>(stark *strong* stärker *stronger* →R107)
>>
>>der Starke *the strong one/man)*
>
>*The survival of the fittest/lit.: stronger one*
>
>Der **Widerspenstigen** Zähmung
>
>>(widerspenstig *unruly, wilful, stubborn*
>>
>>Die Widerspenstige *the wilful woman)*
>
>*The Taming of the Shrew*

Note: Adjectives used as nouns nevertheless retain the appropriate adjective endings (→**R106**), e.g.

>Dem **Erstaunlichen** an der Sache auf die Spur zu kommen . . .
>
>*To find out about the amazing aspect of the matter . . .*

R181 Looking up Compound Words

1. Compound words are a particular feature of German. So being able to analyse their structure and work out their meaning is an essential skill. There is virtually no limit to the number of word combinations which can be formed by joining, e.g.

NOUN + NOUN	**Weltkrieg** (Welt + Krieg) *world war* [T2:3]
VERB (STEM) + NOUN	**Denkweise** (denk + Weise) *way of thinking* [T12:1]
ADJECTIVE + VERB (PAST PARTICIPLE)	**weitgereist** (weit + gereist) infinitive: reisen *widely travelled*
ADJECTIVE + NOUN	**Großstadt** (groß + Stadt) *city* [T3:4]
NOUN + VERB (PRESENT PARTICIPLE)	**gewichtsmindernd** (Gewicht + mindern(d)) [T18:5] *weight-reducing*

2. The BASE COMPONENT, i.e. the last part of a compound, gives the basic meaning of the word and determines the gender of the compound. The first part(s) modify the general meaning. Thus

$$
\left.
\begin{array}{lll}
A & B & \\
A & B & C \\
A & B & C & D
\end{array}
\right\} \text{ is some kind of } \left\{
\begin{array}{l}
B \\
C \\
D
\end{array}
\right.
$$

e.g.   der **Großstadtverkehr** [T19:8]   groß/Stadt/Verkehr

der Verkehr	main meaning given in dictionary: *traffic*
die Stadt	*town*
der Stadtverkehr	*town traffic, traffic in town*
groß	large, big, great
die Großstadt	*city*
	city traffic, urban traffic

die **Selbsthilfeorganisation** [T14:10]	selbst/Hilfe/Organisation
die Organisation	organization. What kind?
die Hilfe	help. An organization to help.
	To help whom?
selbst	*self*
	self-help organization

3. Where two or more compounds with the same component, usually the base component, are given in a text, a hyphen often replaces the base component, e.g.

Glaubens-, Gewissens-, Meinungs- und Versammlungs**freiheit**

freedom *of religion, of conscience, of opinion and assembly*

mehr Kriegs- als Friedens**jahre** [T2:2]

*more **years** of war than (**years**) of peace*

4. Compounds are listed in their alphabetical place in the dictionary. If there are several compound forms with the same first component the first word is usually replaced by a dash or swung dash (tilde), e.g.

Arbeits-:	~ stelle (Arbeitsstelle)	*place of work; job*
	~ tag (Arbeitstag)	*work/ing day*
	~ zimmer (Arbeitszimmer)	*work room, study*

However, dictionaries only list compound words which are frequently used or have, as a compound, acquired a new meaning, e.g.

Wasserstoff

| Wasser | *water* |
| Stoff | *material* |

BUT: **Wasserstoff** means ***hydrogen***

Zeitgeschichte [T11:9]

| Zeit | *time* |
| Geschichte | *history* |

BUT: **Zeitgeschichte** means ***contemporary history***

It is therefore essential to be able to work out the meaning of compounds by first splitting them up into their original parts, then looking up the meaning for the individual components (→**R182**).

R182 Splitting up Compound Words

1. A compound form may consist of complete words simply written together or of only parts of words, e.g. the verb stem.

Individual components are often joined together by the following letters:

(e) s   (e) n   er

The second (or third or fourth!) part of the compound therefore often starts after these letters, e.g.

Geschichtsbücher [T15:2]	*history books*
Nachkriegsjahre [T13:6]	*post-war years*
Bundesversammlung [T2:12]	*Federal Assembly*
Elektronenrechner [T3:7]	*electronic calculator/computer*

Sometimes, however, these letters are not 'joining' letters but part of the individual component!

e.g. **Bühnenstücke** [T15:2] > Bühnen/Stücke *stage plays*

Very occasionally this can lead to reading problems:

Wachstube   NOT: Wach/s/Tube

BUT: Wach/Stube

(Stube *room*, Wach(e) *guard*)

guard(s)-room

OR: Wachs/Tube

(Tube *tube*, Wachs *wax*]

tube of wax

In such cases be guided by the context.

If a compound has no joining letters you can, nevertheless, often see where roughly the 'seams' of a compound are, as frequently consonant clusters are found at the joint, e.g.

Da**mpfm**aschine [Dampf + Maschine] [T3:2]   *steam engine*

2. Familiarize yourself with common PREFIXES (→**R174**) and SUFFIXES (→**R186**) to speed up the recognition of word structures, e.g.

Entwick**lung**sstadien (Entwicklung/s/stadien) [T12:1]

stages of development

Sicher**heit**sschloß (Sicherheit/s/schloß) [T17:1]

safety (Yale) lock

Note that **er** can be either a genuine PREFIX or the plural indicator of a component noun, e.g.

Umfrage**er**gebnis [T20:2] (Umfrage/Ergebnis)

survey result

Bild**er**buch (Bild/er/buch)

book of pictures/picture book

3. If you do not recognize individual components, there is no other way but to look up the compound as a whole in the dictionary. Check how much of the word is given, then look up the next part etc., **working strictly from left to right**, e.g.

Temperaturschutzschalter [T23:10]

Temperatur

⟶ schutz

⟶ schalter

⟶

Once the components have been identified put together the individual meanings to get the meaning of the whole compound, **now working from right to left**, e.g.

Temperaturschutzschalter

Schalter	The dictionary gives you *switch* or *counter*. The context tells you it has to be some sort of *switch*. What sort of switch?
Schutz	*protection, safeguard*. So it is some sort of safety switch.
Temperatur	*temperature*. So literally it is a temperature safety switch.
	thermal circuit breaker

R183 Looking up Adjectives and Adverbs

Adjectives are listed in the dictionary in their undeclined form (without endings), i.e. the same form as the equivalent adverb. (➔R109)

Since the meanings of adjectives and adverbs can differ it is important to check the right section of the dictionary entry, e.g.

schwer adj.: (a) *heavy*; (b) *strong*; (c) *serious, grave*; (d) *hard, difficult*.

adv.: *really, deeply, heavily*

Er war **schwer** gekränkt.

*He was **deeply** hurt.*

Aspects of Word Formation

R184 Derivatives

Word formation is a subject of great complexity and, for reasons of space, cannot be dealt with comprehensively here. But here are a few points to bear in mind when you are dealing with derivatives.

1. An infinite number of new words can be formed by adding PREFIXES (→R174) and/or SUFFIXES (→R186) to words or word stems, e.g.

antworten	*to answer*
verantworten	*to accept responsibility for*
Verantwort**ung**	*responsibility*
verantwortungs**los**	*irresponsible*
frei	*free*
Frei**heit**	*freedom, liberty*
befreien	*to free/release*
hören	*to hear/listen*
hör**bar**	*audible*
Hörbar**keit**	*audibility*

2. Nouns can be derived from:

other nouns:	Nachbar**schaft**	*neighbourhood*
	Nachbar	*neighbour*
adjectives:	Bestimmt**heit**	*certainty*
	bestimmt	*certain, particular, definite*
verbs:	Bewerb**ung**	*application*
	bewerben	*to apply*

3. Adjectives can be derived from:

other adjectives:	**un**veränderlich	*unchanging, invariable*
	veränderlich	*changeable, variable*
nouns:	ahnungs**los**	*unsuspecting*
	Ahnung	*suspicion, premonition*
verbs:	übersetz**bar**	*translatable*
	übersetzen	*to translate*

4. Verbs can be derived from:

other verbs:	**zu**hören	*to listen*
	hören	*to hear*
nouns:	**be**bildern	*to illustrate*
	Bild	*picture*
adjectives:	**be**schönigen	*to gloss over*
	schön	*beautiful*

5. Most common derivatives and those derivatives which have acquired a totally new meaning are listed in larger dictionaries. As sometimes, however, authors use unusual combinations or form new derivatives, it is useful to be able to analyse such words, i.e.

- to recognize PREFIXES (→**R174**) and SUFFIXES (→**R186**),
- to trace the derivative back to its original stem form,
- then derive the meaning by combining the original meaning with the meaning of the prefixes/suffixes used.

e.g.: **Unausgeglichenheit**

ausgeglichen	is (a) the past participle of **ausgleichen** *to balance, to even out*
	(b) an adjective, meaning *balanced, even, equal, consistent.*
un	is a prefix used for negation (→**R130**)
unausgeglichen	*not balanced unbalanced*
heit	is a suffix which turns an adjective or past participle into an abstract noun (→**R186**)
Unausgeglichenheit	*the state of being unbalanced* *imbalance, inequality, disharmony, instability*

R185 Prefixes

For a list of prefixes which can be attached to verb stems see **R174**. Good dictionaries also list common prefixes. If the general meaning of a prefix is not given in the dictionary, it can often be derived by comparing those words beginning with the same prefix listed in the dictionary. Also, there are many prefixes which have clearly recognizable English equivalents (→**R165**), e.g.

desinteressiert	*disinteressiert*... *disinterested*
Unrecht	*injustice*
Indifferenz	*indifference*
Überproduktion	*overproduction*

R186 Suffixes

Good dictionaries list common suffixes. There are also many suffixes which have clearly recognizable English equivalents (→**R165**), e.g.

Virtuos**ität**	*virtuosity*
Sozial**ismus**	*socialism*
infekt**iös**	*infectious*

The examples and explanations given in the following alphabetically arranged section are intended to help you to deal with some suffixes which may not be given in the dictionary.

(m masculine, f feminine, n neuter. For explanation of other abbreviations after noun entries →R178)

-bar   Corresponds to the English *-ible/-able*. (→R78.5)
Added to verb stems it forms adjectives and adverbs, e.g.

bezahl**bar**	*pay**able***
bezahl(en)	*to pay*
denk**bar**	*conceiv**able***
denk(en)	*to think*

[T21:6] fühl**bar** lit.: *feel**able***, i.e. *can be felt, is to be felt, percept**ible***

-chen   n. Pl.: – The diminutive form of nouns. Often an umlaut is added, e.g.

das Sträß**chen**	*small/narrow street*
die Straße	*street or road*
das Schiff**chen**	*little ship/boat*
das Schiff	*ship*

-e   m, f, n. Pl.: -n Added to verb stems and adjectives, turns them into nouns. Often an umlaut is added.
(This must not be mixed up with the DATIVE -e →R101), e.g.

das Falsch**e**	*that which is wrong* [T21:2]
falsch	*wrong*
das Erkennbar**e**	*that which is recognisable* [T21:6]
erkennbar	*recognizable*
die Such**e**	*the search*
such(en)	*to search*

-(er)ei   f. Pl.: -en Turns verb stems into nouns, e.g.

die Schreib**erei**	*writing, paperwork*
schreib(en)	*to write*
die Verschwend**erei**	*act of wasting, squandering*
verschwend(en)	*to waste*

-(er)isch   Turns verb stems and nouns into adjectives/adverbs, e.g.

schöpf**erisch**	*creative*
schöpf(en)	*to create*
verrät**erisch**	*treacherous, perfidious*
der Verräter	*traitor*

-es   Turns adjectives and verbs into nouns. Note that the noun is used without a determiner. (→R91.2), e.g.

Bekannt**es** [T12:4]	*that which is (well) known, familiar*
bekannt	*well known, familiar*

-heit   f. Pl.: -en Turns adjectives and nouns into abstract nouns, e.g.

die Verkehrt**heit** [T22:3]	*wrongness*
verkehrt	*wrong*
die Kind**heit**	*childhood*
das Kind	*child*

-in f. Pl.: -innen Turns masculine nouns (usually job titles etc.) into feminine forms, e.g.

die Student**in**	*female student*
der Student	*male student*
die Künstler**in**	*female artist*
der Künstler	*male artist*

-isch see **-(er)isch**

-(ig)keit f. Pl.: -en Turns adjectives into abstract nouns, e.g.

die **F**reundlich**keit**	*friendliness*
freundlich	*friendly*
die **A**hnungslosig**keit**	*ignorance, cluelessness*
ahnungslos	*unsuspecting, clueless*

-(er)lei Adjective/adverb suffix added to numerals linked by 'er', e.g.

manch**erlei**	*various*
manch	*many, many a*
hundert**erlei**	*hundreds, 'a hundred and one things'*
hundert	*hundred*

-lein n. Pl.: – Like the suffix **-chen** it turns nouns into their diminutive forms. Often there is a an added umlaut, e.g.

das Rös**lein**	*little rose*
die Rose	*rose*
das Büch**lein**	*little book, booklet*
das Buch	*book*

-lich Adjective/adverb suffix added to verb stems and nouns. Corresponds to the English *-able/-ably* and *-ly*, e.g.

begreif**lich**	*understandable*
begreif(en)	*to understand*
täg**lich**	*daily*
Tag	*day*

But note that not all words ending in **-lich** follow this pattern:

vornehm**lich**	*adv: principally, above all*
	adj: principal, main
vornehm	*distinguished, elegant.*
	(Dated: *First and foremost*)

-s Turns nouns and other word forms into adverbs, e.g.

morgen**s**	*in the morning(s)*
Morgen	*morning*
anfang**s**	*at first, initially*
Anfang	*beginning, start*
zusehend**s**	*visibly, noticeably*
zusehend	*present participle (→R43) of*
zusehen	*to watch*

-schaft   f. Pl.: -en Noun suffix added to other nouns, sometimes with the linking letters -**(e)n**. Corresponds to *-ship*, e.g.

die Freund**schaft**	*friendship*
Freund	*friend*
die Patenschaft	*godparenthood, sponsorship*
der Pate	*godfather, sponsor*

-tum   n. Pl.: -er Added to nouns, sometimes with the linking letters -**en/-(e)s**, e.g.

das Herzog**tum**	*dukedom, duchy*
der Herzog	*duke*
das Held**entum**	*heroism*
der Held	*hero*

-ung   f. Pl.: -en Noun suffix added to verb stems, e.g.

die Übereinstimm**ung** [T12: 4]	*agreement*
übereinstimmen	*to agree*
die Beschwör**ung** [T2: 10]	*entreaty, plea*
beschwören	*to implore, to beseech*
die Glieder**ung** [T11: 3]	*structure, subdivision*
glieder(n)	*to structure, subdivide*

Directions

R187 The Imperative

Formal form of address (→R25), singular and plural (*Sie*):

 INFINITIVE STEM + *en Sie*, e.g.

Lesen Sie diesen Artikel!	*Read this article.*
Übersetzen Sie den Text!	*Translate the text.*
Denken Sie an . . .	*Think of* . . .
Schalten Sie das Videogerät **ein**!	*Switch the video machine on.*

 (**einschalten** is a separable verb (→R39))

Familiar form of address (→R25)

 Singular (*du*):

  PRESENT TENSE STEM of *du* (+ e), e.g.

Hol das Buch!	*Fetch the book.*
Beantworte die Frage!	*Answer the question.*
Öffne das Fenster!	*Open the window.*
Gib ihm das Geld!	*Give him the money.*
Siehe Seite 36.	*See page 36.*
Nimm bitte das Geld!	*Please take the money.*

  Note: the UMLAUT added to some strong verb forms is dropped in the IMPERATIVE:

Halt(e) an der Ecke!	*Stop at the corner.*
[Du hältst an der Ecke.]	
Fahr nicht, geh zu Fuß!	Don't drive, walk!
[Du fährst nicht.]	

 Plural (*ihr*):

  PRESENT TENSE form of *ihr*, e.g.

Vergleicht Abbildung X.	*Compare illustration X.*
Gebt ihm das Geld!	*Give him the money.*
Haltet an der Ecke!	*Stop at the corner.*

There is also a quasi IMPERATIVE form for *wir* (→R25). In meaning this corresponds to the English 'Let's . . . '

 INFINITIVE STEM + *en wir*, e.g.

Nehmen wir an . . . [T7:15]	*Let's assume* . . .
Vergleichen wir die Ergebnisse!	*Let's compare the results.*

R188 Instructions

An INSTRUCTION can be conveyed by a number of different grammatical forms. All sentences below are instructions to

switch on the projector with button 4. [T23:1]

1. INFINITIVE (→R21):

Den Projektor mit Taste 4 **einschalten.**

The infinitive appears in final position. (→R15)
Both infinitives and participles (→R34) can be used in this way, e.g.

Nicht **hinauslehnen!**   *Do not lean out!*
Rauchen **verboten!**   *Smoking prohibited!*

2. IMPERATIVE (→R187):

Schalten Sie den Projektor mit Taste 4 **ein!**

einschalten is a separable verb (→R39)

3. STATEMENT (→R3):

Sie schalten den Projektor mit Taste 4 **ein.**

4. MODAL VERB (→R66 and R69) + PASSIVE (→R73-4)

Der Projektor **soll/muß** mit Taste 4 **eingeschaltet werden.**

The modal verb can be either FACTUAL or NON-FACTUAL. (→R66):

Der Projektor **sollte** mit Taste 4 **eingeschaltet werden.**

Modal verbs are found especially in instructions with a negation word. (→R124–134), e.g.

Das Einlegen des Films **sollte nicht** in greller Sonne erfolgen.
The film ought not to be loaded in bright sunlight.

5. *ist . . .* ZU INFINITIVE (→R78.2):

Der Projektor ist mit Taste 4 **ein<u>z</u>uschalten.**

6. man + NON-FACTUAL VERB (→R48 and R58):

Man schalte den Projektor mit Taste 4 **ein.**

Note: Achtung (lit.: *Attention! Watch out!*) and **bitte [beachten Sie]** (*please [note]*) may be used as introductions to instructions.

Conventions

R189 The Gothic Script (Fraktur)

You may wish to read older publications printed in Gothic script, or *Fraktur* as the Germans call it. Here is the Gothic alphabet to help you decipher texts in Gothic script.

𝕬	𝕭	𝕮	𝕯	𝕰	𝕱	𝕲	𝕳	𝕴	𝕵	𝕶	𝕷	𝕸	𝕹
𝖆	𝖇	𝖈	𝖉	𝖊	𝖋	𝖌	𝖍	𝖎	𝖏	𝖐	𝖑	𝖒	𝖓
A	B	C	D	E	F	G	H	I	J	K	L	M	N
a	b	c	d	e	f	g	h	i	j	k	l	m	n

𝕺	𝕻	𝕼	𝕽	𝕾		𝕿	𝖀	𝖁	𝖂	𝖃	𝖄	𝖅
𝖔	𝖕	𝖖	𝖗	𝖘 𝖟		𝖙	𝖚	𝖛	𝖜	𝖝	𝖞	𝖟
O	P	Q	R	S		T	U	V	W	X	Y	Z
o	p	q	r	s ß		t	u	v	w	x	y	z

R190 Numbers, Dates, etc.

Here is a list of numbers spelt out. You may wish to learn them in order not to have to look them up in the dictionary all the time.

1. Cardinal numbers

0 null		*Note the different sequence in German:*
1 eins	11 elf	21 einundzwanzig (*lit.*: one and twenty)
2 zwei	12 zwölf	22 zweiundzwanzig (*lit.*: two and twenty)
3 drei	13 dreizehn	23 dreiundzwanzig (*lit.*: three and twenty)
4 vier	14 vierzehn	24 vierundzwanzig
5 fünf	15 fünfzehn	25 fünfundzwanzig
6 sechs	16 sechzehn	26 sechsundzwanzig
7 sieben	17 siebzehn	27 siebenundzwanzig
8 acht	18 achtzehn	28 achtundzwanzig
9 neun	19 neunzehn	29 neunundzwanzig
10 zehn	20 zwanzig	30 dreißig

40 vierzig	49 neunundvierzig
50 fünfzig	51 einundfünfzig
60 sechzig	67 siebenundsechzig
70 siebzig	73 dreiundsiebzig
80 achtzig	88 achtundachtzig
90 neunzig	96 sechsundneunzig
100 (ein)hundert	185 (ein)hundertfünfundachtzig (*lit.*: one hundred five and eighty)
200 zweihundert	204 zweihundert(und)vier
300 dreihundert	319 dreihundert(und)neunzehn
1000 (ein)tausend	1265 (ein)tausendzweihundertfünfundsechzig

But for years:

e.g. 1998   neunzehnhundertachtundneunzig

in 1945   (im Jahre) neunzehnhundertfünfundvierzig

2. Ordinal numbers

Note that these have endings like adjectives (→R108).

erst–	*1st*
zweit–	*2nd*
dritt–	*3rd*
viert–	*4th*
fünft–	*5th*
sechst–	*6th*
siebt–	*7th*
acht–	*8th*
neunt–	*9th*
zehnt– etc.	*10th*
neunzehnt–	*19th* (from 10th until 19th t is added,
zwanzigst–	*20th* then st)
einundzwanzigst–	*21st*
zweiundzwanzigst– etc.	*22nd*

im neunzehnten Jahrhundert	*in the nineteenth century*
der zweite April	*2 April*
am zweiten April	*on 2 April*

3. Fractions

	Drittel	*a third*
	Fünftel	*a fifth*
ein	Achtel	*an eighth*
	Zwanzigstel	*a twentieth*
	Hundertstel	*a hundredth*
	etc.	
eine	Hälfte	*a half*

4. - **mal** corresponds to the English 'times', e.g.

einmal	*once*
zweimal	*twice*
dreimal	*three times*
fünfzigmal	*fifty times*
hundertmal	*hundred times*

5. Note that German uses a **comma** where English uses a decimal point, e.g.

3,7 **Millionen** instead of *3.7 million*

1,5 **Kilometer** instead of *1.5 kilometres*

6. Also compare:

German   198 456 Einwohner

English   *198,456 inhabitants*

i.e. in German there is a space where you would use a comma in English.

R191 Spelling Reform

In January 1996 it was announced that proposals for a reform of the German spelling conventions, in force since 1901/2, were accepted by the relevant government bodies. The reform proposals had been put forward by German, Austrian and Swiss specialist working groups and are the result of many years of research and discussions.
The new spelling is to be taught in schools from August 1998 onwards and by 2005 the old spelling conventions will be considered outdated, though not wrong.

Unlike earlier, quite radical reform plans (one idea, for example, was to abolish capitals for nouns), this latest proposal is moderate in its approach and does not suggest very drastic changes. However, for the non-native reader problems may occasionally arise because the spelling of some words in any pre-1997/8 (?) text may differ from the spelling given in a dictionary published later, and of course the other way round, the spelling in any newly published text may be different from the spelling given in an older dictionary.

Note, for example, the following differences, where problems could arise:

	EXAMPLES:	
	OLD	NEW
■ **ss** instead of **ß** (after a short vowel)	daß muß	**dass** mu**ss**
■ sometimes an **ä** instead of an **e** (if the word is derived from another word which contains an 'a')	Stengel überschwenglich	Stängel überschwänglich
■ three consonants instead of two (to retain both parts of compound words)	Schiffahrt Flußsand	Schifffahrt Flusssand
■ an extra **h** (to retain both the original word and the abstract ending which turns it into a noun →**R186**)	Zäheit Roheit	Zähheit Rohheit

■ **z** instead of **t** (because derived from 'Substanz/Differenz')	substantiell Differential	substanziell Differenzial
■ an **h** omitted (analogous to 'blau, grau' etc.)	rauh Känguruh	rau Känguru
■ the spelling of 'foreign' words (to adapt them more closely to other similar words in German)	Ketchup Panther Megaphon	Ketschup Panter Megafon
■ other differences, e.g. the use of capitals, or whether a word is spelt as one word or two	übrigbleiben haltmachen Sonntag abends im allgemeinen wieviel irgend etwas radfahren	übrig bleiben Halt machen sonntagabends im Allgemeinen wie viel irgendetwas Rad fahren

The reform also includes proposals concerning PUNCTUATION, mainly the use of commas.

It suggests, for example, the **abolition of the comma** which

■ separates **main clauses linked by a connector (→R160).**

■ splits off **'zu'+ infinitive clauses (→R149).**
This particular change would be in line with the English convention. However, dropping the comma will make it harder to spot 'zu' + infinitive constructions and thus make analysing the structure of complex sentences a bit more difficult.

Part III

Further Exercises

E1 (→R167)

A. Underline the letter sequence 'ei' in the following list of words. This is not a text, so do not try to read it as a text. Instead, try to scan the words as fast as you can in order to pick out all the 'ei' sequences. Then test your accuracy:

klein aber auch heiß und stieg mit Eiweiß oder fieberhaft und unbegreiflich europäisch wenn Kleinigkeit stiegen und hieß oder bittet vielleicht auf Seide oder lieber steigt schon eitel steigen und hielt dann ergiebig geheißen aber bietet und heilt die Eule und sieden mit Leib oder eilige eiskalt gießen die Liebe ist neugierig in Eile

B. Now underline the letter sequence 'ie' in the following set of words:

klein und heiß stieg das Eiweiß oder fieberhaft und unbegreiflich ist europäisch eine Kleinigkeit aber stiegen hieß und bittet vielleicht mit Seide dann lieber steigt auf eitel in steigen oder hielt ergiebig und geheißen bietet oder heilt mit Eule an sieden auf Leib ist eilige und eiskalt für gießen in Liebe und neugierig in Eile

E2 (→R167)

A. Skim through any German text and pick out the letter sequence 'ei'. This has been done for Corpus Text 1 in the key.

B. Skim through any German text and pick out the letter sequence 'ie'. This has been done for Corpus Text 1 in the key.

E3 (→R167)

Underline the umlauted letters in the following list of words. This is not a text, so do not try to read it as a text. Instead, try to scan the words as fast as you can in order to pick out all the umlauts. Then test your accuracy:

Alter alte älter Mutter Mütter Mutter Bruder Brüder gesunder gesünder Sohn Söhne Ölpreis Mobilität abgeholt ausgehöhlt vertraglich verträglich Apfel Äpfel waren wären konnte könnte durften dürften konnte dürften waren Bruder gesünder älter Mütter Äpfel verträglich Mutter könnte Sohn alte wären Mutter älter durften vertraglich gesunder Mutter verträglich ausgehöhlt Söhne durften

E4 (→R3, R6, R27–30, R39)

Identify the FINITE VERB and its COMPLETION in the following sentences:
1. Handwerker nehmen sogar bei den Ostdeutschen den Platz drei ein. [T1:4]
2. Dies geht aus einer Umfrage hervor. [T1:2]
3. Erasmus von Rotterdam rief vor fast 500 Jahren die Völker Europas zu einem Völkerbund auf. [T2:11]
4. Victor Hugo kündigte 1851 die Vereinigten Staaten von Europa an. [T2:13]
5. Da aber drehten die Gesandten den Spieß um. [T15:9]
6. Die Schweiz wies die höchste Krebsrate in der Alten Welt aus. [T16:4]
7. Die gleichen Probleme treten auch bei Messungen in psychologischen Experimenten auf. [T7:9]

8. Holz schwimmt; Metalle und andere Stoffe dagegen gehen unter. [T18:10]
9. Die restlichen 0,2 Liter Holz tauchen nicht ein. [T18:9]
10. Dennoch legt die Umfrage auch einige Schattenseiten bloß. [T20:4]

E5 (→R3, R6, R33, R74)

Identify the FINITE VERB and its COMPLETION in the following sentences.

1. Dieser Kontinent hat in seiner Geschichte mehr Kriegs- als Friedensjahre erlebt. [T2:2]
2. Für alle Bundesregierungen ist der Ausgleich mit den westlichen Partnern ein Kernpunkt bundesdeutscher Außenpolitik gewesen. [T2:18]
3. Der Mensch hat bisher rund 800 Lebensspannen auf Erden gelebt. [T3:1]
4. Vor einigen Jahren hat eine neue Epoche in der Geschichte begonnen. [T5:8]
5. Durch den Beitritt der ehemaligen DDR hat sich diese Zahl nur unwesentlich verändert. [T13:2]
6. Es wurde viel erreicht. [T2:19]
7. In ihrer Zeit wurde die erste Atombombe gezündet. [T3:7]
8. Die Entstehung der Menschheit wurde in vielen Mythen beschrieben. [T5:7]

E6 (→R3, R6, R63)

Identify the FINITE VERB and its COMPLETION in the following sentences.

1. Das schlechte Ergebnis mag mit der Enttäuschung über die wirtschaftliche Situation zusammenhängen. [T1:9]
2. Wir müssen eine Art Vereinigter Staaten von Europa schaffen. [T2:6]
3. Das Proletariat kann nur in England in allen seinen Verhältnissen studiert werden. [T4:4]
4. Die Musik der Atome, der Sterne und der Tiere muß umgewandelt werden. [T5:6]

E7 (→R6)

Identify the FINITE VERB and its COMPLETION in the following sentences.

1. Der Wunsch nach Frieden stand bei der Gründung der Europäischen Gemeinschaft Pate. [T2:4]
2. Alle diese Einrichtungen stellen die bestehende soziale Ordnung nicht in Frage. [T14:12]
3. Wir haben es hier nicht mit der Geschichte dieser Revolution zu tun. [T4:5]

E8 (→R8, R97–100)

Identify the SUBJECT of the verb in the following sentences.

1. Nach Meinung von Emnid mag das schlechte Ergebnis mit der Enttäuschung über die wirtschaftliche Lage zusammenhängen. [T1:9]
2. Nun besitzt Holz eine geringere durchschnittliche Dichte als Wasser. [T18:10]
3. Die Arbeiter wohnen in oft menschenunwürdigen Behausungen. [T14:8]

4. Die Freiheit zu bewußtem Handeln sollten wir uns erhalten. [T19:11]
5. Erst nach dem Schrecken zweier Weltkriege nahm man die Appelle ernst. [T2:17]

E9 (→R8, R97–100)

Identify the SUBJECT of the verb in the following sentences.

1. In Karl Marx findet der Sozialismus seinen führenden Theoretiker. [T14:14]
2. Neben einem wohlhabenden Industriebürgertum entsteht ein Industrieproletariat. [T14:6]
3. Auf den Aluminiumwürfel wirkt eine entgegengesetzte Kraft. [T18:5]
4. Auffallend ist, daß der Rückstand nicht bestritten wird. [T20:8]
5. Den Talar leiht man Ihnen sicher von der Universität. [T10b:5]

E10 (→R10.3–5)

Identify the SUBJECT of the verb in the following sentences.

1. Es besteht die Gefahr von neuen Kriegen in Europa.
2. Mit der Industrialisierung verändert sich vor allem in Preußen die soziale Landschaft von Grund auf. [T14:5]
3. Bedeutsam für diese Entwicklung war außerdem die Wirtschaftspolitik der Regierung. [T14:17]
4. Es wohnen in dieser Region viele Dialektsprecher.
5. Im ersten Versuch wird ihr erlaubt, sich zu üben. [T7:16]

E11 (→R19)

Identify the FIRST CONCEPT in the following sentences and say whether it is:

> the SUBJECT (Sub.)
> a TOKEN subject (Tok.)
> an OBJECT of the verb (Obj.)

1. Etwa 30 Prozent aller Menschen reagieren jederzeit auf ein Placebo wie auf ein Arzneimittel. [T9:8]
2. Es wurde der Verdacht geäußert, Milch könne krebserregend sein. [T16:1]
3. Einige Schattenseiten legt diese Umfrage bloß. [T20:4]
4. Es können in dieser Region mehrere Dialekte gesprochen werden.
5. Die tiefste Wahrheit spricht der Komponist aus. [T21:5]
6. Die Überlegenheit der Planlosigkeit begründen weder der Hinweis auf Fehlleistungen noch die Identifizierung der Planung mit Staatsdirigismus. [T19:10]

E12 (→R19)

Identify the FIRST CONCEPT in the following sentences and say whether it is:

> an ADVERBIAL (Adv.)
> a VERB COMPLETION (Com.)

an ADJECTIVE (Adj.)

a DEPENDENT CLAUSE (Dep.)

1. Zur Schematisierung seines Gegenstandes teilt der Historiker das bisherige Geschehen in große Zeitabschnitte ein. [T11:1]
2. Wenn das Thermometer kälter ist als das Wasser, wird es die Temperatur des Wassers leicht senken. [T7:13]
3. Damit ein eisernes Schiff schwimmt, muß sein Inneres sehr viel Luftraum enthalten. [T18:11]
4. Genannt werden häufiger andere Gründe. [T20:13]
5. Überraschend ist das Ergebnis, das aus Bochum kommt. [T20:2]

E13 (→R11–14)

Underline the FINITE VERBS OR INFINITIVES in the following sentences which are in FINAL position.

1. Victor Hugo, der 1851 die Vereinigten Staaten von Europa ankündigte, erntete nur Hohn und Spott. [T2:13–14]
2. Die Erfindung der Dampfmaschine ist wichtig, weil sie den Anstoß zu einer industriellen Revolution gab, die die bürgerliche Gesellschaft umwandelte. [T4:1–2]
3. Ich habe es getan, obwohl der Scherz 4 Pfund kostete. [T10b:7]
4. Wenn diese Voraussetzung zutreffend ist, wird eine Vergleichung zahlreiche Übereinstimmungen aufweisen. [T12:4]
5. Neue Finanzmethoden machen es möglich, moderne Produktionsverfahren im großen Stil einzusetzen. [T14:2]

E14 (→R27–30, R44)

a. Find the FINITE verbs in the following sentences.
b. Give the tense used, whether it is singular or plural, and infinitive form.

1. Da kam einem Statistiker der beruhigende Einfall. [T16:8]
2. Wir urteilen so über die sogenannten Wilden und halbwilden Völker. [T12:3]
3. Gottlob bedarf es in den meisten Fällen keines besonderen Fachwissens. [T16:15]
4. In Europa zeigte sich ähnlich Alarmierendes. [T16:3]
5. Er erntete Hohn und Spott. [T2:14]
6. Seit meiner Kindheit glaube ich, daß ich nicht von dieser Welt bin. [T5:11]
7. Der eigentliche Anlaß zu diesem Prozeß erwuchs aus dem Eroberungskrieg Philipps II. gegen die Griechen. [T15:4]
8. Die gleichen Probleme treten auch bei Messungen in psychologischen Experimenten auf. [T7:9]
9. Ihr Verdienst liegt meist an der Grenze des Existenzminimums. [T14:9]
10. Erst nach dem Schrecken zweier Weltkriege nahm man die Appelle ernst. [T2:17]

E15 (→R31–34, R44)

Underline the AUXILIARY VERB and the PAST PARTICIPLE:

1. Dieser Kontinent hat mehr Kriegs- als Friedensjahre erlebt. [T2:2]

2. Sie haben auf gepackten Koffern gesessen. [T13:6]
3. Für alle Bundesregierungen ist das ein Kernpunkt bundesdeutscher Außenpolitik gewesen. [T2:18]
4. Der Aluminiumwürfel ist um das Gewicht der von ihm verdrängten Wassermenge leichter geworden. [T18:4]
5. Vor einigen Jahren hat eine neue Epoche in der Geschichte begonnen. [T5:8]
6. . . ., daß das menschliche Leben auf der Erde, im Tier- und Pflanzenbereich entstanden ist. [T5:9]
7. Ich habe es leichtsinniger Weise getan. [T10b:6]
8. Ich bin bei allen Universitätsanlässen darin herumgelaufen. [T10b:6]
9. Sie haben erlebt, wie das Automobil zur Alltäglichkeit wurde. [T3:6]
10. . . ., wenn er seine Eltern schlecht behandelt, den Wehrdienst verweigert, Fahnenflucht begangen, sein Erbe durchgebracht oder sich gegenüber anderen Männern prostituiert hatte. [T15:10]

E16 (→R39, R44, R171)

The following sentences from the Text Corpus contain SEPARABLE VERBS. Identify them and find correct meanings in the dictionary.

1. Den breitesten Raum in Dovers Buch nimmt ein Prozeß gegen den Athener Timarchos ein. [T15:3]
   The greatest space in Dover's book . . . by a lawsuit against the Athenian Timarchos.
2. Da aber drehten die Gesandten den Spieß um. [T15:9]
   But then the delegates . . .
3. Dennoch legt die Umfrage auch einige Schattenseiten bloß. [T20:4]
   Yet the survey also . . . some negative points.
4. Auch in Mitteleuropa setzt sich die industrielle Revolution durch. [T14:1]
   In Central Europe too the industrial revolution . . .
5. Erst nach dem Schrecken zweier Weltkriege nahm man die Appelle ernst. [T2:17]
   It was only after the shock of two world wars that people . . . the appeals.
6. Sieben Prozent der Frankfurter Firmen aus der Eisen-, Blech- und Metallindustrie, aber auch ein Teil der Feinmechanikhersteller und Maschinenbauer geben an, [T20:5]
   Seven per cent of the Frankfurt firms in the iron, sheet metal and metal industries but also some of the precision engineering firms and mechanical engineering companies . . .
7. Dann weicht eine Messung leicht von der anderen ab. [T7:2]
   Then the measurements . . . slightly from each other.
8. Wir kommen überhaupt nicht mehr durch. [T19:6]
   We no longer . . . at all.
9. Die restlichen 0,2 Liter Holz tauchen nicht ein. [T18:9]
   The remaining 0.2 litres of wood do not . . .
10. Ein falscher Schlüssel hebt nur einen Teil der Sperrstifte auf die richtige Höhe an. [T17:8]
    A wrong key . . . only some of the blocking pins to the correct height.

E17 (→R40-1)

In the following sentences the verb appears with a REFLEXIVE PRONOUN. Work out the meaning of these reflexive constructions.

1. Dann schaltet sich die Lampe wieder ein. [T23:12]
   Then the lamp . . . . again.
2. Dann verkehrt sich sein Sinn ins Gegenteil. [T21:10]
   Then its meaning/purpose . . . .
3. Demosthenes hatte sich von den anderen Gesandtschaftsteilnehmern distanziert. [T15:7]
   Demosthenes . . . . the other members of the delegation.
4. . . . jene, die sich nicht zur Spitzenstellung bekennen, . . . [T20:10]
   those who do not . . . . to be in a leading position
5. Man begnügt sich mit den Wirkungen ihres Materials. [T21:3]
   One . . . . with the effects of its material.
6. In Europa zeigte sich ähnlich Alarmierendes. [T16:3]
   In Europe similarly alarming factors . . . .
7. Demnach stellt sich eine schematische Gliederung der abendländischen Geschichte folgendermaßen dar: [T11:3]
   Accordingly a schematic division of Western history . . . . like this
8. . . . , weil sie sich von Zeit zu Zeit ändern. [T7:10]
   . . . because they . . . . from time to time.

E18 (→R21–44)

In Corpus Text 3 pick out all

a. FINITE VERBS
b. PAST PARTICIPLES

E19 (→R47–8)

Divide the following verb forms into three groups:

[+] those which are **always** non-factual
[±] those which can **sometimes** be non-factual
[−] those which are **never** non-factual

1. könnte [   ]; kann [   ]; könne [   ]
2. wollte [   ]; wolle [   ]; will [   ]
3. dürfte [   ]; durfte [   ]; dürfe [   ]; darf [   ]
4. muß [   ]; mußte [   ]; müßte [   ]; müsse [   ]
5. bin [   ]; ist [   ]; sei [   ]; sind [   ]; seien [   ]; war [   ]; wäre [   ]
6. hat [   ]; habe [   ]; hatte [   ]; hätte [   ]
7. gibt [   ]; gebe [   ]; gebt [   ]; gäbe [   ]

E20 (→R46–7)

Give the INFINITIVE of the following non-factual forms.

1. käme
2. gäbe
3. brächte
4. ginge
5. ließe
6. täte

E21 (→R47–62)

Identify all the non-factual verb forms in Corpus Text 19.

E22 (→R50–1)

Say whether the following non-factual forms refer to (**a**) the past, or (**b**) the present and/or future.

PAST   PRESENT/FUTURE
1. hätte
2. wäre
3. könnte
4. hätte gehabt
5. wäre gewesen
6. hätte sein können
7. gäbe
8. hätte gegeben

E23 (→R54)

The following sentences are reported versions of **either**

    a. 'There is no correlation' **or**
    b. 'There was no correlation'.

For each sentence, say whether it is a report of (**a**) or of (**b**):

1. Er behauptete, es gebe keine Korrelation.
2. Er behauptete, es habe keine Korrelation gegeben.
3. Er behauptete, es gäbe keine Korrelation.
4. Er behauptete, es hätte keine Korrelation gegeben.
5. Er behauptete, es gibt keine Korrelation.

Now say for each of the above whether the reported version implies:

    [+] that the speaker may be inclined to accept the truth of what was asserted;
    [±] that the speaker is being careful to pass on the information in a neutral way;
    [−] that the speaker *might* be sceptical as to the truth of the assertion.

E24 (→R63, R66, R67, R69, R71)

Identify the MODAL VERB + the dependent INFINITIVE in the following sentences and work out their meanings:

1. Wir wollen die Freiheit erhalten.
   Wir müssen die Freiheit sicherstellen.
   Wir müssen die Freiheit planen. [T19:1]
   We . . . . freedom.
2. Wir können die Temperatur messen. [T7:12]
   We . . . . the temperature.

3. Das Placebo soll dem Medikament in Größe, Farbe, Geschmack, völlig gleich sein. [T9:3]
   The placebo . . . . completely identical in size, colour, taste.
4. Die Meßvorrichtung kann einen Einfluß auf das Ergebnis haben. [T7:11]
   The measuring device . . . . an influence on the result.
5. . . . , daß sie ihre Gesandten vor Gericht stellen wollten. [T15:6]
   . . . , that they . . . . their delegates to court.
6. Statistik kann nicht alles beweisen. [T16:14]
   Statistics . . . . not . . . . everything.
7. Darf ich Sie um eine Auskunft bitten? [T10a:1]
   . . . . . . I . . . . you for some information?
8. Leute, die alles wissen möchten, aber nichts lernen wollen [T22:1]
   People, who . . . . everything, but . . . . nothing
9. Die Gesandten, die mit schwersten Strafen rechnen mußten, [T15:9]
   The delegates, who . . . . with most severe punishment,
10. Hauptankläger sollte Timarchos sein. [T15:8]
    Timarchos . . . . chief/main prosecutor.

E25 (→R67, R69, R7)

Number the verb complex in the order required in English, then translate.

e.g.: Die Alten unter uns haben die Mondlandung ansehen können. [T3:5]
   The older ones among us . . . . the landing on the moon.
Key: Die Alten unter uns **haben** die Mondlandung **ansehen können**.

$$\qquad\qquad\qquad\qquad \underset{1}{} \qquad\qquad\qquad\qquad\qquad \underset{3}{} \quad \underset{2}{}$$

   (1) have (2) been able (3) to watch (were able to watch)

1. Ich werde Sie auf der Durchreise besuchen können. [T10a:11]
   I . . . . you on the way through.
2. Wir haben die Wassertemperatur messen können. [T7:12]
   We . . . . the water temperature.
3. Haben Sie ein Kostüm erstehen müssen? [T10a:7]
   . . . . . . you . . . . a costume?
4. . . . , weil wir uns auf das Wenige haben beschränken müssen, [T4:7]
   because we . . . . ourselves to the few (aspects)
5. Hätte es eine deutlichere Korrelation geben können? [T16:7]
   . . . . a clearer correlation ?

E26 (→R68)

Match the English translations to the German sentences:

e.g.: **a.** Sie haben die Temperatur messen wollen.
   b. Sie wollen die Temperatur gemessen haben.

   I. *They wanted to measure the temperature. (lit.: They have wanted . . .)*
   II. *They claim to have measured the temperature.*
Key: **a**I, **b**II.

1. **a.** Er hat das Rätsel nicht lösen können.
   b. Er kann das Rätsel nicht gelöst haben.

I. *He cannot have solved the puzzle (i.e. it's not possible that he has)*
II. *He has not been able to solve the puzzle.*

2. **a.** Er hätte sich ändern sollen.
   b. Er soll sich geändert haben.

   I. *He ought to have changed.*
   II. *He is said to have changed.*

3. **a.** Sie hat die Wahrheit sagen wollen.
   b. Sie will die Wahrheit gesagt haben.

   I. *She claims to have told the truth.*
   II. *She wanted to tell the truth. (lit.: has wanted to tell)*

4. **a.** Er hätte den Vertrag nicht unterschreiben sollen.
   b. Er soll den Vertrag nicht unterschrieben haben.

   I. *He is said not to have signed the contract.*
   II. *He should not have signed the contract.*

5. **a.** Er hätte früher nach Deutschland fahren können.
   b. Er kann früher nach Deutschland gefahren sein.

   I. *He may have travelled to Germany earlier.*
   II. *He would have been able to travel to Germany earlier.*

E27 (→R74–5)

Which of the following sentences contains a passive?

1. Das Thermometer wird die Temperatur des Wassers leicht senken.
2. Das Thermometer wird in das Glas getaucht.
3. Die Öffentlichkeit wurde aufgeschreckt.
4. Die Öffentlichkeit würde erstaunt sein.
5. Der Film ist durch diesen Preis berühmt geworden.
6. Der Film ist von der Akademie ausgezeichnet worden.

E28 (→R78)

Underline the alternative constructions with a passive meaning in the following text.

Es läßt sich denken, daß man viele Jahre brauchen wird, um in einer fremden Sprache authentische Texte lesen zu können. Ohne viel Arbeit ist das leichte Verstehen schwieriger Texte sicherlich nicht zu erreichen, doch ist nicht zu vergessen, daß man in der eigenen Muttersprache schon ein bestimmtes, zum Teil übertragbares Wissen hat, das diesen Lernprozeß erleichtern wird. Einen Text in der Fremdsprache versteht man schneller und besser, wenn man in der eigenen Sprache ein kompetenter Leser ist. Denn die wichtige Rolle von „Transfer skills" ist einfach nicht zu leugnen:— das hat sich mehrmals in der Forschungsliteratur gezeigt. Immerhin ist ein gutes Wörterbuch, in dem die unbekannten Vokabeln nachzuschlagen sind, unverzichtbar.

E29 (→R74–80)

One of the Corpus Texts listed in each set has no passive constructions of any kind. Which one?

a. Text 5, Text 6, Text 7
b. Text 11, Text 12, Text 13
c. Text 15, Text 16, Text 17

E30 (→R74–80)

In Corpus Text 16, passives are found in only one of the three paragraphs. In which paragraph?

E31 (→R86)

A. Read the four sentences below and analyse the core sentence structure which they have in common:

1. Die Überlegenheit der USA als wissenschaftlich führendes Land bedeutet eine neue Rolle für das Deutsche als Wirtschaftssprache in Europa.
2. Die Überlegenheit der USA als wissenschaftlich führendes Land bedeutet, daß das Deutsche eine neue Rolle bekommt als Wirtschaftssprache in Europa.
3. Die Tatsache, daß die USA jetzt das wissenschaftlich führende Land ist, bedeutet eine neue Rolle für das Deutsche als Wirtschaftssprache in Europa.
4. Die Tatsache, daß die USA jetzt das wissenschaftlich führende Land ist, bedeutet, daß das Deutsche eine neue Rolle als Wirtschaftssprache in Europa bekommt.

B. Read the four sentences below and analyse the core sentence structure which they have in common:

1. Man versteht heute die schweren Folgen der Umweltverschmutzung besser.
2. Man versteht heute besser, wie schwer die Folgen der Umweltverschmutzung sind.
3. Jedes Schulkind versteht heute, daß die Umweltverschmutzung schwere Folgen hat.
4. Welche schwere Folgen die Umweltverschmutzung hat, versteht heute jeder, der Auto fährt.

E32 (→R88)

All of the following sentences contain a VERB + PREPOSITION phrase. Analyse the core sentence structure of each, following the example given below.

e.g.: Heute versteht man unter einem Placebo ein Leerpräparat. [T9:3]
1. Dies geht aus einer Umfrage hervor. [T1:2]

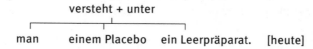

```
              versteht + unter
        ┌──────────┴──────────┐
    man     einem Placebo   ein Leerpräparat.   [heute]
```

2. Erasmus von Rotterdam rief die Völker Europas zu einem Völkerbund auf. [T2:11]

3. Zur Schematisierung seines Gegenstandes teilt der Historiker das bisherige Geschehen in große Zeitabschnitte ein. [T11:1]
4. Auf den Aluminiumwürfel wirkt eine entgegengesetzte Kraft. [T18:5]
5. Eine Messung weicht leicht von der anderen ab. [T7:2]
6. Bach beschäftigte sich nie mit dieser Form. [T8:4]
7. In das natürliche Geschehen und das Denken des Menschen greifen die übernatürlichen Mächte ein. [T6:6]

E33 (→R97)

Say whether the underlined nouns are in the singular or the plural.

der Preis der Karte
die Farbe des Wagens
die Bewertung der Ergebnisse
die Zahl der Studenten
die Zahl der Lehrer
die Sprecher dieses Dialekts
das Zusammenspiel der Farben

E34 (→R94–5, R97)

Try to predict the gender of the nouns in the following phrases. Then look them up in your dictionary and translate the phrase. (All these phrases are taken from Text Corpus 1.)

aus einer Umfrage
hinter dem Arzt
bei der Bewertung des Hausfrauenberufs
über die Berufsgruppe
mit dem geringsten Ansehen
mit der Entäuschung
über die wirtschaftliche Situation
nach der Wiedervereinigung

E35 (→R96)

Translate:

1. Mir fehlt die Zeit.
2. Sie ist ihrer Mutter sehr ähnlich.
3. Das Examen ist ihm nicht gelungen.
4. Wilhelm von Humboldts Ideen über die Sprache sind denen Chomskys sehr nahe.

E36 (→R101, R105)

Say whether the nouns below are in the accusative or the dative, and whether they are in the singular or the plural (you may need to read the sections on prepositions and case, R94–5).

| | ACCUSATIVE | | DATIVE | |
| | SING. | PLUR. | SING. | PLUR. |

für den Produzenten
mit diesen Menschen
mit diesem Gedanken
von den Chirurgen
in dem Franzosen
durch diesen Jungen
zwischen die Kontrahenten
von den Photographen

E37 (→R101, R105)

Say whether the nouns below are in the accusative or the dative, and whether they are in the singular or the plural (you may need to read the sections on prepositions and case, R94–5).

| | ACCUSATIVE | | DATIVE | |
| | SING. | PLUR. | SING. | PLUR. |

durch den Produzenten
von den Produzenten
Man dankt den Produzenten.
Man beschuldigt den Produzenten.

E38 (→R94–5)

Using your knowledge of which prepositions dictate which case, say whether the nouns in the following phrases are in the accusative or the dative.

durch diesen Fall
für jede Möglichkeit
in das Geschehen
an diesem Beispiel
nach der Besichtigung
in dem Geschehen
dieser Statistik zufolge
in den Ofen
in den Öfen
von der Kraft
ans Telefon
ohne den Unterschied
hinter der Mauer
am Telefon
hinter die Mauer

E39 (→R103, R97)

Say which case or cases the following determiners can signal, and whether they can be singular or plural.

	NOM.		ACC.		DAT.		GEN.	
	SING.	PLUR.	SING.	PLUR.	SING.	PLUR.	SING.	PLUR.
den								
das								
der								
dieses								
des								
dem								
die								
diese								

E40 (→R107)

Say whether the adjective in the following phrases is a simple adjective, a comparative, or a superlative.

A. ein großes Problem
   größere Probleme
   die größten Probleme

B. ein geringer Unterschied
   geringere Unterschiede
   der geringste Unterschied

C. ein schwerer Unfall
   schwerere Unfälle
   schwere Unfälle
   der schwerste Unfall
   ein schwererer Unfall

E41 (→R108)

Match the phrase on the left to the appropriate translation on the right.

1. der italienischen Weine   A. Italian wine (subject)
2. den italienischen Wein   B. the Italian wine (subject)
3. der italienische Wein   C. of Italian wines
4. des italienischen Weins   D. of the Italian wines
5. italienische Weine   E. the Italian wine (accusative)
6. italienischer Weine   F. of Italian wine
7. italienischer Wein   G. of the Italian wine
8. italienischen Weins   H. Italian wines (nominative or accusative)

E42 (→R108)

Say whether the following phrases are singular or plural:

A. 1. der neue Mitarbeiter
   2. der neuen Mitarbeiter
   3. die neuen Mitarbeiter
   4. des neuen Mitarbeiters
B. 1. der neuen Situation
   2. die neue Situation
   3. der neuen Situationen
   4. die neuen Situationen

E43 (→R109)

Underline the adverbs and translate.

ein ausgesprochen schwieriges Problem
diese denkbar schlechten Bedingungen
nach dem unvergeßlichen, schönen Sonnenuntergang
nach dem unvergeßlich schönen Sonnenuntergang
diese starken Ergebnisse
diese stark abweichenden Ergebnisse

E44 (→R110–14)

Underline the subject in the following relative clauses.

1. die bestehende soziale Ordnung, die die karitativen Institutionen nicht in Frage stellen [T14:12]
2. diese Appelle, denen immer nur Kriege folgten [T2:15]
3. Diese Erfindungen gaben den Anstoß zu einer Revolution, die die ganze bürgerliche Gesellschaft umwandelte. [T4:2]
4. die Musik, die die Menschen hören [T5:5]
5. die Bedingungen, unter denen die Messungen durchgeführt werden [T7:6]
6. der doppelte Blindversuch, bei dem auch der Arzt nicht weiß, . . . [T9:10]

E45 (→R115–23)

Underline the extended adjective phrase (EAP) in each of the following, and translate the whole. The examples in this exercise are adapted from the Text Corpus and you may like to look more closely at the particular context of each example when working out the meaning.

A.
1. der nach William Penn genannte Bundesstaat [T2:12]
2. diese erst nach dem Schrecken zweier Weltkriege ernstgenommenen Appelle [T2:17]
3. dieser in seiner Geschichte mehr Kriegs- als Friedensjahre erlebende Kontinent [T2:2]
4. die vor vier Generationen eigentlich beginnende Industrialisierung [T3:2]
5. die erste, 1946 gebaute Elektronenrechner [T3:7]

6. die mit der Erfindung der Dampfmaschine beginnende Geschichte der arbeitenden Klassen in England [T4:1]

B.

1. England ist der klassische Boden dieser gewaltigen, geräuschlos vor sich gehenden Umwälzung. [T4:3]

2. Der Durchmesser einer an einem warmen Tag sich ausdehnenden Stahlstange ist größer als an einem kalten Tag. [T7:7]

3. Damals bezeichnete das Wort Placebo ein mehr dem Patienten zum Gefallen als zu dessen Nutzen verordnetes Medikament. [T9:2]

4. Bei diesen schon 1843 zur Widerlegung der Wirksamkeit homöopathischer Mittel durchgeführten Blindversuchen wurden teilweise erstaunliche Placebo-Wirkungen registriert. [T9:6–7]

5. Händel stellte den größten Teil seines Lebens in den Dienst der Oper, anders als der sich nie mit dieser Form beschäftigende Bach. [T8:3–4]

6. Das neue Proletariat rekrutiert sich aus den in die großen Städte strömenden Landarbeitern. [T14:6]

E46 (→R124–34)

Insert the correct NEGATION WORD/S.

1. Günstige Einflüsse gehen auch von der Kooperationsbereitschaft von Gewerkschaften und Arbeitgebern und **nicht zuletzt** der staatlichen Wirtschaftspolitik aus.
   Lit.: *Favourable influences emanate also from the trade unions' and employers' willingness to co-operate and* . . . . *from the economic policy of the government.*

2. Die fünfziger Jahre sind allerdings **nicht nur** eine Periode stürmischen wirtschaftlichen Wachstums und Wiederaufbaus.
   However, the 1950s are . . . . *a period of rapid economic growth and reconstruction.*

3. Überraschend ist, daß der **unzureichende** Zugang zu Forschungsergebnissen **keineswegs** als Hemmnis angesehen wird. [T20:11]
   What is surprising is that the . . . . *access to research data is* . . . . *considered to be a hindrance.*

4. 30% aller Menschen reagieren **niemals**. [T9:8]
   30% of all people . . . . *react.*

5. Während sie **nichts** anderes tun, als . . . [T19:8]
   Whilst they do . . . . *other than . . .*

E47 (→R141–62)

For conventions used in this exercise, **→R159, R162**.

Identify the DEPENDENT CLAUSES in the following sentences. Mark the key indicators FINITE VERB , <CONJUNCTION>, <RELATIVE PRONOUNS, ZU + INFINITIVES, [NON-CLAUSE INSERTIONS].

1. Der unzureichende Zugang zu Forschungsergebnissen wird keineswegs als Hemmnis angesehen, um in internationale Spitzenstellung vorzudringen. [T20:11]

2. Mit den Bedingungen waren die Athener so wenig einverstanden, daß sie ihre Gesandten wegen Landesverrats vor Gericht stellen wollten. [T15:6]

3. In der Schweiz mietete Brecht ein kleines Haus am Züriberg und stürzte sich wieder in die Arbeit, obwohl er seinen Aufenthaltsort in der Schweiz nur als Zwischenstation auf dem Wege nach Deutschland ansah.

4. Einzelne Vorträge in der Öffentlichkeit oder vor einem intimen Kreise von Vorbereiteten wechselten mit den großen Vortragszyklen, die in einzelnen Städten sich oft über zwei Wochen hinzogen.

5. Aber erst im Sommer, als Nietzsche wiederum ins Engadin ging, besserte sich sein Zustand merklich.

6. Schaut man sich die Entwicklung während der letzten hundert Jahre an, so zeigt sich ein anderes Bild.

7. Aber man glaubt nur, was man zu glauben bereit ist.

8. Aus den USA liegen zahlreiche empirische Untersuchungen über das Ausmaß vor, in dem Unterricht und Schulerziehung Vorurteile, vornehmlich gegenüber Minderheiten, abbauen.

9. Im übrigen hängt das Abschneiden beim Intelligenztest beträchtlich von der Umwelt ab, in der die Versuchsperson aufgewachsen ist.

10. Wir haben unserem Beitrag eine kurze Erörterung der einzelnen Begriffe vorangestellt, weil sie für unser Thema notwendig zu sein scheinen.

E48 (→R141–62)

Find out the function of **und** in the following sentences, i.e. does it link clauses [. . .] or does it link individual words or phrases [**und**] ?

1. Die zukünftigen Probleme der Gesellschaft werden aber immer komplexer **und** sind ohne bewußte, sorgfältige Analyse **und** optimale Entscheidung überhaupt nicht mehr zu ordnen. [T19:9]

2. Nun besitzt Holz eine geringere durchschnittliche Dichte als Wasser **und** schwimmt; Metalle **und** andere Stoffe dagegen haben eine größere durchschnittliche Dichte **und** gehen unter. [T18:10]

3. Der Sozialismus dagegen zieht radikale Konsequenzen **und** ruft zum Umsturz des kapitalistischen Systems auf. [T14:13]

4. Günstige Einflüsse gehen auch von dem parallelen Aufschwung der Weltwirtschaft, mit der die Bundesrepublik im Zuge der Westintegration schon bald wieder eng verflochten ist, der Kooperationsbereitschaft von Gewerkschaften **und** Arbeitgebern **und** nicht zuletzt der staatlichen Wirtschaftspolitik aus.

5. Die Rolle des Staates soll sich darauf beschränken, die für das Funktionieren des Marktes notwendigen Rahmenbedingungen zu schaffen, Störungen des Wettbewerbs, etwa durch übermäßige Konzentrationsprozesse, zu unterbinden **und** vor allem auch soziale Fehlentwicklungen auszugleichen.

E49 (→R141–62)

In the following sentences find and mark

- the MAIN CLAUSE:
- SUBORDINATE CLAUSES:
- RELATIVE CLAUSES:
- ZU + INFINITIVE CLAUSES:
- Other NON-CLAUSE INSERTIONS:

	Finite Verb	
<CONJUNCTION>	FV	
<RELATIVE PRONOUN	FV	
ZU + INFINITIVE		
[	]	

1. Der Zylinder, der mit dem Riegel in Verbindung steht, kann gedreht, das Schloß also geöffnet werden. [T17:7]
2. Allerdings lassen die Unternehmen, zumindest jene, die sich nicht zur Spitzenstellung bekennen, keinen Zweifel daran, daß sie trotzdem Probleme haben. [T20:10]
3. Verhaltensweisen können nicht genau gemessen werden, weil sie sich von Zeit zu Zeit ändern, da die Voraussetzungen nicht immer die gleichen sind und da sich die Meßvorrichtungen gelegentlich verändern können. [T7:10]
4. Kann ein Körper bei restlosem Untertauchen mehr Flüssigkeitsgewicht verdrängen, als er selbst wiegt, so wird er nur so tief in die Flüssigkeit eintauchen, bis der entstehende Auftrieb gleich seinem Gewicht ist. [T18:7]
5. Den Menschen der Vorzeit kennen wir in den Entwicklungsstadien, die er durchlaufen hat, durch die unbelebten Denkmäler und Geräte, die er uns hinterlassen, durch die Kunde von seiner Kunst, seiner Religion und Lebensanschauung, die wir entweder direkt oder auf dem Wege der Tradition in Sagen, Mythen und Märchen erhalten haben, durch die Überreste seiner Denkweisen in unseren eigenen Sitten und Gebräuchen. [T12:1]
6. Es gibt relativ wenig Menschen, die imstande sind, rein musikalisch zu verstehen, was Musik zu sagen hat. [T21:1]

E50 (→R141–62)

After analysing the basic structures of the sentences in the above exercise, show them in diagrammatic form.

e.g.:

6. Es gibt relativ wenig Menschen, die imstande sind, rein musikalisch zu verstehen, was Musik zu sagen hat. (→R159.2)

```
1  _____| gibt |_____ ,
2                      <die . . . | sind, |
3                            . . . zu verstehen ,
4                                       <was . . . | hat. |
```

E51 (→R141–62, R259)

a. 'Strip' the following complex sentences of all DEPENDENT CLAUSES and CONSTRUCTIONS leaving the MAIN CLAUSE only.
b. Work out the meaning of the MAIN CLAUSE. Then consider which of the DEPENDENT CLAUSES to tackle first in order to get the maximum amount of completing information.

1. Das Gesetz, auf das Aischines und Demosthenes sich stützten, besagte, daß ein Bürger nicht einmal mehr in der Volksversammlung sprechen, geschweige denn irgendein Amt

ausüben durfte, wenn er seine Eltern schlecht behandelt, den Wehrdienst verweigert, Fahnenflucht begangen, sein Erbe durchgebracht oder sich gegenüber anderen Männern prostituiert hatte. [T15:10]

2. In den gleichen Jahren, in denen Rudolf Steiner durch den Protestanten K. J. Schröer in die Lebens- und Geisteswelt Goethes eingeführt wurde und dadurch den Ansatzpunkt für seinen eigenen "Goetheanismus" fand, begegnete ihm im Hause Müller ein kultivierter Katholizismus, der sich mit innerer Konsequenz Goethe gegenüber abgeneigt verhält.

3. Ob C. G. Jung in alchimistischen Folianten den Wandlungsprozess der Psyche verfolgt oder östliche Geistlehren kommentiert, ob er politisch-gesellschaftliche Verhältnisse (etwa Vorgänge während des Dritten Reiches) deutet oder berichtet, in welcher Stimmung er einst als junger Mensch der Natur gegenübertrat, immer ist diese religiöse Komponente gegenwärtig.

4. Wie alle Autos, die Brecht je besaß, nahm es nach kurzer Zeit ein Aussehen an, als habe er es unlängst von einem Autofriedhof geholt.

5. Da es das Vermögen Teilhards überstieg, die von der Paläontologie seiner Zeit erarbeiteten Begriffe durch geistigen Einblick in die Bewußtseinsentwicklung des Vor- und Frühmenschen zu ergänzen und zu vertiefen, mußte er sich mit Scheinlösungen begnügen.

E52 (→R169)

Find out the meaning of the following FINITE VERBS by first working out their INFINITIVE form then looking up the meaning.

1. spricht [T21:5]	6. könnten [T2:5]	11. tat [T21:8]
2. gaben [T4:2]	7. nannten [T20:14]	12. lag [T16:11]
3. erwuchs [T15:4]	8. hält [T10b:2]	13. genügt [T16:16]
4. beschwor [T2:12]	9. nahm [T2:17]	14. begann [T3:7]
5. erfand [T3:2]	10. hätten [T19:8]	15. bezeichnete [T9:2]

E53 (→R175, R176)

In the following sentences the VERB is used together with (an)other word(s), e.g. a NOUN or PREPOSITION, to form an idiomatic unit. Find the appropriate entry in the dictionary. (Note that idioms are often listed under the NOUN entry.)

1. Aber die Gesandten drehten den Spieß um. [T15:9]
2. Japanerinnen nahmen zu jener Zeit noch keine Milch zu sich. [T16:6]
3. Der Wunsch nach Frieden stand bei der Europäischen Gemeinschaft Pate. [T2:4]
4. Die Erde ist nicht nur eine Stätte, die mit Ordnung und Regel rechnet. [T6:5]
5. Das wird Ihnen Spaß machen. [T10b:12]
6. Der Rektor hält beim Essen eine Ansprache. [T10b:2]
7. Die Welt gilt als in drei Stockwerke gegliedert. [T6:2]
8. Sie nehmen den Großstadtverkehr nicht zur Kenntnis. [T19:8]

E54 (→R170)

Is the ge- part of the VERB STEM or a PAST PARTICIPLE form?
Translate:

1. **a.** Er hat sich nicht in die Kirche **getraut**.
   b. Sie wurden in der Kirche **getraut**.
2. **a.** Das Konzert hat ihm **gefallen**.
   b. Im Schnee ist das Kind immer **gefallen**.
3. **a.** Der Aufsatz ist ihm gut **geraten**.
   b. Das scheint mir nicht **geraten**.
   c. Er hat ihm dazu **geraten**.
4. **a.** Er hat ein Wörterbuch **gebraucht**.
   b. Er **gebraucht** oft ein Wörterbuch.
5. **a.** Er hat nicht an der Tür **gehorcht**.
   b. Das Kind **gehorcht** der Mutter nicht.

E55 (→R177)

The following sentences contain various combinations of the verb **kommen** + PREPOSITIONS or (and) separable/inseparable PREFIXES. Note the word order!
Translate:

1. Plötzlich kommt er auf einen Gedanken.
2. So etwas ist noch nie vorgekommen.
3. Es kommt auch auf den Kontext an.
4. Sie kam ums Leben.
5. Er kam im Krieg um.
6. Wir kommen gut mit ihm aus.
7. Sie bekommt die Stelle nicht.
8. Sie sagte, er sei auf den Hund gekommen.
9. Sie kommt später nach.
10. Er kommt von diesem Problem nicht mehr los.

E56 (→R184–6)

The following nouns are derived from verbs or adjectives. Work out their meaning by looking up the original verb/adjective.

1. Alarmierendes [T16:3]
2. das Banale [T21:2]
3. ein (eingehenderes) Beschäftigen [T8:8]
4. eine Vergleichung [T12:4]
5. (alles) Vibrierende [T5:4]
6. das Erkennbare [T21:6]
7. das Einsetzen [T11:4]
8. (anderes) Beachtenswertes [T10a:9]

E57 (→R181–2)

Split up the following COMPOUND WORDS into their original components. Then work out the meaning of the compound.

1. Verkehrssignalanlagen [T19:4]
2. Gesandtschaftsteilnehmer [T15:7]
3. Feinmechanikhersteller [T20:5]
4. gewichtsmindernde (Kraft) [T18:5]
5. Produktionsverfahren [T14:3]
6. Beliebtheitsskala [T1:3]
7. Selbstüberschätzung [T20:16]
8. Meßvorrichtung [T7:10]
9. Scheinmedikament [T9:3]
10. Forschungsergebnisse [T20:11]

E58 (→R180–2, R184–6)

Analyse the following DERIVATIVES and COMPOUNDS.

1. die Überbewertung [T20:15]
2. unvorhergesehen [T9:5]
3. Erschöpfendes [T21:5]
4. Schwimmfähigkeit [T18:1]
5. pilzförmig [T17:3]
6. Urzeit [T11:4]
7. Auslastung [T20:13]
8. unüberblickbar [T21:7]
9. das Gemessene [T7:11]
10. das Nichterreichen [T20:14]

E59 (→R187–8)

Which of the following sentences are not INSTRUCTIONS?

1. Bitte Namen und Adresse angeben.
2. Der Film sollte bald belichtet werden.
3. Film in Versandbeutel packen.
4. Um Schaden zu vermeiden, Projektor ausschalten.
5. Die Gebrauchsanweisung ist zu beachten.
6. Das Gerät ist mit einem Schutzschalter ausgestattet.
7. Lüftungsöffnungen stets freihalten.
8. Schalten Sie die Lampe wieder ein.
9. Die Sicherung ist vom Fachmann auszuwechseln.
10. Störungen im Bildtransport können vorkommen.

Key to Further Exercises

E1

A.

klein aber auch heiß und stieg mit Eiweiß oder fieberhaft und unbegreiflich europäisch wenn Kleinigkeit stiegen und hieß oder bittet vielleicht auf Seide oder lieber steigt schon eitel steigen und hielt dann ergiebig geheißen aber bietet und heilt die Eule und sieden mit Leib oder eilige eiskalt gießen die Liebe ist neugierig in Eile

B.

klein und heiß stieg das Eiweiß oder fieberhaft und unbegreiflich ist europäisch eine Kleinigkeit aber stiegen hieß und bittet vielleicht mit Seide dann lieber steigt auf eitel in steigen oder hielt ergiebig und geheißen bietet oder heilt mit Eule an sieden auf Leib ist eilige und eiskalt für gießen in Liebe und neugierig in Eile

E2

A.

(1) Im Westen wie im Osten Deutschlands ist der Arztberuf am beliebtesten. (2) Dies geht aus einer Umfrage des Emnid-Instituts hervor. (3) Während aber im Westen von den zehn angesehensten Berufen neun eine Hochschulausbildung voraussetzen, werden im Osten auch die Handwerker, Landwirte und Sozialarbeiter in der Beliebtheitsskala ganz vorn eingestuft. (4) Handwerker nehmen bei den Ostdeutschen sogar den Platz drei ein, gleich hinter dem Arzt und dem Zahnarzt, während er im Westen nicht einmal unter den ersten zehn auftaucht.

(5) Anders verhält es sich bei der Bewertung des Hausfrauenberufs. (6) Während die Hausfrau im Westen den zehnten Platz einnimmt, gehört sie im Osten nicht zu den beliebtesten zehn. (7) Einig sind sich Ost und West über die Berufsgruppe mit dem geringsten Ansehen—die Versicherungsvertreter, die auf Platz 25 ganz hinten rangieren, und wenig angesehen sind hier wie dort auch Offiziere und Werbeleute. (8) Nicht viel besser geht es den Bundestagsabgeordneten, die im Westen auf Platz 19 kommen und im Osten auf Platz 22 sogar noch

negativer eingestuft werden. (9) Nach Meinung von Emnid mag das schlechte Ergebnis für die Parlamentarier im Osten mit der Enttäuschung über die wirtschaftliche Situation nach der Wiedervereinigung zusammenhängen.

B.

(1) Im Westen wie im Osten Deutschlands ist der Arztberuf am beliebtesten.

(2) Dies geht aus einer Umfrage des Emnid-Instituts hervor. (3) Während aber im Westen von den zehn angesehensten Berufen neun eine Hochschulausbildung voraussetzen, werden im Osten auch die Handwerker, Landwirte und Sozialarbeiter in der Beliebtheitsskala ganz vorn eingestuft. (4) Handwerker nehmen bei den Ostdeutschen sogar den Platz drei ein, gleich hinter dem Arzt und dem Zahnarzt, während er im Westen nicht einmal unter den ersten zehn auftaucht.

(5) Anders verhält es sich bei der Bewertung des Hausfrauenberufs. (6) Während die Hausfrau im Westen den zehnten Platz einnimmt, gehört sie im Osten nicht zu den beliebtesten zehn. (7) Einig sind sich Ost und West über die Berufsgruppe mit dem geringsten Ansehen—die Versicherungsvertreter, die auf Platz 25 ganz hinten rangieren, und wenig angesehen sind hier wie dort auch Offiziere und Werbeleute. (8) Nicht viel besser geht es den Bundestagsabgeordneten, die im Westen auf Platz 19 kommen und im Osten auf Platz 22 sogar noch negativer eingestuft werden. (9) Nach Meinung von Emnid mag das schlechte Ergebnis für die Parlamentarier im Osten mit der Enttäuschung über die wirtschaftliche Situation nach der Wiedervereinigung zusammenhängen.

E3

Alter alte älter Mutter Mütter Mutter Bruder Brüder gesunder gesünder Sohn Söhne Ölpreis Mobilität abgeholt ausgehöhlt verträglich verträglich Apfel Äpfel waren wären konnte könnte durften dürften konnte dürften waren Bruder gesünder älter Mütter Äpfel verträglich Mutter könnte Sohn alte wären Mutter älter durften verträglich gesunder Mutter verträglich ausgehöhlt Söhne durften

E4

1 Handwerker <u>nehmen</u> sogar bei den Ostdeutschen den Platz drei <u>ein</u>.
2 Dies <u>geht</u> aus einer Umfrage <u>hervor</u>.
3 Erasmus von Rotterdam <u>rief</u> vor fast 500 Jahren die Völker Europas zu einem Völkerbund <u>auf</u>.
4 Victor Hugo <u>kündigte</u> 1851 die Vereinigten Staaten von Europa <u>an</u>.
5 Da aber <u>drehten</u> die Gesandten den Spieß <u>um</u>.
6 Die Schweiz <u>wies</u> die höchste Krebsrate in der Alten Welt <u>aus</u>.
7 Die gleichen Probleme <u>treten</u> auch bei Messungen in psychologischen Experimenten <u>auf</u>.
8 Holz schwimmt; Metalle und andere Stoffe dagegen <u>gehen</u> <u>unter</u>.
9 Die restlichen 0,2 Liter Holz <u>tauchen</u> nicht <u>ein</u>.
10 Dennoch <u>legt</u> die Umfrage auch einige Schattenseiten <u>bloß</u>.

E5

1 Dieser Konitinent <u>hat</u> in seiner Geschichte mehr Kriegs- als Friedensjahre <u>erlebt</u>.
2 Für alle Bundesregierungen <u>ist</u> der Ausgleich mit den westlichen Partnern ein Kernpunkt bundesdeutscher Außenpolitik <u>gewesen</u>.
3 Der Mensch <u>hat</u> bisher rund 800 Lebensspannen auf Erden <u>gelebt</u>.
4 Vor einigen Jahren <u>hat</u> eine neue Epoche in der Geschichte <u>begonnen</u>.
5 Durch den Beitritt der ehemaligen DDR <u>hat</u> sich diese Zahl nur unwesentlich <u>verändert</u>.
6 Es <u>wurde</u> viel <u>erreicht</u>.
7 In ihrer Zeit <u>wurde</u> die erste Atombombe <u>gezündet</u>.
8 Die Entstehung der Menschheit <u>wurde</u> in vielen Mythen <u>beschrieben</u>.

E6

1 Das schlechte Ergebnis <u>mag</u> mit der Enttäuschung über die wirtschaftliche Situation <u>zusammenhängen</u>.
2 Wir <u>müssen</u> eine Art Vereinigter Staaten von Europa <u>schaffen</u>.
3 Das Proletariat <u>kann</u> nur in England in allen seinen Verhältnissen <u>studiert</u> <u>werden</u>.
4 Die Musik der Atome, der Sterne und der Tiere <u>muß</u> <u>umgewandelt</u> <u>werden</u>.

E7

1 Der Wunsch nach Frieden <u>stand</u> bei der Gründung der Europäischen Gemeinschaft <u>Pate</u>.
2 Alle diese Einrichtungen <u>stellen</u> die bestehende soziale Ordnung nicht in <u>Frage</u>.
3 Wir <u>haben</u> es hier nicht mit der Geschichte dieser Revolution <u>zu</u> <u>tun</u>.

E8

1 Nach Meinung von Emnid mag <u>das schlechte Ergebnis</u> mit der Enttäuschung über die wirtschaftliche Lage zusammenhängen.
2 Nun besitzt <u>Holz</u> eine geringere durchschnittliche Dichte als Wasser.
3 <u>Die Arbeiter</u> wohnen in oft menschenunwürdigen Behausungen.
4 Die Freiheit zu bewußtem Handeln sollten <u>wir</u> uns erhalten.
5 Erst nach dem Schrecken zweier Weltkriege nahm <u>man</u> die Appelle ernst.

E9

1 In Karl Marx findet <u>der Sozialismus</u> seinen führenden Theoretiker.
2 Neben einem wohlhabenden Industriebürgertum entsteht <u>ein Industrieproletariat</u>.
3 Auf den Aluminiumwürfel wirkt <u>eine entgegengesetzte Kraft</u>.
4 Auffallend ist, daß <u>der Rückstand</u> <u>nicht</u> <u>bestritten</u> <u>wird</u>.
5 Den Talar leiht <u>man</u> Ihnen sicher von der Universität.

E10

1 Es besteht <u>die Gefahr</u> von neuen Kriegen in Europa.
2 Mit der Industrialisierung verändert sich vor allem in Preußen <u>die soziale Landschaft</u> von Grund auf.
3 Bedeutsam für diese Entwicklung war außerdem <u>die Wirtschaftspolitik</u> der Regierung.
4 Es wohnen in dieser Region <u>viele Dialektsprecher</u>.
5 Im ersten Versuch wird <u>[es]</u> ihr erlaubt, sich zu üben.

(This last sentence is an example of a 'subjectless' passive sentence, →R10.5.)

E11

1 Etwa 30 Prozent aller Menschen (Subj.)
2 Es (Tok.)
3 Einige Schattenseiten (Obj.)
4 Es (Tok.)
5 Die tiefste Wahrheit (Obj.)
6 Die Überlegenheit der Planlosigkeit (Obj.)

E12

1 Zur Schematisierung seines Gegenstandes (Adv.)
2 Wenn das Thermometer kälter ist als das Wasser (Dep.)
3 Damit ein eisernes Schiff schwimmt (Dep.)
4 Genannt (Com.)
5 Überraschend (Adj.)

E13

1 Victor Hugo, der 1851 die Vereinigten Staaten von Europa ankündigte, erntete nur Hohn und Spott.
2 Die Erfindung der Dampfmaschine ist wichtig, weil sie den Anstoß zu einer industriellen Revolution gab, die die bürgerliche Gesellschaft umwandelte.
3 Ich habe es getan, obwohl der Scherz 4 Pfund kostete.
4 Wenn diese Voraussetzung zutreffend ist, wird eine Vergleichung zahlreiche Übereinstimmungen aufweisen.
5 Neue Finanzmethoden machen es möglich, moderne Produktionsverfahren im großen Stil einzusetzen.

E14

1 **kam** — simple past tense, singular; infinitive: **kommen** *to come*
2 **urteilen** — present tense, plural; infinitive: **urteilen** *to judge*
3 **bedarf** (inseparable prefix be- (→R174) + modal verb 'darf'(→R66) Modal verbs have irregular singular present tense forms); Present tense, singular; infinitive: **bedürfen** *to need, to require*
4 **zeigte** — simple past tense, singular; infinitive: **zeigen** *to show*
5 **erntete** — simple past tense, singular; infinitive: **ernten** *to harvest, to reap, to get*
6 **glaube, bin** — present tense (subject for both is **ich**); infinitive: **glauben** *to believe*, **sein** *to be*
7 **erwuchs** (inseparable prefix er- (→R174) + wuchs) — simple past tense, singular; infinitive: **erwachsen** *to grow*. **erwachsen aus** *to arise, to develop from* (→R175 verbs with prepositions)
8 **treten + auf** (separable verb) present tense, plural (NB infinitive: **auftreten** *to occur* (→R39) the second t is part of the STEM and not past tense indicator);
9 **liegt** — present tense, singular; infinitive: **liegen** *to lie*
10 **nahm + ernst** infinitive: (→R39) separable verb — past tense, singular (subject: man) — **ernstnehmen** *to take seriously*

E15

1 Dieser Kontinent hat mehr Kriegs- als Friedensjahre erlebt.
2 Sie haben auf gepackten Koffern gesessen.
3 Für alle Bundesregierungen ist das ein Kernpunkt bundesdeutscher Außenpolitik gewesen.
4 Der Aluminiumwürfel ist um das Gewicht der von ihm verdrängten Wassermenge leichter geworden.
5 Vor einigen Jahren hat eine neue Epoche in der Geschichte begonnen.
6 . . ., daß das menschliche Leben auf der Erde, im Tier- und Pflanzenbereich entstanden ist.
7 Ich habe es leichtsinniger Weise getan.
8 Ich bin bei allen Universitätsanlässen darin herumgelaufen.
9 Sie haben erlebt, wie das Automobil zur Alltäglichkeit wurde.
10 . . ., wenn er seine Eltern schlecht behandelt, den Wehrdienst verweigert, Fahnenflucht begangen, sein Erbe durchgebracht oder sich gegenüber anderen Männern prostituiert hatte.

E16

1 **nimmt . . . ein** — infinitive: **einnehmen**, here: *to take up (is taken up)*
2 **drehten . . . um** — infinitive: **umdrehen** *to turn round* den Spieß umdrehen (Idiomatic phrase. Look up under 'Spieß') *to turn the tables (turned the tables)*
3 **legt . . . bloß** — infinitive: **bloßlegen**, here: *to bring to light (brings to light)*
4 **setzt sich . . . durch** — infinitive: **sich durchsetzen** *to be successful, to win through (is successful)*
5 **nahm . . . ernst** — infinitive: **ernstnehmen** *to take seriously (took seriously)*
6 **geben . . . an** — infinitive: **angeben**, here: *to maintain, state (state)*
7 **weicht . . . ab** — infinitive: **abweichen** *to diverge, differ (diverge)*
8 **kommen . . . durch** — infinitive: **durchkommen** *to get through (get through)*
9 **tauchen . . . ein** — infinitive: **eintauchen** *to immerse (immerse)*
10 **hebt . . . an** — infinitive: **anheben** *to raise, to lift (raises)*

E17

1 **schaltet sich ein** — the reflexive meaning the dictionary gives for **sich einschalten** is *to intervene*. This, of course, does not make sense in the context. This is because **sich** here has a separate meaning and thus an equivalent in English: *itself*. **einschalten** *to switch on* (*switches itself on*)
2 **verkehrt sich** — most dictionaries list the whole phrase **sich ins Gegenteil verkehren** *to become reversed* (*becomes reversed*)
3 **sich . . . distanziert hatte** — **sich distanzieren von** *to dissociate oneself from* (*had dissociated himself from*)
4 **sich . . . bekennen** — **sich bekennen zu** *to declare oneself to be* (*declare themselves*)
5 **begnügt sich** — **sich begnügen mit** *to be content or satisfied with* (*is satisfied with*)
6 **zeigte sich** — **sich zeigen** *to appear, to show* (*appeared*)
7 **stellt sich . . . dar** — **sich darstellen** *to appear, to show itself* (*appears, looks*)
8 **sich . . . ändern** — **sich ändern** *to change* (*change*)

E18

1a. sagen hat	**b.** gelebt
2a. erfand baute begann	**b.** —
3a. war existierte gilt	**b.** —
4a. war	**b.** —
5a. hörten haben	**b.** können (→**R67**)
6a. haben wurde	**b.** erlebt
7a. wurde (→**R74, R163**) begann	**b.** gezündet gebaut enträtselt

E19

1 könnte [+]; kann [−]; könne [+]
2 wollte [±]; wolle [+]; will [−]
3 dürfte [+]; durfte [−]; dürfe [+]; darf [−]
4 muß [−]; mußte [−]; müßte [+]; müsse [+]
5 bin [−]; ist [−]; sei [+]; sind [−]; seien [+]; war [−]; wäre [+]
6 hat [−]; habe [±]; hatte [−]; hätte [+]
7 gibt [−]; gebe [±]; gebt [−]; gäbe [+]

E20

1 käme   is from kommen
2 gäbe   is from geben
3 brächte is from bringen
4 ginge   is from gehen
5 ließe   is from lassen
6 täte   is from tun

E21

FALSCH PROGRAMMIERT

(1) Wenn wir in der Komplexität der zukünftigen gesellschaftlichen Realität die Freiheit des Menschen erhalten wollen, dann müssen wir diese Freiheit mit den besten Mitteln menschlichen Denkens sicherstellen, kurzum, wir müssen die Freiheit planen. (2) Es wird in unserer Gesellschaft die Täuschung aufrechterhalten, Planung und Freiheit <u>schlössen</u> sich gegenseitig aus. (3) Daß dies ein rechter Trugschluß ist, <u>sei</u> durch einen Vergleich veranschaulicht:

(4) Wenn wir in einer verkehrsarmen Dorfstraße eine Verkehrssignalanlage <u>aufstellen</u> <u>würden</u>, dann <u>wäre</u> dies eine unnötige Einschränkung unserer Freiheit: (5) Es <u>würde</u> uns plötzlich <u>verwehrt</u>, zu manchen Zeiten die Straße zu passieren, ohne daß es einen ersichtlichen Grund gibt. (6) Ganz anders bei einem Großstadt-Verkehrszentrum: Ohne Verkehrssignalanlage ist es verstopft, und wir kommen überhaupt nicht mehr durch. (7) Dieser Vergleich zeigt uns, daß es möglich ist, einfache gesellschaftliche Probleme dem ungeregelten Spiel der Kräfte zu überlassen, daß aber mit zunehmender Komplexität die Planung unvermeidbar ist, wenn nicht das Chaos herrschen soll. (8) Den Ideologen der Planlosigkeit in unserem Lande ist vorzuwerfen, daß sie so tun, als ob sie eine Möglichkeit <u>hätten</u>, die Großstadt-Straßenkreuzung ohne Verkehrssignalanlage zu ordnen, während sie in Wirklichkeit nichts anderes tun, als den Großstadtverkehr nicht zur Kenntnis zu nehmen, und dann behaupten: Es gibt nur Dorfstraßen.

(9) Die zukünftigen Probleme der Gesellschaft werden aber immer komplexer und sind ohne bewußte, sorgfältige Analyse und optimale Entscheidung unter Beachtung der in demokratischer Weise gewählten Wertsysteme überhaupt nicht mehr zu ordnen. (10) Weder der Hinweis auf Fehlleistungen planender Gesellschaften noch die irreführende Identifizierung der Planung mit Staatsdirigismus begründen eine Überlegenheit der Planlosigkeit.

(11) (Um einer möglichen Kritik zuvorzukommen: 'Freiheit' von Naturgesetzen gibt es wohl nicht, die 'Freiheit' zu bewußtem, verantwortlichem und sittlichem Verhalten <u>sollten</u> wir uns aber erhalten.)

E22

	PAST	PRESENT/FUTURE
1. hätte		√
2. wäre		√
3. könnte		√
4. hätte gehabt	√	
5. wäre gewesen	√	
6. hätte sein können	√	
7. gäbe		√
8. hätte gegeben	√	

E23

1a; 2b; 3a; 4b; 5a.
1[±]; 2[±]; 3[−]; 4[−]; 5[+]

E24

1. wollen . . . erhalten — *want to preserve*
   müssen . . . sicherstellen — *must guarantee*
   müssen . . . planen — *must plan (for)*
2. können . . . messen — *can measure*
3. soll . . . sein — *should/ought to be*
4. kann . . . haben — *can/may have*
5. (vor Gericht) stellen wollten — *wanted to take (to court)*
6. kann . . . beweisen — *can prove*
7. darf . . . bitten — *may ask*
8. wissen möchten, lernen wollen — *would like to know, want to learn*
9. (mit) rechnen mußten — *had to reckon (with)*
10. sollte . . . sein — *was to be*

E25

1. (1)werde . . . (3)besuchen (2)können
   (1)shall (2)be able to (3)visit
2. (1)haben . . . (3)messen (2)können
   (1)have (2)been able to (3)measure
3. (1)Haben . . . (3)erstehen (2)müssen
   (1)Have (2)had to (3)buy/did . . . have to
4. (1)haben (3)beschränken (2)müssen
   (1)have (2)had to (3)restrict/had to restrict
5. (1)Hätte es . . . (3)geben (2)können
   (1 + 2)Could have (3)been
   es gibt — *there is/are (→R42)*
   es kann geben — *there can be*
   es hätte geben können — *there could have been*
   Could there have been . . . ? (→R68)

E26

1 a: II   b: I
2 a: I   b: II
3 a: II   b: I
4 a: II   b: I
5 a: II   b: I

E27

2, 3, and 6 contain passives:
2 The thermometer is put into the glass. [T7:13]
3 The public were alarmed. [T16:1]
6 The film has been awarded a prize by the academy.

1, 4, and 5 contain **werden** but not in a passive construction:

1 The thermometer will lower the temperature of the water slightly. (Future tense) [T7:13]
4 The public would be amazed. (**würde** + infinitive)
5 The film has become famous because of this prize. (**geworden** is the past participle of the full verb 'werden' meaning 'to become')

E28

Es läßt sich denken, daß man viele Jahre brauchen wird, um in einer fremden Sprache authentische Texte lesen zu können. Ohne viel Arbeit ist das leichte Verstehen schwieriger Texte sicherlich nicht zu erreichen, doch ist nicht zu vergessen, daß man in der eigenen Muttersprache schon ein bestimmtes, zum Teil übertragbares Wissen hat, das diesen Lernprozeß erleichtern wird. Einen Text in der Fremdsprache versteht man schneller und besser, wenn man in der eigenen Sprache ein kompetenter Leser ist. Denn die wichtige Rolle von 'Transfer skills' ist einfach nicht zu leugnen: – das hat sich mehrmals in der Forschungsliteratur gezeigt. Immerhin ist ein gutes Wörterbuch, in dem die unbekannten Vokabeln nachzuschlagen sind, unverzichtbar.

(Note also that the sentence beginning 'Einen Text in der Fremdsprache . . . ' has an OVS word order. →R78.6)

E29

a Text 6
b Text 13
c Text 15

E30

The first paragraph in Corpus Text 16 contains passives. The other two paragraphs have no passive constructions.

E31

A.

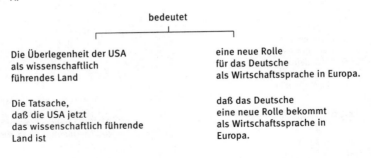

bedeutet

Die Überlegenheit der USA als wissenschaftlich führendes Land

eine neue Rolle für das Deutsche als Wirtschaftssprache in Europa.

Die Tatsache, daß die USA jetzt das wissenschaftlich führende Land ist

daß das Deutsche eine neue Rolle bekommt als Wirtschaftssprache in Europa.

B.

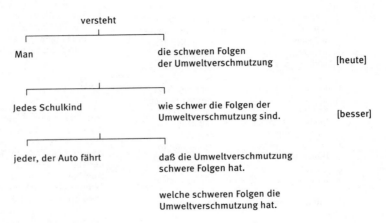

versteht

Man

die schweren Folgen der Umweltverschmutzung

[heute]

Jedes Schulkind

wie schwer die Folgen der Umweltverschmutzung sind.

[besser]

jeder, der Auto fährt

daß die Umweltverschmutzung schwere Folgen hat.

welche schweren Folgen die Umweltverschmutzung hat.

E32

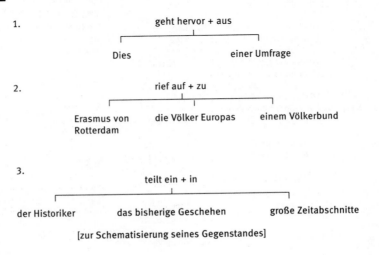

1.

geht hervor + aus

Dies

einer Umfrage

2.

rief auf + zu

Erasmus von Rotterdam

die Völker Europas

einem Völkerbund

3.

teilt ein + in

der Historiker

das bisherige Geschehen

große Zeitabschnitte

[zur Schematisierung seines Gegenstandes]

4.

wirkt + auf

eine entgegengesetzte Kraft   den Aluminiumwürfel

5.

weicht ab + von

Eine Messung   der anderen   [leicht]

6.

beschäftigte sich + mit

Bach   dieser Form.   [nie]

7.

greifen ein + in

die übernatürlichen Mächte   das natürliche Geschehen und
das Denken des Menschen

E33

der Preis der Karte: SINGULAR ('the price of the card/
ticket')
die Farbe des Wagens: SINGULAR ('the colour of the
car')
die Bewertung der Ergebnisse: PLURAL ('the
evaluation of the results')
die Zahl der Studenten: PLURAL ('the number of
students')
die Zahl der Lehrer: PLURAL ('the number of
teachers')
die Sprecher dieses Dialekts: SINGULAR ('the
speakers of this dialect')
das Zusammenspiel der Farben: PLURAL ('the
interplay of the colours')

E34

die Umfrage: 'from an opinion poll'
der Arzt: 'behind the doctor'
die Bewertung (→R186); der Hausfrauenberuf: 'in the
assessment of the occupation of housewife'
die Berufsgruppe: 'about the professional group'
das Ansehen: 'with the least esteem'
die Entäuschung (→R186): 'with the disappointment'
die Situation: 'about the economic situation'
die Wiedervereinigung (→R186): 'after reunification'

E35

1. I don't have the time (lit.: 'To me the time is
   lacking').
2. She is very like her mother ('She is to her mother
   very similar').
3. He did not pass the exam ('The exam did not go
   well for him').
4. Wilhelm von Humboldt's ideas on language are
   very close to those of Chomsky.

E36

	ACCUSATIVE		DATIVE	
	SING.	PLUR.	SING.	PLUR.
für den Produzenten	x			
mit diesen Menschen				x
mit diesem Gedanken			x	
von den Chirurgen				x
in dem Franzosen			x	
durch diesen Jungen	x			
zwischen die Kontrahenten		x		
von den Photographen				x

E37

	ACCUSATIVE		DATIVE	
	SING.	PLUR.	SING.	PLUR
durch den Produzenten	x			
von den Produzenten				x
Man dankt den Produzenten.				x
Man beschuldigt den Produzenten.	x			

E38

durch diesen Fall	ACCUSATIVE	through this case
für jede Möglichkeit	ACCUSATIVE	for every possibility
in das Geschehen	ACCUSATIVE	into the events
an diesem Beispiel	DATIVE	with this example
nach der Besichtigung	DATIVE	after the viewing
in dem Geschehen	DATIVE	in the events
dieser Statistik zufolge	DATIVE	according to this statistic
in den Ofen	ACCUSATIVE	into the oven
in den Öfen	DATIVE	in the ovens
von der Kraft	DATIVE	of the force
ans Telefon	ACCUSATIVE	to the phone
ohne den Unterschied	ACCUSATIVE	without the difference
hinter der Mauer	DATIVE	behind the wall
am Telefon	DATIVE	on the phone
hinter die Mauer	ACCUSATIVE	behind the wall (motion)

E39

	NOMINATIVE		ACCUSATIVE		DATIVE		GENITIVE	
	SING.	PLUR.	SING.	PLUR.	SING.	PLUR.	SING.	PLUR.
den			x			x		
das	x		x					
der	x				x		x	x
dieses	x		x				x	
des							x	
dem					x			
die	x	x	x	x				
diese	x	x	x	x				

E40

A. SIMPLE: 'a large problem'
COMPARATIVE: 'larger/quite large problems'
SUPERLATIVE: 'the largest problems'

B. SIMPLE: 'a small difference'
COMPARATIVE: 'smaller/quite small   differences'
SUPERLATIVE: 'the smallest difference'

C. SIMPLE: 'a serious accident'
COMPARATIVE: 'more serious/fairly serious accidents'
SIMPLE: 'serious accidents'
SUPERLATIVE: 'the most serious accident'
COMPARATIVE: 'a more serious/fairly serious accident'

E41

1D; 2E; 3B; 4G; 5H; 6C; 7A; 8F

E42

A.
1. SINGULAR: 'the new colleague'
2. PLURAL: 'of the new colleagues'
3. PLURAL: 'the new colleagues'
4. SINGULAR: 'of the new colleague'

B.
1. SINGULAR: 'of the new situation/to the new situation'
2. SINGULAR: 'the new situation'
3. PLURAL: 'of the new situations'
4. PLURAL: 'the new situations'

E43

ein <u>ausgesprochen</u> schwieriges Problem
('an extremely difficult problem')
diese <u>denkbar</u> schlechten Bedingungen
('these conditions which are as bad as can be imagined')
nach dem unvergeßlichen, schönen Sonnenuntergang
('after the unforgettable, beautiful sunsest')
nach dem <u>unvergeßlich</u> schönen Sonnenuntergang
('after the unforgettably beautiful sunset')
diese starken Ergebnisse
('these strong results')
diese <u>stark</u> abweichenden Ergebnisse
('these significantly diverging results')

E44

1. die bestehende soziale Ordnung, die <u>die</u> karitativen <u>Institutionen</u> nicht in Frage stellen
2. diese Appelle, denen immer nur <u>Kriege</u> folgten
3. Diese Erfindungen gaben den Anstoß zu einer Revolution, <u>die</u> die ganze bürgerliche Gesellschaft umwandelte.
4. die Musik, die <u>die</u> <u>Menschen</u> hören
5. die Bedingungen, unter denen <u>die</u> <u>Messungen</u> durchgeführt werden
6. der doppelte Blindversuch, bei dem auch <u>der</u> <u>Arzt</u> nicht weiß, . . .

E45

A.
1. der <u>nach William Penn genannte</u> Bundesstaat
   the federal state named after William Penn
2. diese <u>erst nach dem Schrecken zweier Weltkriege ernstgenommenen</u> Appelle
   these appeals, which were were taken seriously only after the horror of two world wars
3. dieser <u>in seiner Geschichte mehr Kriegs- als Friedensjahre erlebende</u> Kontinent
   this continent, which has experienced more years of war than of peace
4. die <u>vor vier Generationen eigentlich beginnende</u> Industrialisierung
   the industrialisation which really began four generations ago
5. die erste, <u>1946 gebaute</u> Elektronenrechner
   the first electronic calculator, built in 1946
6. die <u>mit der Erfindung der Dampfmaschine beginnende</u> Geschichte der arbeitenden Klassen in England
   the history of the working classes in England, which begins with the invention of the steam engine

B.

1. England ist der klassische Boden dieser <u>gewaltigen, geräuschlos vor sich gehenden</u> Umwälzung.

   England is the classic location for this huge upheaval, which proceeded quietly.

2. Der Durchmesser einer <u>an einem warmen Tag sich ausdehnenden Stahlstange</u> ist größer als an einem kalten Tag.

   The diameter of a steel rod which expands on a warm day is larger than on a cold day.

3. Damals bezeichnete das Wort Placebo ein <u>mehr dem Patienten zum Gefallen als zu dessen Nutzen verordnetes</u> Medikament.

   At that time the word placebo designated a medicine which was prescribed more to please the patient than for his benefit.

4. Bei diesen <u>schon 1843 zur Widerlegung der Wirksamkeit homöopathischer Mittel durchgeführten</u> Blindversuchen wurden teilweise erstaunliche Placebo-Wirkungen registriert.

   In these blind trials, which were conducted as early as 1843 in order to refute the effectiveness of homeopathic substances, some astonishing placebo effects were registered.

5. Händel stellte den größten Teil seines Lebens in den Dienst der Oper, anders als der <u>sich nie mit dieser Form beschäftigende</u> Bach.

   Handel placed the largest part of his life in the service of opera, unlike Bach, who never occupied himself with this form.

6. Das neue Proletariat rekrutiert sich aus den <u>in die großen Städte strömenden</u> Landarbeitern.

   The new proletariat was recruited from the agricultural workers who were streaming into the large cities.

E46

1. *not least*
2. *not only*
3. *insufficient; not at all / by no means*
4. *never*
5. *nothing*

E47

1. , um in internationale Spitzenstellung <u>vorzu</u>dringen. (INFINITIVE CLAUSE)
2. , ‹daß› sie ihre Gesandten wegen Landesverrats vor Gericht stellen [wollten] . (DEPENDENT CLAUSE introduced by the CONJUNCTION daß)
3. , ‹obwhol› er seinen Aufenthaltsort in der Schweiz nur als Zwischenstation auf dem Wege nach Deutschland [ansah] . (DEPENDENT CLAUSE introduced by the CONJUNCTION obwohl)
4. , ‹die in einzelnen Städten sich oft über zwei Wochen [hinzogen] . (RELATIVE CLAUSE)
5. , ‹als› Nietzsche wiederum ins Engadin [ging] , (DEPENDENT CLAUSE introduced by the CONJUNCTION als)
6. [Schaut] man sich die Entwicklung während der letzten hundert Jahre an, ('if'-clause, without 'wenn')
7. , ‹was man zu glauben bereit [ist] . (RELATIVE CLAUSE)
8. , in ‹dem Unterricht und Schulerziehung Vorurteile [. . .] [abbauen] . (RELATIVE CLAUSE)
   [vornehmlich gegenüber Minderheiten] (Non-clause insertion)
9. , in ‹der die Versuchsperson aufgewachsen [ist] . (RELATIVE CLAUSE)
10. , ‹weil› sie für unser Thema notwendig zu sein [scheinen] . (DEPENDENT CLAUSE introduced by the CONJUNCTION weil)

E48

1. Die zukünftigen Probleme der Gesellschaft ⸢werden⸣ aber immer komplexer . . . ⸢sind⸣ ohne bewußte, sorgfältige Analyse **und** optimale Entscheidung überhaupt nicht mehr zu ordnen.

2. Nun ⸢besitzt⸣ Holz eine geringere durchschnittliche Dichte als Wasser . . . ⸢schwimmt⸣ ; Metalle **und** andere Stoffe dagegen haben eine größere durchschnittliche Dichte . . . ⸢gehen⸣ unter.

3. Der Sozialismus dagegen ⸢zieht⸣ radikale Konsequenzen . . . ⸢ruft⸣ zum Umsturz des kapitalistischen Systems auf.

4. Günstige Einflüsse ⸢gehen⸣ auch von dem parallelen Aufschwung der Weltwirtschaft, mit der die Bundesrepublik im Zuge der Westintegration schon bald wieder eng verflochten ⸢ist⸣, der Kooperationsbereitschaft von Gewerkschaften **und** Arbeitgebern **und** nicht zuletzt der staatlichen Wirtschaftspolitik aus.

5. Die Rolle des Staaates ⸢soll⸣ sich darauf beschränken, die für das Funktionieren des Marktes notwendigen Rahmenbedingungen zu schaffen, Störungen des Wettbewerbs, etwa durch übermäßige Konzentrationsprozesse, zu unterbinden . . . vor allem auch soziale Fehlentwicklungen auszugleichen.

E49

1. Der Zylinder, ‹der mit dem Riegel in Verbindung ⸢steht⸣, ⸢kann⸣ gedreht, das Schloß also geöffnet werden.

2. Allerdings ⸢lassen⸣ die Unternehmen, Izumindest jenel, ‹die sich nicht zur Spitzenstellung ⸢bekennen⸣, keinen Zweifel daran, ‹daß› sie trotzdem Probleme ⸢haben⸣.

3. Verhaltensweisen ⸢können⸣ nicht genau gemessen werden, ‹weil› sie sich von Zeit zu Zeit ⸢ändern⸣, ‹da› die Voraussetzungen nicht immer die gleichen ⸢sind⸣ und ‹da› sich die Meßvorrichtungen gelegentlich verändern ⸢können⸣.

4. ⸢Kann⸣ * ein Körper bei restlosem Untertauchen mehr** Flüssigkeitsgewicht verdrängen, als** er selbst wiegt, so wird er nur so tief in die Flüssigkeit eintauchen, ‹bis› der entstehende Auftrieb gleich seinem Gewicht ist.
   (*** Kann** introduces an if-Clause without 'wenn'. (→R16,144.2)
   ** mehr als *more than*)

5. Den Menschen der Vorzeit ⸢kennen⸣ wir in den Entwicklungsstadien, ‹die er durchlaufen ⸢hat⸣, durch die unbelebten Denkmäler und Geräte, ‹die er uns hinterlassen ⸢∅⸣, durch die Kunde von seiner Kunst, seiner Religion und Lebensanschauung, ‹die wir entweder direkt oder auf dem Wege der Tradition in Sagen, Mythen und Märchen erhalten ⸢haben⸣, durch die Überreste seiner Denkweisen in unseren eigenen Sitten und Gebräuchen.

6. Es ⸢gibt⸣ relativ wenig Menschen, ‹die imstande sind, rein musikalisch zu verstehen, ‹was Musik zu Sagen ⸢hat⸣.

E50

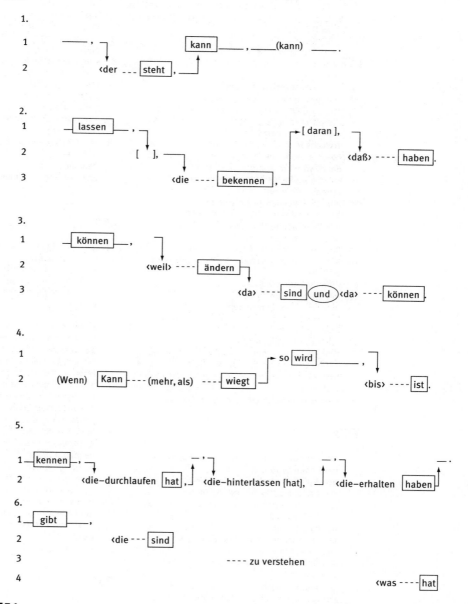

E51

1. **a.** <u>Das Gesetz</u>, . . . , <u>besagte</u> . . . (*the law said . . .*)
   b. The next clause to tackle would be the daß-clause.

2. **a.** <u>In den gleichen Jahren</u>, . . . , begegnete ihm im Hause Müller ein kultivierter Katholizismus . . . (*During the same years he encountered at the home of Müller a cultured catholicism . . .*)

   b. Either of the two RELATIVE CLAUSES could be tackled next.

3. **a.** <u>immer ist diese religiöse Komponente gegenwärtig</u> (*this religious component is always present*)
   b. The MAIN CLAUSE here can stand on its own. The ob(*whether*)-clauses only elaborate on the immer (*always*).

4. **a.** <u>nahm es nach kurzer Zeit ein Aussehen an</u> (*it took on the appearance of*)
   b. Obviously both DEPENDENT CLAUSES have to be worked out.

5. **a.** mußte er sich mit Scheinlösungen begnügen.
   (*he had to be content with mock solutions*)

   b. One has to tackle both DEPENDENT CLAUSES to find out why.

E52

1. infinitive: **sprechen** *to speak*
2. infinitive: **geben** *to give*
3. **er-** is a prefix. (➔R174) infinitive: **wachsen**.
   (Note the **-s** is here not 2nd person singular indicator, but part of the stem.)
   erwachsen *to arise, to develop*
4. **be-** is a prefix. (➔R174) infinitive: **schwören**.
   beschwören *to implore, to beseech*
5. **er-** is a prefix. (➔R174) infinitive: **finden**.
   erfinden *to invent*
6. infinitive: **können** *to be able to*
   (But here NON-FACTUAL. (➔R48, R66)
7. infinitive: **nennen** *to name*
8. infinitive: **halten** *to hold*
9. infinitive: **nehmen** *to take*
10. infinitive: **haben** *to have* But here NON-FACTUAL.
    (➔R48)
11. infinitive: **tun** *to do*
12. infinitive: **liegen** *to lie*
13. infinitive: **genügen** *to suffice*
    Note that the **ge-** is here an integral part of the verb stem.
14. infinitive: **beginnen** *to begin*
    (The **be-** is here not a prefix to be detached before looking up the verb in the list of strong and irregular verbs but an integral part of the verb stem.)
15. infinitive: **bezeichnen** *to call, to describe*

E53

1. Aber die Gesandten **drehten den Spieß um**.
   umdrehen *to turn around*
   den Spieß umdrehen *to turn the tables*
   But the delegates turned the tables.
2. Japanerinnen **nahmen** zu jener Zeit noch keine Milch **zu sich**.
   nehmen *to take*
   etw. zu sich nehmen *to partake of s.th., to consume s.th.*
   At that time Japanese women did not yet consume milk.
3. Der Wunsch nach Frieden **stand** bei der Europäischen Gemeinschaft **Pate**.
   stehen *to stand*
   Pate stehen lit. *to stand (as) godfather, to be the force behind something*
   The wish for peace was the force behind the foundation of the European Community.
4. Die Erde ist nicht nur eine Stätte, die **mit** Ordnung und Regel **rechnet**.
   rechnen *to calculate, to count*
   rechnen mit etw. *to reckon with s.th./s.b., to count on*
   Earth is not just a place which counts on order and rules.

5. Das wird Ihnen **Spaß machen**.
   machen *to make*
   Spaß machen *to enjoy (doing) s.th.* OR: *to joke*
   In the context of Text 10b:12: *You'll enjoy it.*
6. Der Rektor **hält** beim Essen **eine Ansprache**.
   halten *to hold*
   eine Ansprache halten *to make a speech.*
   The rector makes a speech at dinner.
7. Die Welt **gilt als** in drei Stockwerke gegliedert.
   gelten *to be valid*
   gelten als *to be regarded as*
   The world is regarded as being divided into three levels.
8. Sie **nehmen** den Großstadtverkehr nicht **zur Kenntnis**.
   nehmen *to take*
   etw. zur Kenntnis nehmen *to take note of s.th.*
   They do not take note of the city traffic.

E54

1. **getrauen** (a reflexive verb) *to dare*
   trauen *to marry*
   a. *He did not dare to go into the church.*
   b. *They were married in church.*
2. **gefallen** *to please* But **gefallen** + dative (➔R96)
   to like
   fallen *to fall*
   a. *He liked the concert.*
   b. *The child always fell down in the snow.*
3. **geraten** *to turn out*
   scheint **geraten** *to seem advisable*
   raten *to advise; to guess*
   a. *His essay turned out well.*
   b. *That does not seem advisable to me.*
   c. *He advised him to do it.*
4. **gebrauchen** *to use; to apply*
   brauchen *to need, to require; to use*
   a. *He used a dictionary* (gebrauchen) OR: *He needed a dictionary.* (brauchen)
   b. *He often uses a dictionary.* (As **gebraucht** here appears in finite position it is clear that the 'ge-' is part of the verb stem.)
5. **horchen** *to listen, to eavesdrop*
   gehorchen *to obey; to respond*
   a. *He did not listen at the door.* OR: *He did not obey.*
   b. *The child does not obey the mother.*

E55

1. Plötzlich **kommt** er **auf** einen Gedanken.
   kommen . . . auf (verb + preposition)
   Note: This cannot be the separable verb **aufkommen** since **auf** is not in Position IV
   to come upon/hit on something
   He suddenly thought of/had an idea.
2. So etwas **ist** noch nie **vorgekommen**.
   vorkommen (separable verb). past participle: **vorgekommen** (➔R172)
   to happen, to occur
   Something like this has never happened before.
3. Es **kommt** auch **auf** den Kontext **an**.

ankommen (separable verb) *to arrive*
BUT: **ankommen auf** *to depend on s.th.*
It also depends on the context.

4. Sie **kam ums Leben.**
kommen ... um ... *to be deprived of*
(*something*)
ums Leben kommen (check under **Leben**)
to die
She died.

5. Er **kam** im Krieg **um.**
umkommen (separable verb) *to die, to be killed,*
to perish
He was killed in the war.

6. Wir **kamen** gut **mit** ihm **aus.**
auskommen mit (separable verb) *to get on with*
somebody;
to make do with something
We got on well with him.

7. Sie **bekommt** die Stelle nicht.
bekommen (inseparable verb) *to get, to obtain,*
to receive
She does not get the job.

8. Sie sagte, er sei **auf den Hund gekommen.**
kommen ... auf + Hund (check under **Hund**)
to go to the dogs
She said that he had gone to the dogs.

9. Sie **kommt** später **nach.**
nachkommen (separable verb) *to follow/to*
come later
She will come later.

10. Er **kommt von** diesem Problem nicht mehr **los.**
loskommen ... von *to get away, to get free from*
He cannot get away from the problem.
ALSO: *He cannot get the problem out of his*
mind.

E56

1. **Alarmierendes**
alarmieren   *to alarm*
alarmierend   *alarming*
Alarmierendes   *something alarming, i.e. news*

2. das **Banale** (→R 186)
banal   *banal*
das **Banale**   *the banal*

3. **ein** (eingehenderes) **Beschäftigen** (→R180)
beschäftigen several meanings. Here: *to deal*
with s.th.
a (detailed, thorough,) dealing with

4. **eine Vergleichung** (→R186)
vergleichen   *to compare*
a comparison

5. (alles) **Vibrierende** (→R186)
vibrieren   *to vibrate*
vibrierend   *vibrating*
(*all/everything*) *that is vibrating*

6. das **Erkennbare** (→R186)
erkennen   *to recognize*
erkenn**bar**   *recognizable*
Erkennbare   *that which is recognizable*

7. das **Einsetzen** (→R180)
einsetzen   here: *to start, to begin*
the beginning

8. (anderes) **Beachtenswertes**

beachten   *to note*
beachtens**wert**   *worth noting, noteworthy*
Beachtens**wertes**   *s.th. noteworthy,*
                    (*other*) *things worth noting*

E57

1. **Verkehrssignalanlagen**
                    Anlagen
                    Signal
                    Signalanlagen
Verkehr
Verkehr/s/Signal/Anlagen
Pl. of Anlage *installations*
signal
installations for signalling
traffic
installations for giving signals to traffic
traffic lights

2. **Gesandtschaftsteilnehmer**
                    Teilnehmer
Gesandtschaft
Gesandtschaft/s/teilnehmer
participant, member
delegation
member of the/a delegation

3. **Feinmechanikhersteller**
                    Hersteller
            Mechanik
Feinmechanik
Fein/Mechanik/Hersteller
manufacturer
mechanics
precision engineering
manufacturer in precision engineering

4. **gewichtsmindernd**
                    mindern
                    mindernd
Gewicht
Gewicht/s/mindernd
to reduce
reducing
weight
weight-reducing

5. **Produktionsverfahren**
                    Verfahren
Produktion
Produktion/s/verfahren
procedure, process, method,
production
production process or method

6. **Beliebtheitsskala**
                    Skala
Beliebtheit
Beliebtheit/s/skala
scale, range
popularity
scale of popularity

7. **Selbstüberschätzung**
   Überschätzung
   Selbst
   Selbst/Überschätzung
   overestimation
   Selbst self
   overestimation of oneself

8. **Meßvorrichtung**
   Vorrichtung
   Meß
   Meß/Vorrichtung
   gadget, device
   messen to measure
   measuring device

9. **Scheinmedikament**
   Medikament
   scheinen
   Schein
   Schein/Medikament
   medicine
   to seem, to appear
   pretence
   'pretend' medicine
   placebo

10. **Forschungsergebnisse**
    Ergebnisse
    Forschung
    Forschung/s/Ergebnisse
    results
    research
    research results

E58

1. die **Überbewertung**
   bewert(en)
   überbewerten
   ung
   to judge, value, assess
   to overvalue, overrate
   noun suffix (→R186)
   overvaluation, overrating

2. **unvorhergesehen**
   gesehen
   vorher
   un
   past participle of **sehen** (*to see*) *seen*
   before
   un/not (→R130)
   unforeseen

3. **Erschöpfendes**
   erschöpfen
   erschöpfend
   Erschöpfendes (→R186)
   to exhaust
   exhaustive
   something exhaustive (here: **comments**)

4. **Schwimmfähigkeit**
   schwimmen
   Fähigkeit
   to swim
   ability
   ability to swim. here: **buoyancy**

5. **pilzförmig**
   förmig
   Pilz
   in the form of, shaped like
   mushroom, fungus
   mushroom-shaped

6. **Urzeit**
   ur
   Zeit
   original, first
   time
   primeval times, prehistory

7. **Auslastung**
   auslasten
   ung (→R186)
   to use to capacity
   full use

8. **unüberblickbar**
   Blick
   blicken
   überblicken
   bar
   überblickbar
   un
   unüberblickbar
   view, glance
   to look, to glance
   to oversee, to grasp
   (→R186, R78.5)
   lit: *'graspable'*
   un, not (→R130) Negation
   lit.: *not graspable* **incomprehensible,**
   incalculable

9. das **Gemessene**
   gemessen
   Gemessene
   past participle of **messen** (*to measure*)
   measured
   (→R186)
   that which has been measured

10. das **Nichterreichen**
    erreichen
    nicht
    to reach, achieve, attain
    not
    (Note the capital, i.e. here used as a noun.)
    failure to reach/achieve

E59

6 and 10 are not instructions.

Part IV

....

German–English
Text Corpus

List of Texts

21 ****** Schönberg: Was Musik zu sagen hat
What music has to say
22 **** Schopenhauer: Nach dem Tode
After death
23 **(*) Bedienungshinweise: Projektor
User instructions: projector

The approximate level of difficulty is indicated by the number of asterisks, i.e. a single asterisk denotes a relatively easy text.

1 Das Ansehen der Berufe*

(1) Im Westen wie im Osten Deutschlands ist der Arztberuf am beliebtesten. (2) Dies geht aus einer Umfrage des Emnid-Instituts hervor. (3) Während aber im Westen von den zehn angesehensten Berufen neun eine Hochschulausbildung voraussetzen, werden im Osten auch die Handwerker, Landwirte und Sozialarbeiter in der Beliebtheitsskala ganz vorn eingestuft. (4) Handwerker nehmen bei den Ostdeutschen sogar den Platz drei ein, gleich hinter dem Arzt und dem Zahnarzt, während er im Westen nicht einmal unter den ersten zehn auftaucht.

(5) Anders verhält es sich bei der Bewertung des Hausfrauenberufs. (6) Während die Hausfrau im Westen den zehnten Platz einnimmt, gehört sie im Osten nicht zu den beliebtesten zehn. (7) Einig sind sich Ost und West über die Berufsgruppe mit dem geringsten Ansehen – die Versicherungsvertreter, die auf Platz 25 ganz hinten rangieren, und wenig angesehen sind hier wie dort auch Offiziere und Werbeleute. (8) Nicht viel besser geht es den Bundestagsabgeordneten, die im Westen auf Platz 19 kommen und im Osten auf Platz 22 sogar noch negativer eingestuft werden. (9) Nach Meinung von Emnid mag das schlechte Ergebnis für die Parlamentarier im Osten mit der Enttäuschung über die wirtschaftliche Situation nach der Wiedervereinigung zusammenhängen.

Source: 'Arztberuf hat höchstes Ansehen', Nachrichten, DAAD Letter, *Hochschule und Ausland*, 4 (Dec. 1991).

1 The standing of the professions

(1) In the west as in the east of Germany the profession of doctor is the best loved. (2) This is the result of an opinion poll by the Emnid-Institute. (3) But whereas in the west nine of the ten most respected occupations require a university education, in the east the craftsmen, farmers, and social workers are also placed near the top in the scale of popularity. (4) Craftsmen even occupy third place with the East Germans, just behind the doctor and the dentist, whereas they do not even appear in the first ten in the west.

(5) It is quite different when it comes to evaluating the occupation of housewife. (6) Whilst the housewife occupies tenth place in the west, she does not belong to the most popular ten in the east. (7) East and west are at one concerning the occupational group with the least standing — the insurance representatives, who come right at the bottom in twenty-fifth place, and in both parts of Germany officers and advertising professionals are not respected much. (8) The delegates in the Bundestag fared not much better, coming in nineteenth place in the west and being placed even lower in the east, in twenty-second place. (9) In the opinion of Emnid the poor result for the parliamentarians in the east may be connected with disillusionment about the economic situation after reunification.

2 Brauchen wir Europa?*

(1) Europas Geschichte ist eine Geschichte von Kriegen: 100 jährigen, 30 jährigen, 7jährigen Kriegen, die ganze Städte, halbe Völker vernichteten. (2) Dieser Kontinent hat in seiner Geschichte mehr Kriegs- als Friedensjahre erlebt. (3) Noch lange nach dem Ende des zweiten Weltkriegs erörterten europäische Politiker ernsthaft, ob wieder ein Krieg zwischen den Staaten Westeuropas — ein Konflikt vor allem mit Deutschland — ausbrechen könnte.

(4) Der Wunsch nach Frieden stand bei der Gründung der Europäischen Gemeinschaft Pate: (5)„Wenn Europa einmal einträchtig sein gemeinsames Erbe verwalten würde, dann könnten seine drei- oder vierhundert Millionen Einwohner ein Glück, einen Wohlstand und einen Ruhm ohne Grenzen genießen. . . . (6) Wir müssen eine Art Vereinigter Staaten von Europa schaffen . . . (7) Der Weg dahin ist einfach. (8) Es ist nichts weiter dazu nötig, als daß Hunderte von Millionen Männern und Frauen Recht statt Unrecht tun und Segen statt Fluch ernten." (9) So sagte der bedeutende britische Premierminister Winston Churchill schon 1946, ein Jahr nach dem Ende des zweiten Weltkrieges.

(10) Solche Beschwörungen sind alt. (11) Erasmus von Rotterdam, der große niederländische Theologe und Philosoph, rief vor fast 500 Jahren die Völker Europas zu einem Völkerbund auf. (12) William Penn, der Quäker (nach dem der US-Bundesstaat Pennsylvania benannt wurde), beschwor 150 Jahre später die Staaten, eine Europäische Bundesversammlung zu schaffen. (13) Victor Hugo, der große französische Dichter, kündigte 1851 die Vereinigten Staaten von Europa an. (14) Er erntete Hohn und Spott. (15) Und den Appellen und Aufrufen folgten immer nur neue Kriege. (16) Denn Europa war dem Krieg stets näher als dem Frieden. (17) Erst nach dem Schrecken zweier Weltkriege nahm man die Appelle ernst.

(18) Für alle Bundesregierungen ist der Ausgleich mit den westlichen Partnern, das Bemühen um die Einigung Europas, ein Kernpunkt bundesdeutscher Außenpolitik gewesen. (19) Und es wurde viel erreicht.

Source: *Europa. Chronik, Probleme, Ziele* (Presse- und Informationsamt der Bundesregierung, Bonn, 1979).

2 Do we need Europe?

(1) Europe's history is a history of wars: hundred-year, thirty-year, seven-year wars which destroyed whole cities, half-nations. (2) In its history this continent has experienced more years of war than of peace. (3) Long after the end of the Second World War European politicians were still seriously discussing whether a war between the states of Europe — in particular a conflict with Germany — could break out again.

(4) The desire for peace was the godparent at the founding of the European Community: (5) 'If Europe were to manage its common heritage harmoniously, then its three or four hundred million inhabitants could enjoy a boundless good fortune, prosperity and reputation. . . . (6) We must create a kind of United States of Europe . . . (7) The way to this goal is simple. (8) Nothing more is needed than that hundreds of millions of men and women do right instead of wrong and reap happiness instead of misery.' (9) These were the words of the important British prime minister Winston Churchill as early as 1946, one year after the end of the Second World War.

(10) Such invocations are old. (11) Erasmus of Rotterdam, the great Dutch theologian and philosopher, summoned the peoples of Europe almost 500 years ago to form a federation of nations. (12) William Penn, the Quaker (after whom the US state Pennsylvania is named), called on the states 150 years later to create a European federal assembly. (13) Victor Hugo, the great French writer, announced the United States of Europe in 1851. (14) This brought him scorn and derision. (15) And all these appeals were always followed only by more new wars. (16) For Europe was always closer to war than to peace. (17) Only after the horror of two world wars did people take these appeals seriously.

(18) For all Federal German governments, a central point of foreign policy has been rapprochement with the western partners, working for the unification of Europe. (19) And much has been achieved.

3 Die moderne Welt*(*)

(1) Der Mensch, so sagen uns die Historiker, hat bisher rund 800 Lebensspannen auf Erden gelebt, die meisten davon in Höhlen. (2) Gutenberg erfand seine beweglichen Lettern vor fünfzehn Generationen, Watt baute die erste Dampfmaschine vor sechs, die eigentliche Industrialisierung begann vor vier Lebensspannen. (3) Bis dahin war die Gesellschaft statisch, ein Unterschied zwischen Vergangenheit und Gegenwart existierte kaum, aber seitdem gilt das Gesetz der Akzeleration. (4) Eine Großstadt des Jahres 1886 war einer Metropole des Jahres 86 n.Chr. ähnlicher als einer heutigen Großstadt. (5) Die Alten unter uns, die als Kind im Jahre 1903 vom ersten Flug der Gebrüder Wright erzählen hörten, haben am Fernsehschirm die Mondlandung der Apollo XI mit ansehen können. (6) Sie haben erlebt, wie das Automobil zur Alltäglichkeit wurde. (7) In ihrer Zeit wurde die erste Atombombe gezündet (1945), der erste Elektronenrechner gebaut (1946), die Doppelhelix enträtselt (1953) — das Zeitalter der Atomkraft, des Computers, der Biotechnik begann.

Source: Theo Sommer, 'Das letzte Jahr', *Die Zeit*, 2 Jan. 1987.

4 Engels: Die Geschichte der arbeitenden Klassen in England*(*)

(1) Die Geschichte der arbeitenden Klassen in England beginnt mit der letzten Hälfte des vorigen Jahrhunderts, mit der Erfindung der Dampfmaschine und der Maschinen zur Verarbeitung der Baumwolle. (2) Diese Erfindungen gaben bekanntlich den Anstoß zu einer industriellen Revolution, einer Revolution, die zugleich die ganze bürgerliche Gesellschaft umwandelte, und deren weltgeschichtliche Bedeutung erst jetzt anfängt erkannt zu werden. (3) England ist der klassische Boden dieser Umwälzung, die um so gewaltiger war, je geräuschloser sie vor sich ging, und England ist darum auch das klassische Land für die Entwicklung ihres hauptsächlichsten Resultates, des Proletariats. (4) Das Proletariat kann nur in England in allen seinen Verhältnissen und nach allen Seiten hin studiert werden.

(5) Wir haben es hier einstweilen nicht mit der Geschichte dieser Revolution, nicht mit ihrer ungeheuren Bedeutung für die Gegenwart und Zukunft zu tun. (6) Diese Darstellung muß einer künftigen, umfassenderen Arbeit vorbehalten bleiben. (7) Für den Augenblick müssen wir uns auf das Wenige beschränken, das zum Verständnis der gegenwärtigen Lage der englischen Proletarier notwendig ist.

Source: Friedrich Engels, '*Die Lage der arbeitenden Klasse in England*', in Karl Marx, Friedrich Engels, *Historisch-Kritische Gesamtausgabe. Werke, Schriften, Briefe*, hrsg. von V. Adoratskij, Marx-Engels — Verlag GmbH, Berlin, 1932 (Erste Abteilung, Bd. 4).

3 The modern world

(1) Mankind, so the historians tell us, has lived some 800 generations on earth so far, most of them in caves. (2) Gutenberg invented his movable letters fifteen generations ago, Watt built the first steam engine six generations ago, real industrialization began four generations ago. (3) Up till then society was static: a difference between past and present hardly existed; but since then the law of acceleration has applied. (4) A large city of the year 1886 was more like a metropolis of AD 86 than a modern city. (5) The old ones amongst us, who as children in 1903 heard tell of the first flight of the Wright brothers, were amongst those who witnessed the moon landing of Apollo XI on the television screen. (6) They have seen how the automobile has become an everyday object. (7) In their lifetime the first atom bomb was exploded (1945), the first electronic computer built (1946), the double helix unravelled (1953) — the age of atomic power, of the computer, of biotechnology began.

4 Engels: The history of the working classes in England

(1) The history of the working classes in England begins with the latter half of the last century, with the invention of the steam engine and the machines for the processing of cotton. (2) As is well known, these inventions provided the impetus for an industrial revolution, a revolution which at the same time transformed the whole of bourgeois society and whose world-historical significance is only now beginning to be recognized. (3) England is the classic location of this upheaval which was all the more huge for happening silently, and England is therefore also the classic country for the development of its principal result, the proletariat. (4) Only in England can the proletariat be studied in all its relations and with regard to all its aspects.

(5) For the time being we are not concerned here with the history of this revolution, nor with its enormous significance for the present and the future. (6) This account must be left to a future, more comprehensive work. (7) For the moment we must restrict ourselves to the little that is necessary for an understanding of the present situation of the English labouring classes.

5 Stockhausen: Die Entstehung der Musik*

(1) Die Entstehung der Musik ist nicht von der Entstehung der Menschheit zu trennen. (2) Seitdem der Mensch existiert, gibt es Musik. (3) Doch auch die Tiere, die Atome, die Sterne erzeugen Musik. (4) Alles Vibrierende erzeugt Musik. (5) Die für Menschen wahrnehmbare Musik ist die von den Menschen geschaffene Musik. (6) Die Musik der Atome, der Sterne und der Tiere muß umgewandelt werden, damit der Mensch sie hören kann. (7) Die Entstehung der Menschheit wurde in vielen Mythen beschrieben. (8) Vor einigen Jahren hat eine neue Epoche in der Geschichte begonnen, und die Geschichte der Menschen bekommt einen Sinn.

(9) Ich bin davon überzeugt, daß das menschliche Leben auf der Erde im Tier- und Pflanzenbereich entstanden ist. (10) Andererseits glaube ich auch, daß vor 400 000 oder 450 000 Jahren fremde Lebewesen aus dem Universum dem Menschen die Kultur und auch die Musik brachten. (11) Seit meiner Kindheit glaube ich, daß ich nicht von dieser Welt bin. (12) Meine wichtigste Aufgabe hier auf Erden ist, durch die Musik die Beziehungen zwischen den Bewohnern dieser Erde und denen anderer Planeten herzustellen.

Source: Interview with Karlheinz Stockhausen. Published in *Moderne Musik. Von den Regeln der Klassik zum freien Experiment* (Hamburg: Rowohlt, 1977).

6 Bultmann: Das mythische Weltbild**

(1) Das Weltbild des Neuen Testaments ist ein mythisches. (2) Die Welt gilt als in drei Stockwerke gegliedert. (3) In der Mitte befindet sich die Erde, über ihr der Himmel, unter ihr die Unterwelt. (4) Der Himmel ist die Wohnung Gottes und der himmlischen Gestalten, der Engel; die Unterwelt ist die Hölle, der Ort der Qual. (5) Aber auch die Erde ist nicht nur die Stätte des natürlich alltäglichen Geschehens, der Vorsorge und Arbeit, die mit Ordnung und Regel rechnet; sondern sie ist auch der Schauplatz des Wirkens übernatürlicher Mächte, Gottes und seiner Engel, des Satans und seiner Dämonen. (6) In das natürliche Geschehen und in das Denken, Wollen und Handeln des Menschen greifen die übernatürlichen Mächte ein; Wunder sind nichts Seltenes. (7) Der Mensch ist seiner selbst nicht mächtig; Dämonen können ihn besitzen; der Satan kann ihm böse Gedanken eingeben; aber auch Gott kann sein Denken und Wollen lenken, kann ihn himmlische Gesichte schauen lassen, ihn sein befehlendes oder tröstendes Wort hören lassen, kann ihm die übernatürliche Kraft seines Geistes schenken.

Source: Rudolf Bultmann, 'Neues Testament und Mythologie. Das Problem der Entmythologisierung der neutestamentlichen Verkündigung', in Manfred Baumotte (ed.), *Die Frage nach dem historischen Jesu* (Gütersloh, 1984). First printed in Hans Werner Bartsch (ed.), *Kerygma und Mythos I: Ein theologisches Gespräch* (H. Reich Evangelischer Verlag: Hamburg, 1948).

5 Stockhausen: The origin of music

(1) The origins of music are not to be divorced from the origins of mankind. (2) Since mankind has existed, there has been music. (3) But animals too, the atoms, the stars produce music. (4) Everything that vibrates produces music. (5) The music perceptible to mankind is the music created by mankind. (6) The music of the atoms, the stars, and the animals has to be transformed in order that human beings can hear it. (7) The origin of mankind has been described in many myths. (8) Some years ago a new epoch began in history, and the history of mankind has been made meaningful.

(9) I am convinced that human life began on earth, in the animal and plant kingdom. (10) On the other hand I also believe that 400,000 or 450,000 years ago alien beings from the universe brought humankind culture and also music. (11) Since my childhood I have believed that I am not of this world. (12) My most important task here on earth is through music to create the connections between the inhabitants of this earth and those of other planets.

6 Bultmann: The mythical world-view

(1) The world-view of the New Testament is a mythical one. (2) The world is regarded as being divided up into three levels. (3) The earth is in the middle, above it is the heaven, below it the underworld. (4) The heavens are the place of residence of God and the heavenly figures, the angels; the underworld is hell, the place of torment. (5) But the earth too is not just the place of the natural everyday happenings, of provision for the future and work, which counts on order and predictability; it is also the stage on which supernatural powers work their effects, the powers of God and his angels, of Satan and his demons. (6) The supernatural powers intervene in the natural events and in mankind's thoughts, intentions, and actions; miracles are not at all unknown. (7) Human beings are not in full control of themselves: demons can possess them, Satan can implant evil thoughts in them, but God too can guide their thoughts and intentions, can let them see heavenly visions, can let them hear his commanding or consoling word, can grant them the supernatural power of his spirit.

7 Alle Messungen sind Schätzungen*(*)

(1) Alle Messungen sind Schätzungen. (2) Der Durchmesser einer Stahlstange kann sehr genau mit einer Mikro-Schublehre gemessen werden, aber wenn von einer Stahlstange verschiedene Messungen gemacht werden, weicht eine Messung leicht von der anderen ab. (3) Der Durchschnitt dieser Messungen ist die beste Schätzung des Durchmessers. (4) Dieser Durchschnitt ist nicht der genaue Durchmesser; um eine gute Schätzung zu erhalten, werden verschiedene Messungen zusammengenommen. (5) Die Schätzung kann durch eine größere Anzahl Messungen verbessert werden, aber es ist nie möglich, den genauen Durchmesser zu bestimmen.

(6) Messungen werden durch die Bedingungen, unter denen sie durchgeführt werden, beeinflußt. (7) Der Durchmesser der Stahlstange ist an einem warmen Tage größer als an einem kalten Tage, weil das Metall sich ausdehnt, sobald die Temperatur steigt. (8) Die Temperatur verursacht eine Veränderung des Durchmessers der Stahlstange und sie verändert auch die Länge.

(9) Die gleichen Probleme treten auch bei Messungen in psychologischen Experimenten auf. (10) Verhaltensweisen können nicht genau gemessen werden, weil sie sich von Zeit zu Zeit ändern, da die Voraussetzungen nicht immer die gleichen sind und da sich die Meßvorrichtungen gelegentlich verändern können.

(11) Die Messungen werden außerdem noch durch die Tatsache erschwert, daß die Meßvorrichtung selbst einen Einfluß auf das Gemessene haben kann. (12) Wir können die Wassertemperatur in einem Glas mittels eines Thermometers messen. (13) Wenn das Thermometer kälter ist als das Wasser, wird es die Temperatur des Wassers leicht senken, sobald es in das Glas getaucht wird.

(14) In gleicher Weise kann sich in der Psychologie das Verhalten als Ergebnis der Tatsache, daß es gemessen wird, ändern. (15) Nehmen wir an, die Fähigkeit einer Person, arithmetische Probleme zu lösen, werde durch Zeitmessungen ermittelt. (16) Im ersten Versuch wird ihr erlaubt, sich zu üben; damit wird sie es in ihrem nächsten Versuch sehr wahrscheinlich besser machen. (17) Dadurch steigt ihre Leistung, weil die Testsituation selbst ihr die Möglichkeit zur Übung gibt.

Source: *Grundlegende statistiche Begriffe*, ins Deutsche übertragen und adaptiert von M, Nüßli-Marolt and H. Fischer (Bern, 1963).

7 All measurements are estimates

(1) All measurements are estimates. (2) The diameter of a steel rod can be measured very precisely with a micrometer, but when different measurements are made of the same steel rod, one measurement will deviate slightly from the other. (3) The average of these measurements is the best estimate of the diameter. (4) This average is not the precise diameter — in order to obtain a good estimate, different measurements are taken together. (5) The estimate can be improved by means of a larger number of measurements but it is never possible to determine the precise diameter.

(6) Measurements are influenced by the conditions under which they are carried out. (7) The diameter of the steel rod is greater on a warm day than on a cold day, because the metal expands as soon as the temperature rises. (8) The temperature causes a change in the diameter of the steel rod and it also changes the length.

(9) The same problems also occur with measurements in psychological experiments. (10) Modes of behaviour cannot be measured exactly because they change from time to time, since the circumstances are not always the same and since the measuring devices can alter occasionally.

(11) What is more, the measurements are further complicated by the fact that the measuring device itself can have an influence on the thing being measured. (12) We can measure the water temperature in a glass by means of a thermometer. (13) If the thermometer is colder than the water, it will slightly depress the temperature of the water as soon as it is put into the glass.

(14) In the same way, in psychology, behaviour can alter as a result of the fact that it is being measured. (15) Let us suppose that the ability of a person to solve arithmetic puzzles is being calculated using time measurements. (16) On the first attempt this person is allowed to practise; and as a result s/he will very probably do it much better in his or her next attempt. (17) Because of this, the person's performance increases because the test situation itself has given them the opportunity to practise.

8 Bach und Händel**

(1) In Bach und Händel fand das Barockzeitalter seine Krönung. (2) So unterschiedlich wie ihr Lebenslauf ist auch ihr Lebenswerk. (3) Händel stellte den größten Teil seines Lebens in den Dienst der Oper. (4) Bach beschäftigte sich nie mit dieser Form. (5) Händel war Repräsentant barocker Pracht. (6) Bach war der Typus des nach innen gerichteten Musikers, der „alles zur größeren Ehre Gottes" schrieb und an den Anfang seiner Werke das demütige „Jesu hilf" setzte. (7) Händels Musik eröffnet sich dem Hörer oft schon beim ersten Hören und ist damit ausgesprochen volkstümlich. (8) Bachs Tonsprache erfordert ein eingehenderes Beschäftigen, wenn man ihre Schönheit voll erfassen will. (9) Daraus erklärt es sich wohl, daß Bachs Werk erst viele Jahrzehnte nach seinem Tod durch Mendelssohn für die Nachwelt wiederentdeckt wurde; Händels Oratorien blieben dagegen vor allem in England stets lebendig.

Source: K. Aichele and B. Binkowski (eds.), *Unser Liederbuch* (Stuttgart, 1959).

9 Placebo**

(1) Das Wort Placebo wird in der Medizin in Amerika seit 200 Jahren benutzt (in Deutschland seit 1946). (2) Man bezeichnete damit früher ein Medikament, das mehr dem Patienten zum Gefallen (placebo: ich werde gefallen) als zu dessen Nutzen verordnet wurde. (3) Heute versteht man unter einem Placebo ein Leerpräparat, ein Scheinmedikament, das mit einem zu prüfenden Mittel in Größe, Farbe, Geschmack völlig gleich sein soll. (4) Beide Mittel, das Placebo und das Originalmittel, werden verordnet, um den pharmakodynamischen vom psychodynamischen Anteil eines Medikamentes zu trennen, d. h. um den suggestiven und den chemischen Anteil der Wirkung auseinanderzuhalten. (5) Es handelt sich hierbei um eine absichtliche, für den Patienten dagegen unvorhergesehene Suggestion, daher *Blindversuch* genannt. (6) Solche Versuche wurden schon 1843 zur Widerlegung der Wirksamkeit homöopathischer Mittel durchgeführt. (7) Mit diesem *einfachen* Blindversuch wurden teilweise erstaunliche Placebo-Wirkungen registriert, doch waren diese schwankend in ihrer Intensität. (8) Etwa 30 Prozent aller Menschen reagieren jederzeit auf ein Placebo wie ein Arzneimittel. (9) 40 Prozent reagieren ungleichmäßig, 30 Prozent niemals. (10) So wurde der *doppelte Blindversuch* entwickelt, bei dem nicht nur der Patient, sondern auch der Arzt nicht weiß, welches das zu prüfende Medikament und welches das Leerpräparat ist.

Source: Bernt Hoffmann, *Handbuch des autogenen Trainings* (dtv, Munich, 1977).

8 Bach and Handel

(1) In Bach and Handel, the baroque period reached its height. (2) The differences in the course of their lives are as great as the differences in their life's work. (3) Handel placed the greatest part of his life at the service of opera. (4) Bach never occupied himself with this form. (5) Handel was the representative of baroque splendour. (6) Bach was the type of the inward-looking musician who wrote 'everything for the greater honour of God' and put the humble 'Jesus help me' at the start of his works. (7) Handel's music often appeals to the listener at the very first hearing and is thus extremely populist. (8) Bach's musical language requires more detailed attention if one wants to grasp its beauty fully. (9) It is perhaps for this reason that Bach's work was not rediscovered for posterity, by Mendelssohn, until many decades after his death. whereas Handel's oratorios were always popular, especially in England.

9 Placebo

(1) The word placebo has been used in medicine in America for 200 years (in Germany since 1946). (2) In earlier times one used the word to designate a medicine that was prescribed more to please the patient (placebo: I will please) than for his benefit. (3) Today one understands by a placebo an empty preparation, a pseudo-medication, which is intended to be completely identical with a medication that is to be tested, in size, colour, and taste. (4) Both substances, the placebo and the authentic substance, are prescribed in order to separate the pharmacological part of a medication from the psychological part, that is, in order to distinguish the portion of its effect which is suggestive from that which is chemical. (5) What we have here is a deliberate, but for the patient unforeseen suggestion, which is accordingly called a *blind test*. (6) Such experiments were carried out as early as 1843 in order to refute the effectiveness of homeopathic substances. (7) With this *simple* blind test, placebo effects, some of them astonishing, were noted, but they were uneven in their intensity. (8) About 30 per cent of all people react every time to a placebo as if it were a medicine. (9) Forty per cent react unevenly, and 30 per cent never react. (10) For this reason the *double blind test* was developed, in which not only the patient but also the doctor does not know which is the medicine that is being tested and which is the empty preparation.

10 Briefwechsel**

A

Prof. D. R. Bultmann   Marburg, 29.III.1935
Marburg a. d. Lahn,
Calvinstr. 14

Lieber Herr Barth!

(1) Darf ich sie um eine Auskunft bitten? Die University St.Andrews will mir den D.D. verleihen u. lädt mich auf den 28. Juni zum Empfang des Diploms ein. (2) Sie sind dieser Ehre ja schon früher teilhaftig geworden. (3) U. ich bitte Sie, mir Anweisungen über das richtige Verhalten zu geben. (4) Muß man dabei eine Rede halten, eine Erwiderungsansprache? (5) Bes. schwierig scheint die Frage der Kleidung zu sein. (6) Man tritt wohl im Frack an? (7) Muß man sich dort ein Doktor-Kostüm erstehen, ganz oder teilweise? (8) (Eine Offerte von einem Edinburgher Geschäft ist bereits eingetroffen.) (9) Ich wäre Ihnen sehr dankbar, wenn Sie mir in diesen Fragen Rat geben wollten u. etwa noch anderes Beachtenswertes sagten. (10) Sind Sie im Juni voraussichtl. in Bonn ? (11) Dann könnte ich Sie auf der Durchreise noch besuchen u. Ratschläge einholen. — (12) Wie geht es Ihnen u. Ihrer Familie? (13) Bei uns steht es wohl. (14) Herzliche Grüße von Haus zu Haus! Ihr

R. Bultmann

B

Bonn, 31.III.1935

Lieber Herr B.!

(1) Nein, Sie brauchen dort keine Rede zu halten. (2) Das tut jeweilen, vermutlich auf Grund vorausgehender Verabredung, irgend ein Angelsachse unter den Doktorierten. (3) Dagegen hält der Rektor beim Essen eine Ansprache, bei der Sie gut aufpassen müssen, um im rechten Augenblick, wenn Sie erwähnt werden, liebenswürdig zu lächeln. (4) Frack ist nicht nötig. (5) Den Talar leiht man Ihnen sicher von der Universität; so wars jedenfalls in Glasgow. (6) Man wird Ihnen nachher den *hood*, eine Art Kapuze in leuchtenden Farben, das eigentliche Ehrenzeichen, zum Kauf anbieten. (7) Ich habe es leichtsinniger Weise getan, obwohl der Scherz 4 Pfund kostete, und bin nachher bei allen Universitätsanlässen hier darin herumgelaufen. (8) Wenn schon, denn schon, dachte ich und erklärte hier den staunenden Medizinern etc: ich sei nämlich der päpstliche Legat. (9) Der Doktorierungsakt selber ist überaus feierlich: ich mußte knien, wie s.Z. bei der Konfirmation und dazu wurde etwas in unverständlichem Latein über mich gemurmelt. (10) Die Studenten aber dürfen nach alter Übung Krakehl dazu machen. (11) St. Andrews ist eine putzige herrlich gelegene Miniaturuniversität. . . . (12) Das Ganze wird Ihnen in jeder Hinsicht Spaß machen, was man ja heutzutag wirklich nötig hat. (13) Ich gratuliere Ihnen und wünsche Ihnen alles Gute. (14) Wo ich im Juni bin, ist noch ganz unübersehbar. Mit herzlichem Gruß!   Ihr

Karl Barth

Source: Karl Barth, *Briefe, v. Karl Bart–Rudolf Bultmann, Briefwechsel 1922–1966*, ed. Bernd Jaspert (Theologischer Verlag, Zürich, 1971).

10 Correspondence

A

Dear Mr Barth,

(1) May I ask you something? The University of St Andrews wants to award me the DD and is inviting me over on the 28th June to receive the degree. (2) You have of course already been the recipient of this honour. (3) And I ask you to give me some tips on correct behaviour. (4) Does one have to give a speech at the ceremony, a response? (5) The question of dress seems particularly difficult to me. (6) I suppose one turns up in a dress suit? (7) Does one have to buy the doctoral attire, in full or in part? (8) (An advertisement from an Edinburgh company has already arrived.) (9) I would be very grateful to you if you could advise me in these matters and could perhaps tell me other things that need to be known. (10) Do you expect to be in Bonn in June? (11) Then I could visit you on the way and pick up some tips. (12) How are you and your family? (13) We are well. (14) Friendly greetings from house to house!
Your
R. Bultmann

B

Dear Mr B.,

(1) No, you don't need to make a speech there. (2) That is always done by one of the Anglo-Saxons amongst those receiving doctorates, presumably on the basis of a prior arrangement. (3) On the other hand the rector gives an address at the dinner during which you must be sure to pay attention so that you smile politely at the right moment when you are mentioned. (4) Formal dress is not necessary. (5) You can certainly hire the gown from the university; at least that's how it was in Glasgow. (6) Afterwards you will be asked whether you want to buy the hood, a kind of cap in brilliant colours. (7) In a moment of recklessness, I did so, although this foolishness cost me four pounds, and since then I have gone around in it at all university occasions here. (8) In for a penny, in for a pound! I thought, and explained to the amazed medics etc. here that I was the papal legate. (9) The graduation ceremony itself is extremely formal: I had to kneel, like for my confirmation, and then something in incomprehensible Latin was mumbled over me. (10) But the students were allowed to make a noise, by old tradition. (11) St Andrews is a quaint, beautifully situated miniature university. . . . (12) The whole thing will be enjoyable in every way, which one really does need nowadays, after all. (13) I congratulate you and wish you all the best. (14) Where I am in June is still not at all certain.
With best wishes, Your
Karl Barth

11 Einteilung der Geschichte**(*)

(1) Zur Schematisierung seines Gegenstandes teilt der Historiker das bisherige Geschehen in große, zusammenhängende Zeitabschnitte ein. (2) Dabei wurde es seit dem 17. Jahrhundert üblich, in den geschichtlichen Lehrbüchern die Weltgeschichte in Vorgeschichte, Alte, Mittlere und Neuere Geschichte zu gliedern und seit 1945 dazu auch die Begriffe Neueste Geschichte und Zeitgeschichte zu verwenden.

(3) Demnach stellt sich eine schematische Gliederung der abendländischen Geschichte folgendermaßen dar:

(4) Urzeit: — Älteste Geschichte der Menschheit und der einzelnen Völker von den Anfängen bis zum Einsetzen schriftlicher Quellen

(5) Altertum
3000 v. Chr.–5. Jh. n. Chr. — Zeitraum von den Anfängen geschichtlicher Kunde (vor 3000 Keilschrift und Hieroglyphen, 2000 chinesische Schrift, 900 griechisches Alphabet) bis zum Ende der griechisch-römischen Antike

(6) Mittelalter
5. Jh.–15. Jh. — Medium aevum = die Zwischenzeit, die Zeit zwischen Altertum und Neuzeit; ein von den Humanisten geprägter Begriff für die Zeit zwischen dem Verfall der Antike und ihrer Wiedergeburt (Renaissance); die Zeit also von 476 n. Chr. bis zum Ende des 15. Jahrhunderts

(7) Neuzeit
16. Jh.–18. Jh. — Die Geschichtsperiode von etwa 1500 bis zur Französischen Revolution

(8) Neueste Zeit
19. Jh.–20. Jh. — Die Zeit nach der Französischen Revolution bis zum Ende des 1. bzw. 2. Weltkrieges

(9) Zeitgeschichte
seit 1945 — Die Jüngste Vergangenheit

Source: Diether Raff, *Deutsche Geschichte* (Munich, 1985).

11 The division of history

(1) In order to schematize his subject the historian divides up past events into large, coherent periods of time. (2) In doing so it has been the custom since the seventeenth century to divide up world history in history textbooks into prehistory, ancient, medieval, and modern history.

(3) Accordingly, a schematic division of Western history looks like this:

(4) Prehistory	Earliest history of mankind and the individual peoples from the beginnings up to the onset of written records
(5) Antiquity 3000 BC– 5th cent. AD	The period from the beginnings of historical sources (3,000 years ago cuneiform and hieroglyphs, 2,000: Chinese writing system, 900: Greek alphabet) up until the end of Graeco-Roman antiquity
(6) Middle Ages 5th–15th cent.	Medium aevum = the intervening age, the time between antiquity and the modern age; a term coined by the humanists for the time between the decline of antiquity and its rebirth (Renaissance); the time, that is to say, from AD 476 until the end of the fifteenth century
(7) Early Modern History 16th–18th cent.	The historical period from about 1500 up to the French Revolution
(8) Modern History 19th–20th cent.	The time from the French Revolution up to the end of the First or Second World War
(9) Contemporary History Since 1945	The most recent past

12 Freud: Totem und Tabu**(*)

(1) Den Menschen der Vorzeit kennen wir in den Entwicklungsstadien, die er durchlaufen hat, durch die unbelebten Denkmäler und Geräte, die er uns hinterlassen, durch die Kunde von seiner Kunst, seiner Religion und Lebensanschauung, die wir entweder direkt oder auf dem Wege der Tradition in Sagen, Mythen und Märchen erhalten haben, durch die Überreste seiner Denkweisen in unseren eigenen Sitten und Gebräuchen. (2) Außerdem aber ist er noch in gewissem Sinne unser Zeitgenosse; es leben Menschen, von denen wir glauben, daß sie den Primitiven noch sehr nahe stehen, viel näher als wir, in denen wir daher die direkten Abkömmlinge und Vertreter der früheren Menschen erblicken. (3) Wir urteilen so über die sogenannten Wilden und halbwilden Völker, deren Seelenleben ein besonderes Interesse für uns gewinnt, wenn wir in ihm eine gut erhaltene Vorstufe unserer eigenen Entwicklung erkennen dürfen.

(4) Wenn diese Voraussetzung zutreffend ist, so wird eine Vergleichung der „Psychologie der Naturvölker", wie die Völkerkunde sie lehrt, mit der Psychologie des Neurotikers, wie sie durch die Psychoanalyse bekannt geworden ist, zahlreiche Übereinstimmungen aufweisen müssen, und wird uns gestatten, bereits Bekanntes hier und dort in neuem Licht zu sehen.

Source: Sigmund Freud, *Totem und Tabu*, (in *Gesammelte Werke*, ix (Fischer, Frankfurt a. M., 1940)).

12 Freud: Totem and taboo

(1) We are familiar with the human being of prehistory in the developmental stages which he passed through, through the inanimate monuments and tools which he has left behind for us, through the knowledge of his art, his religion, and his world-view which we have received either directly or by way of tradition in sagas, myths, and fairy-tales, through the remnants of his ways of thinking in our own customs and usages. (2) Also, however, he is still in a certain sense our contemporary; there are people living now about whom we believe that they are still very close to the primitives, a lot closer than we are, and in whom we therefore glimpse the direct descendants and representatives of earlier human beings. (3) This is how we judge the so-called primitive and semi-primitive peoples, whose spiritual life acquires a special interest for us if we are able to see in them a well-preserved earlier stage of our own development.

(4) If this assumption is justified, then a comparison of the 'psychology of primitive tribes', such as anthropology teaches, with the psychology of the neurotic, such as has become familiar through psychoanalysis, will be bound to reveal numerous points of agreement and will enable us to see our present knowledge in a new light in some instances.

13 Die Juden in Deutschland heute***(*)

(1) Heute zählen die jüdischen Gemeinden in der Bundesrepublik etwa 30 000 Mitglieder. (2) Durch den Beitritt der ehemaligen DDR hat sich diese Zahl nur unwesentlich verändert, da den jüdischen Gemeinden auf dem Gebiet der ehemaligen DDR nur einige Hundert Menschen angehören. (3) Die Mehrzahl der Juden, die nach dem Ende der nationalsozialistischen Herrschaft in Deutschland ansässig wurden und neue Gemeinden aufbauten, kam aus osteuropäischen Ländern.

(4)„Die wenigen deutschen Juden, die die Vernichtungslager überlebt haben oder aus der Emigration zurückgekehrt sind, fallen zahlenmäßig kaum ins Gewicht. (5) Die jüdische Gemeinschaft stellt im wesentlichen eine Gemeinschaft der der Massenvernichtung entronnenen, zufällig überlebenden, ungewollt in der Bundesrepublik gestrandeten osteuropäischen Juden dar. (6) Es ist eine Gemeinschaft, die in den Nachkriegsjahren auf gepackten Koffern gesessen hat und die heute bemüht ist, sich mit der Realität in der Bundesrepublik zu arrangieren—wenn auch unter Schmerzen und Schuldgefühlen."[1]

[1] Quoted from *Jüdisches Leben in Deutschland nach* 1945 (iudicium Verlag, Frankfurt, 1986), 8.

Source: Ulrich Ruh, *Religion und Kirche in der Bundesrepublik Deutschland* (iudicium Verlag, Munich, 1990).

13 The Jews in Germany today

(1) Today the Jewish communities in the Federal Republic have about 30,000 members. (2) This number has risen only marginally with the accession of the former GDR, since only a few hundred people belong to Jewish communities on the territory of the former GDR. (3) The majority of Jews who became resident in Germany and built up new communities after the end of the National Socialist rule came from eastern European countries.

(4) 'The few German Jews who survived the extermination camps or returned from emigration are numerically of little significance. (5) The Jewish community is essentially a community of eastern European Jews who escaped the mass extermination, survived by chance, and were stranded unwanted in the Federal Republic. (6) It is a community which sat on packed suitcases in the years following the War and which is today at pains to fit into the reality of life in the Federal Republic—even though this means pain and feelings of guilt.'

14 Die 50er Jahre***

(1) In den Fünfziger Jahren, der Zeit der politischen Reaktion, schafft die wirtschaftliche Entwicklung eine völlig neue politische und soziale Situation: auch in Mitteleuropa setzt sich jetzt die industrielle Revolution durch. (2) Die Schwerindustrie wächst sprunghaft; industrielle Ballungsräume entstehen vor allem im Ruhr- und im Saargebiet und in Oberschlesien. (3) Neue Finanzierungsmethoden über Aktiengesellschaften und Wirtschaftsbanken erlauben den Einsatz moderner Produktionsverfahren im großen Stil und die rasche Erweiterung der Märkte. (4) Deutschland ist auf dem Wege zu einem modernen Industrieland.

(5) Mit der Industrialisierung verändert sich die soziale Landschaft von Grund auf. (6) Neben einem wohlhabenden und selbstbewußten Industriebürgertum entsteht ein ständig wachsendes Industrieproletariat, das sich vor allem aus ehemals selbständigen Handwerkern und aus den in die großen Städte strömenden Landarbeitern rekrutiert. (7) Mit sinkenden Reallöhnen verschlechtert sich dessen Situation zunehmend. (8) Die Arbeiter wohnen in oft menschenunwürdigen Behausungen. (9) Ihr Verdienst liegt meist an der Grenze des Existenzminimums. (10) Selbsthilfeorganisationen wie Konsumgenossenschaften, Krankenversicherungen und Darlehenskassen versuchen, die ärgste Not zu lindern. (11) In die gleiche Richtung zielen karitative Institutionen wie Kolpings Gesellenvereine. (12) Alle diese Einrichtungen stellen die bestehende wirtschaftliche und soziale Ordnung nicht in Frage. (13) Der Sozialismus dagegen zieht radikale Konsequenzen und ruft zum Umsturz des kapitalistischen Systems auf. (14) In Karl Marx findet er seinen führenden Theoretiker. (15) Das Kernland der industriellen Entwicklung ist Preußen, das—noch dazu als Führungsmacht des Zollvereins—ein immer stärkeres wirtschaftliches Gewicht innerhalb Deutschlands gewinnt. (16) Damit wird zugleich auch seine politische Stellung gegenüber Österreich gestärkt. (17) Bedeutsam für die weitere politische Entwicklung ist außerdem, daß bereits in den Jahren der Reaktion die Wirtschaftspolitik Preußens den Interessen weiter Kreise des Bürgertums entspricht.

Source: 'Fragen an die deutsche Geschichte'. Historische Ausstellung im Reichstagsgebäude in Berlin, 1985.

14 The 1850s

(1) In the fifties, the time of political reaction, the economic development creates a completely new political and social situation: in central Europe, too, the industrial revolution takes hold. (2) Heavy industry grows rapidly; industrial conurbations come into being, especially in the Ruhr and the Saar regions, and in Upper Silesia. (3) New methods of financing using share-ownership companies and merchant banks make possible the use of modern production methods on a grand scale and the rapid expansion of markets. (4) Germany is on the way to becoming a modern industrial country.

(5) With industrialization the social landscape changes completely. (6) Alongside a wealthy and self-confident industrial middle class there arises a steadily growing industrial proletariat which above all is recruited from previously independent craftsmen and from the agricultural workers who are streaming into the large cities. (7) With falling real wages, their situation increasingly deteriorates. (8) The workers often live in dwellings unfit for human habitation. (9) Their earnings are usually on the border of the minimum subsistence rate. (10) Self-help organizations such as the consumer societies, health insurance schemes and lending societies attempt to alleviate the worst poverty. (11) Charitable institutions such as the Kolping journeymen's societies aim in the same direction. (12) All these institutions do not question the prevailing economic and social order. (13) Socialism, on the other hand, draws radical conclusions and calls for the overthrow of the capitalist system. (14) In Karl Marx it finds its leading theoretician. (15) The heartland of industrial development is Prussia, which—being also a leading power in the customs union—gains an ever stronger economic position within Germany. (16) And with that its political position in comparison with Austria is also strengthened. (17) Moreover, what is also significant for the future political development is that, already in the years of political reaction, Prussia's economic policy corresponds to the interests of broad sections of the middle classes.

15 Homosexualität in der Antike***

(1) Kenneth J. Dover: „Homosexualität in der griechischen Antike"; aus dem Englischen von Susan Worcester; Verlag C. H. Beck, München 1983; 244 S., 48,-DM.

(2) Die Quellen (aus der Zeit vom 8. bis zum 2. vorchristlichen Jahrhundert) sind Darstellungen in der Vasenmalerei (in der das Thema offenbar sehr beliebt war), entsprechende Szenen in den Werken archaischer und klassischer Dichter, Beschreibungen, beziehungsweise Meinungen in Geschichtsbüchern, philosophischen Schriften und in Komödien (etwa in den Dialogen Platons und in den Bühnenstücken des Aristophanes), ferner Vaseninschriften und Graffiti, vor allem aber Gerichtsreden.

(3) Den breitesten Raum in Dovers Buch nimmt ein Prozeß gegen den Athener Timarchos ein, aus dem Jahr 346 v. Chr. in Athen. (4) Der eigentliche Anlaß zu diesem Prozeß erwuchs aus dem Eroberungskrieg Philipps II. gegen die Griechen. (5) Es ging um die Friedensbedingungen, die Philipp im Frühsommer 346 mit einer Gesandtschaft aus Athen, der auch die berühmten Rhetoren und Politiker Aischines und Demosthenes angehörten, vereinbart hatte. (6) Mit den Bedingungen waren die Athener so wenig einverstanden, daß sie ihre Gesandten, vor allem Aischines, wegen Landesverrats vor Gericht stellen wollten. (7) Treibende Kraft dabei war Demosthenes, der sich nach der Rückkehr aus Makedonien von den anderen Gesandtschaftsteilnehmern distanziert hatte. (8) Hauptankläger sollte der bereits erwähnte Timarchos sein.

(9) Da aber drehten die Gesandten, die für den Fall einer Verurteilung mit schwersten Strafen rechnen mußten, den Spieß um, indem Aischines den Timarchos verklagte; Timarchos dürfe das Amt eines Klägers nicht ausüben, weil er sich in seiner Jugend prostituiert habe. (10) Das Gesetz, auf das Aischines und Demosthenes sich stützten, besagte, daß ein Bürger nicht einmal mehr in der Volksversammlung sprechen, geschweige denn irgend ein Amt ausüben durfte, wenn er seine Eltern schlecht behandelt, den Wehrdienst verweigert, Fahnenflucht begangen, sein Erbe durchgebracht oder sich gegenüber anderen Männern prostituiert hatte. (11) Im Prozeß gegen Timarchos ging es allein um den letzten Punkt, und Timarchos verlor den Prozeß.

Source: Gerhard Prause, 'Aber Geld durften sie nicht nehmen. . .', review in *Die Zeit*, 28 Sept. 1984.

15 Homosexuality in the ancient world

(1) Kenneth J. Dover: 'Homosexuality in Ancient Greece', translated from the English by Susan Worcester, published by C. H. Beck Verlag, Munich 1983, 244 pp., 48 DM.

(2) The sources (from the period from the eighth to the second century BC) are depictions in vase painting (where the topic was obviously very popular), relevant scenes in the works of ancient and classical poets, descriptions or opinions in history books, philosophical texts, and in comedies (for instance in Plato's dialogues and in the plays of Aristophanes), and, further, vase inscriptions and graffiti, but particularly court speeches.

(3) The greatest space in Dover's book is taken up by a lawsuit against the Athenian Timarchos, from the year 346 BC in Athens. (4) The actual cause of this trial arose from Philip II's war of conquest against the Greeks. (5) It concerned the conditions for peace which Philip had agreed in the early summer of 346 BC with a delegation from Athens which also included the famous orators and politicians Aischines and Demosthenes. (6) The Athenians were so little in agreement with the conditions that they wanted to put their emissaries, and especially Aischines, on trial for high treason. (7) The driving force in this was Demosthenes, who had distanced himself from the other members of the delegation after his return from Macedonia. (8) The chief plaintiff was to be the aforementioned Timarchos.

(9) But then the emissaries, who had to reckon with the most severe punishment if they were convicted, turned the tables when Aischines brought a charge against Timarchos: Timarchos, it was alleged, did not have the right to perform the office of prosecutor, because he had prostituted himself in his youth. (10) The law on which Aischines and Demosthenes based their case stated that a citizen could not even speak in the assembly any more, let alone hold office, if he had treated his parents badly, had avoided military service, had committed desertion, had squandered his inheritance, or had prostituted himself with other men. (11) In the case against Timarchos this last point alone was at issue, and Timarchos lost the case.

16 Statistik***(*)

(1) Wie von einem Erdbeben wurde die Öffentlichkeit aufgeschreckt, als in einem amerikanischen Medizin-Fachblatt der Verdacht geäußert wurde, Milch könne krebserregend sein. (2) Er basierte auf einer Statistik, derzufolge in Neu-England und in den US-Staaten Minnesota und Wisconsin, in Gegenden also, in denen viel Milch produziert und konsumiert wurde, die Rate der Krebserkrankungen ungewöhnlich hoch war. (3) In Europa zeigte sich ähnlich Alarmierendes. (4) Die Schweiz, das Land mit dem höchsten Milchverbrauch, wies die höchste Krebsrate in der Alten Welt aus. (5) Und das war noch nicht alles. (6) Unter den englischen Frauen, Milchtrinkerinnen aus alter Tradition, war die Krebshäufigkeit achtmal so hoch wie bei Japanerinnen, die zu jener Zeit noch so gut wie keine Milch zu sich nahmen. (7) Hätte es eine deutlichere als diese einfach bestätigte Korrelation geben können?

(8) Ehe noch eine weltweite Kampagne für Milchabstinenz einsetzte, kam einem Statistiker der beruhigende Einfall. (9) Am Krebs erkranken die meisten Menschen erst im fortgeschrittenen Alter. (10) Je älter also jemand wird, desto größer ist die Wahrscheinlichkeit, daß er an Krebs stirbt. (11) Darin lag die Lösung. (12) Neu-England, Minnesota, Wisconsin und die Schweiz hatten eines gemeinsam: Ihre Bewohner erreichten im Schnitt ein deutlich höheres Alter als die der anderen Länder ihres Kontinents. (13) Die Engländerinnen überlebten—statistisch betrachtet—die japanischen Frauen gar um zwölf Jahre.

(14) Statistik, das lehrte auch dieser Flop eindrucksvoll, kann zwar nicht alles beweisen, doch es fällt uns nicht schwer, aus ihr just das herauszulesen, was uns frönt. (15) Gottlob bedarf es in den meisten Fällen keines besonderen Fachwissens, um hinter die Schliche der statistischen Lügner zu kommen. (16) Dazu genügt allenthalben gesunde Skepsis. (17) Besonders angebracht ist sie, wenn auf Statistik beruhende Aussagen allzu plausibel klingen. (18) Es gibt keinen größeren Feind der Erkenntnis als die Plausibilität.

Source: Thomas von Randow, 'Wie lügt man mit Statistik?', *Die Zeit*, 17 Jan. 1986.

16 Statistics

(1) As if by an earthquake the public were frightened when the suspicion was expressed in a specialist American medical journal that milk could be carcinogenic. (2) It was based on a statistic according to which the rate of cancers in New England and in the US states of Minnesota and Wisconsin, that is in areas in which a lot of milk is produced and consumed, was unusually high. (3) In Europe there was similarly alarming evidence. (4) Switzerland, the country with the highest milk consumption, had the highest cancer rate in the Old World. (5) And that was not all. (6) Amongst English women, milk drinkers by ancient tradition, the frequency of cancer was eight times as high as in Japanese women, who at that time consumed practically no milk. (7) Could there have been a clearer correlation than this simply confirmed one?

(8) Before a world-wide campaign for milk abstinence got under way, the soothing solution came to a statistician. (9) Most people fall ill with cancer only at an advanced age. (10) Therefore the older one becomes, the greater the probability that one will die of cancer. (11) Therein lay the solution. (12) New England, Minnesota, Wisconsin, and Switzerland had one thing in common: their inhabitants reached on average a significantly higher age than those in the other states on their continents. (13) The English women outlived–in statistical terms–the Japanese women by twelve years, no less.

(14) Statistics, as this débâcle has taught us emphatically, cannot prove everything, but it is not difficult for us to take just what we want out of them. (15) Thankfully, in most cases it does not require any specialist expertise to see through the tricks of the statistical liers. (16) For this, all we need is plenty of healthy scepticism. (17) It is especially appropriate when statements resting on statistics sound all too plausible. (18) There is no greater enemy of understanding than plausibility.

17 Sicherheitsschloß ***(*)

(1) Das Kernstück des Sicherheitsschlosses ist ein Zylinder (daher auch Zylinderschloß). (2) Er ist drehbar im Gehäuse gelagert. (3) In geschlossenem Zustand (Abb. 1) drücken Federn die pilzförmigen, senkrecht zur Achse angeordneten Stifte im Gehäuse nach unten. (4) Im Zylinder selbst sind getrennt unterschiedlich lange Stifte angeordnet. (5) Weil die Oberstifte nach unten gedrückt werden, sperren sie die Trennlinie zwischen Zylinder und Gehäuse, wodurch der Zylinder nicht gedreht werden kann. (6) Wenn nun der richtige Schlüssel in den Zylinder gebracht wird (Abb. 2), werden die Stifte so weit hochgedrückt, daß ihre Trennlinie gerade mit der Trennlinie zwischen Zylinder und Gehäuse übereinstimmt. (7) Der Zylinder, der mit dem Riegel in Verbindung steht, kann gedreht, das Schloß also geöffnet werden. (8) Ein falscher Schlüssel hebt nur einen Teil der Sperrstifte auf die richtige Höhe an, so daß die restlichen Stifte immer noch ein Öffnen verhindern.

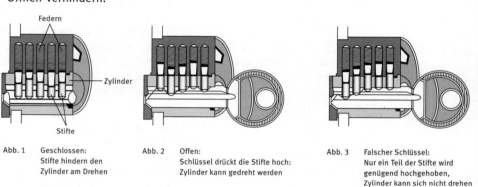

Abb. 1 Geschlossen: Stifte hindern den Zylinder am Drehen	Abb. 2 Offen: Schlüssel drückt die Stifte hoch: Zylinder kann gedreht werden	Abb. 3 Falscher Schlüssel: Nur ein Teil der Stifte wird genügend hochgehoben, Zylinder kann sich nicht drehen

Source: *Wie funktioniert das? Die Technik im Leben von heute* (Mannheim, 1978).

17 Yale lock

(1) The main piece of a Yale lock is a cylinder (hence also cylinder lock). (2) It is rotatably housed in a casing. (3) When closed (Fig. 1) springs press down the mushroom-shaped pins which are positioned vertically in the casing. (4) In the cylinder itself, pins of different lengths are positioned independently of one another. (5) Because the upper pins are pushed down they close off the dividing line between cylinder and casing, as a result of which the cylinder cannot be turned. (6) But when the correct key is inserted in the cylinder (Fig. 2) the pins are pushed up until their line of separation coincides exactly with the line of separation between cylinder and casing. (7) The cylinder, which is connected to the bolt, can be turned, and thus the lock opened. (8) The wrong key raises only some of the barring pins to the correct height, with the result that the other pins still prevent opening.

FIG. 1. Closed: pins prevent the cylinder from turning
FIG. 2. Open: key raises the pins; cylinder can be turned
FIG. 3. Wrong key: Only some of the pins are raised sufficiently; cylinder cannot turn

18 Warum ein Schiff schwimmt ****

(1) Grundlage der Schwimmfähigkeit eines Schiffes ist das Archimedische Prinzip. (2) Nach diesem Prinzip wird jeder Körper, der in eine Flüssigkeit getaucht wird, um so viel leichter, wie die von ihm verdrängte Flüssigkeitsmenge wiegt. (3) So wird man feststellen, daß ein massiver Würfel aus Aluminium, sofern er gerade einen Liter Rauminhalt hat, 2,7 kg wiegt (Abb. 1*a*); taucht man ihn aber nach Abbildung 1*b* in Wasser, so wiegt er nur noch 1,7 kg. (4) Der Aluminiumwürfel ist, da er 1 Liter Volumen hat und infolgedessen 1 Liter bzw. 1 kg Wasser verdrängt, um das Gewicht der von ihm verdrängten Wassermenge leichter geworden. (5) Auf ihn wirkt also eine in ihrer Richtung der Schwerkraft entgegengesetzte (gewichtsmindernde) Kraft, die Auftriebskraft. (6) Diese senkrecht nach oben wirkende, wie jede Kraft in Newton (N) gemessene Auftriebskraft greift am Formschwerpunkt des Volumens an, das von dem in die Flüssigkeit eingetauchten Körper eingenommen wird (gleich Volumen der verdrängten Flüssigkeitsmenge). (7) Kann ein Körper bei restlosem Untertauchen mehr Flüssigkeitsgewicht verdrängen, als er selbst wiegt, so wird er nur so tief in die Flüssigkeit eintauchen, bis der entstehende Auftrieb gleich seinem Gewicht ist. (8) Ein Würfel aus Holz, der bei einem Liter Rauminhalt etwa 0,8 kg wiegt, taucht so weit ins Wasser ein, bis er 0,8 Liter, d.h. 0,8 kg Wasser verdrängt hat (Abb. 2). (9) Die restlichen 0,2 Liter Holz tauchen nicht ein, weil schon vorher Gleichgewicht zwischen dem Eigengewicht und dem Auftrieb besteht; man sagt in diesem Fall: der Körper schwimmt. (10) Nun besitzt Holz eine geringere durchschnittliche Dichte als Wasser (die Dichte ist gleich der Masse m geteilt durch das Volumen V eines Körpers) und schwimmt; Metall und andere Stoffe dagegen haben eine größere durchschnittliche Dichte und gehen unter. (11) Damit ein eisernes Schiff schwimmt, muß sein Inneres sehr viel Luftraum (s. Abb. 3) enthalten, so daß seine durchschnittliche Dichte geringer wird als die des Wassers.

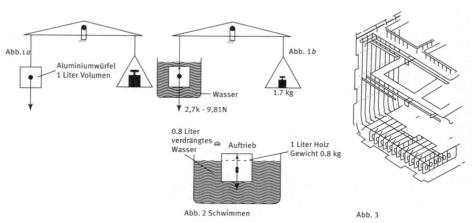

Abb. 1*a*

Aluminiumwürfel
1 Liter Volumen

Abb. 1*b*

Wasser

1.7 kg

2,7k - 9,81N

0.8 Liter verdrängtes Wasser ≙ Auftrieb

1 Liter Holz Gewicht 0.8 kg

Abb. 2 Schwimmen

Abb. 3

Source: Wie funktioniert das? Die Technik im Leben von heute (Mannheim, 1978).

18 Why a ship floats

(1) The basis of a ship's buoyancy is the Archimedian principle. (2) According to this principle any body which is placed in a liquid becomes lighter by the amount which the quantity of liquid displaced by it weighs. (3) Thus one will find that a solid cube of aluminium, if it has a volume of exactly one liter, weighs 2.7 kg. (Fig. 1a); but if one places it as in Fig. 1b in water, then it weighs only 1.7 kg. (4) The aluminium cube, since it has a volume of 1 litre and consequently displaces 1 litre or 1 kg. of water, has become lighter by the weight of the quantity of water displaced by it. (5) Therefore there is acting upon it a (weight-reducing) force which is opposed to the force of gravity in its direction — the upthrust. (6) This upthrust, which acts vertically and upwards and is measured, like any force, in Newtons (N) attaches to the centre of gravity of the volume taken up by the body immersed in the liquid (equals the volume of the displaced quantity of liquid). (7) If a body can displace more weight of liquid, when completely immersed, than the body itself weighs, then it will sink into the liquid only until the upthrust which is created is equal to its weight. (8) A cube made of wood, which with a volume of 1 litre weighs about 0.8 kg., sinks into the water until it has displaced 0.8 litres or 0.8 kg. of water (Fig. 2). (9) The remaining 0.2 litres of wood do not sink, because equilibrium between the weight of the object and the upthrust already exists, and one says in this case: the body floats. (10) Now wood has a lower average density than water (the density is equal to the mass m divided by the volume V of a body), and floats; metals and other materials on the other hand have a greater average density and sink. (11) In order for an iron ship to float, its inside must contain a lot of air (see Fig. 3), so that its average density becomes less than that of the water.

Fig. 1a. Aluminium cube, 1 litre volume
Fig. 1b. Water
Fig. 2. Floating
         0.8 litres of displaced water
         Upthrust
         1 litre of wood, weight 0.8 kg.

19 Falsch programmiert ****

(1) Wenn wir in der Komplexität der zukünftigen gesellschaftlichen Realität die Freiheit des Menschen erhalten wollen, dann müssen wir diese Freiheit mit den besten Mitteln menschlichen Denkens sicherstellen, kurzum, wir müssen die Freiheit planen. (2) Es wird in unserer Gesellschaft die Täuschung aufrechterhalten, Planung und Freiheit schlössen sich gegenseitig aus. (3) Daß dies ein rechter Trugschluß ist, sei durch einen Vergleich veranschaulicht:

(4) Wenn wir in einer verkehrsarmen Dorfstraße eine Verkehrssignalanlage aufstellen würden, dann wäre dies eine unnötige Einschränkung unserer Freiheit. (5) Es würde uns plötzlich verwehrt, zu manchen Zeiten die Straße zu passieren, ohne daß es einen ersichtlichen Grund gibt. (6) Ganz anders bei einem Großstadt-Verkehrszentrum: Ohne Verkehrssignalanlage ist es verstopft, und wir kommen überhaupt nicht mehr durch. (7) Dieser Vergleich zeigt uns, daß es möglich ist, einfache gesellschaftliche Probleme dem ungeregelten Spiel der Kräfte zu überlassen, daß aber mit zunehmender Komplexität die Planung unvermeidbar ist, wenn nicht das Chaos herrschen soll. (8) Den Ideologen der Planlosigkeit in unserem Lande ist vorzuwerfen, daß sie so tun, als ob sie eine Möglichkeit hätten, die Großstadt-Straßenkreuzung ohne Verkehrssignalanlage zu ordnen, während sie in Wirklichkeit nichts anderes tun, als den Großstadtverkehr nicht zur Kenntnis zu nehmen, und dann behaupten: Es gibt nur Dorfstraßen.

(9) Die zukünftigen Probleme der Gesellschaft werden aber immer komplexer und sind ohne bewußte, sorgfältige Analyse und optimale Entscheidung unter Beachtung der in demokratischer Weise gewählten Wertsysteme überhaupt nicht mehr zu ordnen. (10) Weder der Hinweis auf Fehlleistungen planender Gesellschaften noch die irreführende Identifizierung der Planung mit Staatsdirigismus begründen eine Überlegenheit der Planlosigkeit.

(11) (Um einer möglichen Kritik zuvorzukommen: „Freiheit" von Naturgesetzen gibt es wohl nicht, die „Freiheit" zu bewußtem, verantwortlichem und sittlichem Verhalten sollten wir uns aber erhalten.)

Source: Karl Steinbuch, *Falsch Programmiert* (Stuttgart, 1968).

19 Wrongly programmed

(1) If we want to retain the freedom of the human being in the complexity of the social reality of the future, then we must secure this freedom with the best means of human thinking, in short, we must plan freedom. (2) In our society the illusion is maintained that planning and freedom are mutually exclusive. (3) That this is simply a fallacy can be illustrated by a comparison.

(4) If we were to put up a set of traffic lights on a street in a village with hardly any traffic, then this would be an unnecessary restriction of our freedom. (5) We would suddenly be prevented from crossing the street at some times without there being an obvious reason. (6) It is quite different in the case of a busy junction in a large city: without traffic lights it is blocked and we cannot get through at all any more. (7) This comparison shows us that it is possible to leave simple social problems to the unregulated play of forces, but that as complexity increases planning is unavoidable if chaos is not to rule. (8) The ideologues of non-planning in our society have to face the charge that they behave as if they had a possibility of regulating the city intersection without traffic lights, whereas in reality they are not doing anything other than ignoring the traffic in large cities and then claiming that there are only village streets.

(9) But the future problems of society are becoming ever more complex and can no longer be sorted out at all without deliberate, careful analysis and optimal decision-making taking into account the democratically elected value systems. (10) Neither pointing out the failures of societies that have planning nor the misleading identification of planning with state control demonstrates the superiority of non-planning.

(11) (In order to anticipate a possible criticism: it may be that 'freedom' from the laws of nature does not exist, but we should hold on to the 'freedom' to behave consciously, responsibly, and ethically.)

20 Deutsche an der Spitze? ****

(1) Bei einer Umfrage bestritten die meisten Unternehmen einen technologischen Rückstand in der Bundesrepublik.

(2) Überraschend ist das Umfrageergebnis, das aus dem Bereich der Industrie und Handelskammer Bochum kommt — einer Ruhrgebietsregion, von der es oft hieß, sie habe den Anschluß verpaßt. (3) Die Bochumer Kammer meldet es anders: „Unternehmen, die in Teilbereichen einen gewissen Nachholbedarf im technischen Entwicklungsstand vermuten, sind die Ausnahme."

(4) Dennoch legt die Umfrage auch einige Schattenseiten bloß: 'Gewisse Andeutungen und Hinweise sind nicht zu übersehen, die deutlich machen, daß es da und dort Schwachstellen und einen Nachholbedarf gibt.'

(5) Sieben Prozent der Frankfurter Firmen aus der Eisen-, Blech- und Metallindustrie, aber auch ein Teil der Feinmechanikhersteller und Maschinenbauer geben an, sie hätten einen technologischen Nachholbedarf. (6) Im Nürnberger Bereich wird vielfach auf die Überlegenheit der USA und Japans in der Elektronik- und Computerbranche verwiesen. (7) Beklagt wird hier insbesondere die Abhängigkeit der Deutschen von Vorlieferungen aus diesen Ländern.

(8) Auffallend ist, daß der zeitweilig vorhandene Rückstand etwa bei der Aufwendung der Mikroelektronik nicht bestritten wird, die befragten Unternehmen zugleich aber den Eindruck vermitteln, den Rückstand aufzuholen. (9) Vielfach sei er bereits aufgeholt worden. (10) Allerdings lassen die Unternehmen, zumindest jene, die sich nicht zur Spitzenstellung bekennen, keinen Zweifel daran, daß sie trotzdem Probleme haben. (11) Überraschend ist, daß der unzureichende Zugang zu Forschungsergebnissen keineswegs — wie vielfach vermutet — als Hemmnis angesehen wird, um in internationale Spitzenstellung vorzudringen. (12) Nur ganz wenige Unternehmen — vorwiegend Mittel- und Kleinbetriebe — sehen darin eine Ursache ihres Problems. (13) Andere Gründe werden häufiger genannt: die mangelnde Auslastung neuer Anlagen ebenso wie das Fehlen qualifizierter Arbeitskräfte. (14) Darüber hinaus nannten viele Unternehmen auch den „Mangel an Kapital als Grund für das Nichterreichen des internationalen Spitzenstandards".

(15) Obwohl die Ergebnisse seiner Umfrage eindeutig positiv sind, warnt der Industrie- und Handelstag vor ihrer Überbewertung. (16) Denn es fehlt auch nicht der Hinweis, daß die Unternehmen geneigt sein könnten, „in einer gewissen Art von Selbstüberschätzung ihre internationale Wettbewerbsposition zu hoch einzuordnen."

Source: Wolfgang Hoffmann, *Die Zeit*, 9 Nov. 1984.

20 Germans in the Lead?

(1) In an opinion survey most companies denied that there was a technological deficit in the Federal Republic.

(2) The survey finding which comes from the area of the chamber of trade and commerce in Bochum—a region of the Ruhr about which it was often said that it had missed the boat—is surprising. (3) The chamber in Bochum has different news: 'Companies which detect a certain need to catch up in their level of technology are the exception.'

(4) Nevertheless the survey also lays bare a few negative aspects: 'Certain suggestions and indications cannot be overlooked which make it clear that here and there there are weak spots and a need to catch up with competitors.'

(5) Seven per cent of the Frankfurt firms in the iron, sheet metal, and metal industry, but also a proportion of precision engineering companies and mechanical engineering firms, say that they have a technological deficit. (6) In the Nuremberg area the superiority of the USA and Japan in electronics and computer sector is frequently pointed out. (7) What is lamented here is particularly the dependency of the Germans on deliveries from these countries.

(8) What is striking is that the temporary deficit in, say, the application of microelectronics is not contested, but that the companies in the survey give the impression that they are closing the gap. (9) In many cases, it is claimed, it has already been closed. (10) For all that, the companies, at least those which do not claim to be leaders in their field, leave no doubt that they have problems nevertheless. (11) What is surprising is that the inadequate access to research findings is not at all seen as a bar—as is frequently supposed—to forging ahead into the leading position. (12) Only a very few companies—predominantly small and middle-sized firms—see this as a cause of their problem. (13) Other reasons are mentioned more often: the below-capacity use of new plant and the absence of qualified workers. (14) In addition, many firms also blamed the 'shortage of capital as a reason for not reaching the international top flight'.

(15) Although the results of its survey are unambiguously positive, the Chamber of Industry and Commerce warns against setting too much store by them. (16) For there is also evidence that the companies could be inclined 'in a certain kind of self-overestimation to put their international competitive position too high'.

21 Schönberg: was Musik zu sagen hat *****

(1) Es gibt relativ wenig Menschen, die imstande sind, rein musikalisch zu verstehen, was Musik zu sagen hat. (2) Die Annahme, ein Tonstück müsse Vorstellungen irgendwelcher Art erwecken, und wenn solche ausbleiben, sei das Tonstück nicht verstanden worden oder es tauge nichts, ist so weit verbreitet, wie nur das Falsche und Banale verbreitet sein kann. (3) Von keiner Kunst verlangt man Ähnliches, sondern begnügt sich mit den Wirkungen ihres Materials, wobei allerdings in den anderen Künsten das Stoffliche, der dargestellte Gegenstand, dem beschränkten Auffassungsvermögen des geistigen Mittelstandes von selbst entgegenkommt. (4) Da der Musik als solcher ein unmittelbar erkennbares Stoffliches fehlt, suchen die einen hinter ihren Wirkungen rein formale Schönheit, die andern poetische Vorgänge. (5) Selbst Schopenhauer, der erst durch den wundervollen Gedanken: „Der Komponist offenbart das innerste Wesen der Welt und spricht die tiefste Weisheit aus, in einer Sprache, die seine Vernunft nicht versteht; wie eine magnetische Somnambule Aufschlüsse gibt über Dinge, von denen sie wachend keinen Begriff hat", wirklich Erschöpfendes über das Wesen der Musik sagt, verliert sich später, indem er versucht, Einzelheiten dieser Sprache, die die Vernunft nicht versteht, in unsere Begriffe zu übersetzen. (6) Obwohl ihm dabei klar sein muß, daß bei dieser Übersetzung in die Begriffe, in die Sprache des Menschen, welche Abstraktion, Reduktion aufs Erkennbare ist, das Wesentliche, die Sprache der Welt, die vielleicht unverständlich bleiben und nur fühlbar sein soll, verloren geht. (7) Aber immerhin ist er berechtigt zu solchem Vorgehen, da es ja sein Zweck als Philosoph ist, das Wesen der Welt, den unüberblickbaren Reichtum, darzustellen durch die Begriffe, durch die nur allzuleicht zu durchschauende Armut. (8) Und auch Wagner, wenn er dem Durchschnittsmenschen einen mittelbaren Begriff von dem geben wollte, was er als Musiker unmittelbar erschaut hatte, tat recht, wenn er Beethovenschen Symphonien Programme unterlegte.

(9) Verhängnisvoll wird solch ein Vorgang, wenn er Allgemeingebrauch wird. (10) Dann verkehrt sich sein Sinn ins Gegenteil: man sucht in der Musik Vorgänge und Gefühle zu erkennen, so als ob sie drin sein müßten.

Source: Arnold Schönberg, 'Das Verhältnis zum Text', in Wassily Kandinsky and Franz Marc (eds.), *Der Blaue Reiter. Dokumentarische Neuausgabe von Klaus Lankheit* (Munich, 1965).

21 Schoenberg: What music has to say

(1) There are relatively few people who are capable of understanding in purely musical terms what music has to say. (2) The assumption that a piece of music has to awaken ideas of some kind, and that if these are not present the music has not been understood or is worthless, is as widespread as only the false and banal can be. (3) One does not demand this kind of thing of any art, but on the contrary one is satisfied with the effects of its material, though it is true that in the other arts the material aspect, the depicted object, accommodates itself to the limited understanding of the intellectually average person. (4) Since music as such lacks an immediately recognizable material aspect, some people look for purely formal beauty behind its effects, and others look for poetic processes. (5) Even Schopenhauer, who in the wonderful idea: 'The composer reveals the innermost essence of the world and expresses the profoundest truth in a language which his reason does not understand; as a magnetic somnambulist gives insight into things about which she has no conception when awake', says something really meaningful about the nature of music, loses himself later when he attempts to translate details of this language which reason cannot comprehend into our concepts. (6) Although in doing so it must be clear to him that in this process of translation into concepts, into the language of human beings, which is abstraction, reduction to what can be perceived, what is essential, the language of the world, which ought perhaps to remain incomprehensible and ought to be only capable of being felt, is lost. (7) But even so he is justified in proceeding like this since it is after all his purpose as a philosopher to present the essence of the world, its uncompassable wealth, by means of concepts, by means of all too transparent inadequacy. (8) And Wagner too, when he wanted to give the average person an approximate concept of what he as a musician had glimpsed directly, acted correctly when he put programmes to Beethoven's symphonies.

(9) Such a process becomes fateful when it becomes general usage. (10) Then its sense is turned around into its opposite: one attempts to recognize processes and feelings in music, as if they had to be in there.

22 Schopenhauer: Nach dem Tode ****

Wenn man, so im täglichen Umgange, von einem der vielen Leute, die Alles wissen möchten, aber nichts lernen wollen, über die Fortdauer nach dem Tode befragt wird, ist wohl die passendeste, auch zunächst richtigste Antwort: „Nach deinem Tode wirst du seyn was du vor deiner Geburt warst." Denn sie implicirt die Verkehrtheit der Forderung, daß die Art von Existenz, welche einen Anfang hat, ohne Ende seyn solle; zudem aber enthält sie die Andeutung, daß es wohl zweierlei Existenz und, dem entsprechend, zweierlei Nichts geben möge. Imgleichen jedoch könnte man antworten: „Was immer du nach deinem Tode seyn wirst, — und wäre es nichts, — wird dir alsdann eben so natürlich und angemessen seyn, wie es dir jetzt dein individuelles, organisches Daseyn ist: also hättest du höchstens den Augenblick des Uebergangs zu fürchten."

(1) Wenn man, so im täglichen Umgange, von einem der vielen Leute, die Alles wissen möchten, aber nichts lernen wollen, über die Fortdauer nach dem Tode befragt wird, ist wohl die passendeste, auch zunächst richtigste Antwort:

(2) „Nach deinem Tode wirst du seyn[1] was du vor deiner Geburt warst." (3) Denn sie implicirt[2] die Verkehrtheit der Forderung, daß die Art von Existenz, welche einen Anfang hat, ohne Ende seyn solle; zudem aber enthält sie die Andeutung, daß es wohl zweierlei Existenz und, dem entsprechend, zweierlei Nichts geben möge. — (4) Imgleichen jedoch könnte man antworten: (5) „Was immer du nach deinem Tode seyn wirst, — und wäre es nichts, — wird dir alsdann eben so natürlich und angemessen seyn, wie es dir jetzt dein individuelles, organisches Daseyn[3] ist: (6) also hättest du höchstens den Augenblick des Uebergangs zu fürchten."

Note: corresponding modern spellings: [1] sein;
[2] impliziert;
[3] Dasein

Source: Arthur Schopenhauer, *Parerga und Paralipomena* (1851).

22 Schopenhauer: After death

(1) When one is asked, in everyday conversation, by one of the many people who would like to know everything but do not want to learn anything, about the continuation of life after death, the most appropriate, and to begin with the most correct answer is probably:

(2) 'After your death you will be what you were before your birth.' (3) For this implies the wrong-headedness of the demand that the kind of existence which has a beginning should be without end; however it also contains the indication that there may be two kinds of existence and, correspondingly, two kinds of nothing. (4) In the same way, however, one could answer: (5) 'Whatever you will be after your death — even if it is nothing — will be just as natural and right for you as your individual, organic existence is now. (6) Therefore, at the most, you would have to fear the moment of transition.'

23 Bedienungshinweise: Projektor **(*)

Projektion

(1) Gerät mit Taste 4 einschalten. (2) Magazin von hinten in die Magazinführung bis Diaschieber vorschieben. (3) Zur automatischen Bildvorführung Taste 5 drücken. (4) Kurzer Druck (bis 500 ms) = Bildwechsel vorwärts. (5) Langer Druck (ab 750 ms) = Bildwechsel rückwärts. (6) Durch Drücken bei 7 kann die angehobene Fernbedienung herausgenommen werden (nicht bei Perkeo compact IR autofocus). (7) Achtung! Lüftungsöffnungen 12 stets freihalten!

Beheben von Störungen

(8) Durch unsachgemäß gerahmte oder in ihren Abmessungen nicht normgemäße Dias können Störungen im Bildtransport vorkommen. (9) Um Schäden am Projektor zu vermeiden, Projektor ausschalten und das verklemmte Dia von Hand lösen. (10) Das Gerät ist mit einem Temperaturschutzschalter ausgestattet, der im Falle einer Überhitzung (z.B. durch mangelnde Luftzufuhr) die Lampe ausschaltet. (11) Dabei bleibt das Gebläse in Funktion und der Projektor wird abgekühlt. (12) Nach kurzer Dauer schaltet sich die Lampe wieder ein. (13) Sollte der Projektor in seinen elektrischen Funktionen ausfallen, so ist vom Fachmann gegebenenfalls die durch Demontage des Oberteils zugängliche Sicherung „0,5 A träge" auszuwechseln.

Source: Bedienungshinweise für Zeiss Ikon Perkeo Projektor, Zeiss Ikon AG, Braunschweig, 1986.

23 User Instructions: Projector

Projection

(1) Switch on the apparatus with switch no. 4. (2) Push the magazine into the magazine holder from behind, as far as the slide mover. (3) For automatic presentation of pictures press switch no. 5. (4) Short press (up to 500 milliseconds) = picture change forwards. (5) Long press (from 750 milliseconds) = picture change in reverse. (6) By pressing 7 the raised remote control can be removed (not on Perkeo compact IR autofocus). (7) Important! Always keep the ventilation openings 12 free.

Correcting faults

(8) Disruptions in moving the slides into position can come about through incorrectly framed slides or slides whose dimensions do not comply with the norm. (9) To avoid damage to the projector, switch off the projector and remove the stuck slide by hand. (10) The apparatus is fitted with an automatic thermal circuit breaker, which switches off the lamp in the event of overheating (e.g. because of insufficient ventilation). (11) In this case the fan still works and the projector is cooled. (12) After a short while the lamp switches on again. (13) If the projector fails in its electrical functions, the fuse '0.5 A delayed action', access to which is gained by dismantling the upper section, may need to be changed by a suitably qualified person.